Unemployment,
Imperfect Competition and
Macroeconomics

Unemployment, Imperfect Competition and Macroeconomics

Essays in the Post Keynesian Tradition

Malcolm C. Sawyer
Professor of Economics
University of Leeds

Edward Elgar

Published by
Edward Elgar Publishing Limited
Gower House
Croft Road
Aldershot
Hants GU11 3HR
England

Edward Elgar Publishing Company
Old Post Road
Brookfield
Vermont 05036
USA

British Library Cataloguing in Publication Data
Sawyer, Malcolm C.
    Unemployment, Imperfect Competition and
    Macroeconomics: Essays in the Post
    Keynesian Tradition
    I. Title
    330.1

Library of Congress Cataloguing in Publication Data
Sawyer, Malcolm C.
    Unemployment, imperfect competition and macroeconomics : essays in
    the post Keynesian tradition / Malcolm C. Sawyer
        224p. 23 cm.
        1. Keynesian economics. 2. Unemployment . 3. Competition,
    Imperfect. 4. Macroeconomics. I. Title.
    HB 99.7.S29 1995
    330.15'6—dc20   94–37277
                                                              CIP

ISBN 1 85278 957 3

Printed in Great Britain at the University Press, Cambridge

Contents

List of Illustrations   vi

Acknowledgements   vii

1. Introduction   1

2. Unemployment and the dismal science   6

3. Post Keynesian macroeconomics: a survey   30

4. Post Keyensian economics: the state of the art   50

5. Conflict and aggregate demand in post Keynesian economics: the problem of over-determinacy   70

6. The relationship between imperfect competition and macroeconomic analysis   92

7. Keynes's macroeconomic analysis and theories of imperfect competition   118

8. On the origins of post Keynesian pricing theory and macroeconomics   133

9. Post Keynesian analysis and industrial economics   146

10. Prices, pricing, capacity utilisation and unemployment in the post Keynesian traditions   170

References   193

Index   210

Illustrations

Figures

3.1 Interaction of price and wage determination 43

5.1 Interaction of aggregate demand, price and wage determination 80

5.2 Interaction of aggregate demand, price and wage determination 81

6.1 Real wage/employment relationship based on price/output decisions 95

6.2 Real wage/employment configurations 98

6.3 Aggregate demand and pricing decisions 100

6.4 Shift in p-curve consequent on new entry 102

7.1 Interaction of supply of labour and p-curve 129

Tables

9.1 Sources of capital funds: industrial and commercial companies: UK 168

Acknowledgements

Many people have contributed to the development of the papers printed below. Most of the papers have been presented at conferences and seminars and the subsequent discussion on those occasions has led to a sharpening up of the arguments. Victoria Chick, Amitava Dutt, Bill Gerrard, Geoff Harcourt, John Hillard, Marc Lavoie, Fred Lee, Gary Mongiovi, Peter Reynolds, Christof Rhul, Peter Skott, Jan Toporowski, Casper van Ewijk have commented on at least one of the essays which follow. Nina Shapiro has supplied pertinent comments on many of the essays and our more general discussions have generated a number of new insights. Philip Arestis has commented on nearly all the papers below and his comments have led to many improvements in them. Our discussions and work together over the years have added significantly to the development of my ideas. I would also like to thank Edward Elgar not only for publishing this volume of essays and many of the volumes in which earlier versions of the essays appeared, but for the stimulus he has provided for publication of some of my previous books in the area of post Keynesian and radical political economy.

Many of the essays have appeared in print before, but all have been rewritten for this volume, in some cases extensively. Duplication between chapters has been reduced as much as possible. The origin of the essays is as follows:

Chapter 2: Expanded version of the text of an inaugural lecture delivered at the University of Leeds, 16 November 1992. The text of the lecture was published under the same title in *Leeds Review*, 1993.

Chapter 3: Originally published in D. Greenway et alia. (eds) *Companion to Contemporary Economic Analysis*, London: Routledge, 1991.

Chapter 4: This chapter was presented at the 10th annual conference of the Dutch-Belgian Association of Post-Keynesian Studies held at University of Utrecht, 6 October 1989. Published in W.L.M. Adriaansen and J. van den Linden (eds.) *Post Keynesian Thought in Perspective*, Wolters-Noordhoof, 1991, pp.31–56.

Chapter 5: This chapter is previously unpublished but is based on a discussion paper of the same title from the University of York, 1986

Chapter 6: This is a revised version of the paper presented to the conference on Recent Developments in the Theory of Industrial Organisation held in Naples April 28/29 1989. Originally published in A. del Monte (ed.), *Recent Developments in Industrial Economics*, London: Macmillan, 1992, pp.79–113.

Chapter 7: This chapter was presented at the *Review of Political Economy* conference, Malvern, August 1990. Published in B. Gerrard and J. Hillard (eds) *The Philosophy and Economics of Keynes*, Aldershot: Edward Elgar, 1992.

Chapter 8: An earlier version of this chapter was presented to the Post Keynesian Economics Study Group in February 1989. Published in P. Arestis and V. Chick (eds) *Recent Developments in Post Keynesian Economics*, Aldershot: Edward Elgar, 1992.

Chapter 9: A version of this chapter was presented at the *Review of Political Economy* conference held at Malvern in August 1989. This chapter is based on the paper 'On the Post Keynesian tradition and industrial economics', *Review of Political Economy* vol. 2, from which sections that overlap with other chapters have been excised and other parts of the paper expanded and updated.

Chapter 10: This chapter was originally written as a rather long paper which was presented at the conference on Alternative Traditions in Macro economics: Diversity and Convergence held at the University of Hohenheim, Stuttgart, 26 – 28 July 1990, and at the conference on Analytical Political Economy held at the University of Notre Dame, March 1991. One part of the paper was published in G. Mongiovi and C. Ruhl (eds) *Macroeconomic Theory: Diversity and Convergence*, Aldershot: Edward Elgar, 1992, and the other part in A. Dutt (ed) *New Directions in Analytical Political Economy*, Aldershot: Edward Elgar, 1994.

I am grateful to the following for their permission to reproduce here in a revised form previously published material: University of Leeds in respect of Chapter 2, Routledge Ltd. in respect of Chapter 3, the Dutch-Belgian Post Keynesian Association in respect of Chapter 4, Macmillan Ltd. in respect of Chapter 6, Edward Arnold Ltd. in respect of Chapter 9, and Edward Elgar Ltd. in respect of Chapters 7, 8 and 10.

1. Introduction

One of the central concerns of post Keynesian economists has long been that of unemployment and its causes in decentralised market economies. This concern is, of course, not limited to post Keynesian economists, though the 1980s and 1990s have been characterised by a lack of concern about unemployment by many economists, politicians and others in the face of high levels of unemployment. Some economists (and others), as noted by Romer (1993), 'deny the existence of significant involuntary unemployment'.[1]

A quarter of a century after the Second World War, during which time unemployment was rather low in many industrialised countries, the past twenty years have seen high and often increasing levels of unemployment. Many of the origins of modern post Keynesian economics can be dated in the 1930s in response to the high levels of unemployment current at the time.[2] The emergence of macroeconomics as a distinct subject within economics can also be placed in the 1930s, as can the development of theories of imperfect competition. The essays in this book have been written from within the post Keynesian tradition and, as the title of the book suggests, the essays focus on unemployment, macroeconomics and imperfect competition. The central concern is, though, with the understanding of the causes of unemployment. This will be most evident in Chapter 2 where I discuss some of the causes of and possible remedies for unemployment.

There have been varying responses by economists to the persistence of unemployment. One response, which can be particularly though not exclusively associated with the 'new classical macroeconomics' and real business cycle theorists (see, for example, Plosser, 1989), has been close to a denial of the possibility of unemployment in any genuine sense. In that approach, any unemployment which does arise is mainly by choice (though mistaken expectations may also play a role). 'Real business cycle models view aggregate economic variables as the outcomes of the decisions made by many individual agents acting to maximise their utility subject to production possibilities and resource constraints' (Plosser, 1989). Another response has been to ascribe unemployment to departures from 'flexible' markets (particularly labour mar-

---

1. Romer is specifically referring here to real business cycle theorists and to Plosser (1989) in particular.
2. The work of Keynes (1936) and Kalecki (1933, 1971a) was particularly important in this respect, even though precursors to their important ideas can be identified.

kets) (see, for example, Romer, 1993). A notable aspect of these (and other) responses is the denial of any problems of demand deficiency. There is also an (often implicit) assumption that a pure market economy (in some form) would not result in unemployment, and hence the occurrence of unemployment has to be ascribed in some way to imperfections in the real world, some or all of which could potentially be removed. The essays in this book start from a quite different perspective. In a monetary economy, there is always a threat of a deficiency of aggregate demand (as compared with that required to sustain full employment). Further, markets do not work as pictured in neo-classical economics and in particular do not tend to generate full employment. Hence my approach is based (as will be seen in Chapter 2) on a different perception of how market economies operate and the view that unemployment is pervasive in market economies.

The first main chapter (Chapter 2), entitled 'Unemployment and the dismal science', seeks to argue two major themes. The first is that conventional economic analysis (largely neo-classical) cannot comprehend unemployment because of its definition of economics as the study of the use of scarce resources for competing ends, and that its obsession with (perfectly competitive) markets makes it difficult to provide a convincing explanation for the occurrence of unemployment. Although my prime concern in this chapter is with unemployment, it can be noted that this same obsession with (perfectly competitive) markets (and with methodological individualism) has served to isolate economic analysis from both other social sciences and from organisational and management studies. An alternative view of the purpose of economics and of the economic analysis of markets is then required, which we seek to sketch in that chapter (for further elaboration see Sawyer, 1992a and 1994a). This alternative analysis of the operation of markets provides a number of reasons as to why unfettered market economies will have inherent tendencies to generate unemployment, and this leads into the second theme. This is that, since market economies are observed to generally operate with unemployment, a whole range of interventions and institutional changes are required for the achievement of full employment (and if those changes were implemented many would question whether the resulting economy was a market one). It is not sufficient to regard the removal of market imperfections (e.g. monopoly) or just the creation of sufficient aggregate demand as the route to full employment. In later chapters, I return to the theme of the role of imperfections (in the sense of imperfect competition) in the generation of unemployment, and argue that they do not provide any adequate explanation of unemployment. That is not to say that there are not supply-side limitations on the achievement of full employment but these limitations arise from, for example, an inadequacy of capital equipment to sustain the full employment of labour and the balance of trade constraint.

The next two essays complement each other in a discussion of the nature of post Keynesian economics. Chapter 3 provides an overview of post Keynesian macroeconomics with its emphasis on the nature and role of money, pricing and investment, cycles and growth. It seeks to show that there is a post Keynesian approach to macroeconomics which is both coherent and quite separate and different from orthodox Keynesian macroeconomics (and even more so from monetarist and new classical macroeconomics). Chapter 4 is also a review of post Keynesian economics, taking a broader and more critical perspective than Chapter 3. It is argued that there is not yet (and perhaps never will be) a fully coherent and universal post Keynesian theory, for the simple reasons that the world is immensely complex, economies change over time and differ across societies. This chapter is intended to show both the vitality of the post Keynesian approach to economics as well as the remaining issues and disagreements within that broad school of thought.

Chapter 5 continues the theme of identifying differences within post Keynesian economics (in this case with a focus on the roles of the demand-side and the supply-side of the economy in the determination of the level of economic activity), which involves what I label a problem of over-determinacy. In effect, the post Keynesian approaches have too many forces at work in the determination of the level of economic activity. But this chapter also introduces the basis of models of price, wage and aggregate demand determination which are extensively used in the subsequent chapters.

Chapters 6 and 7 share an essentially common theme, which is to explore the relationship between macroeconomics and imperfect competition. It is often commented that the modern origins of both forms of analyses are to be found in the 1930s and both have strong elements of suggesting unemployment and excess capacity will arise in market economies. Imperfect competition is often seen as involving some rigidity of price, and the Keynesian analysis is often portrayed as suggesting that unemployment arises from a failure of prices to adjust, thereby creating an apparent link between imperfect competition and (Keynesian) macroeconomics. I argue in these chapters that the explanation of unemployment does not need to be rooted in imperfect competition (and specifically that Keynes did not need to invoke imperfect competition to explain unemployment). But, since the economy is characterised by imperfect competition, economic analysis should incorporate that, and further that there is a complementarity between aggregate demand analysis and theories of imperfect competition.

Chapter 8 considers four seminal contributions to the post Keynesian theory of pricing (those of Kalecki, Hall and Hitch, Means, and Sweezy). It argues that, with the partial exception of Means, none of these contributions sees prices as being fixed or rigid, though each of them would envisage that changes in demand do not have much impact on prices. A major aspect of these (and other) post Keynesian approaches to pricing starts from the observation that firms set prices in their own interests (though it is also the case as discussed in the previous chapter that prices have to conform at the systemic level). This means that prices do not play the co-ordinating and allocative functions which are envisaged in neo-classical theory.

The aim of Chapter 9 is to consider some aspects of the post Keynesian approach (or perhaps it should be approaches) to industrial economics. It begins, however, by a consideration of the uneasy relationship between neo-classical economics and industrial economics, and suggests that there has been a significant influence of orthodox industrial economics on many post Keynesian economists, and in particular the influence of industrial structure on profitability and prices. This is followed by an elaboration of some of the different themes within post Keynesian economics which are relevant to the theme of the chapter, and in particular discusses different views of the objectives of firms and of their controllers, which leads to a further consideration of the relationships between profits and investment. The remaining sections of the chapter seek to sketch out some themes which should feature in a post Keynesian approach to the area of industrial economics.

Some important features of post Keynesian economics (particularly the Kaleckian stream) are highlighted in Chapter 10. A first feature is the interplay between microeconomic and macroeconomic forces, such that one set forces cannot be adequately analysed without consideration of the other set.. This is illustrated by the approach to pricing and prices in this chapter. On the one side, the general level of demand and of costs influences the pricing decisions made by firms. On the other side, the prices established must have some consistency with each other and with the level of demand that is generated by the wages and profits resulting from the prices set. A second feature is the role of aggregate demand in setting the level of economic activity. It is argued in this chapter that the influence of aggregate demand is operative in the short run in the setting of the levels of capacity utilisation and of unemployment and in the long-run in the determination of the over-all scale of the economy.

In a book of essays, it is sometimes difficult for the reader to immediately identify continuing themes running through the book. Here I would point to three themes which (at least to me) recur and which are central to post Keynesian economics (and which help to sharply distinguish it from neo-classical economic analysis). The first theme is the relevance of the level of aggregate demand for the level of economic activity. This is, of course, a well-worn Keynesian theme, but I would argue that the level of demand is relevant not only for the setting of the levels of capacity utilisation and of employment in the short run but also influences the scale of the economy (in terms of the productive capacity of the economy). The second theme is that post Keynesian economics does not involve any notion of price rigidity but rather sees prices as fulfilling roles other than the allocative one assigned to them by neo-classical economics. Much of the misunderstanding of Keynesian and post Keynesian economics has flowed from the neo-classical perception than the only role of price is the allocative one, with prices set in perfectly competitive markets. The post Keynesian perception is that prices are by economic agents in their own interests, and there are many roles which can be attributed to price. The third theme is the interrelationship of the supply-side and the demand-side of the economy, and that a full analysis of the causes of unemployment must pay due attention to both. In particular, economic policies designed to reduce unemployment have to encompass both demand-side and supply-side: high levels of demand would not lead to full employment if there is an inadequate supply-side, but equally a high level of demand is necessary for the sustenance of full employment.

2. Unemployment and the dismal science

INTRODUCTION

Seeking to understand the causes of unemployment, of poverty and of differences in living standards has drawn many, including myself, to the study of economics.[1] Yet conventional economic analysis provides little insight into these problems for reasons discussed later. I can only agree with Malinvaud when he wrote that '[e]conomics as a science has failed at this moment of history to convey to the general public a useful message on what ought to have been done in order to contain unemployment' (Malinvaud, 1984), but adding that it is the lack of a useful message rather than any failure of communication. Recently, the control of inflation has generally been seen as a much more important concern of economic policy than the control of unemployment. It is difficult to understand on the basis of any consideration of the economic costs involved why this should be so, for not only does unemployment cause clear hardship and waste, there is evidence of a much wider range of detrimental effects on psychological well-being, occurrence of stress-related disease and suicide.[2,3] In contrast, it is difficult to pin down any comparable costs associated with inflation *per se* (though inflation may go along with other difficulties).[4] But there are distributional aspects (e.g. unemployment is concentrated and not generally experienced by the economically and politically powerful) which does help to explain the concern over inflation rather than unemployment.

I began the formal study of economics in October 1966 which can be seen, in retrospect, to have been about the time of the beginning of the end of the post-war full employment era in the UK. Three months earlier a deflationary

---

1. Seeking a solution for unemployment has influenced many to become economists, as evidenced in a number of biographies in Arestis and Sawyer (1992), and as surveyed in Harcourt (1992a, ch. 9).
2. There is evidence of substantial social costs of unemployment, e.g. effect on suicide rates (Shapiro and Ahlburg, 1983), mental illness and crime (Brenner, 1979). For a recent overview see Burchell (1992).
3. Economists have found it difficult to pin down any significant costs associated with inflation *per se*, especially when inflation is fully anticipated with prices, wages and other incomes rising in line. There may be redistribution by unanticipated inflation but in my view that should be ascribed to the underlying cause of inflation, rather than inflation *per se*.
4. The situation in the former Yugoslavia at the time of writing is an extreme example of this. Inflation is running at 100 000 per cent alongside the destruction of that country.

package had been introduced in response to a balance of payments crisis, and this in effect signalled the end of government commitment to full employment. Unemployment rose rapidly and reached over 600 000 in January 1967, up from just over quarter of a million in July 1966. Previously, unemployment had fluctuated around 300 000 though there had been years when it had exceeded 450,000. But from 1966 onwards there has been a tendency for unemployment to ratchet upwards – to over 900,000 in early 1972, to a million and half in the summer of 1976, and then to over three million in early 1983. I have used the figures as they were reported at the time, but as is well known there have been many revisions to the basis on which unemployment statistics are compiled, with the effect that the general upward trend in unemployment is understated. Some estimates of the current (1994) levels of unemployment measured on a basis comparable to that used in the 1960s would put unemployment at closer to four million than the near three million recorded in official statistics.

This general rise in the level of unemployment has not been confined to Britain, for as Solow has written '[t]here is a fact, a big unmistakable unsubtle fact: essentially everywhere in the modern industrial capitalist world, unemployment rates are much higher than they used to be two or three decades ago' (Solow, 1986). Of particular relevance for the remainder of this chapter is the observation that an

exceptional and equally beneficial phenomenon was the achievement in the 1960s of full employment, at least in the north-western part of the area [Europe]. This was an unprecedented success for industrial societies. Bouts of full employment for the urban labour force had occurred at cyclical peaks in the past, but a prolonged period of peace-time full employment, including the virtual disappearance of underemployment on the land, was something which the more cyclically sensitive and agriculturally dependent pre-war economies had not experienced (Boltho, 1982, pp.1–2).

During the 1950s and 1960s there had been considerable faith amongst economists that unemployment (at least in Western Europe though it remained higher in the United States) had been conquered through the acceptance of Keynesian ideas and the commitment of governments to full employment as an objective of policy. The contribution of demand management policies to the low levels of unemployment during the post-war boom was later to become a matter of some debate (Matthews, 1968, Stafford, 1970, Boltho, 1982). In a Penguin paperback, which was widely used in the teaching of A-level economics, we find the following written in 1972:

It is true that not everyone believed [in 1945] in the government's willingness to preserve full employment .... It is also true that some economists were still doubtful about the government's ability to control demand in such a way as to maintain full employment .... But such worries and sceptics were proved totally wrong. Full employment has been maintained year in and year out. [Further,] one can perhaps say that Britain and other Western countries have had full employment since the war because governments have been committed to full employment, and knew how to secure it; and they knew how to secure it because Keynes had told them (Stewart, 1972).

Indeed, even after the rise in unemployment in the UK in the second half of the 1960s there was little suggestion that unemployment would re-emerge as a major problem. In 1977, a high-powered OECD group of experts concluded that 'our reading of recent history is that the most important feature [of the recession of the mid-1970s] was an unusual bunching of unfortunate disturbances unlikely to be repeated on the same scale, the impact of which was compounded by some avoidable errors in economic policy' and that growth could resume at much the same pace as during the long post-war boom (OECD, 1977). [5]

This optimism, false as it turned out, no doubt arose from many sources, including the tendency to project the present into the future and the undoubted transformation of economic prospects between the inter-war and post-war years. However, there are two elements which are relevant for my later arguments. The first is that Keynesian macroeconomic analysis as it developed in the 1950s and 1960s focused on the demand-side with little attention paid to the supply-side. The treatment of the supply-side in Keynesian economics, such as it was, essentially disregarded any significant problems arising from that side of the economy. This is not to accept the frequently levied charge that Keynes failed to consider the supply side but rather that '[i]t is in determining the volume, not the direction, of actual employment that the existing system breaks down' (Keynes, 1936, p.379), i.e. there is *not* a malfunctioning of the supply-side. The second was a tendency to overlook the financing implications of a prolonged government budget deficit. During the 1950s and 1960s, the maintenance of high levels of employment had not generally required deficits (at least on government current account) but substantial deficits may accompany Keynesian macroeconomic policies when the latter are actually required to offset inadequate long-term private-sector demand. Indeed it is paradoxical that many governments have run substantial budget deficits since the mid-1970s when Keynesian macroeconomic policies have been perceived as superseded by monetarist policies.

THE DISMAL SCIENCE

The label of the 'dismal science', given to economics by Carlyle (1849), arose in part from the arguments of the classical economists that any tendency for wages to rise above subsistence would lead to an increased population and labour force which would push wages back down, and in part for other reasons mentioned below. Some economists appear to delight in a modern-day equivalent of the 'dismal science' approach, stressing the limits of resources and the consequent need to economise and make efficient use of the available resources. This view is summarised in the oft-quoted phrase of Friedman

---

5. Ernest Mandel is one of the few who can claim to have foreseen the end of the post-war boom. In Mandel (1964), he predicted the probable turning point around the late 1960s, and there are arguments that 1968/69 was the turning point marking the end of the post-war boom.

'there's no such thing as a free lunch'. Economic analysis often appears to be confined to studying the efficiency or otherwise of exchange. I will argue later that whilst the efficient use of available resources is worthy of study, it is rather more important to focus on ways of increasing resources at the disposal of an economy, to investigate the way in which the resources are used within the productive process and how the proceeds of production (income) are distributed. This broader conception of the scope of economic analysis can be related to the fundamental distinction which Baranzini and Scazzieri (1986), amongst others, have drawn between the exchange paradigm (i.e. the neo-classical one) and the production paradigm. The former paradigm is only concerned with exchange and its representation of production is as an exchange of inputs for outputs as dictated by a production function. The latter paradigm encompasses the study of production (e.g. of the labour process) and is concerned with questions such as the distribution of economic benefits, the creation and use of surplus and the growth of productive forces.

I have argued elsewhere (Sawyer, 1987) that one of the attractions of the Phillips curve with its purported trade-off between inflation and unemployment was that it involved the idea that more of one good thing (less unemployment) involved less of another (more inflation). Low unemployment was not a free 'good', as suggested in the simple Keynesian multiplier approach (since lower unemployment could be readily obtained by an increase in government or other spending), but rather could only be secured at the price of higher inflation. Being the holder of the chair in economics at the University of Leeds provides me with an added incentive to call this curve the Brown curve for, as Thirlwall (1972) has argued, there are good reasons to see the scatter diagrams between inflation and unemployment drawn by my predecessor Arthur Brown (Brown, 1955) as anticipating Phillips. Professor Brown did not attempt to draw any curve through the points nor to claim that the wage change–unemployment relationship was a stable one. He thus presented a more accurate picture of the wage change–unemployment nexus but at the cost of not having a curve to his name. This episode perhaps tells us something about the nature of economics as a discipline and the desire for firm conclusions and for simple diagrams.

There is though a strand in the general approach of many economists which is in one respect the opposite of the 'dismal science' view, namely the Panglossian one, with its tendency to see the actual world as the best of all possible worlds. The underlying argument is simple: if improvements could be made, they would have been made. It is encapsulated in the story concerning two economists walking down the street. One sees a £10 note lying in the road and points it out to her companion with a view to picking it up. The companion responds that there cannot be a £10 note lying there, for if there was someone would have already picked it up. In other respects, this Panglossian approach can be seen as further evidence of the dismal science, in that if the existing world were the best that is available and no improvements are possible this would be a rather dismal prospect for billions of people throughout the world.

In the context of unemployment this general Panglossian approach leads to a disbelief in the existence of genuine (involuntary) unemployment, rather than a search for explanations of unemployment and its persistence. The Panglossian view involves treating actual outcomes (unemployment) as revealed to be preferred to others (employment), with the assumption that the other option of employment was available. The latter is ensured by an appeal to Say's Law that supply will always create its own demand, so that there will be sufficient demand to hire all those willing to supply labour.

The second part of the 'dismal science' tag is of course science, and space constraints preclude any serious discussion of whether 'economics is yet a science' (to use the title of Eichner, 1983). Let me rather boldly state that if 'science' is taken to mean the generation and testing of predictions from hypotheses, then, in my view, there is no possibility of economic analysis being or becoming a science. For, simply, the testing of any hypothesis requires too many auxiliary assumptions to be made (including the essential replication of the economy over time) for any definitive conclusions to be drawn. This difficulty is, of course, not unique to economics though economists have perhaps been less conscious of these difficulties than those working in other disciplines. Further, most concepts used in economic theory (e.g. firm, market) are essentially theoretical concepts which may be useful for the purposes of analysis but do not have a necessary correspondence with like-named features of the real world (and this argument is mentioned below in the context of markets, and for further discussion see Sawyer, 1992a). However, if we use the term in the German sense that science consists of systematic enquiry then economic analysis can be viewed as a science.

UNEMPLOYMENT AND ECONOMIC ANALYSIS

A one-time standard interpretation of the emergence of Keynesian economics was that most previous (essentially neo-classical) analysis could only cope with the clear evidence of unemployment by making a variety of ad hoc assumptions – it had become a degenerate research programme. It was compared to the earth-centred Ptolemaic model of the universe, which had been made compatible with the observed motions of the stars and planets by adding epicycles to their assumed orbits around the earth; similarly neo-classical economics added trade unions, rigid wages etc. to explain unemployment. Keynesian economics, as it was interpreted from the neo-classical mind-set, was later to be often charged with using these same assumptions for its own explanation of unemployment: this was despite the fact that Keynes rarely mentioned trade unions and monopolies and assumed flexible wages and prices. But it is a reflection of the strong hold which neo-classical analysis and the market-clearing assumption have that there is a strong tendency to interpret any explanation of unemployment in terms of exogenously imposed imperfections viewed as divergences from the perfection of the clearing competitive market in theory.

The first major point to be argued here is that unemployment and excess capacity strike at the very heart of standard economic analysis and the defined purpose of economics. Robbins, in 1932, defined the scope of economics as 'the science which studies human behaviour as a relationship between ends and scarce means which have alternative uses' and thereby economic analysis 'focuses attention on a particular *aspect* of behaviour, the form imposed by the influence of scarcity' (Robbins, 1932). As Joan Robinson remarked (Robinson, 1972), 1932 was not the most appropriate time to make this definition since the major economic problem of the time was not the scarcity of resources but rather a scarcity of demand for those resources. Both of the two major theoretical advances in economic analysis in the 1930s implied demand, rather than supply or costs, as the limiting factor. The theory of imperfect competition (Chamberlin, 1933; Robinson, 1933) suggests the expansion of the firm as constrained by demand with the firm operating subject to decreasing unit costs: but the marginal revenue for an expansion of output would be less than the marginal cost of its production. The macroeconomics of Kalecki and Keynes, of course, strongly suggests that firms collectively are demand-constrained.

There is also the paradox to which Hodgson (1994) points, namely that whilst economics is often defined in terms of scarcity of resources, neo-classical economics assumes that knowledge, information and the ability to process that information (the assumption of unbounded rationality) are avail-able in abundance. This has become particularly evident in the 'rational expec-tations' literature. Further, there are some resources, of which skills and knowledge are the best examples, which are enhanced by usage, rather than depleted, through the phenomenon of 'learning-by-doing'. 'Use of a resource such as a skill has the immediate effect of improving the skill, of enlarging (rather than depleting) its availability' (Hirschman, 1985)

The way in which resources are used is worthy of study, and often resources are scarce. Many of us struggle every day with the scarcity of perhaps the ultimate resource of time, though many others suffer from time on their hands. The conditions under which resources will be efficiently used is also clearly worthy of study, though there is little reason to restrict that to the role of markets in achieving efficiency nor to forego the study of the creation of additional resources, of the distribution of income etc. and of the conditions of demand. Further, it is because unemployment is unequally distributed that it is such a social as well as an economic problem. If unemployment were equally distributed so that everyone worked say 20 per cent fewer hours than they would wish rather than 15 per cent of them having no job, others working fewer hours than desired whilst the rest work as many or more hours than they wish, unemployment would be of much less concern. It must be doubtful that the many undoubted adverse social and psychological impacts of unemployment would still arise if everyone were working 20 per cent fewer hours than they wished.

The concern with individual behaviour and rationality interacting through markets has led many economists to state that there is no such thing as macroeconomics. That is to say there are no phenomena which cannot be explained through consideration of individual behaviour and the simple summation thereof. This methodological individualism has tended to isolate economic analysis from that used in other social sciences, though this form of economic analysis has sought to colonise subjects which had previously been seen as the province of other disciplines:[6] in the words of Geoff Harcourt (Harcourt, 1982), economists have often been social science imperialists. Indeed recent attempts to extend conventional economic analysis to the behaviour of animals have been reported in prestigious economics journals (e.g. rats in Battalio, Kagel and McDonald, 1985 in *American Economic Review*, pigeons in Morgan and Tustin, 1992 in *Economic Journal*). A comparison of experiments using humans and those using other animals might well suggest that economic analysis is more applicable to non-humans than to humans since the rationality postulate is frequently broken by humans.[7] It is worth recalling that Carlyle 'charged [the utilitarian calculus] with ignoring all those sentiments, aspirations and interests which distinguished the human from other animals and was dubbed by Carlyle "the Pig Philosophy"' (Milgate, 1987, quoting Carlyle, 1850).

The emphasis on the individual also has the effect of denying the operation of systemic forces (including macroeconomic ones) and obscuring the interplay between society, institutions and individuals. For clearly the existing society and its mores influence and mould individuals, whose actions collectively change that society. Similarly, particular institutions have their norms of behaviour, working practices etc. to which individuals have to some degree to conform and yet are able to influence. 'We are faced at every turn with the problem of organic unity, of discreteness, of discontinuity – the whole is not equal to the sum of the parts, comparisons of quantity fail us, small changes produce large effects, the assumptions of a uniform and homogeneous continuum are not satisfied' (Keynes, 1972, p.262).[8]

---

6. This is most clearly reflected in the work of Becker on racial discrimination, marriage, crime etc. (e.g. Becker 1957, 1966, 1973) for which he was recently awarded the Nobel prize.

7. For example Morgan and Tustin (1992) conclude that 'Each bird's chosen input rates are compared to the efficient rates for the chosen work rate. Welfare losses from inefficient allocations of the work rate are measured in two ways and are almost always small, indicating that the birds do very well in solving their problems, and supporting the use of neo-classical models of labour supply and allocation in analysing these types of choice problem'. In contrast Loomes and Taylor (1992) conclude that their paper 'reports a series of experiments which supplement existing evidence of non-transitive behaviour in cases that involve gains' noting that 'Many economists regard transitivity as a fundamental tenet of rational behaviour.' Further, 'systematic violations of transitivity are repeatedly observed' (p.364).

8. Also 'I have called my theory a general theory. I mean by this that I am chiefly concerned with the behaviour of the economic system as a whole – with aggregate incomes, aggregate profits, aggregate output, aggregate employment, aggregate investment, aggregate saving rather than with the incomes, profits, output, employment, investment and saving of particular industries, firms or individuals. And I argue that important mistakes have been made through extending to the system

In economic analysis (as in other disciplines) it can readily be observed that theories continue to be widely accepted and taught even when their predictions are clearly contradicted by observation. This may be a necessary feature of advance in knowledge, with new observations appearing to conflict with established theory. However, in economic analysis, theories gain acceptance even when their predictions are contrary to observation. The clearest case of this is the new classical macroeconomics (though that school also sought to redefine full employment and hence unemployment). Unemployment in the new classical macroeconomic approach is ascribed to misperceptions of wages and prices and over employment is viewed as occurring as often as underemployment. This thinking enjoyed considerable popularity in the first half of the 1980s despite record post-war levels of unemployment in this country and much of Europe (though not in the USA as unemployment was reduced by the, perhaps unintended, fiscal stimulation in the guise of Reagonomics with tax cuts and budget deficits). To use a further example, the Harrod–Domar growth model with its prediction of instability continues to be taught despite the clear evidence that although capitalist economies display some instability, it is not of the dramatic form suggested by that model.

The point being made here is not just that there is dissonance between theory and observation, but that the persistence of unemployment runs counter to the widely used definition of the subject matter of neo-classical economics, derived from Robbins (1932) quoted above. Thus neo-classical economic analysis finds great difficulty in reconciling its definition of its own subject matter with the evidence of unemployment and excess capacity. Similarly, although unbounded rationality is rather dear to the heart of most economists, the waste of resources evidenced by unemployment and excess capacity appear as clear evidence of irrationality. Since in this approach society is the summation of individuals, this irrationality must spring from the individual level, in obvious contradiction to the presumed individual rationality. As a consequence, there has been much recent effort to explain unemployment as a rational decision in the sense that the occurrence of unemployment is in the interests of those who make the effective decisions concerning wages and employment. Models are constructed (under the general heading of insider/outsider approach) in which the unemployed are effectively excluded from participation in decision-making.[9] Further, evidence of the effects of unemployment on psychological well-being raises many doubts about modelling individuals as making rational choices between employment and unemployment.[10]

---

as a whole conclusions which have been correctly arrived at in respect of a part of it taken in isolation' (Keynes from preface to French edition of *General Theory*, 1971, p. xxxii).

9. See, for example, Lindbeck and Snower(1988) and Weiss (1990).

10. For example, Clark and Oswald (1994) conclude that their paper 'explores, and rejects, the hypothesis that unemployment is voluntary. Unemployed people in Great Britain in 1991 have much lower levels of mental well-being than those in work. As a rough illustration, being unemployed is worse, in terms of "lost" utility units, than divorce or marital separation.'

The widespread experience of significant levels of unemployment in most countries in most eras suggests an important question: can any decentralised industrialised economy operate over the long term with full employment? , and hence be subject to a generalised scarcity of resources? Or perhaps the question should be put as: what are the peculiar conditions under which a few economies do exhibit something approaching full employment for say a decade or more? The definition of full employment is, of course, problematic: apart from the question of what percentage of the work-force being unemployed would constitute full employment, there are also difficulties with the treatment of discouraged workers and those working part-time when their preference would be for full-time work etc. OECD countries experience with something approaching full employment (on conventional measures etc.) ended in *circa* 1973, and in many countries full employment only lasted for a few years. Soviet-style economies have generally been characterised as resource-constrained or shortage economies, in contrast with the demand-constrained capitalist economies (Kalecki, 1970). Shortages and queues were pervasive. It could be argued that these shortages, including those of labour, helped to undermine the economic system with the associated removal of pressures to maintain labour productivity, technical innovation etc.[11] Indeed, '*[r]esponsible* monetary policy works by creating enough unemployment to control inflation ... substantial unemployment is in fact an inevitable price that is paid for freedom and prosperity' (Richard Layard as adviser to Russian ministry of labour, reported in *Financial Times* 29 June 1992 emphasis added)

This may indicate that unemployment has some functional roles to play even though it is wasteful at the level of the individual (though I am aware of the trap of assuming that because something occurs it must have some purpose or function or that the results of something tells us about its cause). The occurrence of unemployment may often be due to some failure of the economy to achieve adequate performance (e.g. balance of trade difficulties constraining private and public expenditure which thereby lead to unemployment). But it is suggested here that even otherwise successful economies (however that may be defined) appear to generally operate with a degree of unemployment and excess capacity. Excess capacity can simultaneously be in the interests of the firms themselves (e.g. as an inhibition on other firms entering their market), provide a degree of flexibility in the co-ordination of economic activity and place competitive pressure on firms in their search for sales. In a not dissimilar way, unemployment serves to restrain the power of workers in terms of wage demands and places on them pressure to maintain work effort, ideas which can be traced back as least as far as Marx ('the industrial reserve army [which] during the periods of stagnation and average prosperity weighs down the active army of workers: during periods of over-production and feverish activity, it

---

11. There were no doubt many other causes as well. This should not be taken to indicate that the Soviet experiences were wholly negative ones.

puts a curb on their pretensions' (1976[1867]), but see also Kalecki (1943a), Shapiro and Stiglitz (1984) and Bowles (1985).

The idea that unemployment performs one or more systemic functions such as restraining wage inflation and enforcing worker discipline, is hardly a novel one. Unemployment is not an efficient instrument for these functions but if unemployment is to be avoided alternative instruments have to be found. It is difficult to overstate the importance of the implications of adopting this idea. It is also difficult to overstate the constricting nature of the contrary and more widely accepted (amongst economists) idea that unemployment arises from features of the real world which are assumed absent in the theory and can be labelled as imperfections. This idea put simply is that since a perfect market system is seen to involve a clearing labour market with full employment, then observed unemployment must be attributable to some features of the real world which are absent from the model. These imperfections can be lack of information, trade unions, misplaced government activity or whatever are not considered in the perfectly competitive model.

In contrast, it is postulated here that unemployment may perform a variety of functions, and the reduction of unemployment requires the development of institutions and policy instruments which would perform those functions instead. Further, the research agenda is changed from one in which full employment is viewed as the norm and deviations from it are to be explained to one in which unemployment is regarded as the usual situation and occasions of full employment require special explanation.

DEMAND AND SUPPLY, DEMAND AND SUPPLY

There are a number of jokes directed against starting from the jibe that asking six economists a question generates seven different answers. Another is one person telling another that she has taught her parrot economics. How? By teaching him to say 'demand and supply, demand and supply' in response to any question on economics. Like many 'economist' jokes, both of these contain more than a grain of truth. The central focus on demand and supply can be readily seen by looking at most economics texts, whether at the introductory, undergraduate or graduate level or at sophisticated theoretical journals. Throughout, the focus is on the market within which the forces of demand and supply interact to define market-clearing equilibrium. The basic question which has to be addressed (Sawyer,1992a) concerns the relationship between the theoretical construct of the market and the reality of actual exchange and production.

The particular concern here is with the implications of the focus on the market for the analysis of unemployment. The hold which the metaphor of market has over the thinking of most economists helps to explain why the new and fundamental ideas of Kalecki and Keynes faced such difficulties in being widely accepted (and later were to a large extent rejected). For although there was some acceptance of Keynesian notions,[12] I would argue that this was rather superficial and did not grapple with the revolutionary ideas which Keynes advanced.[13] In a battle for the hearts and minds of economists between 'the market' and 'aggregate demand', the latter stood no chance. Simply since it was assumed that the labour market was sooner or later going to clear at full employment, other elements of the economy (and notably here the level of aggregate demand) would have to adjust to that. In my view, a key failure of Kalecki and Keynes was not to confront head-on this market analysis of wages and employment and not to try to replace the market metaphor with a more appropriate one. This led first to the view that unemployment might be a short-term problem but not a long-term one (to which the Keynesian response has generally been to draw on Keynes's phrase written in a different context that 'in the long run we are all dead').[14] The eventual operation of market forces could not be denied and the labour market would eventually clear to restore full employment.[15] It then led to the conclusion that unemployment would quickly or immediately return to the 'natural' rate of unemployment. In the macroeconomic analyses of both Kalecki and Keynes, little attention is paid to the labour sector other than the setting of money wages. Real wages, being the ratio of money wages to prices, are settled by the pricing decisions of producers: employment is derived from output, which producers determine according to their expectations of demand. Thus in their analyses there is *no* labour market in the sense that the interaction of the demand and supply of labour settle real wages and employment. In effect, the economic analyses of Kalecki and Keynes can only be fully appreciated through the explicit rejection of the notion of a labour market in which real wages and employment levels are simultaneously determined.[16]

12. There was only a loose relationship anyway between the ideas of Keynes and Keynesian economics as a vast literature in the past 25 years has shown (e.g. Chick, 1983). Indeed the post Keynesian tradition emphasises its inheritance from Keynes and its differences from Keynesian economics (by which we mean that grounded in IS-LM equilibrium analysis).

13. Another revolutionary aspect of Keynes (which is particularly evident in Keynes, 1937) was the rejection of the probability calculus as a way of understanding economic behaviour in the context of pervasive uncertainty. This aspect had no discernible influence on Keynesian economics, but has been revived in recent years. See Carabelli (1988) and O'Donnell (1989) for discussion of the evolution of Keynes's ideas in this area and Davidson (1991) and Lawson (1988) for more general discussion.

14. The view that there would be full employment in the long run (exemplified in the neo-classical growth model of Solow, 1956) presupposes the existence of a long run towards which the short run tends (and it is usually assumed that the long run is not influenced by the short run). In contrast, the approach of Kalecki denies both of those propositions: for example, 'the long term trend is but a slowly changing component of a chain of short-period situations; it has no independent entity ' (Kalecki, 1971a, p.165).

15. Denied is used both in the sense that market forces will in practice come through and in the sense that economic theorists found it difficult to deny their role within the chosen theoretical framework.

16. This is not a point about the existence, or otherwise, of a single aggregate labour market, but rather that the ways in which wages and employment are determined in the real world are remote from the ways envisaged in the analysis of competitive labour markets in theory.

There have been interesting developments in the past ten years or so relating to the setting of wages by firms (e.g. efficiency wages, insider/outsider models), though the motivating force for these developments has been to search for an equilibrium microeconomic explanation of unemployment rather than to understand the mechanisms of wage determination itself. However, it is still the case that the demand/supply model has considerable hold over the thinking of most economists. 'Their research seems to be oriented less to a better and better theoretical understanding of labor market reality but rather to a search for more and more refined methods which shall bring undeniable unemployment in line with the premises of the general market and equilibrium theory' (Rothschild, 1978 as translated in Schettkat, 1992).

I have argued elsewhere (Sawyer, 1992a) that the notion of market is poorly defined and have expressed considerable doubts on the usefulness of the market metaphor. Here, the parts of the argument which are particularly relevant to labour are outlined. One clear aspect of neo-classical economics is that in many respects labour is treated like any other 'good' for which there is demand and supply. For example, '[i]n a market economy, the compensation of labour is determined by the interaction of demand and supply in each labour market: relative compensation by the interaction of relative demand and supply' and '[t]he forces of demand and supply ... are filtered through the wage formation institutions of the labour market. While these institutions do not supplant the forces of demand and supply they can constrain them sufficiently to alter wage outcomes' (Flanagan, 1992). However, even when the market metaphor is used, there is limited empirical support for competitive labour markets.

In local labour markets (where competitive forces are clearly defined and appear powerful) the empirical results are a challenge [to the neo-classical approach]. First, wages for a given type of labour vary notably (there are many examples). Second, non-wage terms are more generous in high wage plants than in low – inequality of net advantage appears to be greater than inequality of wages. Third, there is no clear market rate determined by impersonal forces of supply and demand. Fourth, there is no clear tendency to equality of wages (or net advantage) over time. Fifth, competitive forces are recognised as important by employers, but they tend to produce rough equality of wage increases rather than a tendency to equality of reward. A hierarchy emerges – with high and low wage employers – and this often shows substantial stability over time. (MacKay, 1993).

There are in my view compelling reasons for *not* treating labour like peanuts, for example that labour, being human, can vary effort and work intensity. But those arguments are put to one side here since whilst they would reinforce my argument they are not central to it.[17] My basic argument is that there is little correspondence between the market metaphor as portrayed in (neo-classical) economic analysis and the actual processes of the exchange of labour services and the setting of wages.

First, there are well-known difficulties in defining a specific market. In theory there is a well-defined commodity for which there are demand and

---

17. For some further discussion see Sawyer (1989, Part 2).

supply curves. But in practice the definition of the 'commodity' is problematic. Should the investigation focus on the market for professors of economics, all teachers of economics, all academics, all forms of employment for those labelled economists etc. etc.? There are also relevant spatial aspects: for example does the relevant market extend over a locality, a region, a nation etc., the world? The often sharp split amongst economists between theorists and applied economists has led to this difficulty being regarded as one for the applied economists to tackle in their empirical work, and one which the theorist does not need to address. However, I would argue that this is a much more serious issue than is generally realised, for the following reasons:

(i) since the concept of market is a central one in economic analysis, the inability to provide a precise definition to which there are clear real-world counterparts is significant;

(ii) setting the limits to the boundaries of a specific market for empirical work is in the hands of the investigator, and there is no particular reason to think that the boundaries adopted are those which participants would recognise as relevant;

(iii) the boundaries of a specific market are constructed in terms of a uniformity of price, which itself is an equilibrium phenomenon. Thus the definition of the scope of a particular market cannot comprehend price adjustment in disequilibrium. Hence, in practice, the definition of a particular market is undertaken on pragmatic grounds, with an inevitable gap between the theoretical definition of a market and the empirical one.

Second, there is the question of what distinguishes market activities from non-market ones. This is a broad question and here I can only focus on a part of it which relates to labour. The relevance of the question is that non-market activities are often identified as imperfections within a market context with the clear connotation that they are a problem to be dealt with.[18] In contrast, it should be argued that many imperfections such as long-term contracts, trade unions, co-operation over training etc. can have a clear positive role to play in economic development. A related aspect is that any promotion of the market requires a demarcation between market and non-market, particularly as there is often an implicit assumption that non-market activities interfere with and hamper market activities. Thus, the notions of the promotion of the market and 'leave it to the market' are vacuous until the concept of the market concept is defined.

The dominant view in economic analysis of the market is the neo-classical one in which economic relationships are mediated by price only and in which there is anonymity between economic agents. Since the commodity being exchanged is well defined and it is implicitly assumed that there is a system of

---

18. Money can also be seen as an 'imperfection' in that it has proved difficult to find a rationale for the existence of money within the confines of general equilibrium analysis. But as Keynes, Davidson and other have argued, money is an institutional arrangement which allows people to deal with the inherent uncertainty of the future (see Keynes, 1936, Davidson, 1977).

contract law backing up the exchanges, no attention need be paid to personal qualities such as reputation, reliability, trust etc. It is, of course, the case that much effort has been made to analyse situations in which there is product variety so that reputation, reliability and trust become potentially relevant.

Many institutions and other arrangements can only be appreciated by reference to those features which are *absent* from the neo-classical concept of the market. There is then a tendency to label them as imperfections and to seek to blame them for any failure of the economy to work as indicated by the market model (and perhaps to seek legislative remedies for them, which raises interesting issues on the relationship between government and market). But those imperfections may have arisen to cope with real-world aspects which are denied by the market concept. For example, a trade union can be labelled (in my view rather inaccurately) a monopoly seller of labour, but can also be viewed as an institution which protects workers from exploitation (which would be denied by the market paradigm), one which economises on transactions costs (Williamson, 1986) or one which provides workers with a voice and involvement (Hirschman, 1971).

Another view of the market arises from the Austrian school and notably the work of Hayek. The distinction is drawn between unconscious or spontaneous order arrived at through the market and conscious order imposed by the State. This dichotomy (and there is a corresponding one in the neo-classical tradition which has been particularly influential) should be seen as rather unhelpful. It is clearly the case that all existing economies (perhaps necessarily) combine elements of market and plan. The counterpoising of the market and the plan overlooks the complementarities between market and plan, and also neglects the obvious fact that economic agents within markets plan and that the outcome of much State activity is not exactly in line with intentions.[19]

A major function of the market is seen to be the matching of demand and supply through the adjustment of relative prices (and the associated variations in demand and supply). There are, of course, in practice numerous ways in which demand and supply are matched, or perhaps more accurately the degree of mismatch is reduced. For example, the employer may hire someone with greater qualifications than required for the job, which reduces, but does not eliminate, the mismatch between demand and supply. Similarly, a shortage of labour of a particular skill level can lead to lowering of entry requirements, provision of training etc.

Third, there is the question of the correspondence between the labour market metaphor and reality. Economists have typically paid little attention to methodological issues and one aspect of that is a general failure to address issues such as the correspondence between theoretical constructs and reality and the rhetoric of argument in economics (though see, for example, McCloskey 1986). Whilst demand and supply curves have adorned millions of chalkboards, that does not mean there is a close relationship between demand

19. This point has been argued by, *inter alia,* Auerbach (1988, 1992) and Hodgson (1988).

and supply analysis and exchange in the real world (and *a fortiori* production).[20] Indeed, the demand and supply analysis could be seen as a Weberian ideal type from which actual exchange processes will diverge in a variety of ways. As such, the real-world experience of exchange processes will always diverge from the theoretical expectations, so that the demand and supply analysis cannot be subject to testing by accuracy of predictions.

Demand and supply analysis has considerable rhetorical appeal to most economists. In other words, an explanation of some real-world phenomena in terms of demand and supply analysis (which in turn is based on optimising behaviour) will generally be deemed an acceptable explanation. But, for reasons hinted at above, such an explanation cannot be fully empirically investigated, and relies for its acceptance (or otherwise) on its rhetorical appeal.

WHY UNEMPLOYMENT?

Having discussed why conventional economic analysis fails to understand and explain unemployment, it is incumbent on me to provide my own approach. This is done by means of discussing three sets of factors which interact to generate unemployment in decentralised market economies.

The first broad factor is essentially a re-assertion of the key Keynesian notion, namely that in a decentralised monetary economy there is no automatic market mechanism which ensures that aggregate demand is sufficient to purchase full employment aggregate supply (even in the absence of other constraints such as balance of trade, insufficient capital equipment). The problems of co-ordination between aggregate demand and potential aggregate supply can be viewed as an inevitable consequence of a decentralised monetary economy, even if some of the problems can be reduced by appropriate policies and institutional arrangements. There are economic benefits from the existence of money and of exchange, but there are also some inevitable costs, arising from failures of co-ordination in a decentralised economy.

The key Keynesian idea that the level of aggregate demand is relevant for the level of economic activity remains intact though the precise effect that demand has will depend on the supply characteristics of an economy. But the influence of aggregate demand comes through in a range of ways additional to those analysed by Keynes, most notably that the size and quality of the supply-side (of labour and of capital equipment) is influenced over the long haul by the demand-side. For not only are additions to the stock of capital equipment (investment) influenced by the general level of demand, but also the effective supply of labour is likely to be influenced by the demand for labour. High

---

20. In a similar vein, Coase (1992) argues, in connection with much recent industrial economics, that '[w]hat is being studied is a system which lives in the minds of economists but not on earth. I have called the result 'blackboard economics'. The firm and the market appear by name but they lack any substance.'

levels of demand for labour draw people into the work-force, whilst low levels of demand push people out of the measured work-force, back into the home, into early retirement etc. Thus it is not only ratios such as the rate of unemployment and capacity utilisation that are influenced by aggregate demand, but also the scale of the economy (labour force, capital stock).

The second set of factors arises from the view that there are significant economic, social and political forces which generate and reinforce disparities and inequalities, whether between individuals, between regions or countries etc. This is an application of the notion that 'success breeds success' and the corollary 'failure breeds failure': and that '[f]or to everyone who has will more be given, and he will have abundance but from him who has not even what he has will be taken away' (St Matthew 25:29).[21] In the economic sphere, the operation of market forces (by which I mean here the spontaneous interaction of individuals) generates cumulative causation (Myrdal, 1957) and centrapetalism (Cowling, 1987, 1990). An economically successful region generates profits which enable further investment; it can attract mobile, often highly skilled, labour from other regions; it can benefit from static and dynamic economies of scale (which feature heavily in the work of Kaldor, e.g. Kaldor 1972). Other forces also arise: for example, local government revenue depends on local prosperity, enabling more prosperous areas to enjoy better public services. Whilst the prosperous regions and groups benefit from growth, prestige etc., the less prosperous do not, and the resources of the less prosperous are under-utilised.

In a world of primary products it would be reasonable to argue that international trade will (or should) be governed by comparative advantage, arising from the endowments of nature. But in a world of manufactured goods and of services, where new products are being continuously developed, where economies of scale, dynamic as well as static, operate and in which investment in equipment, research and people is recognised as important for economic success, *competitive* advantage (Porter 1990) comes to the fore. The notion of competitive advantage contains a strong element of cumulative causation, for clearly success in one time period generates the surplus which can be used to build success in subsequent periods. The availability of that surplus does not guarantee that it will be used to build future success. The surplus can be used in other ways ranging from high levels of luxury and conspicuous consumption through to military expenditure (and the UK and USA have tended recently to indulge in both), which may eventually lead to economic and political decline (Kennedy, 1988). But the availability of a surplus is a pre-condition for future success, which makes the prospects for most third-world countries a very bleak one indeed. Their current poverty does not enable them to generate much of a surplus. Some cannot even meet their minimum consumption requirements; but a surplus is a necessary feature for future prosperity. Competitive advantage can to some degree be created (as is clear from the Japanese economic success

21. For discussion see Sawyer (1989, ch. 13) and Skott(1985).

over the past 50 years) whereas comparative advantage is given by nature. The creation of competitive advantage is not something which comes about through the spontaneous market forces, but rather through the planned actions of government and others.

The consequence of this general view is that, whilst there are forces for convergence between regions and countries, there are also strong forces for divergence. Regions which are relatively backward will display both lower levels of *per capita* income and higher levels of unemployment, and find considerable difficulty in catching up with more prosperous regions.[22,23] The forces making for a lack of convergence also apply to the individual as people can become trapped in a cycle of relatively low wages, poor employment prospects etc.[24]

The third set of forces relates to the constraints on the achievement of full employment. I will discuss these later, and so here will just mention them as those arising from balance of trade considerations, inflationary pressures and the difficulties of securing satisfactory productivity levels and growth.

It would be naive to think that correct economic analyses of the causes of unemployment and of the conditions for full employment will lead to full employment, or even to the implementation of policies designed to achieve that end. For such to occur there clearly has to be a political will arising from socio-political forces pushing for full employment (Kalecki, 1943a). The experience of the last 20 years would suggest that those forces are relatively weak.

CONDITIONS FOR FULL EMPLOYMENT

When the conditions required for sustainable full employment to be achieved are listed, we soon start to think that it cannot be reached. Indeed we wonder how Western European countries came so close to full employment for so many years in the 1960s. Five considerations are outlined which I would see as important for the achievement of full employment. The discussion of these

---

22. Forces of cumulative causation would suggest that the beneficial effects of the Single European Market will be concentrated in the already rich core areas of the Community unless there are major transfers of resources to the periphery through, for example, an active regional policy.

23. There has been a considerable debate over whether there has been convergence between countries in terms of level of economic development. Baumol (1986) observed convergence of income levels amongst the richest group of countries but divergence within the poorest group which also fell behind the rest. Amable (1993) finds 'a general pattern of divergence rather than convergence in productivity levels [amongst 59 countries over the period 1960–1985]'. During the 1980s, low-income countries grew (in terms of GNP *per capita*) at an annual average rate of 1.0 per cent (excluding India and China which averaged 5.6 per cent), lower middle income countries declined by an average of 0.1 per cent per annum, upper-middle-income grew at 0.6 per cent and high-income countries at 2.3 per cent. The world average was 1.2 per cent (Source: World Bank, 1993).

24. Myrdal (1944) provides an extensive discussion of these forces with particular application to the position of black Americans in the 1940s.

points has necessarily to be brief even though each of them raises complex and interesting issues.[25]

The first consideration relates to the maintenance of adequate aggregate demand for full employment. There is perhaps little to add to the discussion of Kalecki (1943a) to the effect that even when the principles of demand management have been discovered it does not follow that they will be implemented. There are socio-political forces which militate against the use of budget deficits to sustain full employment, as can be seen from the experience of the past 20 years or so. As Kalecki wrote in 1943, '[t]he social function of the doctrine of "sound finance" is to make the level of employment dependent on the "state of confidence"' (1943a). It has also to be recognised that there may be political limits the on size of budget deficit which can be sustained.[26] But since the counterpart to a budget deficit is some combination of net private savings and foreign trade deficit, reducing savings or imports, stimulating investment or exports would be appropriate means to tackle the budget deficit, rather than raising tax rates or decreasing public expenditure.

Although there was some superficial acceptance of Keynesian ideas for much of the post-war period, there has not been a deep acceptance, so when the time came for Keynesian notions to be really applied the political will was lacking. This is evident in the way in which government borrowing still raises the spectre of pushing up interest rates and crowding out private borrowing. This overlooks a basic Keynesian point that saving is not a fixed pot from which borrowing can be undertaken: higher levels of income generate higher levels of savings. It also ignores the accumulated evidence that budget deficits are generally not associated with high interest rates,[27] one of the firmest non-facts in economics: and casual observation on the course of interest rates and budget deficits in the past few years in the UK would be consistent with those findings.

The second consideration is the absence of inflationary pressures at or near full employment. I would not wish to subscribe to any simple-minded trade-off between inflation and unemployment, for as I have argued elsewhere (Henry, Sawyer and Smith, 1976; Sawyer, 1987) that view should be rejected on both

---

25. I would not make claim to any originality in this listing of considerations for the achievement of full employment. In particular, much of my subsequent discussion echoes the work of Kalecki (1943a, 1944a) which I have further elaborated on in Sawyer (1985a ch. 7).

26. However, provided that the growth rate of the economy exceeds the post-tax real rate of interest on public debt, any size of budget deficit (defined in terms excluding interest payments on the public debt and also excluding tax paid by the recipients of the interest) maintained relative to GDP will eventually generate a constant public debt to GDP level. In that sense, any size of deficit is sustainable, though it may involve high levels of interest payments.

27. Evans (1985) states that '[o]ne paradigm in economics implies that large deficits produce high interest rates. This paradigm is not supported by the facts in over a century of US history, large deficits have never been associated with high interest rates. Even the post war periods separately offer no support for a positive association between deficits and interest rates.' Findlay and Parker (1992) concluded that 'changes in non-defense expenditure have no significant effect on the one-year [interest] rate' though increases in defence expenditure do.

theoretical and empirical grounds (though those who do subscribe to such a view do arrive at estimates of around 9 or 10 per cent for the rate of unemployment at which inflation would be constant). In many respects it is difficult to say what would happen to inflation at full employment in light of the fact that it is over 20 years since there was full employment and the many institutional changes which have occurred in the interim. But I would suggest that there are reasons to think that full employment would involve considerable inflationary pressures. The 'elasticity' of the stock of money arising from the ease with which money is created through credit and the impossibility of control over it by the State would mean that any inflationary pressures would be little constrained by the stock of money which can evolve in response to price and wage changes. Thus, even if limiting the growth of the stock of money would constrain inflation (rather than reducing output), such a monetary policy is no longer available to the British government (and more generally to governments in industrialised economies) in a deregulated internationalised monetary system.

It may be useful here to state that there are two ways of viewing inflation. The first is that inflation refers to the general rate of increase of prices and as such has to conform to some aggregate requirement. This requirement may be that inflation is in line with the exogenously given growth of the money supply or that domestic inflation has to conform to foreign inflation in a world of fixed exchange rates. The second is that the overall rate of inflation is built up from the absolute changes of individual prices and wages, where the latter may be influenced by the level of and changes in demand, expectations, conflict over income shares etc. The first view leads to simple (not to say simplistic) policy conclusions: namely, set the exogenous limit on inflation (e.g. control the money supply) and inflation will come into line. The second view would stress the conditions which lead to inflation.

The major question which arises here is whether low inflation is compatible with full employment. Having mechanisms (such as membership of a fixed exchange rate system or adherence to a lower monetary growth target) in place to bear down on inflation is not sufficient if the underlying conditions are not consistent with low inflation. Attempts to impose a stringent external constraint on inflation lead either to the constraint being broken (as was generally the case with the setting of monetary targets) and/or to unemployment and low levels of capacity utilisation.

In most countries, wage and price determination mechanisms have evolved in response to a variety of pressures but with little thought to their implications for inflationary pressures. Economies vary considerably in their wage and price setting arrangements and some are clearly more successful in constraining inflation than others. The recent trend in wage determination mechanisms (particularly in the UK) has been in the direction of decentralisation and deregulation. There is no particular reason to think that decentralised wage determination with an emphasis on performance-related pay would be non-inflationary at or near full employment. If atomistic bargaining involves frequent price and wage adjustments, then it is likely to speed up the inflationary process, whereas a degree of institutional rigidity places some brake on upward price and wage adjustments. Further, the more negotiating units there are, the less each one pays attention to the over-all impact of their own settlement, and the less effect will any call for wage restraint have.[28]

The third consideration arises from the requirement for something approaching a balance on the overseas current account at an acceptable level of unemployment which, for a country such as the UK, means an ability to compete in (relatively) high technology sectors. In a world of international financial markets a country may be able to run significant trade deficits for many years (as has been the case of the USA in recent times). But a deficit in trade combined with the interest payments on borrowing to cover previous deficits may be sufficiently large that outstanding debt grows faster than national income, leading into a debt trap situation. It is perhaps not a coincidence that rapid growth in the UK (relative to the other OECD countries, though not to earlier post-war growth experience) in the 1982–89 period came when the advent of North Sea Oil led to a substantial improvement in the current account balance, followed by a gradual deterioration back into deficit.

The current account requirement means that roughly speaking the growth of imports and of exports must be aligned. The growth of the domestic economy is then set by the growth of the world economy, and the relative (marginal) propensities to import by the UK and the rest of the world. A relatively high propensity to import by the UK and/or a low propensity to import (from the UK) by the rest of world generates a low growth rate in the UK (relative to the rest of the world). Further, if that growth rate is below the growth of productivity in the UK then rising unemployment would be the consequence. Whilst there appears to have been some improvement in the relative attractiveness of British produced goods during the 1980s there remains considerable doubt as to whether that has been sufficient to permit growth which is adequate to support full employment.

The growth of exports obviously requires a growth in the demand for them and in the capability of producing them. The growth of export demand will in turn be influenced by the attractiveness of the goods and services produced and, of particular significance, by the general growth of demand for the products concerned. It is plausible to think that relatively fast-growing demand will be concentrated in some service products and in new manufactured products. The former do not feature greatly in international trade whilst the latter tend to be associated with the new technologies and especially, of course, with the development of new and improved products. The development of new products and processes requires not only investment in research and

---

28. The relationship between the degree of centralisation of wage determination, inflationary pressures and employment is much more complex than indicated by the few words in the text. For recent discussion see Rowthorn (1992) and Calmfors and Drifill (1988).

development but also the formation of linkages between companies to develop the whole production system. In other words, an industrial strategy is required.

The essence of an industrial strategy is a commitment by government to the support of industrial development. It springs from the view that government can play a key strategic role in fostering such development. An industrial strategy does not involve detailed central planning but rather the development of an over-all coherent strategy, so that detailed decisions on, for example, support of research and development can be made on an informed basis. It is well known that economic activities such as provision of training and skills and the under-taking of research and development are likely to be under-provided by an unfettered market. Whilst the case for an industrial strategy would draw on such arguments, it involves more than correcting 'market failures'. It provides a framework for decision-making by government and by private enterprise, and commits the government to a developmental role in economic policy.[29] An industrial strategy can take many forms and be organised and implemented in ways which are thoroughly undemocratic. The type of industrial strategy which is advocated here is rather along the lines proposed by Cowling and Sugden (1993b) where they see

the concentration of decision-making within these organizations [large and dominating corporations] that shapes the character of the market. To remedy defects in the free-market economy we must seek to change the nature of strategic decision-making within the modern corporation and, in the longer-term, seek to displace its dominance within the market system. It is this process whereby a concentrated structure of decision-making within the industrial economy is progressively replaced by a democratic structure that constitutes the essence of industrial strategy-making.

It has become commonplace to see many of Britain's economic difficulties as stemming from a (relatively) poorly educated and trained workforce.[30] The precise way in which British education and training is seen as lacking varies over levels of literacy and numeracy, the balance between arts, science and engineering etc.[31] The development and introduction of new products and processes clearly requires people with the appropriate skills and training. But the number of such people required to perform such functions may be relatively small, and it is not self-evident that new production processes always require a workforce most or all of whom have high skill-levels. The benefits of a more highly trained workforce will only flow if production is organised in ways

---

29. For further discussion see Cowling and Sugden (1990, 1993a, 1993b), Sawyer(1992c, 1994b).
30. Concern over education and training levels is not confined to the UK and has become prevalent in the USA, see, for example, Shapiro (1992).
31. Cutler (1992) argues that '[t]he popularity of training as a policy also relates to general political developments in Europe in the 1980s. Faced with the ideological and political onslaught of right wing economic doctrines Social Democratic parties in Europe have moved to the right. Consequently, the critique of market mechanisms has virtually disappeared from their economic programmes. ... It is thus hardly surprising that policies to expand vocational training have been embraced so readily. In this sphere it becomes possible to chatter about 'market failure' but, equally, to make it clear that one is impeccably respectable and that such 'market failure' is only applicable to quite determinant and limited areas.'

which permit the full use of the talents and skills of the workforce. This requires a shift away from a production paradigm which works on the basis that '[i]f skills can be progressively built into machines, then workers need not be especially skilled themselves' (Abernathy, Clark and Kantrow, 1991). It is rather easier for governments and others to devise policies to raise skill levels than it is to ensure that the skills acquired are subsequently used.

The effects of sustained full employment on the position of the workers leads to the fourth consideration. My own interpretation of the end of the long post-war boom would focus on the effects of sustained full employment on the bargaining strength of workers and thereby on inflation, strikes and work effort, producing tensions which the economic system could not cope with and still maintain high levels of employment. Economists have tended to emphasise the role of financial incentives on the supply of labour, though the more recent efficiency wage literature does allow for the effect of wages on work effort (though that literature does not analyse the causes of the variations in work effort). A minority of economists, as indicated earlier, have recognised the effect of the general economic environment, including unemployment, on work effort. It is perhaps in line with the flavour of the 'dismal science' that economists stress the carrot of money and the stick of unemployment.

Other social scientists would generally take a rather more generous attitude towards human behaviour and stress many other factors which influence work effort. Academic economists suffering from relatively low pay but benefiting from significant job security should perhaps not place too much emphasis on the necessity of high wages and unemployment for work effort! I would not wish to argue that unemployment is *necessary* to ensure work effort; indeed unemployment heightens fear and brings demoralisation which serves to undermine work effort. Instead, I would argue that a sustained high level of employment requires the development of other mechanisms to underpin high levels of productivity. These mechanisms are likely to involve worker involvement and participation, job enrichment etc.

A fifth consideration derives from the relationship between the financial sector and the productive sector. There can be little doubt (especially in the Anglo-Saxon world) that the financial sector has become much more important (both economically and politically) in past decades. Further, most parts of the sector have been deregulated and displayed considerable volatility (whether of price as in the foreign exchange markets or of quantity as in loans markets). 'A freely floating exchange rate system and a deregulated financial system mean that neither the exchange rate nor the pattern of rates of interest and prices of financial and other assets reflect underlying economic realities or socially desirable levels' (Harcourt, 1992b, p.8). The thoughts of Keynes are also relevant here when he wrote that

[t]he position is serious when enterprise becomes the bubble on a whirlpool of speculation. When the capital development of a country becomes a by-product of the activities of a casino, the job is likely to be ill done. The measure of success attained by Wall Street, regarded as an institution of which the proper social purpose is to direct new investment into the most

profitable channels in terms of future yield, cannot be claimed as one of the outstanding triumphs of *laissez-faire* capitalism – which is not surprising, if I am right in thinking that the best brains of Wall Street have been in fact directed towards a different object (Keynes, 1936 p.159).

The more widespread influence of the financial sector shows in the concern over financial and nominal variables such as interest rates and inflation, rather than over real variables such as unemployment and poverty. A successfully productive economy capable of generating low levels of unemployment requires a financial sector which serves the needs of the productive sector, rather than the reverse.

The achievement (fully or partially) of these considerations underpinning full employment share the common feature of requiring fundamental changes in both the institutional arrangements of the British economy and in the widespread attitudes of opinion-formers. Further, there are in each case strong arguments as to why 'leaving it to the market' (even if that notion is capable of being defined with any precision) is unlikely to generate the intended results. It is, for example, now widely recognised that 'leaving it to the market' in the financial sector has generated volatility and other problems; that training, research and development are likely to be under-provided, and that the institutional arrangements to secure low inflation at acceptable levels of unemployment do not just appear without conscious planning.

Others may argue that this is an exercise in Utopianism since the social engineering of institutions and attitudes is a difficult, if not impossible assignment, and, more strongly following Hayek, that such attempts at social engineering will bring perverse results. Hayek (1988) argued that the view that 'anything produced by evolution could have been done better by the use of human ingenuity' is untenable. Further, '[m]ost defects and inefficiencies of such spontaneous orders result from attempting to interfere with or to prevent their mechanisms from operating, or to improve the details of their results. Such attempts to intervene in spontaneous order rarely result in anything closely corresponding to men's wishes, since these orders are determined by more particular facts than any such intervening agency can know.' There is some merit in the argument that none of us is far-sighted enough to be able to successfully predict the future. However, that is also an argument for doing nothing, which I would suggest (on past evidence) will involve further high levels of unemployment. I would argue for starting down the road, even if the route is hazy and will change as we proceed and learn.

CONCLUSIONS

The tone of my conclusions, as could easily be guessed from what has gone before, is basically pessimistic: perhaps confirmation that economists (or at least some of us) are still the 'dismal scientists'. Economic analysis has failed to understand the causes of unemployment, in part because of the use of a definition of the scope of economics, which at best marginalises unemployment, giving it the status of an imperfection. The dominance of the market metaphor and the presumption of clearing labour markets have added to the difficulties of comprehending unemployment. I have argued that there is a need to start from the presumption that unemployment is the norm in a decentralised market economy. I have also argued that the prospects for the level of unemployment over the next decade or so are bleak. Finally, the route back to full employment would require major institutional changes to initiate and then sustain full employment.

3. Post Keynesian macroeconomics: a survey

INTRODUCTION

Although many of the key ideas used by post Keynesian macroeconomists can be traced back to at least the 1930s (particularly in the work of Kalecki and Keynes), it is only in the last 20 to 25 years that a distinct school of thought under that title has emerged.[1,2] Eichner and Kregel (1975) and, shortly afterwards, the launch of the *Journal of Post Keynesian Economics* can be seen as marking the consolidation of a range of ideas and people which fell outside of the neo-classical mainstream of economics.

Post Keynesian economics does not make the sharp distinction between microeconomics and macroeconomics that is made in the neo-classical/Keynesian synthesis, so that although this chapter is focused on macroeconomics it must also consider a number of aspects which are generally considered microeconomic (e.g. pricing). The focus on macroeconomics also means that there is an implicit use of a narrow definition of post Keynesian economics.[3] The coverage of this chapter is also limited in (at least) one other respect, namely it does not discuss development and growth. This is a serious omission since many post Keynesian writers have stressed the dynamic nature of capitalist economies and the need for an analysis that overcomes the shortcomings of static equilibrium analysis. However, a proper consideration of growth would require much more space than is available.[4]

The work of Kalecki and of Keynes, which provide the foundations for much of modern post Keynesian macroeconomics, have two important common features.[5] The first is the relevance of aggregate demand for the determination

---

1. The term post Keynesian was frequently used in the 1950s and 1960s to signify economic analyses based on extensions of the IS-LM interpretation of Keynes (1936). The post Keynesian approach discussed in this paper has little relationship with that interpretation.
2. Authors such as Kaldor, Robinson, Sraffa and others made many important contributions during the 1950s and 1960s which have strongly influenced post Keynesian economists. However, the use of the term post Keynesian to signify a range of approaches (of which the short-run macroeconomics is discussed here) dates from the early 1970s.
3. Hamouda and Harcourt (1988) include Sraffian, Marxian etc. under the heading of post Keynesian.
4. Amongst the important post Keynesian writings in this area would be Robinson (1956), Pasinetti (1962, 1981), Kaldor (1957, 1961). Many of the key essays are collected together in Panico and Salvadori (1993).
5. For Kalecki's indication of these common features, see his review of Keynes (1936) which has been translated as Targetti and Kinda-Hass(1982).

of the level of economic activity, which involves the rejection of Say's Law for a monetary economy. Further, both authors distinguished between investment expenditure and consumer expenditure, and saw the former as the active and fluctuating component of demand. The second common feature is the notion that the price level of output, decided upon by producers to maximise their profits (given the level of aggregate demand and money wages), serves to determine the level of real wages. A change in money wages, with a given level of real aggregate demand, would lead to a proportionate change in output price level in the case of a closed economy (and for an open economy the change in output price level would reflect the relative importance of domestic labour and imported inputs). This can be summarised by saying that real wages are set in the output markets, rather than in the labour sectors.[6]

In some respects, the interest in the work of Kalecki and of Keynes in the past decade or so has highlighted a wide range of differences between them, which are reflected in differences between authors working within the post Keynesian tradition (for further discussion of some of these differences see Sawyer, 1985a, ch. 9).

These differences would include:

(i) The assumption of atomistic competitive markets (Keynes) or of oligopolistic markets (Kalecki). It will be argued in Chapter 7 that the assumption on the nature of industrial structure is not crucial to the workings of the principle of effective demand.

(ii) The related difference between the assumption of increasing marginal costs (Keynes) or of (roughly) constant marginal costs (Kalecki). The other side of that coin is whether real wages fall or remain constant as employment expands.

(iii) The nature of money in a developed capitalist economy. In the *General Theory*, Keynes essentially assumed money was created and controlled by the Central Bank, though in the *Treatise on Money* (Keynes, 1930) he did consider money as created by private banks (see Moore, 1984 for further discussion). Kalecki did not give the same central role to money as Keynes did, and the financial system could be portrayed as playing a rather passive role in economic activity. However, Kalecki saw the importance of the creation of money by the banking system for the expansion of aggregate demand since any such expansion has to be financed. Further, the financial system and its willingness to lend increasing amounts to a single firm only at increasing rates of interest placed a significant constraint on the size and growth of the firm (see Sawyer, 1985a, ch. 5, for further discussion).

(iv) The use of equilibrium analysis. With some minor exceptions, Kalecki's analysis was cast in terms of cyclical movements and without use of equilibrium analysis, whereas Keynes made use of equilibrium analysis.

---

6. For reasons explained in the previous chapter I have severe doubts about the usefulness of the notion of a market, and hence prefer to talk of the labour sector rather than the labour market.

(v) Expectations and the predictability of the future. These aspects of post Keynesian economics are further elaborated below, but it suffices to say here that whilst both saw expectations of the future as heavily influenced by past and current experiences, Keynes also emphasised the essential unknowability of the future.

This chapter is organised largely in terms of topics, namely money, prices, investment, labour sector and business cycles. In the discussion of these topics there is some indication of the assumptions of the institutional arrangements of a capitalist economy which post Keynesians make.

MONEY AND FINANCE

A strong theme of post Keynesian macroeconomics is that a monetary economy and a non-monetary economy operate in fundamentally different ways.[7] This stands in contrast to the prevailing orthodoxy, where it can be stated that 'the central characteristic of the market technique of achieving co-ordination is fully displayed in the simple exchange economy that contains neither enterprises nor money' (Friedman, 1982).[8] Since Walrasian general equilibrium analysis does not readily permit the introduction of money with any essential role, this leads to the rejection of any attempt to base a macroeconomic analysis of a monetary economy on Walrasian foundations (see, for example, Davidson, 1977). In a Walrasian world in which there is neither uncertainty nor the passage of time in an essential sense, there would be no reason to hold money as a store of wealth '[f]or it is a recognised characteristic of money as a store of wealth that it is barren, whereas practically every other form of storing wealth yields some interest or profit. Why should anyone outside a lunatic asylum wish to use money as store of wealth?' (Keynes, 1937). In his approach, individuals have a liquidity preference to help insulate themselves against unforeseen events as 'our desire to hold Money as a store of wealth is a barometer of the degree of our distrust of our own calculations and conventions concerning the future' (ibid). But clearly in a static (or predictable) world such as that portrayed in Walrasian general equilibrium analysis, liquidity would be of no benefit.

The existence of financial assets permits the difference between *ex ante* savings and investment for in the absence of financial assets any desire to postpone expenditure (i.e. to save) would still entail the acquisition of goods as a store of value (to provide future spending power). In this discussion, for ease of exposition, the case of a closed economy is used (since none of the essential insights in this section would be affected by the use of an open economy approach).

---

7. A monetary economy is taken to be one with not only money (serving as a medium of exchange) but also with financial assets (including money) which are stores of wealth.
8. The quote is taken from Wray (1990), who provides further quotes in a similar vein as well as a discussion of the post Keynesian approach(es).

The first question relates to the mechanism by which any difference between *ex ante* savings and investment is resolved. The pre-Keynesian answer was, of course, to see the rate of interest as the relevant price which adjusts to bring savings and investment into equality. Patinkin (1982) saw the original contribution of Keynes as being a theory of effective demand which 'in more formal terms is concerned not only with the mathematical solution of the equilibrium equation $F(Y) = Y$, but with demonstrating the stability of this equilibrium as determined by the dynamic adjustment equation $dY/dt = \phi[F(Y) - Y]$ where $\phi' > 0$'. In this quote Y stands for output and $F(Y)$ is the aggregate demand function, and ϕ' is the first derivative of ϕ. Thus any difference between *ex ante* savings and investment (or equivalently between planned output and expenditure) leads to changes in the level of output and income.

The second question refers to the relationship between savings and investment. The simple Keynesian model portrays savings as adjusting (through income changes) to the level of investment, with some forced savings in the short term. Chick (1986) argues that the relationship between savings and investment depends on the stage of development of the banking system. She postulates five stages through which banking systems have generally passed. In the first stage, a rudimentary banking system is only able to act as an intermediary between saver and investor, and then savings have to be made prior to investment. The banking system is then seen as (conceptually) evolving through the second, third and fourth stages until the fifth one is reached, which is the one of contemporary interest. From the second stage onwards, 'investment could precede saving; the matching saving in the first instance is the new bank deposit resulting from loan expansion. Subsequent banking developments have not changed that process; they have intensified it.' (Chick, 1986) By the fifth stage, a sophisticated banking system has developed liability management which entails 'at least from time to time activity seeking lending outlets rather than merely filling all reasonable loan requests' (ibid), and when banks decide to lend much more than hitherto there will be a rapid increase of credit and the stock of money. But the active nature of investment remains a feature of this fifth stage, where the sequence is seen to be plans for investment leading to application for loans, and then the granting of loans and creation of money, and finally the actual investment expenditure and corresponding savings being generated.

Debates over whether money should be treated as endogenous or exogenous (with respect to the actions of the private sector) can be traced back to at least the middle of the last century with the debates between the banking and currency schools.[9] The Radcliffe Report (1959) discussed the difficulties of defining money and whether it is possible to control the money supply in ways which post Keynesian economists would generally accept (for further discus-

---

9 . See Wray (1990) for a survey of previous debates on endogenous money and for the argument that the endogeneity of money is not a result of modern banking arrangements but has been a feature of virtually all economies.

sion see Wulwick, 1987). Kaldor (1970) attacked the then emerging monetarist approach in part on the grounds that the stock of money was not subject to control by the government or Central Bank but rather adjusted to meet the 'needs of trade'. Kaldor and Trevithick (1981) argued that

[u]nlike commodity money, credit money comes into existence as a result of borrowing from the banks (by businesses, individuals or public agencies) and it is extinguished as a result of the repayment of bank debt (which happens automatically under a system where an excess of receipts over outlays is directly applied to a reduction of outstanding overdrafts). Hence in a credit money economy, unlike with commodity money, the outstanding 'money stock' can never be in excess of the amount which individuals wish to hold; and this alone rules out the possibility of there being an 'excess' supply of money which should be the *cause* (as distinct from the consequence) of a rise in spending.

Moore (1989) summarises the post Keynesian view of money in a developed economy thus:

credit money is both a financial asset and a liability of commercial banks. Since bank liabilities are only as good as the assets behind them, bank depositors ultimately are the creditors of bank borrowers. Whenever economic units choose to borrow from their banks, deposits and so bank money are created in the process. Whenever economic units choose to repay their bank loans, deposits are destroyed .... The terms on which credit money is issued, i.e. the interest rate charged on bank loans and paid on bank deposits, play a crucial role in governing the rate of growth of the money stock, and so of aggregate income.

Moore accepts that there is 'a reasonably stable relationship between changes in the base and changes in the broad money stock, and between changes in the broad money stock and changes in aggregate money income', but argues for the causation to run back from aggregate money income rather than forward from base money. The empirical evidence produced (e.g. Moore,1983, 1988, 1989) draws upon both regression analysis and Granger–Sims causality tests. He concludes that 'the evidence appears over-whelmingly consistent with the proposition that the direction of causation runs from commercial bank loans to the money stock to the monetary base. This in turn clearly implies the much noted and documented empirical relationship between money and income reflects primarily reverse causation running from income to money' (Moore, 1989). Wray (1990, ch. 8) provides a review of the evidence supporting the endogenous money approach.

The theoretical argument is relatively straightforward. A planned increase in expenditure (whether arising from a planned real increase or in response to rising prices) has, in a monetary economy, to be backed by money if the expenditure is to take place. Attention is often given to investment expenditure but the argument is quite general for other forms of expenditure. In particular, the expansion of output (say in response to the prospect of a higher level of demand) requires the prior increase of inputs. Increased expenditure by a firm to purchase an increased level of material and labour inputs has to be financed, and may often require an increase in loans and thereby an increase in the money stock.

Four aspects of the significance of credit money in macroeconomic analysis are highlighted here. First, whilst there can be occasions on which an increase in the stock of money originates from changes in the behaviour of banks, the more usual situation is that the stock of money evolves in response to changes in demand. The creation of money occurs as a response to the demand for loans, and whether that money remains in existence or is destroyed (through loan repayment) rests on the desire to hold money. Tooke (1848) called this the 'law of reflux', which 'operates in bringing back to the issuing banks the amount of their notes, whatever it may be, that is not wanted for the purposes which they are required to serve', which now operates more broadly than just for notes.[10]

Second, growth in the money stock is seen as a response to inflation, and not a cause of inflation. For example, when costs rise, producers have to finance a higher nominal value of work-in-progress, and can do so through borrowing from the banks or through depletion of their holdings of money. The former route will then add to the stock of money, which expands as a consequence of cost rises rather than as an initiating cause.

Third, following Kalecki (1944b), doubt is cast on the relevance of the Pigou real-balance effect in an economy where money was largely credit money (and not fully backed by gold). An important feature of credit money is that it does not constitute net worth for the private sector since such money represents an asset for the holder but a liability for the issuer (usually a bank). A fall in the price level then has no net effect on the real value of the stock of credit money though it does redistribute real wealth from banks to others. However, that may understate the effect of a fall in the price level (or more generally prices rising less than anticipated) since such a fall can affect the two sides of a balance sheet differentially. In particular, if the price of assets follows the general decline but liabilities are denominated in nominal terms, a fall in price threatens the existence of the economic unit.

Fourth, the creation of credit money by private banks in response to loan demand from the private sector suggests that control by the government or Central Bank over the stock of money will be difficult. Banks, seeking to maximise profits, will often have incentives to frustrate controls over the size of the stock of money. Thus calls for control over the money supply and for an independent Central Bank to implement such a policy are ill-founded as a misunderstanding of the nature of a modern financial system.

The creation and destruction of credit money will be relevant to cyclical movements in the macro economy. At a minimum, the stock of money has to evolve to permit fluctuations of economic activity. However, the operation of the financial system may be intimately involved with the business cycle. The response of the banking system to a demand for loans (e.g. whether they are granted and at what interest rate) will impinge on the pattern of the cycle.

---

10. Quote from Tooke is taken from Wray (1990), who provides an extensive discussion of the point.

Minsky (1975,1978,1982) advances the 'financial instability hypothesis' which 'is designed to explain instability as a result of the normal functioning of a capitalist economy' (Minsky, 1978). Here we highlight a few aspects of this hypothesis.

Economic activity is seen as generating business cash flows. A part of these cash flows is applied to validate debt. Anticipated cash flows from business operations determine the demand for and supply of debts to be used to finance positions in capital assets and the production of new capital assets (investment output). Money is mainly created as banks finance business and acquire other assets and money is destroyed as debts to banks are repaid or as banks sell assets (Minsky, 1978).

When the economy is relatively tranquil   then, on the whole, firms' expectations are fulfilled and their cash flows are able to meet their debt obligations. But when profits decline (or fail to grow as anticipated) then some firms are left unable to meet their loan repayments. From such an occurrence, a full-blown financial crisis may develop, depending to a large degree on the policy response of the Central Bank. The inability of firms to repay debt places banks in an exposed position as they have incurred financial obligations to other financial institutions. If some banks or other financial institutions collapse, then further pressure is placed on other financial institutions but also on the non-banking sector, part of whose deposits with the collapsing institutions are lost. In the financial crises of the last two decades or so, in practice the Central Banks of the UK and USA (and other countries) have ensured that most troubled financial institutions have survived.

In this discussion some common themes of the post Keynesian approach have been identified. There are, though, continuing differences within the post Keynesian approach. Pollin (1991) argues that 'there are actually two distinct theories of money supply endogeneity within this [post Keynesian] tradition. Both approaches share a common starting point: the idea that the rate of money supply growth and, more importantly, credit availability are fundamentally determined by demand-side pressures within the financial markets.' The differences arise from the manner in which the financial system responds to insufficient reserves. One perspective 'argues that when banks and other intermediaries hold insufficient reserves, central banks must necessarily accommodate their needs', whilst the other view is that 'when central banks do choose to restrict the growth of non borrowed reserves, then additional reserves, though not necessarily a fully adequate supply, are generated within the financial structure itself — through innovative liability management practices' (Pollin, 1991).

Wray (1990, pp.10–11) identifies some broader differences, with four main views on money within the post Keynesian tradition. 'Keynes emphasised money as a unit of account; Minsky emphasises money as a debt which is issued to finance positions in assets; Lavoie emphasises money as credit which finances a flow of spending; and Keynes (and many others) emphasised the holding of money as a safe asset in a world of uncertainty.'

PRICING

There are a number of distinct views of pricing within post Keynesian macroeconomic analysis.[11] Before discussing their differences, three elements of similarity can be noted. First, these theories of pricing suggest that prices will not be very responsive to demand, and indeed prices may react in a way often described as perverse, that is prices move in the opposite direction to demand. Second, prices are set by producers and not by some anonymous auctioneer or market. Thus prices will be set in the interests of the producers, and this usually entails prices set such that the firm plans to supply the demand forthcoming at those prices. In a sense, firms operate to equate planned supply with expected demand at the prices which they determine. Third, whilst prices have some allocative implications they have other roles as well (which Gerrard (1989) labels as conductive, positional, strategic and financial), and these roles are further discussed in the next chapter.

The pricing theory of Keynes (1936) has been much misunderstood, and often associated with a crude price rigidity view.[12] But as Chick (1983) notes '[t]he assumption of fixed prices in Keynesian analysis is most strange, in view of the amount of space devoted in the *General Theory* to the consequences of expansion for prices:' Indeed, a more accurate representation of Keynes would be that of rapid price adjustment (in marked contrast to the temporary equilibrium school) especially in the face of wage changes (as more extensively discussed in Chapters 6 and 7). The equality between the real wage and marginal product of labour is maintained through changes in price, so that a change in the nominal wage or in the level of economic activity (and thereby in the marginal product of labour) leads to a change in price.

Kalecki's approach, often called the degree of monopoly, has also been much misunderstood and frequently dismissed as a tautology (for discussion on the charge of tautology and other criticisms of the degree of monopoly theory see Sawyer (1985a, pp.28–36)). It should first be said that the degree of monopoly analysis is only intended to apply to part, albeit a particularly important part, of the economy. Kalecki made the distinction between cost-determined and demand-determined prices. The former type is associated with manufactured and other industries where supply is elastic as a result of existing reserves of capacity. The latter type is associated raw materials and primary foodstuffs. The cost-determined/demand-determined dichotomy has sometimes

---

11. For purposes of macroeconomic analysis, the view taken of pricing can be a relatively simplified one. In general, the requirement is for a relationship between price and variables such as costs, demand etc. For other purposes, a more sophisticated view of the pricing process may well be required.

12. In my view, the only author who could be described as post Keynesian who comes close to such a view is Means (1936). There is, though, a well-developed school of thought, beginning with Clower (1965) and Leijonhufvud (1968) (e.g. Malinvaud, 1977) which analyses the impact of non-instantaneous price and wage adjustment in the context of atomistic competition. The point here is that such an approach has little to do with the work of Keynesians or of post Keynesians. For further discussion see Chapters 7 and 8.

been aligned with a fixprice/flexiprice dichotomy. There is a correspondence in the sense that in both cases the first-named type of price is viewed as unresponsive to demand. But cost-determined prices are set within the model, i.e. they are endogenous, whereas fixprices are determined exogenously.

Kalecki's analysis evolved over time (for a full discussion see Kriesler, 1987; also Kriesler, 1989, Basile and Salvadori, 1984/85, Lee, 1986), but retained its central features, which can be summarised in the following manner. In light of the history of the industry (e.g. previous collusion or rivalry) and its structure (e.g. level of concentration, barriers to entry), firms strive to maximise profits. The history and structure of the industry are the factors which combine to form the degree of monopoly. The higher the degree of monopoly, the higher will be the mark-up of price over (marginal) costs (for a formal model, which provides similar predictions, see Cowling (1982) based on Cowling and Waterson (1976)). The maximisation of profits is not exactly achieved since 'in view of the uncertainties faced in the process of price fixing it will not be assumed that the firm attempts to maximise its profits in any precise sort of manner' (Kalecki, 1971a). Firms find it costly and difficult to measure marginal costs accurately, and approximate them by average direct costs (and the approximate equality of marginal and average direct costs finds considerable empirical support). In this form, Kalecki's approach has links with the structure-conduct-performance paradigm in industrial economics.[13]

In some respects, Kalecki's particular contribution was to draw out the income distribution implications of pricing decisions. At the level of the firm, price (p) is seen as a mark-up (m) over average direct costs (adc), i.e.:

$$p = (1 + m).adc \qquad (3.1)$$

Writing out adc as average labour costs ($w.l$) and material costs ($n.f$) where w is money wage, f material input price, l and f labour and material inputs per unit of output respectively, this equation can be re-arranged to give:

$$\Pi/S = m/(1 + m) \qquad (3.2)$$

$$w/p = (1/1+m).(1 + n.f/w)^{-1} \qquad (3.3)$$

where Π is profits, so that equation (3.2) links the profits/sales ratio with the mark-up, and similarly equation (3.3) links the real wage with the mark-up. These relationships are derived for the firm level and it is asserted that analogous relationships will hold at the economy level. It is not important that there is a precise aggregation from the firm to the economy, but rather the general idea of the influence of pricing decisions on income distribution and real wages is the important element.

Post Keynesians have generally argued that there is a high propensity to save out of profits and that enterprises have a preference for internal finance

---

13. The structure-conduct-performance approach is discussed in any industrial economics text (e.g. Clarke, 1985, Sawyer, 1985b). For a test of the relationship between industrial structure and profitability with reference to the Kaleckian degree of monopoly approach see Reynolds(1984).

over external finance. This view has underpinned Kaldor's theory of income distribution (Kaldor, 1955). Steindl (1952) portrayed the steady-state position for an industry as being where the profit margin is compatible with financing growth of capital equipment (where the algebraic expression of this is formally identical to equation (3.4) below). The discussion of the approaches that focus on the links between price, profits and investment, for reasons of space only considers the contribution of one author, namely Eichner, but it can be noted that there have been a number of authors who have also elaborated these links in different ways.[14]

In Eichner's approach, the large corporation (megacorp in his terminology) is mainly concerned with growth. 'The megacorp is an organisation rather than an individual .... As an organisation, the megacorp's goal is to expand at the highest possible rate .... It is expansion at the highest rate possible that creates the maximum opportunities for advancement within the organisation, and thus personal rewards for those who are part of the firm's decision-making structure' (Eichner, 1985a). This maximisation of growth is subject to a number of constraints, among them the need to maintain a certain rate of growth of dividends.

'In pursuit of this goal, the megacorp can be expected to follow two behavioral rules. One of these is that it will attempt to maintain, if not actually to enlarge, its share of the market in the industries to which it already belongs while simultaneously undertaking whatever investment is necessary to lower its costs of production. The other behavioral rule is that it will attempt to expand into newer, more rapidly growing industries while simultaneously withdrawing from any older, relatively stagnant industries' (Eichner, 1987).

The use of internal finance is generally preferred by corporations to that of external finance on the basis of lower cost since it can be generally observed that the rate of interest obtained on lending (which is the opportunity cost of internal finance) is significantly below the rate of interest on borrowing. Further, the use of internal finance avoids the transactions cost associated with securing external finance and it also limits outside interference by financial institutions. Prices in mature oligopolistic industries are set by price leaders. Profits and growth are set by the interaction of the demand for and supply of finance (at the level of the firm). For a firm, a higher price generally means higher profits (it being assumed that firms face inelastic demand) and hence more finance for investment. But a higher price reduces demand as well as the growth of demand and the need for investment. The firm then operates where its demand for investment funds is in balance with its ability to provide the finance from its profits.

For simplicity, take the case where the firm decides to rely on internal finance only then $g.K = r.\Pi$, where g is growth rate, K is capital stock (so the left-hand side is investment expenditure), r is retention ratio and Π profits (the

---

14. Authors using this general approach include Harcourt and Kenyon (1976), Ong (1981), Shapiro (1981), Wood (1975) as well as the work of Eichner discussed in the text; subsequent chapters discuss the relationship between the different approaches to pricing in post Keynesian economics.

right-hand side is finance available for investment). This can be re-arranged to give:

$$g.v/r = \Pi/Y \qquad (3.4)$$

where v is the capital-output ratio. These equations are intended to apply for the typical firm, and then by summation for the whole economy. The interpretation of equation (3.4) is that causation runs from left to right – growth expectations, capital-output ratio and retention ratio determining the profit share. Firms are then portrayed as adjusting prices to generate the required profits share with which investment is financed. This relationship has been derived from consideration of pricing, but can be seen more generally as resulting from the equality between savings and investment. The crucial aspect of equation (3.4) should be seen as the links between growth and the distribution of income (reflected here by the profit share Π/Y).

Whilst the approaches of Kalecki and Eichner suggest that prices will be relatively unresponsive to the level of and changes in demand, they still rest on maximisation (even if that maximisation is not precisely achieved). However, starting from Hall and Hitch (1939), there has been a stream of thought which rejects optimising behaviour in favour of satisficing behaviour. Hall and Hitch argued that the results of their interviews with business people on price determination cast 'doubt on the general applicability of the conventional analysis of price and output pricing in terms of marginal cost and marginal revenue, and suggests a mode of entrepreneurial behaviour which current economic doctrine tends to ignore'. They argued that business pricing behaviour could be characterised as the addition of a mark-up to average direct costs, where average direct costs are relatively insensitive to the level of output. From the point of view of macroeconomic analysis, the approach derived from Hall and Hitch can be considered as rather similar to those of Kalecki and others, and empirical such as Godley and Nordhaus (1972), Coutts, Godley and Nordhaus (1978) are in the cost-plus pricing tradition. There are, though, some significant differences between different post Keynesian approaches to pricing, and these are more extensively discussed in Chapters 8 and 10.

LABOUR SECTOR

The post Keynesian analysis of the labour sector has two interrelated elements. The first is that the exchange of labour services and the determination of wages do not take place in a market as that term is usually understood (and for that reason this section is labelled 'labour sector' rather than 'labour market'). Wages are often set through collective bargaining, and relative wages have important status implications. Labour is a human input into production, and as such labour discipline, morale and commitment etc. are important influences on the level of productivity (for an introduction to the post Keynesian approach to the labour sector see Appelbaum, 1979).

The second, and related, element is that bargaining between employer and employee (whether conducted individually or collectively, whether with a balance or imbalance of power) settles money wages but not real wages.

[T]here may be *no* method available to labour as a whole whereby it can bring the wage-goods equivalent of the general level of money-wages into conformity with the marginal disutility of the current volume of employment. There may exist no expedient by which labour as a whole can reduce its *real* wage to a given figure by making revised *money* wage bargains with the entrepreneurs. This will be our contention. We shall endeavour to show that primarily it is certain other forces which determine the general level of real wages (Keynes, 1936).

In its simplest formulation, the level of employment (and the level of economic activity generally) is determined by the level of aggregate demand and the real wage set by the equality between the real wage and the marginal productivity of labour. Any variation in the money wage would be offset by a corresponding variation in the price level, leaving the real wage unchanged. In the formulation of Keynes, prices move rapidly to ensure the equality between the real wage and the marginal productivity of labour. In a Kaleckian approach, the real wage is set by the mark-up of prices over costs (including wages). The common feature is the idea that prices are determined after money wages are set, and that workers (individually or collectively) do not influence real wages.

The original formulation of the Phillips curve (Phillips, 1958) was consistent with this view in that it sought to explain the evolution of money wages but not of real wages. In contrast, Friedman (1968) argued that the original Phillips curve was a mis-specification and real wages (rather than money wages) moved in response to the level of unemployment or excess supply of labour. However, the post Keynesian position remains that real wages are strongly influenced by the product market (as illustrated by equation (3.3) above) rather than set in the labour sector or market.

The post Keynesian approach to money-wage determination is that the labour sector cannot be usefully analysed in terms of a labour market (or markets) in which the supply and demand for labour interact in the manner envisaged by neo-classical economics. There are, though, a variety of ways in which the determination of money wages can be approached. The one that is followed here is based on the view that in industrialised economies wages are often settled or influenced through collective bargaining between trade unions and employers. But even when there is not formal collective bargaining, the influences at work may be rather similar. For as Routh (1980) argues 'it is a mistake to imagine that there is a sharp division between unionised and un-unionised workers, for trade unions cannot do more than institutionalise and direct drives and aspirations that are already present in the individual worker'. Another approach, now often labelled neo-Keynesian, is to consider efficiency wages, implicit contracts etc., which reflect the variable productivity feature of labour (see, for example, Weiss, 1990).

In a simple formulation, for a collective-bargaining setting, the trade union is portrayed as taking the initiative in making a money wage claim (and a more elaborated formulation might consider bargaining over employment, productivity levels etc.). The target money wage of unions in their bargaining is expressed as the multiple of current money wages, expected prices to actual prices and an element which reflects movement towards target real wage, i.e. :

$$w_t^* = w_{t-1}.(p_t^e/p_{t-1}).(T/w_{t-1}/p_{t-1})^c \tag{3.5}$$

where w is the money wage, p an (appropriate) price level, p^e the anticipated price level and T the target real wage.

With allowance for the impact of unemployment on the achievement of this target, we can derive (for details see Sawyer, 1982a, 1982b) the following equation for money wage changes (for some empirical support see Henry, Sawyer and Smith (1976), Arestis (1986)).

$$\dot{w}_t = a + \dot{p}_t^e + b.U_{t-1} + c.(\ln T - \ln w_{t-1}/p_{t-1}) \tag{3.6}$$

It can be seen that either $c = 0$ or a target real wage which always quickly adjusts to the actual real wage (i.e. $T = w_{t-1}/p_{t-1}$) would allow equation (3.6) to simplify to an expectations-augmented Phillips' curve (though without any implication that this equation represents the behaviour of an atomistic competitive labour market). A combination of $a = 0$ and no effect of unemployment on wage bargaining outcome would generate a subsistence real wage view.

It is helpful to consider a steady-state type of outcome in which (i) price expectations are fulfilled and (ii) wages rise in line with prices (where for simplicity a no productivity growth case is considered). This yields:

$$\ln(w/p) = c_0 + c_1.U + \ln T \tag{3.7}$$

where $c_0 = c^{-1}.a$ and $c_1 = c^{-1}.b$.

Thus a steady-state real wage/level of economic activity relationship can be derived from this approach to money wage determination, and this is represented by the w-curve in Figure 3.1. A second real-wage/level-of-economic-activity relationship can be derived from the pricing side (e.g. from equation (3.3) above when the mark-up (m), labour productivity (l) may depend on the level of output and economic activity). Such a relationship is illustrated by the p-curve in Figure 3.1.

The inequalities drawn in Figure 3.1 represent the anticipated price and wage changes. The top inequality in any pair arises from wage determination, whilst the bottom one arises from price determination. It can be seen that zone A would constitute a classic wage/price inflationary spiral, whilst zone D would be a deflationary spiral.[15] From zones B and C, price and wage determination would lead towards the real wage of point Z.

---

15. In this formulation, no essential distinction is made between price (wage) increases and price (wage) decreases. But for many reasons, most post Keynesians would anticipate a degree of downward price and wage inflexibility.

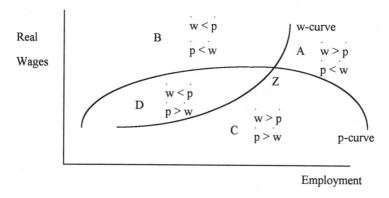

Figure 3.1 Interaction of price and wage determination

This view of inflation is essentially a conflict view of inflation (Rowthorn, 1977, Sawyer, 1983, ch. 1) in that zone A corresponds to the case where the claims on income shares made by enterprises and workers are in conflict. Point Z (at which the rate of inflation would be constant) represents some resolution of that conflict, though it may just mean that unemployment is sufficiently high to restrain real wages. Point Z can also be viewed as a NAIRU (non-accelerating inflation rate of unemployment).

It can be clearly seen that the point Z is determined without reference to the level of aggregate demand. There would appear to be no particular reason why the point Z should be demand-sustainable. By this we mean that there is no reason to think that the wages and profits implicit in the point Z would generate a level of expenditure which would exactly match the output which firms intend to produce at point Z.

This poses the central question which has plagued Keynesian economics, namely: what is the relationship between the demand and supply sides of the economy? The neo-classical/Keynesian synthesis pictures aggregate demand as crucial in the short-term determination of economic activity but with the supply-side dominant in the long-term. Adjustments in the price level, operating on the real value of the money stock, are seen as able to bring the level of demand into line with supply and full employment. In the post Keynesian approach, such adjustments are ruled out on the grounds that money is credit money and, as indicated above, does not constitute net worth.

However, within the post Keynesian approach there are numerous ways through which the supply side (as represented in Figure 3.1) can (partially) adjust to the demand side. Investment raises the capital stock and capacity, which would lead to shifts in the pricing equation. Workers' perceptions of the target real wage can change (say under pressure from government) leading to a shift in the wage equation. The supply of labour can change through variations in age of entry into and exit from the work-force, movements between the workforce and the home as well as migration. The relationship between unemployment and capacity utilisation changes as the size of work-force and capacity change.

The addition of aggregate-demand considerations to a model such as that represented in Figure 3.1 would clearly lead to a problem of over-determinacy (see Chapter 5 for further discussion). In effect, the Kaleckian approach has been to focus on the interaction between aggregate demand and the pricing equation. The NAIRU approach implicitly drops consideration of aggregate demand. The discussion of business cycles below can be viewed in a similar light. The model of Kaldor discussed there focuses only on aggregate demand without reference to the labour sector, whilst the model of Goodwin does not provide for a role for aggregate demand (since it is assumed that all savings are invested).

INVESTMENT

Although investment expenditure has been given a central role in most post Keynesian macroeconomic analysis, there has been relatively little formal theorising on the determinants of investment. This reflects a central problem which arises from the combination of the view that firms cannot easily undo investment decisions and that the forecasting of future events over the lifetime of much capital equipment is impossible. Thus, the use of formal optimising models (such as Jorgenson, 1967) is rejected on the grounds that (at least at the economy level) investment decisions cannot be reversed and that firms cannot make precise profit-maximising (or other) calculations based on well-based expectations of the future. Hence there is little point in economists modelling firms' behaviour as though they can make precise calculations.

The approach of Keynes (1936) to investment decisions has often been identified with the notion that firms will adjust their capital stock up to the point where the marginal efficiency of capital is equated with the rate of interest. This is correct in so far as it goes, but 'it was Keynes's view that "animal spirits" substantially dominated the investment decision'. The equality between the marginal efficiency of capital and the rate of interest 'is merely that *part* of the decision which is amenable to economic analysis' (Chick,1983, emphasis in original).

The marginal efficiency of capital rests on expectations about the future, and these expectations are viewed as insecurely based. 'The outstanding fact is the extreme precariousness of the basis of knowledge on which our estimates of prospective yield have to be made. Our knowledge of the factors which will govern the yield of an investment some years hence is usually very slight and often negligible' (Keynes,1936). Variations of the state of long-term expectations were viewed as particularly significant 'since it seems likely that the fluctuations in the market estimation of the marginal efficiency of different types of capital ... will be too great to be offset by any practicable change in the rate of interest' (Keynes, 1936).

In the approach of Kalecki, investment expenditure is inherently subject to cycles, and generates the business cycle. Kalecki began his analysis with the distinction between investment decisions and actual fixed capital investment, where the lag between the two arises from the period of construction, delivery lags etc. Then current economic variables can be modelled as influencing investment decisions which in turn lead at some future date to actual investment expenditure.

Firms have a preference for internal funds, as indicated above. Since current profits largely determine the volume of internal funds available to a firm they are an important determinant of investment through financial considerations. The use of external funds by a firm is limited eventually by the increasing costs of such funds as the amount of external funds required by a firm increases. Kalecki introduced 'the principle of increasing risk' (Kalecki, 1937b). In effect, the argument is that the greater the volume of borrowing which a firm wishes to undertake (relative to its profits and assets), the greater is the risk that it will be unable to repay the interest charges and the capital sum itself. Financial institutions take this increasing risk into account, and charge higher rates of interest for larger volume of borrowing.

For firms collectively, investment expenditures are constrained by the available finance, which in turn is constrained by the available pool of savings and the willingness of banks to grant loans. Investment decisions are strongly influenced by the currently available savings, though those decisions will lead to levels of future investment expenditure and thereby to future savings levels. When a particular volume of investment expenditure has taken place then it will generate (in a closed private economy) the corresponding amount of savings. But those savings are available only after the investment has taken place and are not available to finance that investment. The finance would have to come from previous savings and the creation of credit by banks.

Firms increase their capital stock as finance becomes available, which arises as profits are made and savings undertaken. Thus some potential investment delayed in the past because of a lack of finance can now proceed as finance becomes available. Further, the incentive for a firm to own and operate capital equipment can be expected to depend on the prospective rate of profit on that capital equipment relative to the rate of interest at which the firm can borrow. The rate of profit would change either because profits change or because the capital stock changes. The latter would automatically change when non-zero net investment occurs. The former would arise from, *inter alia*, fluctuations in the level of output (and thereby profits) and in the degree of monopoly (influencing the profits-to-sales ratio). Although the precise formulation has varied, the factors which Kalecki identified as influencing investment have generally been adhered to by post Keynesians (and indeed incorporated into much econometric modelling of investment behaviour).

The perspective adopted on the modelling of expectations is particularly important in the context of fixed investment since a decision on investment is seen as one which cannot easily be rectified. At the individual level, a firm would often find difficulty in selling second-hand capital equipment; at the aggregate level second-hand equipment can be thrown away (or sold overseas) but the decision cannot otherwise be undone. 'It is by reason of the existence of durable equipment that the economic future is linked to the present. It is, therefore, consonant with, and agreeable to, our broad principles of thought, that the expectation of the future should affect the present through the demand price for durable equipment' (Keynes, 1936). This consideration now leads us to some further discussion on the modelling of expectations.

EXPECTATIONS AND PREDICTABILITY

The post Keynesian approach has always stressed the roles of expectations and perceptions in decision-making, with particular emphasis on their importance for investment decisions. Post Keynesian macroeconomists have generally rejected any notion of 'rational expectations' as an appropriate approach to the modelling of individual expectation formation.[16] 'Rational expectations' would generally be rejected on the grounds that individuals do not have the informational and computational facilities which 'rational expectations' would assume and that history does not repeat itself in the way envisaged in 'rational expectations' (since the future can be forecast by reference to a known model of the economy). However, there has been a wide range of views on approaches to expectations and prediction of the future, ranging from a generalised adaptive-expectations view through to the notion that the future is inherently unknowable.[17]

An oft-quoted starting point for this view is Keynes (1937), where he argued that there are many future events for which 'there is no scientific basis on which to form any calculable probability whatever. We simply do not know'. This line of argument has been particularly developed by Shackle (1972, 1989), where he has focused on the 'human predicament' (of the impossibility of prediction arising from the fact that economic change is linked with changes in knowledge which we cannot know before they have occurred) and individual decision and action as a first cause but with no reference to any necessary relationships between economic variables. Further, the

---

16. For critical discussion of rational expectations see, for example, Colander and Guthrie (1980/81), Bausor (1983), Davidson (1982/83), Gomes (1982), Rutherford (1984), and Wible (1984/85).

17. Some models used by post Keynesians could be said to have incorporated a 'rational expectations' view in one of two senses. The first is most apparent at the level of individual or firm behaviour when actual and expected values are conflated. For example, a distinction is generally not made between the expected demand curve facing a firm (on which a firm's decisions are based) and the actual demand curve facing a firm. The price–quantity decision of the firm is assumed to lie on the actual demand curve as well as on the expected demand curve. The second sense, which is reflected in the model of price/wage interaction presented in the text, is when some steady state is analysed in which expectations are fulfilled, which is algebraically equivalent to rational expectations.

innovativeness of human beings can be stressed (particularly in connection with new ideas and technical progress).

This view has been accused of nihilism (Coddington, 1983; but see Shackle,1983/84). But even if it is not possible to explain say the level of investment expenditure, it may still be worthwhile to explore its consequences. Further, as Earl and Kay (1985) argue, people in uncertain complex situations unable to make detailed optimising decisions may use rules of thumb, which can be analysed (for extensive discussion see Hodgson, 1988,1989). There are also possibilities of extending the post Keynesian analysis in other directions. For example, Gerrard (1994) argues that

the Keynesian uncertainty hypothesis is suggestive of a very fertile research programme. Behaviour depends not only on expectations but also their credence. This implies that additional evidence can affect behaviour in two ways. First, new evidence may lead to a reassessment of relative degrees of belief between alternative expectations, leading to a different best expectation as the basis of action. Second, the new evidence may affect credence, the degree of absolute belief, which, in turn, may affect the propensity to act on the best expectation.

One feature of the *General Theory* was that different decisions are treated differently. Consumer expenditure is a rather passive decision, heavily constrained by available income. Expenditure is influenced by 'social practices and institutions' and by 'habitual behaviour of individuals'. Investment expenditure, in contrast, is an active decision which is not tightly constrained by past income and which is strongly influenced by future prospects. A distinction is drawn between short-term expectations which are largely fulfilled and long-term expectations relating to many years ahead which cannot be checked out and for which the necessary experience on which to base probabilistic estimates of the future cannot be acquired.

BUSINESS CYCLES

For post Keynesian macroeconomists, the fluctuations in economic activity are an important feature of the world, for which an explanation is sought. There are, however, a number of different views on the causes of such fluctuations. Some of the monetary aspects of business cycles have been touched on above. Post Keynesian approaches have focused on two other causes of cycles. The first arises from the fluctuating nature of investment and the impact of changes in the level of economic activity on the level of investment. The second arises from a conflict between workers and capitalists over income shares.

A particular difficulty which has plagued theories of the business cycle has been to find a mathematical formulation which would generate self-perpetuating cycles. The interaction of multiplier and accelerator (Samuelson, 1939) led to a linear second-order difference equation, which would not be capable, in general, of generating a perpetual cycle. Formulations by Kalecki (e.g. Kalecki, 1935, 1937a) led to mixed difference/differential equations which may lead to self-perpetuating cycles (for further discussion of Kalecki's business cycles theories see Sawyer (1985a, pp.54–68)).

Kaldor (1940) realised that a non-linear formulation with multiple equilibria (for the equality between savings and investment) could lead to self-perpetuating cycles, and this was later formalised by Chang and Smyth (1971). The basis of this approach is that income changes in response to the difference between desired investment and savings (both of which are functions of income and the level of the capital stock). Changes in the capital stock depend on desired investment (which is assumed to be realised) minus the depreciation on existing capital stock. Chang and Smyth (1971) show that this pair of first-order differential equations generate a limit cycle (that is a self-perpetuating cycle towards which the relevant economic variable tends). This is a model of pure cycles with no long-term growth, so that cycles take place around stationary values of output and the capital stock.

The analysis of Goodwin (1967) draws upon the 'predator–prey' literature where the 'problem of the symbiosis of two populations – partly complementary, partly hostile –' generates a pair of non-linear differential equations, the solution to which may involve a limit cycle. As such, it avoids having to invoke either ceiling and floors or random shocks to allow the continuation of cycles.

Goodwin's growth cycle, in contrast to Kaldor's approach, does not contain an independent investment function and hence assumes that savings determine the growth of the capital stock. It assumes a classical savings function (all wages spent, all profits saved), so that there is an equality between profits, savings and the increase of the capital stock (where all these variables are in real net terms). The growth rate of employment is equal to growth of output minus the rate of technical change a. The labour force is assumed to grow at a constant rate b so that the rate of change of the employment ratio, e (employment to labour force) is growth of output minus $(a + b)$. There is a struggle between workers and capitalists over real wages, where the power of workers is enhanced by high levels of employment. Goodwin (1967) shows that the resulting equations generate a limit cycle. Desai (1973) extends the analysis by introducing a money wage equation of a Phillips' curve form and a price adjustment equation based on mark-up pricing. Shah and Desai (1981) introduce induced technical change into the Goodwin model, with the effect that the system now converges back to the long-run equilibrium rather than cycling around it.

Skott (1989a) combines two elements of the role of aggregate demand and the class struggle. The ratio of savings to income depends on profit share (reflecting differential savings behaviour) and the ratio of investment to income depends on output–capital ratio and profit share. The *ex post* equality of savings and investment is established through accommodating price adjustments. Output decisions are based on profit share and employment rate. The model is completed by two identities for the growth of the capital stock and of employment. A notable feature of this model is that prices and profit margins are flexible, but that labour market conditions have no impact on real wages or on income shares.

These (and other) approaches to the business cycle illustrate (to varying degrees) a number of post Keynesian themes, namely the cyclical nature of capitalist economics, the role of aggregate demand and the conflict over income distribution.

CONCLUDING REMARKS

This chapter has concentrated on the short-run macroeconomic analysis of the post Keynesians. The focus here has been on the building blocks of macroeconomic analysis, with a neglect of complete post Keynesian models (which are developed in subsequent chapters). There has also been a neglect of the analysis of economic growth. Some of the different approaches within post Keynesian analysis have been indicated (for example, pricing theories). Nevertheless, we hope to have shown that there are solid microeconomic foundations for post Keynesian macroeconomic analysis, which provides a coherent view of the macroeconomics of developed industrialised economies.

4. Post Keynesian economics: the state of the art

INTRODUCTION

This chapter considers the present state of post Keynesian economics, and in particular to focus on some unresolved issues and the possible future developments, rather than reviewing the past achievements. A recent survey of post Keynesian economics (Hamouda and Harcourt, 1988) was entitled 'From Criticism to Coherence?'. This paper follows that one in a number of respects. It defines post Keynesian economics broadly, to cover approaches which are otherwise labelled neo-Ricardian/Sraffian, Kaleckian and neo-Marxian. It is also concerned with the positive contributions of post Keynesian economics rather than the criticism of neo-classical economics. It is clear that post Keynesian economics has progressed a long way from being mainly a criticism of neo-classical economics, though there is still a sense in which the uniting characteristic of post Keynesian economists is a belief that the real world can only be understood by a rejection of neo-classical economics. However, this chapter could be seen as answering the question posed by Hamouda and Harcourt in the negative. This is not because there is any lack of positive contributions by post Keynesians, but rather because as more work is done we have a better understanding of the differences between and within the branches of post Keynesian economics. The decade of the seventies saw not only an explosion of interest in non-neo-classical economics but also different branches exploring their own contributions, and intense debates between different branches (notably between the Marxians and Sraffians). Some have commented (e.g. Eichner, 1985b) on the differences between the tradition emanating from Kalecki with that based on Keynes (e.g. that which stresses the significance of Keynes (1937)). The decades of the 1980s and the 1990s have been marked by rather greater tolerance between different approaches, as well as a broadening out of the issues examined by post Keynesians. Further, much recent post Keynesian literature has been concerned with some of the basic issues in economic analysis (and social science more generally), such as the modelling of human behaviour, the formation of perceptions of the future etc. and this has also tended to highlight the differences between the branches of post Keynesian economics.

There are a number of recent surveys of post Keynesian economics (or parts thereof),[1] and it is not our intention to repeat such surveys here. A notable feature of post Keynesian economics is its pluralistic nature. Neo-classical economics has a central organising principle, namely individuals optimising utility subject to constraints, in the context of (usually) competitive markets, with the use of equilibrium analysis. It is clear that post Keynesian economics does not have a corresponding single organising principle. This means that the definition of post Keynesian economics can be problematic. More importantly, it incorporates a 'horses for courses' type of methodological approach; in other words different modes of analysis, different types of assumptions may be appropriate for different situations. 'Different bodies of theory will reflect different choices as to which facets of the system to concentrate on, derived from different perceptions as to how the system works, no one body of theory purporting to present a complete, closed system' (Dow (1985) in discussing what she labels the Babylonian tradition in methodology). In some circumstances, it may be found appropriate to assume that individuals are well informed about the future, whereas on other occasions stress may be placed on the uncertainty of the future (and different views can be taken of the extent of such uncertainty and how individuals respond to uncertainty). It also means that conflicting modes of analysis co-exist under the general heading of post Keynesian economics. Some find equilibrium analysis of assistance, whilst others argue that such analysis is of little use; some find formal mathematical modelling of use whilst others would reject such modelling. The multi-paradigmatic nature of post Keynesian economics can lead to intense conflict between the adherents of different paradigms. Conflict and competition between paradigms (as between individuals) can be destructive when conducted in an intolerant manner. But the competition of paradigms is also a sign of health, in that it is indicative that the paradigms are alive and vigorous and it can lead, through debate and mutual respect, to advances in analysis and understanding. However, insofar as different branches of post Keynesian economics have different methodologies (if only implicitly) then conversations between the different branches are inhibited since what is regarded as a good argument within one branch may not be so regarded elsewhere.

Any emergence of a single encompassing and coherent post Keynesian paradigm would appear to be a long way off.[2] Indeed I would argue that the vigour of post Keynesian economics during the eighties has in some respects highlighted the divisions within post Keynesian economics as it moved increas-

---

1. For some surveys see Eichner and Kregel (1975), Hamouda and Harcourt (1988), Sawyer (1988c), and Chapter 3 of this volume. Textbooks covering post Keynesian economics include Arestis (1991), Lavoie (1992), Reynolds (1987).
2. This should not be taken to decry the efforts of those who have sought to develop a coherent paradigm. Indeed I have argued (Sawyer, 1985a) that Kalecki developed a coherent approach to macroeconomics. Similarly, Eichner (1987) represents a bold attempt to present a coherent paradigm. The point that I would make is that these (and other) authors have not, for example, explored fully individual behaviour and the relationships between individuals and institutions.

ingly from criticism to positive contributions. As more thought is given to some of the fundamental issues of economic analysis by post Keynesians (e.g. modelling an uncertain future, human behaviour, the appropriateness of short-run and long-run analysis (Carvalho,1984/85), the use of equilibrium analysis), the greater the realisation of the difficulties involved. Differences of approach have to become more apparent before there is the possibility of any consensus emerging. But it may be questioned whether there is any possibility or desirability of an encompassing post Keynesian paradigm emerging. It may be strongly questioned whether an encompassing single paradigm is possible, bearing in mind the stress of many post Keynesian economists on the influence of institutional arrangements and perceptions on economic behaviour. The nature of the influence of any particular set of institutions and perceptions on economic behaviour will always be a matter of debate (as will the appropriate ways of approximating and modelling such influences). Further, economic behaviour and other factors feed back to change institutions and perceptions, so that (at a concrete level) economic analysis has to be modified.

In the space of a chapter, it is only possible to touch on a number of current issues and debates in post Keynesian economics. The issues discussed below reflect my own research interests and perceptions of current debates; I would not claim that others would share my views of the importance of these issues. I have also sought to focus on areas where a lot of further work is required, rather than on areas where considerable advances have already been made.

MACROECONOMIC CONSIDERATIONS

The neo-classical/Keynesian synthesis drew a sharp distinction between microeconomic analysis and macroeconomic analysis, which generated the view that Keynesian macroeconomics lacked any microeconomic foundations. The major contributions of Kalecki and Keynes, on which much of post Keynesian economics has been built, did not make such a distinction but rather combined the economic behaviour of individuals (and in Kalecki's case social classes), the interaction of individuals through markets and macroeconomic forces. A key feature of the post Keynesian approach is, in my view, that it has to include in its analysis forces which are genuinely macroeconomic, not 'in the sense of representing a first simplified rough step towards a more detailed and disaggregated analysis. It is macroeconomic because it could not be otherwise' (Pasinetti,1974). This is a major way in which the post Keynesian approaches differ from the new classical macroeconomics and the Austrian approach where behaviour at the economy level can be derived by the simple summation of behaviour at the individual level. While the analysis of such macroeconomic forces was the innovative contribution on Kalecki and Keynes, that does not mean that the microeconomic forces were overlooked or absent. Although Kalecki wrote little on individual behaviour, he did make a substantial contribution to the analysis of firm behaviour over pricing (and to a lesser extent investment). The pretence that Keynes had nothing to say on microeconomics (and the literature thereby generated on the search for the microeconomic foundations of macroeconomics) has been useful in neo-classical attempts to downgrade his contribution, associated with the portrayal of his approach as nothing more than Walrasian economics with rigid prices. As Chick (1983) makes clear, Keynes had much to say on the supply side even if he 'seems to have assumed that the supply side was easily understood. (How wrong he was !).'

Thus in making a division between macroeconomic and microeconomic considerations, I do not intend to imply that there should be any sharp division between them. Indeed I would argue that the interplay between the individual and the whole which is found in the analyses of Kalecki and Keynes must be extended. Post Keynesian analysis has started to recognise not only the role of bounded rationality and limited information in individual decision-making, and also the ways by which society places constraints on individual decisions and the ways in which tastes and preferences are moulded by society. The interaction between institutionalist economists and post Keynesian ones offers a fruitful way forward in this respect. Hodgson (1989) provides a good entry into such interaction.

The relationship between the demand and the supply sides of the economy (and a corresponding relationship between the macroeconomic forces and the microeconomic ones) has continued to plague both Keynesian and post Keynesian economics. The neo-classical/Keynesian synthesis views the level of economic activity as determined by the IS–LM curves in the short run with prices and wages taken as fixed. In the longer-term, prices and wages adjust, in particular to clear the labour market, and to lead to a supply-side determined level of economic activity. Our commentary on this approach and its relation to post Keynesian economics involves three points. The first relates to the nature of money. Shifts in the IS and LM curves through changes in the price level to bring the demand-side in line with the supply-side depend on money being net worth for the private sector (which in turn generally rules out credit money created within the private sector). The suggestion of Pigou (1943), leading to the Pigou effect and the consequent shift of the IS curve, was soon shown by Kalecki (1944b) to depend on money having some net worth, though credit money itself does not constitute net worth. Despite the empirical doubts on the relevance of the Pigou effect it continued to be taught as a major route through which aggregate demand would adjust to provide full employment, at least in the long run.

The idea that money in a developed capitalist economy is largely credit money, created by a private banking system, has become closely associated with post Keynesian economics.[3] The developments in the financial system and the experience of governments in seeking to control the stock of one (or more) monetary aggregates have enhanced this view of the money stock (for such a

---

3. Moore (1979, 1983, 1989) and Kaldor and Trevithick (1981) for example. See Pollin (1991), Wray (1990) for further discussion.

view from outside the post Keynesian tradition supporting that proposition see Goodhart (1989)).

The second relates to the role of prices. The neo-classical view of prices is that their only role is the allocative one, and that prices change in response to excess demand/supply. Gerrard (1989) makes the point that there are many roles which have been attributed to price, and he suggests four other roles namely conductive, positional, strategic and financial. The conductive role relates to the passing on of costs into prices through say mark-up pricing and of prices into wages. The positional role concerns the relativity of the price of one economic agent with another (e.g. the importance of relative wages). The strategic role of price reflects firms adopting competitive strategies, whilst the financial role is to enable firms to generate sufficient funds to finance expansion. Post Keynesians and others have discussed, generally implicitly rather than explicitly, at considerable length these other roles of prices. A reading of industrial economics texts would show the influence of all these non-allocative factors on the setting of prices by writers who are not generally identified with the post Keynesian approach. For example, the well-known theories on limit-pricing reflect strategic and conductive influences in the setting of prices.

I would suggest that recognition of the many roles of prices is important in at least three respects. The first relates to the macroeconomic discussion, namely that when non-allocative roles for price are considered, the rationale for prices to decline in the face of low levels of demand becomes much less compelling. Outside of perfect competition, the notion of excess demand/supply loses its meaning. Further, even when demand is low (relative to capacity), firms may find it worthwhile to not reduce prices (and correspondingly workers concerned with the positional role of wages will resist wage reductions). Thus the route of declining prices is thereby blocked off.

The second is that any lack of decline of prices in the face of low (or declining) demand is not some aberration or evidence of a lack of competition but rather an integral part of the operation of a decentralised economy. Any constancy of price is not related to any failure of markets to clear, for in the context of imperfect competition, firms generally adjust their output to the expected demand (at the prices which they set).

The third aspect concerns the relationships between economic agents. The neo-classical position is essentially that all economic relationships are exchange/price relationships. Prices are seen to co-ordinate economic activity, and act as signals between economic agents in a specific manner, i.e. rising when there is excess demand and falling when there is excess supply. This in effect confines price to its allocative role. But in a world with no auctioneer to adjust prices, there can be various messages contained in a price signal and different interpretations can be placed on the meaning of such signals. For example, a firm may charge a limit price in order to signal to other firms not to enter the industry concerned. Further, there are many routes other than price through which economic agents communicate with one another and through which economic activity is co-ordinated. Hirschman (1971) drew the distinction between exit and voice mechanisms, with the exit mechanism associated as a market mechanism and voice as a non-market mechanism. Direct communication between economic agents (i.e. voice mechanism) is likely to provide a much clearer message than indirect communication through the price mechanism.

The third comment on the neo-classical synthesis arises from the assumption of atomistic labour markets in the neo-classical synthesis and the interplay of demand and supply to determine real wages and employment. Within the broad post Keynesian tradition, there have been a variety of other ways in which the labour sector has been approached, as to some extent discussed in the section of the previous chapter entitled labour sector.

Keynesian economics became associated with a rigidity of money and/or real wages, and much effort has been expended to devise theoretical justifications for such rigidities (in the face of demand changes). Whilst real wages (relative to productivity) do not fluctuate to a large degree and could be said to exhibit a degree of constancy, nevertheless I would argue that these efforts to explain wage rigidity have been largely misplaced. A much more important question is whether Keynes was right to argue that workers could not influence real wages. If he was right, then aggregate demand side (IS/LM curves) interacting with the demand for labour (suitably defined) serves to determine real wages and the level of economic activity (though this would still omit several important features of Keynes's analysis). If, however, he was wrong, then the issues that are raised relate to the relationship between the demand and supply sides of the economy. It is, of course, the case that if the labour market is modelled in a neo-classical manner with equilibrium imposed then the supply side of the economy will dominate. But that is not the case when other views of the labour market are taken. In order to discuss that I need first to say something about these other views of the labour market.

The Marxian approach stresses the role of unemployment in holding real wages in check and in enforcing labour discipline on workers. This means that a particular level of economic activity (and the associated unemployment and capacity utilisation) is required to sustain profitability and productivity and to restrain real wages. The actual level of economic activity may cycle around, rather than tend towards, this level which restrains real wages. Nevertheless, it is the conflict over income shares (and also the maintenance of factory discipline) which would be the crucial determinant of the average level of economic activity (to which the level of demand would have to adjust), and this could be seen as operating on the supply-side of the economy. A similar problem arises in the more formal conflict theories of inflation, as discussed in the next chapter. It will be seen there that the steady-state level of economic activity then has a considerable similarity with a NAIRU (non-accelerating inflation rate of unemployment). The crucial problem here is that there is no reason to think that the level of economic activity and real wages thereby generated would lead to a level of expenditure which supports that level of economic activity.

There has been a burgeoning literature, generally labelled neo-Keynesian[4] (though I think neo-Walrasian might be more appropriate[5]) concerned with wage (and to a much lesser extent price) determination. This literature introduced a range of concepts such as implicit contracts, efficiency wages with the aim of providing, from a consideration of wage determination, an explanation of involuntary unemployment. Insofar as these approaches have been successful in providing explanations for involuntary unemployment, they face the same problem as indicated in the last paragraph. This can be restated in the following manner: when essentially supply-side considerations determine the level of economic activity and the distribution of income (e.g. through the determination of the real wage), are there reasons to think that the resulting level of demand will exactly match the consequent level of output? To answer yes to that question is in effect to reinstate Say's Law in that income is seen to generate exactly sufficient demand to purchase the corresponding output. But if the answer is no, then we are left with the question of what the mechanisms are by which demand and supply adjust to one another.

In the neo-classical/Keynesian synthesis, the demand for and supply of labour are functions of only the real wage, and their intersection provides a full employment equilibrium position. There appears to be no route through which either the demand or supply of labour schedules could adjust to bring the resulting market-clearing equilibrium position into line with the aggregate demand side. When there are differences between the aggregate demand and the aggregate supply outcomes, the neo-classical/Keynesian view would be that aggregate demand would determine the level of economic activity in the short run. But, in the longer term, aggregate demand is seen to adjust to aggregate supply since there is no mechanism for the supply-side equilibrium to adjust. On the aggregate demand side, it is assumed that the price level can move to bring aggregate demand into line with the supply side. From a post Keynesian perspective matters look rather different. First, the movement in the general price level assumed by the neo-classical/Keynesian synthesis is of the form that prices fall in the face of excess capacity and rise in the face of excess demand; i.e. the general price level retains an allocative role. But when prices have other roles and when they are set by firms (rather than by an auctioneer or an anonymous market) then there is no compelling reason to think that prices will fall in the face of excess capacity.

---

4. For surveys of these approaches, see for example, Frank (1986), Lindbeck and Snower(1986) Weiss (1990).

5. I feel that neo-Keynesian is inappropriate through the lack of reference by this literature to the role of aggregate demand, and its focus on price-determination arrangements which may lead to equilibrium involuntary unemployment. For a critique of the neo-Keynesian approaches, see Davidson (1993).

The second difference is the more important, and in my view has been rather neglected. In the post Keynesian framework, there are many routes through which there can be adjustments on the supply side (broadly defined) of the economy, some of which would be in the direction of bringing the demand-side and supply-side into line though others would not. There are a range of adjustments which can take place in terms of the supply of labour. High levels of unemployment lead to the ejection of people from the labour force (back into the household, the return of migrant labour), with the reverse effects operating during periods of low recorded levels of unemployment. The relationship between employment and the level of economic activity will be changed by additions to or deletions from the stock of capital equipment. Workers' aspirations (as reflected in the target wage) and the market power of firms (as reflected in the mark-up of price over costs) may adjust, so that the relationships between real wages and the level of economic activity (based on wage and price determination) shift.

There are no doubt many other routes through which the demand and supply sides of an economy adjust to one another (and also reasons why adjustment takes a long time). The idea of adjustment processes does not imply that the final outcome would be one of full employment and capacity utilisation. However, the major point which I wish to make here is that there would appear to be no strong reason why supremacy should be given to the supply side in the sense of leaving all adjustment to the demand side. The attention of macroeconomists should also be devoted to the exploration of the various ways in which demand and supply factors interact. But this exploration cannot be undertaken within the framework of the neo-classical/Keynesian synthesis since the demand and supply of labour schedules are treated as given and not subject to endogenous adjustment. Whilst that remains the case, the supply-side of the economy would be determined by the interaction of those schedules, thereby generating full employment. In contrast, as hinted above, the post Keynesian approach opens up numerous possibilities for mutual interaction between demand and supply aspects.

HUMAN BEHAVIOUR AND EXPECTATIONS

Much of the apparent strength of neo-classical economics comes from its use of the paradigm of optimisation subject to constraints. Besides easily lending itself to mathematical techniques, it appears to provide a tool for most, if not all, occasions. Any decision-making situation can be portrayed in these terms, and predictions derived from them. Despite a lack of evidence to support this approach and some evidence at variance with it (see Hodgson, 1988 pp.83–6), it is still widely employed in economic analysis. One can only think that this arises from the lack of a convenient alternative. But it means that many areas of study within economics (e.g. environmental economics, health economics) are dominated by neo-classical economics and utility analysis with very few contributions which could be regarded as post Keynesian.

In the past, post Keynesians have not paid a great deal of attention to individual decision-making. Whilst, as argued above, there has always been some microeconomic underpinnings of post Keynesian macroeconomics, it has often been of a rather simple form, and did not depart a great deal from a neo-classical approach. Kalecki, for example, postulated a modified form of profit maximisation for firms in their pricing decisions, but said virtually nothing about the behaviour of workers and consumers. The analysis was at the level of social classes rather than an individual, and postulated a high propensity to spend by workers. There was very little said about factors influencing the supply of labour nor of the motives of workers and trade unions.

The Sraffian approach is notable for a focus on the objective factors determining long period prices, and for its neglect of discussion of the motivation of either capitalists or workers. In Sraffa (1960), 'there is, for example, no assumption pertaining to economic agents. In particular, there is no specification that producers maximise profit, that consumers choose rationally' (Bradley and Howard, 1982). Capital moves from low profit to high profit sectors, leading to the equalisation of the rate of profit, which implies an element of profit seeking, but it leaves open questions of, for example, how capitalists perceive profit opportunities. But, more generally, there is much post Keynesian macroeconomic analysis that can proceed without directly saying anything about human behaviour, dealing with, for example, the relationship between wages, profits, investment and consumer expenditure.

The debates between 'Chapter 12' (fundamentalist) Keynesians (e.g. Shackle) and the neo-Ricardians (e.g. Eatwell and Milgate) have highlighted some sharp differences between post Keynesians on matters of expectation formation, uncertainty and human behaviour. The (implicit) views on expectations and uncertainty cover the whole range from a position not inconsistent with 'rational expectations'[6] through to a stress on the unknowability of the future, and from an almost total disregard of individual human behaviour through to a stress on the innovative nature of human beings.[7] 'A gulf divides the Sraffian theorists from others like Simon and Shackle who emphasise problems of uncertainty and argue that the economy cannot be captured by a static analysis' (Hodgson, 1989).

It could be argued that the approaches identified as being at the extremes are both rather incomplete. The Sraffian approach portrays some system-level requirements to which prices have to conform without dealing with individual

6. By this I do not mean that post Keynesians adopt a 'rational expectations' perspective for individual behaviour. However, when, for example, a firm is modelled as making a price decision based on expected costs, demand etc., it is often assumed, even within a post Keynesian approach, that the relevant expectations are (on average) fulfilled. It does not generally appear as 'rational expectations' since expected costs and actual costs are not always distinguished. Further, much steady-state analysis implicitly or explicitly assumes that any relevant expectations are fulfilled.

7. 'In so far as economics is about choice as a first *cause*, that is the coming into being of decisive thoughts not in all respects to be explained by antecedents, it is *essential* to talk in terms of what is foreseen, expected and intended' (Shackle, 1989, emphasis in original).

motivation. The Shacklian approach focuses on the 'human predicament' (of the impossibility of prediction arising from the fact that economic change is linked with changes in knowledge which we cannot know before they have occurred) but with little reference to any necessary relationships between economic variables. Carvalho (1984/85) fills out this spectrum with three other approaches (to make a total of five). But as he argues,

major issues separate Post Keynesian gravity center models from historical time theories. This difference seems to be rooted not only in the choice of subjects but, in fact, in the *vision* adopted by each group. Historical time models are not just 'short run' models. It is the dichotomy between short and long run models itself that is rejected. Gravity center models, on the other hand, assume that it is possible to separate long run forces from short run occurrences, ignoring the latter.

There is a rather fundamental question here, namely whether the differences between branches of post Keynesian economics are so profound that they should be regarded as quite separate schools of thought. It may be that they will eventually turn out to be complementary in the sense of utilising different techniques of analysis to answer rather different questions. However, the argument of Carvalho above would suggest that the differences are rather more fundamental in that these differences involve quite different views of human nature and behaviour and of the relationships between the individual and the whole.

A rather minimalist response to the unbounded rationality assumption frequently used in neo-classical economics has been to focus on the idea of bounded rationality. Although not expressed in those terms, the approaches to pricing of Hall and Hitch (1939) and Kalecki (1943b) contained elements of bounded rationality arguments (as indicated in the discussion in Chapter 9). Hall and Hitch (1939) argued that their approach 'casts doubt on the general applicability of the conventional analysis of price and output pricing in terms of marginal cost and marginal revenue, and suggests a mode of entrepreneurial behaviour which current economic doctrine tends to ignore'. They conclude that 'in pricing they [business people] try to apply a rule of thumb which we shall call 'full cost', and that maximum profits, if they result at all from the application of this rule, do so as an accident (or possibly evolutionary) by-product'. There is some reflection of habit persistence and the influence of the past in that '[t]here is usually some element in the prices ruling at any time which can only be explained in the light of the history of the industry'. Habit persistence and the use of 'rules of thumb' can be seen as derived from bounded rationality in that individuals do not find it worthwhile to persistently recompute their optimal set of actions. Indeed, habit persistence would tend to stabilise decisions, and lead in the direction of aiding rather than hindering forecasting.

One feature of constrained utility maximisation is that the framework used for every type of decision is essentially the same, with the decision-maker always being treated as well informed. In contrast, in the *General Theory*

(Keynes, 1936) different types of decision are treated differently. Decisions relating to consumer expenditure are treated as being rather passive ones, as they are constrained by and respond to available income. Decisions on investment expenditure, in contrast, are active ones not tightly constrained by past income flows and strongly influenced by future prospects. A distinction is drawn between short-period expectations (on, for example, the level of demand) which are largely fulfilled[8] and long-period expectations relating to many years ahead which cannot be checked out and for which the necessary experience on which to base probabilistic estimates of the future cannot be acquired. Further, '[t]he outstanding fact is the extreme precariousness of the basis of knowledge on which our estimates of prospective yield have to be made. Our knowledge of the factors which will govern the yield of an investment some years hence is usually very slight and often negligible' (Keynes, 1936).

It has been argued in connection with Chapter 12 of Keynes (1936) that '[a]lthough subjectivist ideas do provide a wedge of sorts for driving between behaviour and circumstances, it is apparent that it is a thoroughly unwieldy tool with which to operate: it cannot be satisfactorily used in a selective and discriminating way to detach a certain class of behaviour (or the behaviour of a certain group of individuals) from the circumstances in which the behaviour takes place' (Coddington, 1983). The argument here is rather that there are indeed different types of decision and different types of decision-makers. The decision on whether to buy petrol today may be a routinised decision (e.g. respond to amount of petrol in car petrol tank) whereas the decision to buy a car is one to which much more thought is given. Expectations and perceptions are rather more important in a decision to buy a car (which has some aspects of a one-off decision) than in a decision to buy petrol (which in any event is rather consequential on the decision to buy a car). One aspect of the dichotomy between consumer expenditure and investment, especially in Keynes (1936), is that the former is a routinised decision whereas the latter is not. Consumer decisions may then be more predictable (to an outside observer) when arising from habit and rules of thumb than if they arise from re-computation of utility maximisation in each period of time. In some contrast, investment decisions may well be less predictable in the face of uncertainty over the future than they would be with well-based information. This would suggest that which decisions are akin to slowly changing habits and which are innovative leaps into the dark is an important question, the answer to which would strongly influence the modelling of key decisions. The satisficing approach of Simon and others may then be applicable to those decisions which are strongly influenced by habit, whilst much of the analysis of authors such as Shackle is applicable to one-off and innovative decisions.

---

8. 'For the theory of effective demand is substantially the same if we assume that short-period expectations are always fulfilled' (Keynes, 1973).

ORGANISATIONS AND INSTITUTIONS

Much of the discussion of behaviour has taken place at the level of the individual in isolation, but in doing so there‘is considerable danger of forgetting the role of organisations and institutions. Economists from the Austrian school as well as some post Keynesians have been particularly prone to this. But the large corporation is a clear factor of the developed capitalist world, as are governments, trade unions, households etc. One part of the significance of large (and not so large) organisations is that such organisations wield considerable economic and political power. There is a sense in which it is individuals and not organisations who make decisions, though even then the interaction between individuals in the decision-making process may be a significant influence on the decisions made. Even so, the decisions that are made are carried out in the name of the organisation. The organisation continues when individuals leave, and indeed the corporation can be infinitely lived. The impact of decisions made by individuals within an organisation (especially those on investment) can live on because of the continuation of the organisation.

Another part of the significance of organisations and institutions is the impact that they have on the behaviour of individuals who are members of the organisation: to use a phrase in current circulation, people joining an organisation 'go native'. It indicates that people's behaviour within an organisation is influenced by the customs and norms of that organisation. 'If we make the less rigid assumption that individual tastes and preferences are malleable and will change or adapt, then the objectives and behaviour of agents can be moulded or reinforced by institutions' (Hodgson, 1989). There can be seen to be a two-way process involved between individuals and institutions (and society in general). In one direction, an institution is composed of individuals, whose actions and desires influence what the institution does, and perhaps even the form that the institution takes. This has been the traditional route in economic analysis, with some attention given as to how differences between individuals within an organisation can be resolved. But the other direction is also important and has been little explored within economic analysis. The norms and rules of behaviour within an institution (society) strongly influence individuals and their behaviour. Some degree of conformity between the aims of the institution and individuals is necessary for the institution to function effectively. The relationship between the individual and an institution to which she belongs is analogous to that between the micro level and the macro level. There is an essential interdependence between the two on which post Keynesian economics should focus, rather than the neo-classical view that the individual level is the only one that matters (reflected in the phrase of Mrs Thatcher that 'there is no such thing as society') or the other extreme of a form of class imperative governing individual actions.

One branch of post Keynesian economics (which is underplayed in most surveys) has paid particular attention to the market power of large organisations, and this is the monopoly capital school (for a survey see Sawyer, 1988b). The significance of the growth of large, often transnational, enterprises is (at least) four-fold. First, it strongly indicates the absence of atomistic competition over many sectors of the economy. If atomistic competition ever existed, it has now evolved into oligopolistic competition etc. At a minimum that suggests that something like the forces of centralisation and concentration as analysed by Marx are at work generating the elimination of atomistic competition.

Second, a significant proportion of transactions takes place within firms rather than between firms (and it could be added within households). Drawing on the distinction drawn by Coase (1937) between the allocation of resources between firms and that within firm, there has been a replacement of market transactions by administrative transactions as the size of firms has increased over say the last century. This reinforces the point that the analysis of exchange relations exercised through the market is a rather partial analysis of the allocation of resources and the co-ordination of economic activity. Further, since transnational enterprises by definition straddle national boundaries, it means that much international trade takes the form of the movement of commodities within a single organisation rather than the market exchange of international trade theory.

Third, it raises questions of the exercise of economic (and political) power. Some of that power is reflected in the prices charged to consumers and the profits thereby gained. But their power is rather inadequately represented by power over prices. The concentration of decision-making over important economic variables such as investment, research and development and the location of industry and employment provides large corporations with power vis-à-vis workers and governments, and a power to influence the direction in which the economy and society evolve.

Fourth, authors such as Kalecki and particularly Steindl (1952) argued that the growth of concentration would exacerbate stagnationist tendencies. Higher levels of concentration would raise profitability and savings whilst tending to reduce incentives to innovate and to invest. The relevant point here is that it is postulated that differences in industrial organisation (concentration) have implications for macroeconomic performance.

Whilst a part of the construction of post Keynesian economic analysis has to address the issue of individual behaviour, there is a danger in overlooking the significance of the scale of transnational enterprises. The relationship between the individual and the organisation is one in which the norms, rules and ethos of the organisation influence the individual as well as the individual having some (though perhaps close to zero) influence on the organisation. Within the organisation, resources are allocated by administrative and other decisions and not through the market (though this allocation will be influenced by prices etc.). Decisions are made by individuals but propagated in the name of the organisation, and impinge on others. Whilst post Keynesian analysis has addressed the issue of the interaction of economic agents and the macroeconomic level, the argument here is that the relationship between individuals and organisation, and between organisations and the macroeconomic level also has to be addressed.

THE OPERATION OF LAISSEZ-FAIRE MARKETS

There has clearly been a substantial shift in the intellectual and political climate in many countries in the direction of the use of markets and against the use of planning in the past decade or so. In economic analysis, the theoretical basis of such a shift has been a combination of general equilibrium analysis and the views of the Austrian school. The purpose of this section is to consider the nature of a post Keynesian perspective on the operation of markets.

Whilst there are many ideas associated with post Keynesians authors that are relevant, there has so far been an absence of a well-worked-out analysis of the operation of a laissez-faire market economy. At the present time, I would see such an analysis as seeking to combine a number of elements.

The first element draws on the work of Kaldor and Myrdal on the forces of cumulative causation.[9] At the level of a region or nation 'the play of forces in the market normally tends to increase, rather than decrease, the inequalities between regions'. Further, 'trade operates with the same fundamental bias in favour of the richer and progressive regions and against other regions' (Myrdal, 1957). The general idea of cumulative causation complements a rejection of the usefulness of (especially static) equilibrium analysis (Kaldor, 1972). It does pose however a fundamental dilemma, namely that the creation of new resources (investment, training etc.) is intimately involved in the forces of cumulative causation and the growing disparities which that entails. A major policy question which arises is whether it is possible to design forms of government intervention which will limit the operation of the forces of cumulative causation without at the same time damaging the process of resource creation. But otherwise resources in the unsuccessful regions and sectors will be under-utilised and undervalued, with unfettered markets not generating efficient use of the available resources.

The general notion of cumulative causation and the associated disparities can, in my view, be linked with two other aspects of the operation of laissez-faire markets. One of these is the Marxian analysis of competition with the idea that there are forces of concentration and centralisation at work. This links with the idea of cumulative causation in the sense that large firms are cumulatively successful and the small firms tend to disappear. Further, when it is seen that centralisation has a spatial dimension, decision-making becomes regionally concentrated. Cowling (1985) extends the argument into the political sphere. He argues that

9. The major contributions to the notion of cumulative causation being Myrdal (1957) and Kaldor (1972, 1985). See also Skott (1985), Sawyer (1989 ch. 13, 1991a) and Thirlwall (1987) for discussion.

growth in sheer size is not the only threat to democratic control; there are also parallel changes in the organisation of big business which will tend to undermine democracy. Two tendencies which stand out in this regard are transnationalism and centripetal developments .... Centripetal economic tendencies become centripetal political and cultural tendencies and the community enters a vicious circle of relative decline. Thus whole communities lose effective control over their own lives – the essence of true democracy.

The other is the radical political economy analysis of segmented labour markets.[10] For the present argument, that analysis has two important ideas. The first idea is that some markets (the secondary sector) operate in ways akin to the neo-classical atomistic competitive model, whilst other markets (the primary sector) operate in fundamentally different ways. Further, in many respects of wages and working conditions, the performance of the primary sector is superior to that of the secondary sector. The competitive markets of the secondary sector with rapid turnover of workers and low wages are not conducive to acquisition of skills by workers or to the implementation of high technology. The primary sector has features of long-term contracts, rather rigid wages etc., which are characteristics of inflexibility, deemed by neo-classical analysis to be detrimental features. Yet it is expected that the primary sector will exhibit higher levels of training and skill and be more conducive for technological developments.

The second idea is that the operation of the segmented labour markets tends to reinforce rather than reduce inequality. Groups who are socially and economically discriminated against are assigned largely to the secondary sectors with poor wages and employment conditions whilst more favoured groups move into the primary sector with relatively high wages and good employment conditions. Further, those skills that workers in the secondary sector do possess will tend to be under-utilised since the nature of the productive process does not require high skill levels.

The second element of a post Keynesian approach to an analysis of laissez-faire markets is that 'markets are organised and institutionalised exchange. Stress is placed on those market institutions which help to both regulate and establish a consensus over prices and, more generally, to communicate information regarding products, prices, quantities, potential buyers and potential sellers' (Hodgson, 1988). An institutional view of markets has a range of interesting implications. It suggests that 'the market is itself an institution, comprised of a host of subsidiary institutions and interactive with other institutional complexes in society. In short, the economy is more than the market mechanism: it includes the institutions which form, structure and operate through, or channel the operation of the market' (Samuels, 1987). Thus the operation of any market, whether it is regarded as competitive or not, cannot be analysed without specifying the precise institutional arrangements of that market (e.g. rules of operation, laws and customs). If the market is identified as anonymous

---

10. See, for example, Edwards (1979), Gordon, Edwards, and Reich (1982), Edwards, Reich and Gordon (1973), Reich (1984) and for a discussion see Sawyer (1989 ch. 3).

exchange mediated only by price (as suggested by both Walrasian general equilibrium and the Austrian school), then it is clear that 'of the enormous number of transactions in an economy, only a tiny fraction of them take place in what may literally be described as a "market"' (Auerbach, 1988). Transactions within firms, within households etc. take place outside the market. Further, many relations between firms fall outside the range of arms-length exchange relations. These extra-market relations can range from explicit or tacit collusion over prices and pooling information to co-operating over training, research etc.

The third element of a post Keynesian approach relates to the exercise of market power. Much of the post Keynesian literature has assumed that large firms exercise considerable market power (over prices). Eichner (1973) generally portrayed mature industries as dominated by a price leader while Kalecki emphasised the role of the degree of monopoly (influenced by industrial concentration, barriers to entry etc.). Authors such as Clifton (1977) and Auerbach (1988) have argued that competition in the sense of mobility of capital and tendency towards equalisation of the rate of profit has intensified over the past century. However, this does not mean that the economic power of large corporations is diminished. The existence of power of large corporations, whether in terms of their own markets or relative to workers and government, can readily co-exist with competition and rivalry, and specifically with the mobility of capital. Indeed, when that mobility is reflected in the internationalisation of production, the mobility enhances power over workers and government.

The fourth element has already been touched on above, and this is the role of prices and how resources are allocated. Clearly, in the Walrasian general equilibrium analysis, prices have just an allocative role and resources are allocated by that price mechanism. A post Keynesian analysis would recognise that prices have many other roles. It is clearly possible (as in the Sraffian analysis) to construct an analysis of price in which price has no allocative function, with price serving a variety of other roles. Further, as argued above, there are many routes through which resources are allocated other than through the price mechanism.

One of the purposes of a post Keynesian analysis of the operation of markets is to discover the limits of the usefulness of the market as a means of co-ordinating economic activity. A closely related purpose is to influence the formation of public policy. The general idea here can be simply stated: activities which appear harmful when analysed from a general equilibrium standpoint can appear explicable and/or useful when viewed from a post Keynesian perspective. Inflexibility of prices (with respect to demand changes) is viewed unfavourably in general equilibrium terms, but is explicable in post Keynesian analysis. Further, a degree of inflexibility of price may be beneficial; for example such inflexibility injects some stability into the environment against which individuals make decisions (see Hodgson, 1988). In that way, better decisions may be made than would occur with volatile prices. Indeed, the case of flexible exchange rates provides a good example where the volatility which results from competitive markets may be rather high, leading to calls for intervention to reduce the volatility.

SOME METHODOLOGICAL REMARKS

The purpose of this section is to make some remarks on the connections between debates over methodology in economic analysis and post Keynesian economics. There would appear to be a strong tendency for each school of thought to have its own methodology. For, 'what constitutes a good argument within one mode of thought may be a bad argument within another' (Dow, 1985), so that discourse within a particular school of thought requires some general acceptance of a common methodology so that constructive debates can take place. It does mean, however, that discourse between different schools of thought may be rather difficult since each one has its own views on what constitutes a good argument. This is often expressed when the adherents of one school of thought dismiss other schools as unscientific, i.e. that the other schools do not adhere to the methodology advocated by the adherents of the school in question. In this respect, Dow (1985) argues that '[b]ecause the Post Keynesian framework derives primarily from a Babylonian style of thought, however, it cannot accord with the Cartesian/ Euclidean criteria for scientific activity. It is, therefore, straightforward for orthodox theorists to dismiss Post Keynesian theory as unscientific.' Further, insofar as the different branches of thought within post Keynesian economics have distinct methodological approaches, then fruitful discourse between post Keynesian economists is likely to prove difficult.

The naive falsificationist methodology, popularised by Friedman and many others, has generally been used to underpin neo-classical economics (though it is arguable whether there is any necessary link between the two). The widespread appeal to this methodology had two effects of relevance here. First, it was used to support the use of (in some sense) obviously implausible assumptions as central elements of the analysis, and in particular to justify perfect competitive assumptions. Post Keynesian economists have generally sought to build theories which are built on realistic assumptions derived from observation of the world, whereas the neo-classical approach has been based on *a priori* notions on human behaviour (utility and profit maximisation) and many adherents have defended the use of unrealistic assumptions. This difference is perhaps best illustrated by theories of pricing where post Keynesians (e.g. from Hall and Hitch (1939) through to Eichner (1973), as discussed in Chapter 9 below) have based their theories on generalisations of observed behaviour, whereas the neo-classical approaches remain based on *a priori* theorising. A particular example of theorising based on observation was Kaldor, whose approach was generally based on the notion of stylised facts about the world.

Hence the theorist, in choosing a particular theoretical approach, ought to start off with a summary of the facts which he regards as relevant to his problem. Since facts as recorded by statisticians, are always subject to numerous snags and qualifications, and for that reason are incapable to being accurately summarised, the theorist, in my view, should be free to start off with a 'stylised' view of the facts – i.e. concentrate on broad tendencies, ignoring individual detail, and proceed on the 'as if' method, i.e. construct a hypothesis that could account for these 'stylised facts' without necessarily committing himself to the historical accuracy, or sufficiency, of the facts or tendencies thus summarised (Kaldor,1961).

In an extensive discussion of Kaldor's approach, Lawson (1989) argues that Kaldor placed too much weight on induction over deduction, and that both induction and deduction are insufficient by themselves.

Second, when the practice of science is identified with progress through attempted falsification, then economic analysis can only be seen as a science by the generation of precise predictions from theories and the attempted falsification of those predictions. It also encouraged a stress on the distinction between the positive and the normative. The downside of this methodology has been the further encouragement of the use of unrealistic assumptions (since it is only predictions that matter) and the exclusion of theories that do not yield predictions.[11] Recent writings have not been kind to this view. On the one side, there is a realisation that neo-classical economics did not live up to its falsificationist principles (e.g. Eichner, 1983). The difficulties of the exact testing of theories and of establishing that a theory has been empirically rejected have been widely recognised – the Duhem–Quinne thesis on the problems of devising crucial experiments in the face of the need for auxiliary hypotheses etc. On the other side, the narrowness of the prediction criteria has been widely appreciated and a realisation that debates within a scientific community draw on many different types of argument (McCloskey, 1986, Henderson, Dudley-Evans and Backhouse, 1993).

In many respects, post Keynesians have little to fear from a falsificationist approach in the sense that (I would argue) the predictions of post Keynesian economics are generally more accurate than those of neo-classical economics (as I have argued in connection with macroeconomics in Sawyer, 1982a), even taking into account that neo-classical economics generates very few predictions. Nevertheless, a falsificationist approach did serve to narrow down the role of economic analysis (in principle to that of prediction).

Gerrard (1990) identifies three fallacies amongst methodologists: 'the objectivist fallacy of the existence and attainability of objective truth, the infallibilist fallacy that there exists a logical calculus guaranteeing the achievement of objective truth, and the essentialist fallacy that there is one essential aspect of science. All these fallacies are present in the bastardised form of falsification which has found its way into the methodology of economics.' He continues to argue that there

---

11. This was the classic argument advanced by Friedman and Stigler against the use of the theory of monopolistic competition. However, in that case, the argument concerns a class of predictions, namely that monopolistic competition does not yield unambiguous predictions on price and quantity responses to exogenous changes without further specification. It does of course yield prediction on capacity utilisation etc..

is an emerging new view of science seeking to cast off objectivist, infallibilist and essentialist modes of thought. This new view may best be described as the 'concentric circles' model of science. At the core of the scientific process lies the interplay between theory and empirical observation .... Science is a social process involving socio-political and institutional factors both within the scientific community as well as the wider society of which scientists are part .... Last, but by no means least, there is a technological dimension to science. Science has practical implications, providing the capability to do things.

Post Keynesian economics and its general approach sits rather easily with the rejection of the three fallacies identified by Gerrard. It would be widely recognised that our perception of the world and of truth is conditioned by the social environment and our personalities, and that the world (and hence the truth about the world) changes over time. Post Keynesians would accept that there is a wide range of 'tools', not just mathematical ones, that can be useful in economic analysis. The neo-classical approach has developed a single set of first principles from which all economic phenomena are to be explained (perhaps more accurately predicted). As I have suggested above, post Keynesian economics does not have any single organising feature, no set of first principles. The idea that the exploration of different questions requires different techniques of analysis is a welcome one. But it does raise the question of whether the different techniques are essentially complementary or whether they are in some fundamental way contradictory. I would see a major question for post Keynesian economics to be whether the different branches which come under that broad umbrella are complementary or contradictory. In the longer term it may emerge that there is a single set of first principles on which post Keynesian economics can be based, notwithstanding the apparent conflicts within post Keynesian economics indicated above. Alternatively, it may turn out that different branches of post Keynesian economics diverge in terms of first principles.   ·

Post Keynesians would accept that there are many aspects to science and that a theory has to be judged by a range of criteria. Whilst, as I argued above, post Keynesians have little to fear from judging their theories by reference to their predictions, the limitations of such criteria and the immense difficulties of implementation would also be widely recognised. Insight, explanation and realism would also be seen as relevant criteria, though again with a recognition of the considerable difficulties of applying such criteria.

The sociological dimension recognises that the current frames of reference are the result of particular social and historical processes. This principle could be seen to fit in with the general post Keynesian presumption that social and historical processes form current institutions, thought and actions.

Finally, post Keynesians would place emphasis on the practical uses of their analyses. The purpose of economic analysis is seen to be to provide an understanding of the way in which the economy and society operates in order to find ways of improving human welfare.

CONCLUSIONS

Any attempt to survey (however briefly) work under the banner of the post Keynesian forcibly illustrates (at least to those undertaking the survey) the current vigour of post Keynesian economics. The pluralism of post Keynesian economics is also clearly visible. The pluralism and vigour lead to any survey being inevitably partial. A number of frameworks of analysis have been established within which specific questions can be explored, and such exploration will surely happen. At another level, the most exciting yet most difficult step will be to be some degree of synthesis between the branches of post Keynesian economics. Some have already started but more work is required on the issue of how far the adoption of different theoretical perspectives reflects the analysis of different types of problem for which it is not inconsistent to use different approaches. But in some comparisons it may well prove that the different theoretical perspectives reflect fundamentally different world views, leading to yet more fragmentation within economic analysis.

5. Conflict and aggregate demand in post Keynesian economics: the problem of over-determinacy

INTRODUCTION

There are two important ideas concerning the determinants of the level of economic activity advanced by those working outside the mainstream and within a broadly defined post Keynesian tradition. The first one is the influence of the level of aggregate demand with an obvious focus on the role of the demand side of the economy for economic activity. The second is that the level of economic activity (notably the level of unemployment) serves to constrain income claims (particularly wages) and here the focus is on the supply-side of the economy, albeit with an emphasis on the role of conflict. The supply-side is not modelled as being perfectly competitive, and there is no reason to identify the level of employment determined on the supply-side as being that of full employment. But it should be noted that it is difficult (and indeed misleading) to separate demand and supply effects since, for example, the level of effective demand influences the supply-side through capital formation and attachment to the labour force (see Chapter 2).

Neo-classical monetarism suggests that the level of employment and output as well as relative prices are in essence determined on the supply-side of the economy, and the demand-side (essentially the stock of money) determines variables such as the absolute price level and its rate of change.[1] Post Keynesians and some others tend to feel uneasy over any model even when developed within the post Keynesian tradition, which suggests that the level of employment and output are effectively determined on the supply-side of the economy. This may reflect an aversion to being associated with a conclusion which is reminiscent of neo-classical monetarist conclusions. Further, it appears to deny the relevance of aggregate demand in the determination of the level of economic activity, and hence essential parts of Keynes (1936) appear to be abandoned. However, the analysis of the supply-side here is quite

---

1. Interest rates do not fit easily into that categorisation in the sense that interest rates may be seen as demand-side determined (as in an IS-LM analysis) or on the supply-side by the interaction of the forces of thrift and productivity.

different.[2] In particular, there is no suggestion that the supply-side generates full employment or operates in an efficient manner. There is also an interconnection between the supply-side and the demand-side which is further elaborated in later chapters.

Marglin(1984) has pointed to a problem of over-determinacy when insights from what he calls neo-Keynesian economics (which can be seen as a branch of post Keynesian economics) are combined with those from neo-Marxian economics. Expressed crudely, we could say that neo-Keynesian economics stresses the role of aggregate demand (the equality of savings and investment) in the determination of the rates of profit and of growth, whilst the neo-Marxian economics stresses the role of income distribution and savings in the determination of those rates. The formal expression of this below will make it clear that a problem of over-determinacy is involved with the number of equations exceeding the number of variables. Marglin seeks a resolution to this by introducing the rate of inflation as an additional variable, but at the expense of incomplete adjustment by wage bargainers to the rate of inflation.

The purpose of this chapter is to further explore these problems. In effect, the starting point is that within the broad compass of post Keynesian economics there are too many ideas of the determination of the level of economic activity which leads to problems of over-determinacy. It is further argued that it is possible to classify authors in terms of which key post Keynesian idea they have dropped in order to avoid the over-determinacy problem. It can also be argued that periods of history can be identified when one of the ideas (or corresponding equations) were not fully operational. In that way, the over-determinacy problem was overcome through one of the equations being non-operational.

The problem of over-determinacy can be overcome by the introduction of a further variable, of which the interest rate and price level are obvious candidates. However, it is argued, this still means that the supply-side is the dominant force determining the level of economic activity. Finally, these theoretical arguments can be used to illuminate some policy discussions on the effectiveness or otherwise of increasing government expenditure to raise the level of economic activity.

There are a number of important limitations to the approach adopted here. The discussion is limited to a consideration of equilibrium outcomes. The use of equilibrium analysis has considerable limitations in overlooking questions of cyclical movements, the role of uncertainty and the analysis of movements through time. The justification is that of relative simplicity and of sharpening the issues. The analysis is also limited to a consideration of a closed economy.

---

2. A number of people have responded to a previous paper of mine (Sawyer, 1982b) in this way. The analysis of that paper suggested that the conflict arising from wage and price determination set a level of employment which kept the claims of workers and capitalists in balance, and in that sense employment (and real wages) were determined on the supply-side of the economy. The level of aggregate demand then has to adjust to that supply-side determined level of employment and output.

STATEMENT OF THE OVER-DETERMINACY PROBLEM

This section provides the simplest statement of the over-determinacy problem by consideration of price and wage formation and the level of aggregate demand. The modelling of price formation is considered first. A particularly important implication of the formation of prices is the one for the real wage. In the approach considered (but the argument applies more widely) when the firm accepts the money wage as a given (amongst other variables) and then proceeds to set price, the firm's actions over price clearly strongly influence the real (product) wage. This can be interpreted as saying that the real wage is influenced, if not formed, in the product market rather than in the labour market through the interaction of demand for and supply of labour. In an algebraically similar way, efficiency wage considerations lead to the real wage being set by the firms in the pursuit of their interests. [3]

It is also the case (see Sawyer, 1983, 1988d for further details) that a wide range of models of imperfect competition and the model of perfect competition all generate a non-causal relationship (which may be positive or negative) between real wages and the level of output (and of employment). However, whilst this real wage–employment relationship may be given a demand for labour interpretation by many, that is incorrect since the relationship is non-causal and the real wage is non-parametric (Sawyer, 1988d).

The main features of the general approach can be illustrated by a simple monopoly model. The use of the monopoly model has the advantages of simplicity and a coincidence between firm and industry, thereby avoiding problems of interdependence and of aggregation.

Let the demand facing a monopolist be $Q^d = (p/r)^{-k}D^b$ where p is the price of output of the monopolist, r is an index of substitutes and D is a measure of the real level of aggregate demand. The production function is taken for convenience as a homothetic transformation of a Cobb–Douglas function so that $Q^s = f(L^cM^{1-c})$ where L is a measure of labour input, M of material input. The price of material input is m and wage is w. The decision variables for the firm are taken as L and M, with p and Q derivable as a consequence of decisions on L and M. The relationship between L and M is given by:

$$M = ((1-c)w/cm).L \tag{5.1}$$

It is then possible   to derive the equation for labour demand in terms of the exogenous variables $(w, m, r$ and $D)$ as:

$$(k - 1/k).D^{b/k}.c.f'(X).((1-c)w/cm)^{(1-c)} = (w/r) \tag{5.2}$$

where $X = L.((1-c)w/cm)^{(1-c)}$.

---

3. For surveys of these approaches, see for example, Frank (1986), Lindbeck and Snower (1988) and Weiss (1990).

There are numerous ways of expressing the demand for labour which involves endogenous variables. One which involves the real product wage is required for later use and this is:

$$(k - 1/k).f'(X).c.((1 - c)w/cm)^{(1-c)} = (w/p) \quad (5.3)$$

The implied relationship between real product wage and labour employment in equation (5.3) can be positive or negative, depending on f' and f'' (the first and second derivatives of f).[4] A rather similar relationship between real product wage and output can also be derived, and this is done in equation (5.5). This relationship which will be extensively used below.

An oligopoly model along the lines of Cowling and Waterson (1976) which allows for some interdependence between firms' output decisions (in the context of homogeneous product) would yield rather similar results. The one of interest for discussion below relates real product wage with employment level, and at the firm level this is:

$$((k - z)/k).f'(X).c.((1 - c)w/cm)^{(1-c)} = (w/p) \quad (5.4)$$

where z is the perceived elasticity of total output with respect to firm's own output, and X defined as above. Aggregating across firms would yield a similar relationship at the industry level. The nature of the relationship between real wage and the level of economic activity is now complicated by possible variations in both k and z as the level of economic activity varies.

These equations relate employment with the real product wage. But since output and employment are related (with $Q = f(L.(1-c).w/cm)$), it is simple to derive an output, real product wage relationship. It is convenient to normalise output by some notion of full (or desired) capacity written as u and this discussion is summarised as:

$$w/p = F(u, w/m, Z) \quad (5.5)$$

where Z could be labelled the degree of monopoly (cf. Kalecki, 1971a) and is taken to represent factors such as degree of collusion and elasticity of demand which influence the profit mark-up. Equation (5.5) is an association between real wages and capacity utilisation derived from considerations of firm behaviour, based on input prices w and m. Each particular point $(w/p, u)$ corresponds to a specific level of aggregate demand facing firms. A slight re-arrangement would provide a relationship between real wage and employment of the form:

$$w/p = G(L, w/m, Z) \quad (5.6)$$

It is useful to move between the real wage-capacity utilisation space and the real wage–employment space, and noting that a general feature of equations

---

4. In the case of constant returns to the variable factors (f'=1), L does not appear in equation (1), and the employment decision is independent of the real product wage.

(5.5) and (5.6) is a relationship between real wage and level of economic activity.

Equations (5.5) and (5.6) have been derived at the level of the firm, and we now seek to apply them at the economy level. Since the precise functional forms of F and G are not a matter of any concern to the general line of argument, we are not concerned with the properties of F and G in the aggregate. For a particular distribution of aggregate demand across firms, a specific level of aggregate demand would generate a real product wage and employment combination for each firm, which can then be summed across firms to provide the aggregate equivalents of equations (5.5) and (5.6). However, in general, we would expect that variations in the level of aggregate demand would be associated with variations in the distribution of that demand.

The outcome of price formation has been represented in terms of real product wage and output, for this is a convenient representation in the context of discussion of over-determinacy. However, it should be stressed that equation (5.5) has been derived from pricing considerations, and hence it could easily be written as a price equation. Indeed, it is more usual to do so and as such it contains mark-up pricing as a special case.

The approach to money wage determination is based on a bargaining approach. But the approach has the virtue of containing a number of positions as special cases (at least when viewed algebraically). A target real wage approach to money wage determination is used (Sargan, 1964, Henry, Sawyer and Smith, 1976, Sawyer, 1982a, 1982b). The target money wage of workers in their bargaining is expressed as a multiple of current money wages, expected prices to actual prices and an element which reflects movement towards target real wage (labelled T), i.e. :

$$w_t^* = w_{t-1}.(p_t^e/p_{t-1}).(T/w_{t-1}/p_{t-1})^c \qquad (5.7)$$

with allowance for the impact of unemployment on the achievement of this target, the following equation for money wage changes can be derived (for details see Sawyer 1982a, 1982b), where a dot above a variable indicates the rate of change of that variable :

$$\dot{w} = a + \dot{p}^e + b.U_{t-1} + c.(\ln T - \ln w_{t-1}/p_{t-1}) \qquad (5.8)$$

It is useful to consider a steady-state type of outcome in which (i) price expectations are fulfilled and (ii) wages rise in line with prices (where for simplicity a no productivity growth case is considered). This yields:

$$\ln(w/p) = c_0 + c_1.U + \ln T \qquad (5.9)$$

where $c_0 = c^{-1}.a$ and $c_1 = c^{-1}.b$.

There is a presumed negative relationship between the rate of capacity utilisation and unemployment, so that equation (5.9) can be interpreted in terms of a relationship between real wage and capacity utilisation, and this can be written as:

$$w/p = h(u, T) \tag{5.10}$$

Similarly a relationship between real wage and employment can be derived from equation (5.9) which we write as:

$$w/p = i(L, T) \tag{5.11}$$

The combination of equations (5.5) and (5.10) can be seen to provide for the determination in equilibrium of real wages and capacity utilisation by consideration of price and wage determination only. Those two equations form the basis of the idea that real wages and economic activity are determined on the production or supply-side of the economy without reference to the level of aggregate demand. Equations (5.5) and (5.10) can be viewed as a representation of, on the one hand, firms striving for profits and on the other workers striving for real wages. The equilibrium value of capacity utilisation (u) is such that the claims on income by employers and employees are mutually compatible. Alternatively, equations (5.6) and (5.11) serve to determine an equilibrium level of employment.

This derivation has been based on imperfect competition and a bargaining approach. As such there are two features of the resulting equilibrium outcome. The first is that there are no particular reasons to think that the resulting level of employment will be that of full employment. The second is that the resulting equilibrium is effectively the outcome of systemic forces rather than of individual choices. From an algebraic point of view, similar equations could be derived based on perfect competition but their economic interpretation would be somewhat different. On the output side a (negative) relationship between real wage and output can be derived by consideration of the supply schedule of perfectly competitive firms. Similarly, an expectations-augmented Phillips' curve, derived from the market-clearing operation of a competitive labour market, could be viewed from an algebraic point of view as a special case of equation (5.7) above (for further discussion see Chapter 6).

Aggregate demand is now considered and this draws heavily on the model set out by Steindl (1979), which shares a number of features with Kalecki (1971a). This model is used because it incorporates a number of important influences on the level of aggregate demand (e.g. influence of capacity utilisation on investment) and it enables us to focus on the links between level of demand and the distribution of income and by that route it is possible to link real wages with the level of demand.

The components of private sector demand are consumer expenditure and investment (with the economy assumed to be closed). The propensity to spend on consumer goods out of labour income is taken to be much greater than the corresponding propensity out of profits. Investment expenditure relative to capacity output is taken to depend on the level of capacity utilisation, the rate of profitability and the buoyancy of the economy (discussed below). This is written as $g(u, P(u)/v, B)$, where u is the level of capacity utilisation, $P(u)$ the ratio of profits to full capacity output, v the capital–output ratio and B some indicator of buoyancy in the economy.

This formulation differs from Steindl (1979) in two respects. First, there are no lags between capacity utilisation and profitability and investment. This is undertaken for expositional convenience and because the focus here is on equilibrium. Second, whereas Steindl (1979) includes firms' savings $(s_1.P(u))$ as the second argument in the investment function, we have included the rate of profitability. This has been done since the argument for the inclusion of the rate of profitability may be more widely accepted than that for the inclusion of internal savings. However, it can be easily seen that the algebraic difference that this makes is minor.

The basis of the argument for the inclusion of the buoyancy term in the investment function is that the faster the rate of technical progress and the higher the state of business confidence the greater, *ceteris paribus* will be investment expenditure. Steindl and Kalecki both argue along the lines that faster technical change will have a stimulating effect on investment, and the inclusion of B is an algebraic expression of that. Similarly, arguments on the state of confidence and 'animal spirits' could also be seen as captured by the variable B which we label the buoyancy term.

The government sector with a balanced budget is now added. With a balanced budget, the equality between private savings and investment is maintained, but the level of savings and investment will be influenced by the rate of taxation. The condition for equality between investment and savings (both expressed here relative to capacity output) is:

$$g(u,P(u)/v,B) = s_1.P(u) + s_2.lu.(1 - t_w) \qquad (5.12)$$

where l is labour share in gross (of depreciation) output (and hence gross profits share is $(1 - l)$), t_w the tax rate on wages, d is the rate of depreciation and v the capital–output ratio. The share of post-tax profits (net of depreciation) can be written as a function of capacity utilisation as $P(u) = [(1 - l).u - v.d].(1 - t)$ with t the tax rate on net profits.

The relationship between labour share and capacity utilisation embedded in equation (5.12) may be positive or negative. If it is assumed that the marginal effect of a difference in capacity utilisation on savings is greater than the effect on investment, then it can be shown that the relationship between u and l will be initially positive and then negative. The first-order condition for the maximum value of u with respect to l is given by the following equation.

$$g_2/v = s_1 - s_2.(1 - t_w)/(1 - t) \qquad (5.13)$$

It can be shown from equation (5.12) that the effect of a change in buoyancy on capacity utilisation will be positive, provided that the marginal effect of capacity utilisation on savings is greater than that on investment. It is also possible to calculate the effects of changing tax rates (within the context of a balanced budget). The effect of an increase in tax on wages will be (provided $s_2 > 0$) to increase capacity utilisation since the only effect within the context of equation (5.12) is on savings. However, the effect of an increase in profits tax is to reduce (net of tax) profitability which reduces both savings and investment. Hence, as with the share of wages and profits, there can be a rate of profits tax which maximises capacity utilisation. This is given by:

$$g_2/v = s_1 + v.d/(1-l).u \qquad (5.14)$$

Here again this provides a maximum if the effect of capacity utilisation on savings is greater than the effect on investment.

It is generally assumed in this type of approach that since a tax on profits reduces savings, there will be an expansionary effect on output from a rise in profits tax. But the above indicates that, taking into account the impact on investment, there may be an upper limit on this expansionary effect.

The share of labour income, l, is equal to $w.L/p.Q$, and hence the u,l relationship can be translated into a $w/p,u$ relationship which will retain the same basic shape as the u,l relationship. It is the latter relationship which we will use below. For future use the $w/p,u$ relationship is re-written as:

$$g(u,P(u)/v,B) = s_1.P(u) + s_2.(w/p).f(u).(1-t_w) \qquad (5.15)$$

where $L/Q = f(u)$ and $P(u) = (1 - w.f(u)/p - v.d).(1 - t)$

Bringing together the equations for aggregate demand (equation (5.15) above), real wage claims (equation (5.10)) and the price, capacity utilisation relationship derived from considerations of non-perfect competition (equation (5.5)) yields three equations in the two unknowns of real wages and capacity utilisation. For convenience, the three basic equations are repeated here:

$$w/p = F(u, w/m, Z) \qquad (5.5)$$

$$w/p = h(u, T) \qquad (5.10)$$

$$g(u,P(u)/v,B) = s_1.P(u) + s_2.(w/p).f(u).(1-t_w) \qquad (5.15)$$

It is our basic argument that the steady-state model which is formed by equations (5.5), (5.10) and (5.15) is a sufficiently general one which permits the discussion of a number of different views as special cases.

OMISSION OF AN EQUATION AS A RESOLUTION OF THE OVER-DETERMINACY PROBLEM

It can easily be seen that this system of three equations is over-determined with three equations involving two unknowns. In this section we discuss the way in which authors (particularly in the Kaleckian and post Keynesian traditions) have implicitly responded to this over-determinacy. In others words, which of the equations did they drop? Later we discuss which other economic variables have been introduced

The approach of authors such as Kalecki, Keynes and Steindl (and more generally the broad Keynesian tradition) could be said in this respect to concentration on the equivalent of a combination of equations (5.5) and (5.15). As a first approximation, Kalecki and Steindl assumed that average variable costs and the mark-up were constant with respect to capacity utilisation. Thus equation (5.5) would then simplify to $w/p = F(w/m, Z)$. This sets the real wage, leaving the level of capacity utilisation to be read off from equation (5.15). This approach in effect drops the wage formation equation (to resolve the over-determinacy problem) which is equivalent to assuming that workers accept the real wages as determined by employers.[5]

The approach of Rowthorn (1977) can be represented as the level of unemployment being determined so as to balance out the claims for profits and for wages (in light of the claims of government and the foreign sector). This corresponds to our interpretation of the interaction of equations (5.5) and (5.10) above. The level of demand influences wage and profit claims, but has to adjust to the level which generates a level of unemployment and capacity utilisation such that profit and wage claims are consistent with available income and such that inflation is constant. The role of the level of demand in this approach is in terms of influence on wage and profit claims rather than as determining the level of economic activity. The level of demand is set by the money supply, but with the level of economic activity settled as indicated above, the money supply eventually determines the price level and not the level of economic activity. Rowthorn acknowledges that

[s]uperficially, the present analysis looks rather like that of the 'monetarists'. The money supply, through its effect on expenditure, influences demand, and demand influences prices. Moreover, the mechanism of adaptive expectations ensures that the scope for demand management is limited by the possibility of explosive inflation. But this is as far as the similarity goes. The two approaches are based on different theories of wages and prices, and yield different practical implications.

Velupillai (1983) analyses a model with the following characteristics. Money wage changes are determined by a form of Phillips' curve, whilst price changes are an adjustment process towards a pre-determined mark-up. Thus wage and price mechanics are simplified versions of those considered above. Investment is related to growth of output and rate of profit, whilst there is a technical progress function which relates growth of labour productivity to the growth of the capital–output ratio. The model is analysed in terms of equations governing the rate of change of labour's share in national income and of the employment ratio. In effect, Velupillai could be said to have avoided the over-determinacy problem by dropping any reference to savings or consumption. Within his model, there is no independent savings or consumption function nor any national income identity. Hence the model is investment driven but there is no adjustment of savings to that investment.

---

5. Kalecki (1971b) did discuss the pressure of unions on money wages, and argued that it was possible under certain circumstances for this to lead to a rise in real wages. But he represented such a rise as a change in the degree of monopoly, i.e. in the mark-up of price over costs. This can be represented in terms of our approach as rises in money wages leading to a change in Z without introducing the equivalent of equation (5.6).

Layard and Nickell (1985) present a model (their equations (42), (43), and (44)) in which there are three equations describing the demand for labour, price formation and wage formation. The endogenous variables are real wage, employment and the level of aggregate demand, and their model makes use of price and wage equations which are not dissimilar to equations (5.5) and (5.8) above. Their model can be represented for our purposes as follows:

$$N = f(w/p, D).K \tag{5.16}$$

$$p/w = g(D) \tag{5.17}$$

$$w/p = h(N/L) \tag{5.18}$$

where N is actual unemployment, L is full employment, D an index of aggregate demand and K the capital stock. Variables involving expectations and the capital to full employment ratio have been suppressed. There is an element of inconsistency between (5.16) and (5.17). Both equations are derived from profit maximisation considerations with employment as the single decision variable. As far as the firm is concerned aggregate demand is the exogenous variable and p/w and N are the decision variables. For a given level and composition of aggregate demand, a particular p/w and N will be chosen.

There is no equation which could be said to determine the level of aggregate demand (and hence no reason to think that the real wage, profit and employment generated by their model would support the necessary level of aggregate demand). However, a requirement of their model is that the level of aggregate demand is determined within the model in order to avoid over-determinacy.

Layard and Nickell (1986) can be summarised by six equations (where we have suppressed all variables which are treated as exogenous apart from one, for reasons which will be apparent below). In our representation of their model, expectations are fulfilled, and in particular this means that the difference in their model between output and sales (which is assumed to be absorbed in stock changes) disappears (and this reduces the equations representing their model from seven to six). The first number by an equation is our numbering and the second the numbering used in Layard and Nickell (1986)

Employment $N/L = f(w/pA, s).K/AL$ (5.19:9)

Prices $p/w = g(s)$ (5.20:7)

Wages $w/p = h(N/L, p^*/p)$ (5.21:14)

Output $Y/Y_c = D(s)$ (5.22:16)

Aggregate Demand $s = s(x_d, WT, p^*/p)$ (5.23:10)

Competitiveness $p^*/p = i(s, WT)$ (5.24:15)

where N is actual employment, L is full employment, A is a technology variable, s is a measure of aggregate demand, Y_c output which would be produced at full employment, WT world trade variables, x_d government expenditure, w money wages, p domestic prices and p^*/p an index of competitiveness.

In equilibrium (when expectations are fulfilled) this model appears to have six equations, but only five endogenous variables ($N, w/p, s, Y$ and p). Indeed the first four equations, which are regarded by Layard and Nickell as the supply side (p.S144) could be solved for employment, output, real wage and level of aggregate demand (for a given degree of competitiveness). Equation (5.24) would then solve for competitiveness. In terms of the model as presented here, the level of government expenditure or world trade would have to be set in such a way that aggregate demand as set by equation (5.23) is consistent with that determined elsewhere in the model.

The three equations which make up our model (equations (5.5), (5.10) and (5.15)) do not have a common status. Equation (5.5) was seen as the price level charged by firms and hence an equation which holds at all times. This position could be modified to allow for lags in the adjustment of prices to wage and other cost changes. Similarly, the aggregate demand equation (especially in respect of investment) could be seen as operating in the short-run. But, in contrast, the equation (5.10) is a long-term relationship. Thus we would anticipate short-run movements to be determined largely by the interaction of (5.5) and (5.15), with (5.10) exerting a long-term impact.

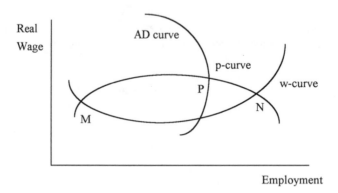

Figure 5.1 Interaction of aggregate demand, price and wage determination

To aid further discussion some possible configurations from equations (5.5) (labelled p-curve), (5.15) (labelled AD) and (5.10) (labelled w-curve) are presented in Figure 5.1. It can be seen that there may be multiple intersections between the p-curve and the w-curve. At real wage levels above the w-curve, the real wage tends to decline and in that way both points M and N would be stable outcomes from the interaction of price and wage formation. The point P, on the intersection of the p-curve and the AD-curve, would be sustainable in the sense that aggregate demand and aggregate supply of output are consistent with one another. However, the point P is above the w-curve, and hence that point involves a real wage which is higher than the one which would be consistent with a constant real wage from the view-point of wage determination. A second configuration is given in Figure 5.2. In this case the point P (supported by aggregate demand and price equation) would lead to upward pressure on money wages in an attempt to raise real wages. The rise in money wages is offset by a rise in prices, immediately according to equation (5.8) but more realistically in a fuller model with some delay. The interaction of the price and wage–formation forms, in effect, an inflation barrier. Thus point P in Figure 5.2 would not be maintainable, involving a price-wage spiral, until the economy moves towards Q. But that would clearly involve the economy being forced off its AD–curve or for that curve to be shifted (e.g. through government action).

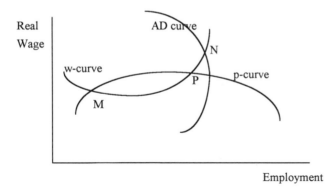

Figure 5.2 Interaction of aggregate demand, price and wage determination

The inflationary barrier can be eased by favourable movements in the price and wage curves. The price curve moves up (in the real wage, capacity utilisation space) with lower foreign prices. This may be through lower input prices (cf. equation (5.3) or (5.5) above) or through lower prices for competing imports which force down domestic prices. Lower government taxation on wages or on consumer goods has the effect of lowering the wage curve (since we are working in terms of pre-tax wages). Government expenditure which brings benefit to workers may also serve to lower the wage curve (for further discussion see Sawyer, 1982a, 1982b).

MARGLIN'S APPROACH

Marglin (1984) faced the problem of a possibly over-determined system when he compared and then combined a neo-Marxian and a neo-Keynesian model. His model of three basic equations can be readily set out. The price of output, p, based on the cost of production is given by:

$$p = w.a_0 + (1+r).p\, a_1 \qquad (5.25)$$

where a_0 is labour-output coefficient and a_1 seed corn requirement for the production of corn in this one-commodity (corn) world, w the wage rate and r the rate of profit.

$$s_c.r = i(r) = g \qquad (5.26)$$

where $i(.)$ is the investment function (expressed relative to capital stock) and s_c is the propensity to save out of profits (with savings out of wages equal to zero) and g is the growth rate.

$$w/p = (w/p)^* \qquad (5.27)$$

where the real wage is fixed by social convention (or physical necessity) at $(w/p)^*$.

This provides three equations in two unknowns, namely the real wage and the rate of profit. The intellectual pedigree of equation (5.25) lies in the neo-Ricardian tradition. Algebraically it plays a similar role to that of our equation (5.3) and also in the sense that a price equation can be given a real wage interpretation. Equation (5.26) corresponds to a special case of equation (5.13) (noting that $P(u)/v$ is equal to the rate of profit r). Equation (5.27) is a special case of equation (5.8) where there is no effect of unemployment on wage change (with $(w/p)^* = T$).

It is notable that the model of Marglin does not make any direct reference to the level of output or equivalent. The two endogenous variables are rate of profit and the real wage, and the scale of the economy is left undetermined. Variables such as consumption and investment are measured relative to the capital stock but as can be seen from equation (5.26) this leaves the growth rate settled but not the level of investment. In that way, the model is scale independent relative to productive capacity and to full employment.

Marglin clearly treats the rate of profit as a key variable rather than a residual one set by capacity utilisation and the mark-up as in the model used in this chapter. This suggests one resolution to the problem of having a missing variable, namely to consider the degree of monopoly as endogenous and we return to that point below.

The main route by which Marglin seeks to complete his 'hybrid' model is by consideration of inflation. Money wage changes are related to the difference between actual and target real wages (his equation (11) which is a special case

of equation (5.8) above) in which $b_0, b_1 = 0$ with $\dot{p}$ omitted. Price changes are related to the difference between investment demands and savings. The model in equilibrium now becomes:

$$p = w\,a_0 + (1+r).p\,a_1 \qquad (5.28)$$

$$-b((w/p) - (w/p)^*) = \dot{p} \qquad (5.29)$$

$$(i(r) - s_c.r)/s_c = \dot{p} \qquad (5.30)$$

$$g = s_c \qquad (5.31)$$

It can be seen that savings behaviour is the effective determinant of growth with some part of investment permanently frustrated. Similarly, there is a permanent discrepancy between actual and target real wages. This model can be seen to be completed with r, w/p, g and $\dot{p}$ as endogenous variables.

The derivation of equation (5.30) relies on investment being planned in prices of period $t - 1$ for implementation in period t. When investment for period t is planned in the prices of period t then Marglin's price inflation equation disappears for equilibrium with savings and investment equal. In other words, equation (5.30) is replaced by:

$$i(r) = s_c.r \qquad (5.30')$$

and this leaves inflation determined by equation (5.29). But that equation also indicates that permanent frustration for workers is involved, and if it were not, then the system would be over-determined (four equations and three variables with $\dot{p}$ dropping out). It also means that workers do not influence real wages but rather their frustration generates inflation.

Although in our view, the solution of the over-determinacy problem through the introduction of inflation as undertaken by Marglin is not ultimately convincing, it may be applicable during certain eras of history. Specifically we argue that there are periods when inflation can acts as a safety valve and in effect operates as an additional variable. But such periods do not last indefinitely.

The Phillips' curve as initially introduced related money wage changes to the level of unemployment, i.e. $\dot{w} = f(U)$. As such it could be seen to complete the Keynesian model with a money wage determination equation. But, crucially, it only refers to money wages and not to real wages. Consideration of the expectations-augmented Phillips' curve of the form:

$$\dot{w} = f(U) + b.\dot{p}^e \qquad (5.31)$$

with $b < 1$ has the effect of adding an equation to the basic model which could be considered as a simple expression of a Keynesian approach (equations (5.5) and (5.15)) but introducing a further variable, namely the rate of inflation. For taking inflationary expectations as fulfilled, and the equilibrium condition that wage and price inflation are equal (since a no productivity growth economy is taken for the sake of simplicity) we have:

$$\dot{p} = f(U)/(1 - b) \tag{5.32}$$

It is, of course, the case that when $b = 1$ the rate of inflation become indeterminate from consideration of the expectations-augmented Phillips' curve.

ADDITIONAL VARIABLES

Returning to the model of three equations discussed above with its problem of over-determinacy, we now consider some of the possibilities of resolving that problem through the introduction of additional variables.

Equation (5.15) can be extended to allow for the rate of interest as a factor influencing the components of demand. Unless there is good reason to allow the interest rate to enter either of the other two equations, the model segments leaving the aggregate demand equation to determine the interest rate with the supply-side equations determining real wage and the level of economic activity.

The extension of the model to incorporate a monetary sector serves to add one equation (demand for money equal supply of money) and to one variable (the price level). From the perspective of our approach here, the important element is that the introduction of the rate of interest and the price level leaves those variables set on the demand-side, with again the supply-side setting the real wage and the level of economic activity.

This suggests that so long as the equivalent of equations (5.5) and (5.10) serves to determine real wages and the level of economic activity, there is only a rather limited role for Keynesian demand-management policies, at least over the longer term. In effect, if real wages and the level of employment are set either by the interaction of the demand and supply of labour (as in the conventional neo-classical approach) or at levels which bring price and wage setting into consistency with one another (as in equations (5.5) and (5.10) above), then there is supply-side dominance. The role for demand management is then heavily constrained. In the approach summarised by equations (5.5) and (5.10), the level of economic activity adjusts to balance off the claims of profits and of wages. This suggests that if those claims could be reconciled by some mechanism other than the level of economic activity (or related variable), that would leave aggregate demand to set the level of economic activity, and we return to this below.

In an earlier paper (Sawyer, 1982b), the over-determinacy problem was avoided by the inclusion of the rate of interest as a variable influencing the level of aggregate demand and a conventional demand and supply of money equation. Whilst this may be satisfactory for a mathematical point of view, it can be challenged in respect of whether the rate of interest is indeed a relevant variable for the aggregate demand equation. Marglin (1984) argued in a somewhat similar context that

it seems to me unrealistic – in the long run as well as the short – to attribute to the rate of interest the equilibrating function on which the neo-classical resolution of the over determination ... depends. It is to dramatise the inability of the interest rate to bear so heavy a weight that it is eliminated altogether from the neo-Marxian and neo-Keynesian analysis of growth, distribution and inflation. Thus non-neo-classical solutions appeal to something other than the price mechanism.

But the model considered above (as with Marglin's model) includes the rate of profit. Clearly for the rate of interest to be an additional variable it would have to be seen to operate independently of the rate of profit.

Both the target real wage of workers and the degree of monopoly of firms have been taken as exogenously determined, though the actual real wage and mark-up are both endogenously determined. It is possible (as could be seen from Figures 5.1 and 5.2) that movements in either the degree of monopoly (shifting the p-curve) or the target real wage (shifting the w-curve) could be the mechanism by which the problem of over-determinacy is resolved. In effect, this would involve either firms or workers accepting whatever real product wage is determined by the interaction of aggregate demand and the actions of workers or firms as the case may be. There is clearly the question of the mechanisms by which the target real wage or the degree of monopoly would adjust. One route would be the use of incomes policy and exhortation by governments, which could be interpreted in terms of shifting the w-curve and the target real wage. A sustained gap between the target real wage and that actually achieved is likely to either produce an explosion of worker militancy or the gradual adaptation of the target real wage towards that which can be achieved.

The final possibility to be mentioned here is the role of government expenditure being adjusted to secure a level of demand which is consistent with the level of economic activity set on the supply-side. Once again this would involve the adjustment of aggregate demand to the dictates of the supply-side of the economy.

One escape from the over-determinacy problem which is indicated (though rejected) by Marglin (1984) is that of a succession of regimes, which we will describe as different eras. We take this to mean, in our context, that whilst each of the ideas that are expressed in the equations (5.5), (5.10) and (5.15) can be accepted as providing some insight into the operation of capitalist economies, they do not necessarily all operate simultaneously. Indeed, we could perhaps go further and say that it is only when all three operate that the economic system finds it difficult to cope. In effect, the reconciliation of equations (5.5), (5.10) and (5.15) would require the adjustment of variables such as interest rate, target real wage or degree of monopoly which are ill-equipped to fulfil that role or are slow to adjust.

Since the model discussed here consists of three equations ((5.5), (5.10) and (5.15)), it would be possible to draw up three categories of eras, each corresponding to the dropping of one of the equations.

We begin by a consideration of removing the wage equation, which we suggest corresponds to the world that Kalecki and Keynes were analysing. In other words, the inter-war economies (and perhaps many other periods) could be characterised by a lack of influence over real wages by workers.

Marglin (1984) argues that

[i]n the eighteenth century, Adam Smith took the rigidity of money wages in the face of a fluctuating price level as important evidence against the idea of a biologically determined subsistence, and Keynes appealed to a less distant past in defending the idea of money wage rigidity. There might thus be a certain plausibility in characterising the first two centuries of capitalism – say 1740–1940 – in terms of a neo-Keynesian regime. But ... rigid money wages are hardly a defensible hypothesis for the post-war period.

We would only amend this to say that the important assumption is not that of constant or rigid money wages, but rather the lack of influence by workers over real wages. Money wages could be changing by any annual amount provided that firms could raise prices to offset those wage changes without altering the tenor of this line of argument.

A related possibility (which has been illustrated in Figure 5.1) is an era in which workers are in a sense satisfied with their real wages. At point P in Figure 5.1, the real wage is above the target level (for the given level of economic activity). A situation like that portrayed in Figure 5.1 could be seen as arising in a period of rapid economic growth. Assuming that the target real wage takes a time to adjust, then a situation like point P could arise, albeit temporarily until the workers' aspirations caught up with reality. We could tentatively suggest that the economic boom of the 1950s may fit in with this view.

The second possibility would be the removal of the price formation equation. In effect, this corresponds to firms accepting whatever profit margin would arise from wage determination. This could arise when workers were very powerful and able to determine real wages. Whilst this is a theoretical possibility, it is difficult to think of concrete examples, though a period of tight price control in the face of wage rises would generate this type of outcome.

The third possibility would be the removal of the aggregate demand equation. It will be recalled that this equation was derived from the familiar Keynesian equality between leakages and injections. This equation would disappear if the equality between leakages and injections was always assured. In the context of a private closed economy, this would mean that planned savings and investment were necessarily equal, which would arise in an economy in which there was an absence of financial assets. For without financial assets, savings can only take the form of purchase of durable goods, i.e. an act of investment.

It would be possible that an era in which workers cannot influence real wages (corresponding to the removal of equation (5.10) from our model) is followed by one in which workers have some partial influence over real wages. This would arise when money wage changes partially but does not completely adjust to price changes, e.g. an expectations-augmented Phillips' curve in which the coefficient on expected inflation is less than unity. For, as we saw above, this leads to a system composed of equations (5.5), (5.15) and (5.32), which is exactly determined with price inflation as the additional variable.

The historical era of the 1950s and 1960s during which the coefficient b in the expectations-augmented Phillips' curve appeared to be less than unity was a Keynesian era in a number of senses. It was Keynesian in that the system of equations (5.5) and (5.15) could be seen as setting real wages and the level of economic activity, whilst equation (5.25) serves merely to set the rate of inflation. It was also Keynesian in that governments were perceived to pursue demand-management policies.

This discussion of different eras could suggest that the adoption of Keynesian demand-management policies to secure high levels of employment would not be possible unless some way is found to lift the restrictions imposed by the interactions of wage and price formation, and this is a topic to which we return below.

POLICY IMPLICATIONS

One implication which could be drawn from the above analysis is that there is little independent role for aggregate demand in the determination of the level of economic activity. The independent determination of prices and wages such that the level of economic activity adjusts to reconcile price and wage claims would leave little role in the longer term for the level of aggregate demand to independently influence the level of economic activity. Indeed the direction of causation is apparently reversed, with the level of aggregate demand having to adjust to the level of economic activity via changes in variables such as interest rates and price level.

It is possible to react to the above line of argument in a number of ways. It may, of course, be concluded that aggregate demand is indeed unimportant in the medium to long term, and hence government-inspired reflation will be frustrated. The impact of a higher level of demand (whether the result of government action or not) would appear to generate inflation as unemployment moves to a lower level. The appropriate level of aggregate demand is required to underpin the level of economic activity as set on the supply-side. It could be further concluded that supply-side policies are to be recommended to seek to change the equilibrium level of economic activity, and we return to this point below.

The challenge to such conclusions would arise, in the first place, from the argument that the unimportance of aggregate demand in the long term arise from incorrect theoretical specifications. In the theoretical domain, this would mean that, for example, it could be argued that workers are unable to influence real wages (though they are able to influence money wages). Then, the equivalent of equation (5.10) above would be eliminated, leaving a model composed of equations like (5.5) and (5.15). It can be easily seen then that it is the interaction of price formation and the aggregate demand equation which determines the level of economic activity. In particular, if it is assumed as a first approximation that prices (relative to costs) are invariant with respect to output, then the level of aggregate demand becomes paramount for the determination of the level of economic activity.

However, more important lines of argument here concern the use of simulations of macro-econometric models in the evaluation of the impact of government expenditure and other changes on the level of economic activity. These lines of argument concern firstly questions of mis-specification and secondly the implications of the fact that the parameters of the models are estimated from previous economic experience.

The mis-specification argument is perhaps most strongly seen in the context of the variables relevant for the determination of wage changes. Some variant of the level of unemployment is usually included. But there has been some argument over, for example, whether it is the actual level of unemployment (U) or the level of unemployment relative to recent experience (U/U^*). Clearly, the former carries implications about the absolute level of unemployment in the long term, whilst the latter only has implications about the relative level of unemployment (i.e. relative to recent experience). In this latter case, given time, the wage formation equation would permit any absolute level of unemployment (though it would be expected that the wage change equation was of the form that real wages growing in line with productivity would be compatible with a constant level of unemployment).

The second aspect of the argument arises from the obvious remark that the estimation of macro-econometric models has to draw upon recent historical evidence, and to some degree the estimated equations provide a best fit to that data (as well as complying with other statistical criteria). It is also the case that when ordinary least squares is used that the estimated equation must pass through the middle of the range of the observations. The question that arises here is the validity of projecting a model estimated during a period of high and rising levels of unemployment to a future period with attempts being made to reduce unemployment. We can illustrate the argument with reference to a wage change equation of the Phillips' curve variety (cf. equation (5.32)). Assuming that an equation is estimated that 'fits', then the following considerations arise. Growth of real wages above average will be associated with (relatively) low levels of unemployment and below average growth of real wages with (relatively) high levels of unemployment. The 'natural rate of unemployment', corresponding to the average growth rate of real wages, will fall in the middle of the range of unemployment observed. The calculated 'natural rate of unemployment' will inevitably lie in the middle of the range of observed unemployment, and hence will rise with rises in the observed unemployment.

The crucial question is then whether the estimated Phillips' curve has captured the reality of the wage–formation process or whether it merely represents determination to represent the data in a particular way. It has to be remembered that considerable effort is devoted to finding price and wage equations that perform satisfactorily (on econometric criteria) for inclusion in a model. The resulting equations may then represent the perceived need for a price and wage equation rather than reflecting some underlying reality.

Easton (1978) has considered some similar questions in the context of wage and price change equations, in the which wage change equation is a linear Phillips' curve:

$$\dot{w} = a_1 - a_2 U + a_3 \dot{p} \qquad (5.33)$$

and price changes by a mark-up equation:

$$\dot{p} = b_1 + b_2 \dot{w} - b_3 \dot{q} \qquad (5.34)$$

where q is growth of labour productivity.[6] With S as labour's share in national income, we have the change in that share as:

$$\dot{S} = [1 - a_3 b_2]^{-1}.[(1 - b_2).(a_1 - a_2 - (1 - a_3).(b_1 - b_3 \dot{q})] - \dot{q} \qquad (5.35)$$

If there are roughly constant labour shares in national income[7] then it can be concluded from equation (5.35) either that the coefficients (a_i and b_i, $i = 1,2,3$)

and q are just such that $\dot{S}$ is zero or that U is to be treated as an endogenous variable. Easton (1978) concludes that many estimated equations are not reconcilable with constant labour share. Further 'if Bowley's law holds [that there is a constant labour share] then the price mark-up equation is likely to be under identified and the estimates of the Phillips curve coefficients could well be biased if unemployment is wrongly treated as an independent variable .... However, more fundamentally, it seems likely that the wage price formation models that are often estimated in econometric studies are misspecified.'

We now return to discuss very briefly policy options when the model formed by equations (5.5), (5.10) and (5.15) is seen as a sufficient approximation to the real world to form the basis of a policy discussion. This would then suggest that ability of economies to return to full employment

---

6. We have simplified Easton's equations slightly by omitting from both equations summary variables which include other influences on wage and price formation.

7. The argument in the text is for the labour share being constant. But it would not be much changed if the labour share were changing at some constant rate.

would then suggest that ability of economies to return to full employment would be seen to depend on, *inter alia*, the restraints placed by price and wage formation being lifted. However, the lifting of those restraints could take many forms, which we now briefly review.

The level of economic activity enters as a variable in equations (5.5) and (5.10) and its equilibrium level brings the competing claims on income into balance. If there was some other way by which those competing claims could be reconciled, then the level of economic activity becomes a free variable with respect to equations (5.5) and (5.10). In the context of our approach, this would leave open the possibility of economic activity being set by the level of aggregate demand. In effect, there appear to be only two routes by which this could happen. The first suggestion is the substitution of centralised wage and price determination for decentralised determination. In our modelling (which was based on decentralised decision-making), firms set prices, given money wages, and unions strive for money wages, given expected prices. In both cases the outcome is seen as regulated by the level of economic activity. Centralised bargaining (even if the outcome in terms of real product wage depended on the level of economic activity) would in effect replace two equations ((5.5) and (5.10)) by one. To state the obvious, this is an algebraic argument which is far removed from consideration of the social and political difficulties that such a substitution would entail.

The second route is that one side (employers or employees) in effect cede the right to influence real wages. This may take the form of employers accepting the real wage (and hence the profit margin) which is consistent with the real wage formed by the interaction of wage–formation and aggregate demand. From an approach different from that which we have adopted, it was seen above that in the paper by Marglin (1984) the neo-Ricardian approach can be viewed in that way, i.e. firms accepting the profitability determined by wage–formation (in that case the subsistence real wage).

In recent years, most attention has been focused implicitly on the idea of workers accepting the real wages as determined by price formation and aggregate demand considerations. We would interpret exhortations for wage restraint, much of recent industrial relations legislation, the adoption of incomes policies as in the main being directed towards cajoling workers into accepting the real wages as determined by price formation. In other words, we could interpret these policies as seeking to restore a world in which workers may have some influence over money wages but not over real wages, which in our model is the equivalent of dropping equation (5.10) above. According to our argument above, this would be equivalent to a return to the world analysed by Keynes, Kalecki and others, in which workers did not influence real wages.

The third route would involve policies designed to encourage a higher real wage to emerge from firms' pricing behaviour. In terms of our Figures above, this would mean a shift upwards in the p-curve. There are two ways in which this can occur – the acceptance of lower profit margins or a rise in productivity.

In either cases, this shift in the p-curve may permit a higher level of economic activity, provided that the level of aggregate demand is sufficient and that the w-curve does not also shift to offset the shift of the p-curve. Supply-side policies designed to improve investment and productivity could be interpreted as seeking to shift both the aggregate demand curve and the p-curve in a manner favourable to the level of economic activity.

The main policy conclusion which flows from the above is that the restoration of full employment requires two aspects. First, aggregate demand has to be set at an appropriate level. Government expenditure may be able to shift the AD–curve, though it was indicated above that there was a limit to the extent to which a balanced budget could shift the AD–curve. Thus, it may not be possible for government expenditure to overcome low investment propensity or high savings propensity. Second, the constraint imposed by wage and price formation needs to be lifted. It is the apparent difficulty of resolving that constraint which must make us gloomy of any prospect of a return to full employment.

CONCLUSIONS

This chapter started from the idea that conflict over income shares and the associated theory of inflation leads to the view that, at least over the medium to long term, it is the interaction of price and wage formation which sets the level of economic activity. This could be described as supply-side determination (since the price equation involves also the determination by firms of their supply of output decision). The use of both a conflict approach and aggregate demand considerations leads to a problem of over-determinacy. This over-determinacy can be removed by omission of one of the key ideas involved in wage and price formation or on the aggregate demand side. Alternatively, it can be resolved by the introduction of additional variable(s). We have argued, however, that the additional variables are usually introduced on the demand-side and not on the supply-side. This has the consequence that it is still the demand-side that is seen to adjust to the supply-side, leaving the supply-side the dominant determinant of the level of economic activity. Finally, we have briefly considered the policy implications of our discussion.

6. The relationship between imperfect competition and macroeconomic analysis

INTRODUCTION

Since the publication of the *General Theory* (Keynes, 1936) there has been the lurking idea that substantial unemployment lasting for a number of years is associated with the existence of imperfect competition. In the late 1930s, ideas such as administered prices (Means, 1935), full cost pricing (Hall and Hitch, 1939) and the kinked demand curve theory (Sweezy, 1939) were concerned in different ways with the notion that prices were sticky, and that this stickiness of prices arose in the context of imperfect competition. To some degree these works interacted with the perception that Keynesian economics involved the assumption of sticky prices. During the 1950s the use of IS-LM analysis based on fixed prices could appeal to the idea that, under imperfect competition, prices tended to be sticky (in some rather undefined sense). Some aspects of the Clower-inspired re-appraisal of Keynesian economics also drew on the view that the source of sticky prices was the pricing policies under imperfect competition (cf. Malinvaud, 1977). Hicks's distinction between fixprice and flexiprice markets has some correspondence with the dichotomy between imperfect competition and perfect competition when he postulated that '[t]here are markets where prices are set by producers; and for those markets, which include a large part of the markets for industrial products, the fixprice assumption makes good sense. But there are other markets, 'flexprice" or speculative markets, in which prices are still determined by supply and demand' (Hicks, 1974).[1] The work of Okun (1981) extended the argument into

---

1. Hicks (1974) also argues that '[t]he major difference between the working of a fixprice market and that of a flexprice market now becomes apparent. In the fixprice market ... actual stocks may be greater, or may be less than, desired stocks; in the flexprice market, on the other hand, actual stocks are always equal to desired stocks–when the stocks of the traders are taken into account'. An important feature of the *fixprice theory* is not that 'prices do not vary, but that the causes of their variation are outside the model. So we suspend the rule that price must change whenever there is an excess of supply or excess of demand.' However '[t]he fixprice commodities ... are not to be supposed to have prices that are fixed, whatever happens; they are characterized, not by that, but by some degree of insulation from the pressures of supply and demand. If their costs of production rise, their prices may well rise; if their costs fall their prices may also fall, though perhaps very gradually.'

many areas of the economy that prices tended to be sticky in the face of demand changes.

Another strand of argument has seen imperfect competition as an essential ingredient in any explanation of unemployment. One expression of this is given by Kaldor (1978) when he wrote that '[i]t is difficult to conceive how production in general can be limited with unutilised capacity at the disposal of the representative firm as well as unemployed labour – unless conditions of some kind of oligopoly prevails'. Its recent manifestation has been largely due to Weitzman (1982) who contended that the existence of increasing returns with the associated market structure of imperfect competition was in a sense at the heart of the causes of unemployment. A number of papers in Worswick and Trevithick (1983) see the work of Weitzman as underpinning the analysis of Keynes; for example, '[w]e now have Weitzman's rigorous demonstration of what Keynes's intuition told him all along' (Thirlwall, 1983).

In this chapter it is argued that the focus on the impact of price and output decisions made under imperfect competition on the output market as in some sense a 'cause' of unemployment is essentially incorrect. The basis of this argument is that the substitution of imperfect competition for perfect competition does not of itself generate equilibrium unemployment. The significance of imperfect competition is however seen to lie in other directions. First, imperfect competition and macroeconomic analysis are mutually supportive. The analysis of imperfect competition requires, for example, that the demand curve facing a firm or industry be positioned by reference to the general level of demand. Macroeconomic analysis requires some microeconomic underpinnings of which imperfect competition would appear to be a more realistic set than perfect competition. Second, the influence which industrial structure (especially the level of concentration) may have on the distribution of income (and thereby the level of aggregate demand) and on the rate of technical progress (with effects on investment demand and growth) is likely to be much more important. In particular, imperfect competition may generate levels of aggregate demand which are insufficient to support full employment. Third, the behaviour in disequilibrium is likely to be different under imperfect competition as compared with perfect competition, although this is not a topic that we explore in this chapter. In particular we would anticipate that price behaviour would be quite different under imperfect competition as compared with perfect competition.

The chapter proceeds in the following way. In the next section a three equation framework is set out which helps to generate the basic conclusion that the price and output decisions under imperfect competition do not generate unemployment of labour. This is followed by an interpretation of the temporary disequilibrium literature and of the idea that any constancy of price under imperfect competition prevents the attainment of full employment. Further sections consider the relationship between imperfect competition and macroeconomics, the importance of income distribution, investment and technical change for the level of employment, and the role of mistakes and expectations.

A FRAMEWORK OF ANALYSIS

The starting point is the view that three building blocks are required, which cover price/output decisions of firms, wage/employment relationships based on labour market behaviour and an aggregate demand equation. Within each of those relationships, a number of alternative equations reflecting different views can be considered. The price/output decisions of firms may arise from perfect competition or from imperfect competition. In either case, it is argued that a real wage/employment relationship is implied, which has the appearance of a demand for labour but which is not in the conventional sense. The real wage/employment relationship from the labour market may be based on a supply–of–labour curve or may be derived from considerations of collective bargaining. The aggregate demand equation is based on a general view of savings and investment behaviour, but it will be seen that the crucial element is whether variables such as interest rates and price level appear in the aggregate demand equation.

The discussion of pricing and of the real wage/employment relationship is conducted at the level of either the firm or the industry. It will be assumed that there is no difficulty in moving from the industry level to the aggregate level, and that the nature of the relationship derived at the industry level will also hold at the aggregate level. The major concern here is with the nature of the real wage/employment relationship (e.g. causal or non-causal) rather than its precise shape. Thus our argument is not materially affected if the particular relationship between real wage and employment derived at the firm or industry level is not preserved at the aggregate level.

The output markets

The profit-maximising condition under perfect competition of price equal to marginal cost is re-written as $(w/p) = mpl$ where w is money wage, p is price level and mpl the marginal productivity of labour, which is conventionally interpreted as a demand for labour function with the implied causation running from real wage to employment. But the interpretation used by Keynes was to focus on the price equals marginal cost aspect and treat it as a pricing equation, and this is discussed further in the next chapter in the section on real wages and employment. Theories of firms (varying from monopolistic competition through oligopoly to monopoly) have a similar structure in the sense that firms are portrayed as facing a demand curve, a production function and a set of input prices. Whatever the objectives of the firms, and whatever the industrial structure within which they operate, the firms can be portrayed as reaching a point price/output outcome. Variations in the level of demand facing the industry will generate different price/output outcomes. With *specified* variations in the level of demand, a curve which might suggest a 'supply' curve relating price and output can be mapped out. Further, and of particular relevance for this chapter, a relationship between the real wage and employment can also be mapped out. However, it is clear that the price/output relationship is not a supply curve in the conventional sense (for it does not map out the response of firms in terms of output to the exogenous price) nor is the real wage, employment relationship a demand for labour curve (for analogous reasons). At the level of the industry, there is an equilibrium relationship between real product wage and employment such that variations in the level of aggregate demand map out that relationship. Aggregating across industries provides a relationship between the real wage and employment, which has the same status as the industry level relationship. For the purposes of this chapter, the important element is the idea of a real wage/employment relationship based on price/output decisions made by producers. The shape of the relationship below is an inverted U-shape, but little said below depends on the precise shape.

A possible real wage/employment relationship is drawn in Figure 6.1 as the p-curve (and has been derived in Chapter 5, cf. equations (5.1), (5.2)). It has been derived from price and output determination considerations but, as argued above, it can be expressed as a relationship between real wages and employment. Two features of that curve need to be highlighted. First, movements along the curve are generated by variations in the level of demand facing the industry. Movements along the curve could be made by the firms themselves but only at the expense of a departure from their objectives.

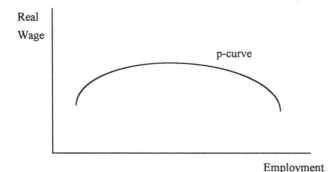

Figure 6.1 Real wage/employment relationship based on price/output decisions

Second, there may well be sections of the curve which are positively sloped. This corresponds to the conclusion drawn by Weitzman (1982), and arises from the possibility of imperfect competitive firms operating along the decreasing portion of their cost curves and/or the mark-up applied by the firms varying with the level of output (and employment). This, of course, undermines the *negative* relationship between real wages and employment which often dominates discussion on the causes of unemployment.

The p-curve is for future reference written as:

$$w/p = f(L,w/m,X) \qquad (6.1)$$

where w is money wage, p output price, L employment and m price of non-labour inputs. The variable X is used to label the factors which influence the firms' mark-up, and these could include the nature of the objectives of the firms, their market power etc. As a shorthand these factors which influence the relationship between price and cost will be referred to as the 'degree of monopoly' though we would not wish to limit the factors to those considered by Kalecki when he discussed the degree of monopoly.

The special case of constant average costs and mark-up corresponds to much (though not all) of the notions of price rigidity. In this case, the real wage/ employment relation becomes horizontal. Since prices vary with costs, it is misleading to talk of fixed prices. Instead it would be preferable to use the distinction drawn by Kalecki (1971a) between cost-determined and demand-determined prices where the predominant influence on the change in price is identified. In the approach here, prices are postulated to change with costs but there would be expected to be little influence of demand (whether the level of or changes in) on price changes.

The general case of imperfect competition can be seen as having three particular implications for macroeconomic analysis. First, it is clear that from the firms' behaviour the real wage/employment relationship can be positive or negative. Under imperfect competition, firms can operate subject to increasing or decreasing returns and the mark-up of price over (marginal or average) costs can vary with the level of output. The combination of those two features means that the real wage/employment relationship can be positive or negative.

Second, firms meet demand at the prices that they set. Hence, there is *no* excess demand for output along the p-curve as drawn in Figure 6.1, for the firms are willingly adjusting supply to meet demand at the prices that they set. In particular, even where price could be considered rigid, demand at the prevailing price is met by the producers. When the rigid price case is applied to perfect competition, the conclusion is drawn that there will be excess demand or supply, and that the complications of disequilibrium trading, quantity adjustment etc. will set in. In the case of imperfect competition, this is *not* the case.

Third, there is a price adjuster under imperfect competition, namely the producers themselves, operating rather like a Walrasian auctioneer. In the tatonnement process as envisaged by Walras, the auctioneer has the two key tasks of adjusting prices in response to excess demand and supply and to prevent disequilibrium trading. However, within each market, firms are pictured by models of imperfect competition as operating in a similar manner. The firms adjust price to eliminate any excess demand (in that supply and demand are balanced) and in these models they do not trade out of equilibrium.

The differences are that prices are adjusted in the interests of the firms and that there is not a single auctioneer who changes all prices simultaneously.

These remarks on imperfect competition relate to the equilibrium outcome without consideration being given to the costs of adjusting the level of output or to the consequences of mistaken expectations. But when firms hold stocks which are able to absorb the consequences of mistaken expectations, the difference in the outcome may be small.

One further implication of interest arises from the firm being seen to set the real wage when determining the output price, and hence the real wage is an endogenous variable at the level of the firm. Thus there is not a causal relationship running from real wage to employment at the level of the firm (and then by summation at the aggregate level). This analysis indicates that the usual neo-classical demand for labour functions differ from those derived from a model of imperfect competition. Symons and Layard (1984) argue that a monopoly model provides 'a relation between employment and the real product wage' comparable with that derived from perfect competition. They also remark that '[at] the very least we have shown there is little in aggregate quarterly data to refute the proposition that the level of employment is *determined* by and large by real factor prices'. (emphasis added). Our analysis would indicate that the status of the real product wage/employment relationship is different under monopoly and imperfect competition from that under perfect competition. In particular, it is not possible to say that employment is *determined* by real factor prices. The estimation of the (apparent) demand curve facing firms requires some variation in the real wage which is usually assumed to occur for exogenous reasons (such as random changes, misperceptions etc.). But in the approach used here the real product wage changes because the firm believes it is in its interest for it to change.

Labour sector considerations

The proposition that imperfect competition does not, through price and output decisions, generate unemployment can easily be seen as follows. In Figure 6.2 three curves have been drawn. One is the p-curve from Figure 6.1, and another is a corresponding curve drawn for perfect competition (and labelled PC here). The relationship between the PC-curve and the p-curve is that the PC-curve involves higher real wages (since the mark-up of price over costs is greater under imperfect competition than under perfect competition) and the slope of the PC-curve is always negative. There may be, of course, circumstances (increasing returns to scale) where perfect competition is not viable and hence a comparison between perfect and imperfect competition could not be drawn. The PC-curve shares one important property with the p-curve, namely that movements along the curve require variations in the level of aggregate demand. The third curve, labelled L_s, is the aggregate labour supply function relating total employment to the level of real wages.

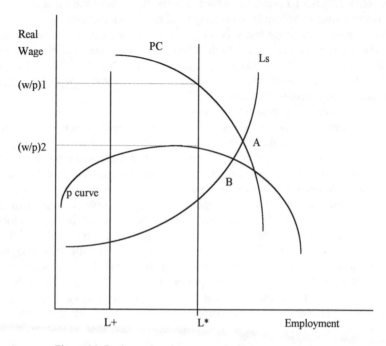

Figure 6.2 Real wage/employment configurations

The status of points A and B in Figure 6.2 is essentially the same even though one arises from imperfect competition and the other from perfect competition. They both involve equilibrium with full employment (defined as workers being on their supply curve). Both equilibrium positions face difficulties in being reached and in being sustained. These difficulties can be illustrated as follows. Suppose the real wage is $(w/p)1$ with employment of L^*, under perfect competition. Assume that money wages began to fall in response to the excess supply of labour. With a constant level of aggregate demand in real terms, the level of employment remains unchanged and prices fall *pari passu* with wages leaving real wages unchanged. The outcome under imperfect competition is essentially similar: take for example a real wage of $(w/p)2$ with employment L^*. With excess supply again, money wage falling in face of excess supply of labour would again leave real wage unchanged if prices fall *pari passu*. If the PC and p-curves are treated as demand-for-labour curves (which in our view would be incorrect but is a widely followed practice) and real wages assumed to move in the labour market according to excess demand and supply, then once again the outcome is similar. However, the difference does arise that there would be occasions when the real wage needs to rise in face of excess supply for equilibrium to be attained (e.g. starting at L^+ in Figure 6.2). Similarly, if there is not a mechanism in the labour market to bring about the required adjustment of real wages, then disequilibrium trade would occur with the usual well- known consequences.

The title of Silvestre(1990), 'There may be unemployment when the labour market is competitive and the output market is not', indicates a converse conclusion to ours (and to Hart, 1982). However, in effect he makes one crucial assumption, namely that the marginal revenue for firms may become negative (whereas Hart assumes that it will always be positive), and hence *'under Hart's assumptions the eventual demand for labour tends to infinity as the wage tends to zero; but under mine the eventual demand for labour at zero wage is not higher than a finite quantity determined by the data of the economy, in particular by the individual initial endowments of the nonproduced good and by the minimum price at which the marginal revenue is positive'* (Silvestre, 1990, italics in original). In terms of Figure 6.2, this would mean that the p-curve would intersect with the *y*-axis at a finite amount of employment and would have no intersection with the supply-of-labour curve.

The full employment at points such as A and B in Figure 6.2 arises from supply-side considerations, but we can ask whether such a position can be sustained from a demand perspective. In other words, do the wages and profits generated in equilibrium lead to a level of expenditure which would sustain that equilibrium in the sense of purchasing the level of output produced and generating the initial level of income. Writing Y as income, E as expenditure, W as wages and $\varPi$ as profits, then $Y = W + \varPi$, but there is no particular reason to think that the consequent E (based on W and $\varPi$) is equal to Y. More generally, any point on the p and PC curves may not be sustainable in this sense.

This point enables us to see why the analyses of Ng (1986) and Weitzman (1982) are incomplete. Ng investigates the reactions of firms to a variety of exogenous changes (e.g. of aggregate demand, of costs) but does not impose the condition on his analysis that the assumed aggregate demand would be generated from the income arising from the price/output outcome. Weitzman's approach suffers from a similar difficulty, though within his model it takes a different form. He parameterises aggregate demand by labour income so that he in effect assumes that aggregate expenditure is equal to labour income. This is the classical savings function with no savings out of wages and with all profits being saved. It transpires that in his model (both in the short run and the long run) profits are zero, which arises from the (implicit) assumption of zero autonomous expenditure. Thus Weitzman's equilibrium position could be said to be sustainable by the assumption that all wages are spent and with the conclusion that there are no profits anyway. The details of this and other arguments are spelt out in the Appendix of this chapter.

This problem of sustainability can be assumed away by appeal to Say's Law of the form that supply sooner or later creates its own demand. In that case, aggregate demand could adjust to support points such as A and B in Figure 6.2 since the supply of labour and capital would generate the corresponding demand. If that were so, then this chapter could end here. However, when the view that '[c]ontemporary thought is still deeply steeped in the notion that if people do not spend their money in one way they will spend it in another' (Keynes,1936) is not accepted then it is necessary to consider the role of aggregate demand. However, before discussing aggregate demand, discussion of the labour market is completed by consideration of wage determination through collective bargaining. This has already been discussed in Chapter 3 and in Chapter 5, where the relationship between real wage and employment was summarised in equation (5.11) which we repeat here for convenience:

$$w/p \;=\; i(L,T) \tag{6.2}$$

where T is the target real wage. The interaction between this real wage/employment relationship (previously labelled the w-curve) and that based on price/output considerations (the p-curve above) has been considered in Chapters 3 and 5.

At a point such as A in Figure 6.2, labour is on its supply curve, and it could be argued from a Say's Law that a willingness to supply labour involves a willingness to spend the resulting income. Whatever the merits of that argument (which we would doubt), it cannot be invoked in Figure 6.3 since the w-curve is not the supply-of-labour curve.

Aggregate demand

In the previous chapter, an equation linking real wage and capacity utilisation was derived from aggregate demand considerations (the main elements of which were differential savings propensities out of wages and profits, and an investment function based on capacity utilisation, profitability and buoyancy). Assuming a positive relationship between labour employed and capacity utilisation (equation (5.15)) the relationship between real wage and labour employed based on aggregate demand consideration is illustrated by the AD-curve in Figure 6.3.

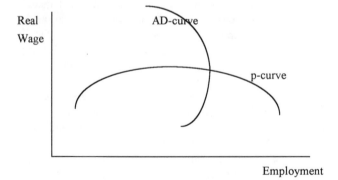

Figure 6.3 Aggregate demand and pricing decisions

Placing the aggregate demand and p-curves together as in Figure 6.3 provides an equilibrium outcome which is sustainable in terms of aggregate demand. If the aggregate demand curve happens to pass through the equivalent of points A, B (Figure 6.2) and Z (in Figure 5.1) then there is a sustainable equilibrium outcome. However, at the level of generality used here, it is not possible to definitely conclude that there would be an intersection between the p-curve and the AD-curve. The greater the market power of firms (higher 'degree of monopoly'), the lower would be the p- curve, and it is quite possible that there is no intersection between the two curves.[2]

The derivation of the p-curve above has been (implicitly) based on a constant number of firms. The analysis of Weitzman (1982) points to the importance of the long-run conditions where firms enter to bid away profits. As is shown in the Appendix to this chapter, the zero profits condition which Weitzman introduces as a long run equilibrium condition is redundant in that it is already present in the short-run conditions. There are numerous possibilities concerning entry (e.g. some industries have free entry, others do not, some firms have lower costs than others), and here we intend to indicate the routes through which changes in the number of firms would have an influence. The first point to make is that in a macroeconomic model the volume of profits is determined by macroeconomic forces (Kalecki, 1971a, Kaldor,1955). Equation (6.3) is relevant here for it can be seen from there that the volume of profits will depend on propensities to save and to invest and the distribution of income.[3] Thus the volume of profits will be affected if any of those parameters are affected. As entry occurs, there will be extra investment to establish the new firms, but it is not clear how steady-state investment would be influenced by the number of firms. The aggregate demand curve may shift as entry occurs since for a given real wage employment combination, profits depend on fixed costs per firm etc.. The distribution of income may be influenced from the pricing side. An increase in the number of firms shifts the p-curve to the right (cf. multi-plant firms) but may also shift the p-curve downwards, as there is further pressure on profit margins. The rightward shift of the p-curve may (cf. Figure 6.4) lead to a reduction in the real wage (when increasing returns to scale operate), leading to a contraction of aggregate demand and a fall in

---

2. McDonald (1985) uses a vintage model in which investment decisions are based on a fixed pay-off period, and concludes that there are plausible values of the profit margin for which there would be no solution for the equation 'investment equals savings'. Further, 'the results are such that one would not be surprised if for some economies at certain times an empirically based investigation found that market power was a cause of aggregate demand deficiency' (McDonald, 1985).

Sylos-Labini (1984) argues that '[i]t might seem strange that an expansion of profits can be such as to prepare the ground for particularly severe crises. But it is so. The Great Depression which began with a collapse of the U.S. economy in 1929 was "caused" by a period of an excessive expansion of profits.'

3. Linearising equations (5.15) gives: $s_w. W + s_p.P = aP + bY + c$, and taking $P/W = x$ then $Y/W = 1 + x$, we can solve for P as $P = c/\{(s_p - a) + s_w x - b(1+x)\}$.

employment (and a fall in profits arising from lower sales and higher unit costs).[4]

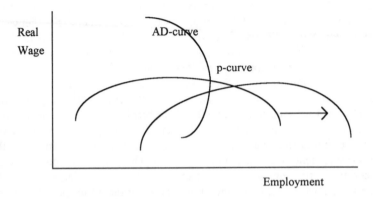

Figure 6.4 Shift in p-curve consequent on new entry

The effect of entry on real wages and employment is seen to depend on the nature of the aggregate demand equation combined with whether firms are typically operating subject to increasing or decreasing costs.

THE RE-APPRAISAL OF KEYNESIAN ECONOMICS LITERATURE

This particular literature may at first sight have little to do with the theme of this chapter since the market structure in that literature has been assumed to be perfectly competitive. Markets are characterised as operating without an auctioneer, leading to quantity rather than price adjustment. There are, however, two links with our theme. The first relates to the nature of the 'auctioneer' under imperfect competition. The idea of an auctioneer with specified functions was a device used by Walras to bring about equilibrium. Arrow (1959) raised the question of how prices adjust in a competitive market in the absence of an auctioneer when all agents are assumed to be price takers.

---

4. Weitzman (1982) assumes constant marginal cost of production so that the p-curve is horizontal and its position is unaffected by the number of firms. However, because of increasing returns to scale, as more firms enter, average output falls, unit costs rise but with marginal cost and price constant, profits per firm decline. Entry in Weitzman's model can only be properly discussed by making a modification to his model to introduce a non–zero component of autonomous demand (for otherwise, as shown in the Appendix, profits are necessarily zero). The aggregate demand simply becomes 'profits equals autonomous component of aggregate demand'. However, as firms enter, average labour productivity declines, which causes the aggregate demand to shift to the right leaving real wages unchanged but employment increased.

There have been a variety of attempts to introduce an element of price making by economic agents whilst preserving the essence of competitive behaviour. An initial point is that all markets operate with a price adjuster, though not with the prevention of disequilibrium trading. But, in some markets, there are people who are not the ultimate buyers or sellers of the product concerned but who do act as price setters (e.g. market makers on the London Stock Exchange, though they combine price setting with some element of buying or selling).

The question is not whether there is a price setter (for there always is) but rather who plays that role. It is our contention that Keynes saw that there are different arrangements for price setting as between the product and labour markets, such that in the product market it is the sellers (producers) who set the price whilst in the labour market it is not solely the sellerswho do so, but it may be the buyers alone or by some agreement amongst buyers and sellers. On that view of part of Keynes's approach, it would appear that Keynes's task might have been easier if he had assumed imperfect competition rather than perfect competition (as we discuss further in the next chapter). For simply the standard analysis of imperfect competition takes precisely that line so far as the product market is concerned as seen above (though how far that would have been clear in the 1930s is debatable). Indeed in the product market it is generally accepted that the producers are the price setters. The price setters will have their own objectives, and this is clearly the case for imperfect competition. However, the usual models of imperfect competition also have it that the firms set price and output jointly and the combination that is chosen lies on the demand curve (apart from mistakes etc.).

The second link is that out of this literature has arisen the fixprice/flexiprice distinction, with the view that fixed price arises from imperfect competition. Malinvaud (1977), for example, argues that '[t]he classical teaching, according to which prices quickly react to excess supplies or demand, is more and more inadequate for short-run macroeconomic analysis as we move into ever-higher degree of organization of society'. He proceeds to argue that '[t]he conclusion therefore emerges that short-term quantitative adjustments are much more apparent and influential than short-term price adjustments', and this conclusion is based on empirical evidence on cost-plus pricing of, for example, Godley and Nordhaus (1972). Hence, '[g]iven the short-run price rigidities that actually exist, the theory under consideration here is justified in assuming full price rigidity, i.e. in working with models in which prices and wage rates are exogenous. This is going to be a "fix-price" theory according to the denomination proposed by J.Hicks'.

This re-appraisal literature has, of course, portrayed quantity adjustment as much faster than price adjustment. There must be considerable doubt whether that would be an accurate portrayal for imperfect competition for generally it would be expected that prices could (if the firms wished) be adjusted very quickly whereas adjustments to the level of production inevitably take time. (though the arguments in this chapter are based on price and quantity adjustment taking place very quickly). Much will depend not so much on the industrial structure *per se* but on the nature of the productive process involved. In those industries (which would surely cover the production of most goods though not services) where production takes a significant time, it may well be argued that quantity adjustment would take a substantial period of time (say between 6 and 18 months) whereas prices can, if required, be adjusted very quickly. The point is that there may often be technical restrictions on the adjustment of output whereas there are not such restrictions on price change. In the models of imperfect competition firms adjust output to satisfy the demand that they face (at the prices that they themselves set). This view can be justified on at least two lines. First, on average, firms have accurate perceptions of demand, and can plan ahead for their production. Second, much fluctuation of demand can be met by variations in stocks (though this would not apply to goods which are made to customer specifications).

CONSTANCY OF PRICES UNDER IMPERFECT COMPETITION

This discussion leads into a consideration of the so-called rigidity of price literature, beginning with Means (administered prices), Sweezy (kinked demand curve) leading up to Okun (1981). This literature is seen as seeking to explaining rigidity of price but tending to forget that firms have chosen the price initially and choose to maintain the price. The distinction is made between constancy of price (i.e. prices do not change because of decisions made by the firms themselves) and rigidity of price (i.e. prices are not permitted to change by some external agency). Further, and of particular significance, firms are generally willing to supply at the chosen price whatever is demanded at that price.

An association has often been made between imperfect competition with inflexibility of price. However, within the imperfect competition approach, since firms are price-makers, when a constant price occurs it does so as a consequence of firms' own decisions, and is not externally imposed. It may be that infrequent price changes reflect the costs of making such changes or that the circumstances which influence prices remain unchanged. Thus there has always been an intrinsic difference between the inflexibility of prices under imperfect competition and the exogenously imposed rigid price which appears in much Keynesian and re-appraisal of Keynesian economics literature.

However, the literature on pricing which supports the view that prices are unresponsive to demand has been cited in support of the assumption of rigid prices (cf. Malinvaud's statement quoted above). There are two difficulties with this argument. First, it relies on the distinction between fixprice and flexiprice, whereas the pricing literature in effect uses the demand-determined/cost-determined distinction. Clearly, in the estimation of most price change equations, prices are not constant or fixed but rather vary with some combination of cost changes and demand, with much empirical evidence supporting the view that cost changes are much more important than demand (or demand changes). But it is a misnomer to call these fixed prices. Indeed, the implicit assumption in the estimation of quarterly price change equations is that prices can be adjusted at least quarterly. But even if prices were held constant for some prolonged period of time (say a number of years), the relevant question would still remain whether firms continued to meet the demand forthcoming at those prices.

Second, under cost-plus pricing formulations, any change in aggregate demand leads to *ceteris paribus*   (mainly) quantity changes and not price changes, nevertheless it is not justified to make a direct translation from behaviour under imperfect competition to perfect competition. In the general model of imperfect competition sketched above, a fall in demand would lead to some combination of price changes (which could be a price increase, decrease or no change) and quantity changes, but the new price, quantity combination will lie on the demand curve facing the firm (mistakes etc. apart) even if the price change is in fact no change. But under perfect competition, a fall in demand without price adjustment would lead to excess supply at the prevailing price, quantity adjusts to the minimum of demand and supply, with the firm forced off their supply curve.

There is, though, the question of the adjustment of the aggregate price level to generate a move back to full employment through the operation of a real balance effect. It can be argued that the combined operation of imperfect competition and collective bargaining is to considerably reduce the possibilities of downward movements of the price level. The practical relevance of the argument that lower prices will stimulate aggregate demand through increasing the real value of the money stock has long been doubted (Kalecki, 1944b). In a credit money world, money does not constitute net worth for the private sector since, for example, a (positive) balance in a bank account (part of the money stock) is an asset for the account holder but a liability for the bank. A lower price level may redistribute wealth between creditors and debtors, but it does not generate a rise in the real value of wealth. Further, there are legitimate doubts about the stability of the financial system in face of declining price level (for example, debtors may find repayment increasingly difficult, default on the loan thereby undermining the position of the lending body). It is anyway the case that a rise in the nominal money supply has the equivalent impact to a fall in the general price level, so that any general downward price rigidity arising from imperfect competition can be overcome in terms of impact on the level of aggregate demand.

This discussion so far has assumed that quantity adjustment presents no difficulties for the firm, which could be perhaps justified by the firms holding sufficient stocks to absorb variations in demand. The circumstances under which the firm would not be able to meet demand would be when capacity is insufficient or when stocks are inadequate. If, for reasons such as those advanced by Okun (1981), firms continue to maintain constant prices, then the view expressed above that supply adjusts to demand in the product markets would not hold. However, this would be a case of relatively high levels of demand, and chronic, if temporary, excess demand in the product markets. Casual observation suggests that chronic excess demand occurs rather rarely. The two examples often cited related to rationing by some car producers in the post-war reconstruction era[5] and the rationing of UK customers by retail outlets faced by a shortage of sugar etc. in 1973. Even if such behaviour were more widely observed, it would be associated with high levels of demand, at least relative to capacity, and with firms employing as much labour as it could. The association of such behaviour with unemployment would arise from an inadequacy of productive capacity rather than an insufficiency of aggregate demand. It may be that firms faced with an upsurge in demand that they perceive as temporary do not raise their prices (and conversely for a reduction in demand) for reasons of protecting consumer loyalty, reputations for fairness etc. But as long as the firms meet demand at those prices, there continues to be no excess demand on the product market side.

However, some different considerations may come into play when goods and services are produced to order. A demand by an individual for say a house built to their specifications cannot realistically be a demand for such a house at this instance, but rather has to be seen as a demand for such a house at some time in the future (where the minimum time is set by the nature of production and to some degree by convention). In these circumstances, a producer can respond to a variation of demand by a combination of variations of price and the length of queue. However, this may suggest that the important differences between industries relate not so much to differences of industrial structure but rather to differences over length of production process and whether goods are sold from stocks or made to order.

There remains the case where firms do not change price because of their perceptions on the response of their rivals. One version of this is the kinked demand curve (Sweezy,1939)[6], where each firm believes it would be unprofitable to change price because of the perceived response of rivals' prices, though firms collectively would benefit from a price change. In particular, it is argued that neither cost nor demand changes would generate a price change. However, the crucial question in the context of macroeconomics is whether at the unchanged prices, firms are prepared to meet the prevailing demand. If they

5. 'For a long time after the war, for example, there were many goods, such as motor-cars, for which a huge pent-up demand existed, and which would have commanded an enormous price in a free market. Yet manufacturers, almost without exception, held prices down to what they considered a "fair" and "reasonable" level, well below the market or profit-maximising price'(Crosland, 1956).

6. The analysis of Hahn (1978) of such a case of firms not changing prices because of rivals' perceived responses is not relevant to our argument since he does 'not assume that the economy *is intrinsically one of monopolistic competition*. The economy to be studied always has a Walrasian equilibrium. I shall show that it also has non-Walrasian equilibria' (emphasis in original).

are, then the economy remains one in which supply and demand are equated in the product markets.[7]

There is a clear difference between the effects of imposed price (or wage) rigidity and of price (or wage) constancy arising as a result of economic agents' decisions. In the first case, apart from a perceived need to explain the rigidity (Drazen 1980), there are usually unexploited gains from further trade. It then becomes difficult to see that the price rigidity can be sustained: the simple way of expressing this is to say that there will be pressures on price from excess demand or supply. In the second case, any decision on price (whether to hold it constant or to change it) is associated with other decisions. For example, with the implicit contract theory, wages and employment are decided upon simultaneously. Indeed in that context there arises the problem noted by Solow (1979), namely that wage constancy is associated with employment constancy rather than with employment variability, which had been the 'stylised fact' proclaimed by Keynesians adapting a wage-rigidity stance. In the case of product prices, Kalecki, Sweezy and Hall & Hitch all saw that price constancy in the face of demand movements could result from firms' own calculations, but that prices may well change in response to cost changes. But it is important to note that all of them appear to accept that firms adjust output to meet demand at the prevailing prices. Thus there is no suggestion here of price constancy leading to excess demand or supply (as would be the case with price rigidity, at least initially), but rather of output adjusting to meet demand.

It may be interesting to ask how a firm would alter price and output in response to variations in the demand that it faces. However, the answer to such a question can only be partial, for it does not address either the question of the origin of demand variation or that of the further repercussions of the price and output decisions. Those decisions will clearly have implications for income, wages, profits etc. At the aggregate level, there is then the question as to whether the wages and profits that result from a specific level of aggregate demand would themselves generate that level of demand. If it does, then there is macroeconomic equilibrium; if not, then there will be further changes to output and price.

The price-inflexibility arguments have been illegitimately carried over from imperfect competition to a form of perfect competition. Price inflexibility in the face of demand change may arise with administered prices, i.e. with the firms as price-setters. This is translated over into a market form in which firms are supposed to be price-takers. The question is not whether price-setters exist but rather who plays that role. The difficulty in identifying a price-setter in

---

7. The p-curve drawn in the figures would become a little more complex. Over a range, neither demand nor cost changes would lead to a price change. For a change in the level of demand, this means that there is a horizontal section in the p-curve. For a change in costs arising from a relatively small wage change, price remains unchanged and the real wage changes in line with money wage change. For a large change in money wages, price would respond leaving a much smaller change in real wages. For a modest change in non-wage costs, the p-curve would not shift.

perfect competition results in falling back on the device of an auctioneer. Imperfect competition clearly identifies the seller as the price-setter (though there may be situations where that may not be so). The disinterested auctioneer is thereby replaced by price-setters with specific interests, which will be pursued through the setting of prices (and other routes).

IMPERFECT COMPETITION AND AGGREGATE DEMAND

The concern of mainstream literature with the macroeconomic implications of imperfect competition have largely focused on price and (to a lesser extent) output decisions, and the flexibility or otherwise of prices (usually in the face of demand changes). In this section, it is argued that the tradition based on authors such as Kalecki and Steindl indicates that imperfect competition does have macroeconomic implications. The argument concentrates on three aspects, namely the distribution of income, investment and technical change. This section makes no claim to originality, but is intended to draw attention to a neglected tradition and to stress some useful links between macroeconomics and industrial economics.

It can be seen by reference to Figure 5.1 in the previous chapter that when the labour market is unable to influence real wages then the level of employment depends on the position of the p-curve. In general, it would be expected that the mark-up of price over costs will be larger the greater the market power of firms. Thus the p-curve would shift downwards with a rise in market power, and the Kaleckian tradition would suggest that the AD-curve is positively sloped. In that case, a rise in market power reduces the level of employment. The general point is that when aggregate demand is relevant, then market power influences the level of employment and unemployment. But when aggregate demand is taken as irrelevant, then the degree of market power influences the level of employment, but does not in itself generate unemployment in that when the supply-of-labour curve in place there is no unemployment.

Some tentative remarks can be made on the influence of industrial structure on the position of the AD-curve. There is not a well-developed theory of investment under conditions of imperfect competition. It would be possible to argue informally as follows. The degree of competition between firms (rivalry) may influence investment, with more intense competition leading to more investment (*ceteris paribus*).[8] When investment is undertaken to secure lower costs and/or to permit the introduction of new products and processes, then the competitive pressures on firms will be seen as relevant for the investment decisions. The structure-conduct-performance paradigm would suggest that

---

8. Using a neo-classical approach (e.g. Jorgenson 1967), which assumes, *inter alia*, malleable capital would suggest that in comparison with perfect competition, monopoly would have a smaller capital stock alongside a smaller labour force and output, for the usual reason that monopolists restrict output when compared with perfectly competitive outcome.

competition decreases as industrial concentration increase, but this is simply using competition in a structural sense. The Marxian view of competition would stress the rivalry between firms, which may be unrelated to the number of firms in an industry. It could be anticipated that the fiercer is rivalry between firms, the greater will be the rate of investment as firms seek to achieve lower costs through investment in new machinery.

The specification of the investment function, and in particular the role of profits, will depend on the development of the financial markets. When financial markets are undeveloped, the possibilities for external finance by firms are highly restricted. In such circumstances, it would be expected that internal finance (retained profits) would be an important influence on the level of investment. Savings out of wages and out of rentier income would have a depressant effect on aggregate demand without any compensating stimulating influence on investment. However, at the limit with savings only from profits and with investment constrained by the availability of internal finance, Say's Law is re-instated. This form of the classical savings function would appear more appropriate for the nineteenth century.[9] The late twentieth century is more appropriately characterised by a highly developed financial system, but one in which there is still a preference by firms for internal over external finance.

The influence of technical change on the pace of investment was crudely represented above by including by the 'buoyancy' term B in the investment function (see Chapter 5). An upward shift in B leads to an outward shift of the AD-curve, and a predicted rise in employment and output. There have been numerous studies within industrial economics literature on the relationship between industrial structure and the pace of technological change. Indeed, it can be argued that the relevance of industrial economics for levels of output and employment is much more substantial through the impact of industrial structure on technical change (and thereby investment and growth) than through the impact on price and output decisions.

THE COMPLEMENTARITY OF IMPERFECT COMPETITION AND MACROECONOMICS

A major part of the argument of Clower and others has been that '*either Walras' law is incompatible with Keynesian economics, or Keynes had nothing fundamentally new to add to orthodox economy theory*' (Clower, 1965, emphasis in original). The traditional modelling of imperfect competition enters this debate through its general assumption that supply adjusts (through price and quantity changes) to demand, so there is a sense in which there is no excess demand in the product markets. Thus, from the application of Walras's Law (in

---

9. Chick (1986) analyses the relationship between savings and investment in different eras as related to the development of the banking system. In particular, whether savings or investment is the active variable to which the other passively adapts is seen to vary depending on the nature of the financial system (see Chapter 3)

the form of the sum of excess demand over all products and labour is zero), then the excess demand for labour as a whole will be zero.

There are some complications in considering Walras's Law in the context of imperfect competition since the usual derivation of that Law involves parametric prices, whereas under imperfect competition the producers set prices. The commodities labelled *1* through to *m* are those supplied by producers and demanded by households, whilst those labelled *m*+ 1 through to *n* are supplied by households to the producers. The prices of the former group are labelled p_i ($i = 1,...,m$) and of the latter group w_j ($j = m+1,...,n$). The vector of ($p_1, p_2,...,p_m$) is signified by **p** and that of ($w_{m+1},...,w_n$) by **w**. A typical producer is faced with a demand function $d_k(\mathbf{p},\mathbf{w})$, ($k$ lying between 1 and m), and sets price p_k^* and intends to supply q_k^* where (p_k^*,q_k^*) lies on the perceived demand function. In the estimation of the demand function facing it, the firm will have to make assumptions about other prices. The analysis here proceeds on the basis that each firm correctly forecasts the prices charged by other producers and treats the price of inputs parametrically.

A profits function covering all producers is defined as:

$$\Pi = \sum_{i=1}^{m} p_i^* . q_i^* - \sum_{j=m+1}^{n} w_j . d_j(\mathbf{p}^*,\mathbf{w}) \tag{6.3}$$

with the demand for each input depending on relative input prices and each firm's demands for inputs are consistent with the intended output.

Households receive income from the supply of inputs to producers and from (lump sum) profits. In the absence of financial assets, households are constrained to have expenditure equal to income, i.e. :

$$\sum_{i=1}^{m} p_i . d_i(\mathbf{p},\mathbf{w}) = \sum_{j=m+1}^{n} w_j . s_j(\mathbf{p},\mathbf{w}) + \Pi \tag{6.4}$$

where the demand for goods and services and the supply of inputs depend on relative prices, and are considered notional in the sense of Clower. A particular case for eqn.(6.4) is where the p_i's are those chosen by the producers (i.e. p_i^*). In that case, adding eqns. (6.3) and (6.4) together yields:

$$\sum_{i=1}^{m} p_i^* . d_i = \sum_{i=1}^{m} p_i^* . q_i + \sum_{j=m+1}^{n} w_j . (s_j - d_j) \tag{6.5}$$

However the producers have acted to ensure that $d_i = q_i^*$, which leads to:

$$\sum_{j=1}^{n} w_j (d_j(\mathbf{p}^*,\mathbf{w}) - s_j(\mathbf{p}^*,\mathbf{w})) = 0 \tag{6.6}$$

In this approach, any failure of the input prices to be at the market-clearing level can lead to unemployment in the manner analysed by Clower and others. Specifically, with the short side of the market dominating, the use of inputs will be demand-constrained for those inputs whose prices are below the market clearing level. Producers will then not be able to produce at the intended level. The sellers of inputs whose prices are above the market-clearing level will of course find themselves demand-constrained.

In this approach, the possibility of unemployment remains, but essentially arises from a lack of price adjustment in the input markets. In the particular case of a single type of input (homogeneous labour), then the above argument would lead to the conclusion of zero excess demand for that input, i.e. there would be no unemployment. The general conclusion arises essentially from the idea that under imperfect competition there are agents who adjust price, namely the producers.

This line of argument suggests that imperfect competition is not a cause of unemployment of labour (though it may be a cause of the under-utilisation of capacity). This conclusion is however drawn from an analysis of a non-monetary economy in which there is no mention of savings and investment. In an analysis where savings and investment are introduced, a rather different conclusion is drawn here, namely, that there is a degree of mutual support between the use of imperfect competition and the macroeconomic analysis of Kalecki and Keynes. In one direction, in analysing the decisions of a firm or industry, it is necessary to locate the position of the relevant demand curve(s), and an important variable in that location would be the level of aggregate demand.

In the other direction, in order to permit imperfect competition to be compatible with unemployment of labour, it is necessary to move away from the equivalent of a barter economy (on which the above derivation of equation (6.6) was based) to a economy with financial assets.[10] This is essentially achieved when the aggregate demand curve is introduced, for although it is derived from the equality between savings and investment, it clearly recognises that they could potentially differ (i.e. at points off the AD-curve). Savings and investment can only potentially differ from one another only in an economy with financial assets, for otherwise a decision to refrain from consumption still requires the acquisition of real goods and services. Without the possibility of a difference between savings and investment, any real wage/employment combination would be sustainable, and in particular the full employment combination would be.

The relationship between Keynesian economics and imperfect competition should not be seen as one in which the latter supports an assumption of rigidity of prices. Indeed, the relationship is seen as rather the reverse of that, namely imperfect competition is more supportive of the notion that the product markets continuously clear (in that price/output combinations lie on the relevant

---

10. Clower argues that his analysis relates to monetary economy. However, Drazen (1980) argues that it is not money *per se* that creates the co-ordination problems but the 'uncoupling of transactions'. I almost said in text a monetary economy (rather than an economy with financial assets). However, in this argument it is not so much the existence of money, but the view that the intention to save does not inexorably lead to the purchase of real goods and services.

demand curve), and hence that output prices adjust rapidly. Another and important implication of the use of imperfect competition refers to the interpretation of any relationship between real wage and employment derived from firm behaviour. It is clear that the real wage/employment relationship is not a demand function since the firms themselves are portrayed as setting both the real wage (via price decision) and employment level. This again fits in with the approach of Keynes in which aggregate demand leads to a particular combination of employment and real wage, such that a different employment/real wage combination would arise only if a different level of aggregate demand were established. It has been seen that the difference between imperfect competition and perfect competition is that the former permits both positive and negative associations between employment and real wage whereas the latter allows only a negative association.

EXPECTATIONS, MISTAKES AND ADJUSTMENT MECHANISMS

The equilibrium position derived from a consideration of wage and price behaviour would be consistent with 'rational' expectations in that all relevant expectations are fulfilled. Firms are assumed to know fully their demand and cost conditions. On the labour market side, suppliers of labour are assumed to know the real wage that they face or, in the case of collective bargaining, that expectations on inflation are fulfilled. Further, any equilibrium including the aggregate demand equation also does not involve any element of expectations being unfulfilled. However, it must be noted that it is expectations on prices and output (i.e. short-term expectations) that are fulfilled. Long-term expectations are particularly relevant for investment decisions, and there is nothing in the model developed above which says whether or not those expectations are fulfilled.[11]

The other aspect of expectation formation which has been ignored above concerns the conjectures that a firm holds on the reactions of other firms to its own actions. The question of conjectures has generated a substantial literature but little by way of a consensus. But in many respects, the particular conjectures adopted by firms are not of fundamental importance here. Whatever the conjectures adopted by firms are, there will an equilibrium outcome in terms of prices and output, given the level of demand and input prices that the firms face. The general relationship summarised in equation (6.1) above is

---

11. 'In his 1937 lecture notes, Keynes himself seems to place even greater relative emphasis on the effects of shifting long-term expectations by suggesting that the *General Theory*, if re-written, should assume at the outset that 'short-period expectations were always fulfilled; and then have a subsequent chapter showing what difference it makes when short-period expectations are disappointed' (Hodgson, 1988 p.218). 'For the theory of effective demand is substantially the same if we assume that short-period expectations are always fulfilled' (Keynes, 1973) and also '[n]ow Hawtrey, as it seems to me, mistakes this higgling process by which the equilibrium position is discovered for the much more fundamental forces which determine what the equilibrium position is' (Keynes, 1973).

maintained, even though the specific shape of the relationship will depend on, *inter alia*, the conjectures adopted by the firms involved.

Suppose that firms generally mis-perceive the demand conditions that they face and over-estimate demand. The resulting output will not all be sold, and stocks accumulate. In the first stage, income remains unchanged, but the evidence of rising stocks lead firms to reduce production (and perhaps to over-adjust to correct previous build-up of stocks) and move towards a level of prices and output consistent with the level of demand. A full model would, of course, be required to model expectations etc., but if we were prepared to assume an unchanging exogenous component of aggregate demand, it would seem reasonable to assume that prices and outputs will move towards the equilibrium outcome.

It could be argued that the equilibrium approach necessarily overlooks problems of co-ordination and ignores the roles of mistakes and business cycles. The co-ordination problem in the re-appraisal of Keynesian economics literature could be seen to arise from the absence of an auctioneer, and the associated inability of unemployed workers to signal their willingness both to work and to purchase. In discussing problems of co-ordination it is useful to distinguish two cases. First, a change in the composition of demand (at an unchanged over-all level of demand) triggers off a deflationary spiral in the Clower-type approach. The short side of the market dominates so that output falls in the market where demand has fallen but does not increase in the market where demand has risen. In the imperfect competition case, it has been argued that this would not be so with price and output adjusting in both rising and falling demand markets. The representation of imperfect competition above does not permit this type of co-ordination difficulty, with supply adjusting upwards and downwards. There is the possibility though of capacity constraints, which may arise from a lack of capacity to provide full employment or from a level of demand that could only be satisfied by a level of employment in excess of full employment. The first case can be a source of unemployment but would not seem to be particularly associated with imperfect competition and is more likely to arise in the aftermath of destruction of capacity through war or through recession. The second case is clearly not one of unemployment.

Second, a change in the level of aggregate demand leads to a change in the level of output, with the relative size of the latter change depending on the price response. In the case of imperfect competition, it may be expected that the effect on prices may be rather small and can be 'perverse' (i.e. prices rise with a fall in aggregate demand). But the difference between perfect competition and imperfect competition is a quantitative one, not a qualitative one.

CONCLUSIONS

The supply side of the economy can be viewed as the determining factor for the level of economic activity provided that one is prepared to assume that aggregate demand can, through changes in interest rates and the price level, adjust to sustain any level of economic activity set on the supply-side of the economy. However, that requires that interest rates, price level etc. can bring about sufficient adjustments on the demand side, and that there are no adjustments on the supply-side (say through changes in the degree of monopoly, the target real wage). Imperfect competition may, for well-known reasons, generate excess capacity, whereas perfect competition would not. However, in the labour market, it has been argued that the industrial structure does not make much difference, and in particular imperfect competition cannot be seen as a cause of unemployment (as a consequence of the price/output decisions).

The view taken here is that industrialised economies are characterised in an imperfectly competitive world, and the question of whether the economy would in some sense operate better under perfect competition is irrelevant since there is no prospect of moving the economy to a state of perfect competition. However, the question can be asked as to how industrial structure influences the macro economy. It has been argued above that the structure will have important implications for the distribution of income, investment and technical progress, all of which feeds into aggregate demand. The position of the aggregate demand curve is a particularly important element in the determination of the level of employment. This is not only a re-assertion of the traditional Keynesian view on the role of aggregate demand, but, as argued above, is a necessary accompaniment of imperfect competition (unless full employment is to be always assumed).

Much has been heard of the need for microeconomic foundations of macroeconomics, and the requirement that such foundations are based on 'rational' behaviour. The approach adopted in this chapter does not require any departure from maximising behaviour (leaving aside whether such behaviour should be labelled 'rational'), though the approach does not require maximising behaviour (with for example pricing and investment based on satisficing behaviour). When unemployment is seen as arising from aggregate demand failure, this is not a question of any absence of maximising behaviour (since both savings and investment could be derived from maximising considerations) but rather the mechanisms by which two sets of decisions (savings, investment) are reconciled. It should be further noted that the use of imperfect competition clearly requires a macroeconomic foundation. In particular, the demand curve facing each firm has to be positioned by reference to the macroeconomic environment. Further, it has been argued that imperfect competition generally involves supply adjusted to demand, and to allow for the possibility of unemployment of labour requires some departure from Walras's Law. This departure was introduced through financial assets which permit savings and investment decisions to be separate from each other.

APPENDIX

The purpose of this appendix is to present a detailed critique of Weitzman (1982) to back up the claims made in the text. The essence of the Weitzman model can be expressed in the following:

$$q = c(L - F) \qquad (A6.1)$$

is the production firm for the firm with q as output, L as labour employed (although note that factors are not distinguished) and c, F are technological constants.

The demand curve for a firm's product is given by:

$$d(p) = a(1/p) + b(1/p).\{(1/p) - (1/\bar{p})\} \qquad (A6.2)$$

where $a = (1-u)Nw/m$, $b = (1-u)Nw^2/Hv$ where u is rate of unemployment, N number of consumers (equal to number of workers), w money wage, m number of firms, H, v parameters of the demand conditions, p firm's own price and $\bar{p}$ price of rivals. The elasticity of demand for the firm is evaluated at $p = \bar{p}$, but the elasticity is calculated for a variation in p which is not followed by a variation in $\bar{p}$.

$$E = 1 + (b/ap) = 1 + wm/Hvp \qquad (A6.3)$$

so that the elasticity of demand is independent of the level of demand. From the profit maximising condition that marginal cost is equal to marginal revenue, price can be derived as:

$$p = w/c\{1 - Hv/cm\} \qquad (A6.4)$$

and for symmetric Nash equilibrium ($p = \bar{p}$) $d = a/p$ and then:

$$d = \{c(1-u)N/m\}.\{1 - Hv/cm\} \qquad (A6.5)$$

It can be noted from equation (A6.4) that the price and number of firms are positively related so that price would be lower under monopoly ($m=1$) than under perfect competition. It will be seen below that within this model profits are always zero, and hence do vary with the number of firms. It is argued that '[i]n the short run, the model treats as exogenously fixed: aggregate demand, the number of firms, and the nominal wage. Endogenously determined by profit maximisation are: prices, output and employment.' This appears to be incorrect, for aggregate demand is treated as exogenous but is parameterised by u, and it can be easily calculated that aggregate demand is treated as $(1-u)Nw$ (i.e. money labour income). However, employment is treated as endogenous, which leads to $(1-u)Nw$, and hence aggregate demand as being endogenous. From the firm's production function with demand satisfied by output ($d = q$) we have $d = c(L - F)$ so that for the firm, $L = (d/c) + F$. Total employment is (with m firms) $(md/c) + mF$ and this would be consistent with the initial employment level if $(1-u)N = (md/c) + mF$. From equations (A6.4) and (A6.5):

$$m.p.d = (1-u)Nw = mw.(d/c + F) \qquad (A6.6)$$

which slightly re-written is:

$$p.d = w.(d/c + F) \tag{A6.7}$$

This is precisely the zero profits condition (equation (21) in Weitzman, 1982) which is said to arise from free entry. But it is contained within the short-run (fixed number of firms) model. Indeed, it is merely a reflection of the well-known conclusion that when there are zero savings out of wages, profits are dependent expenditure out of profits (consumption or investment) (Kaldor, 1955), and so profits are zero because non-wage expenditure is zero. In effect, Weitzman assumed a classical savings function with zero savings out of wages and with all profits being saved.

There are in fact three independent equations in three endogenous variables (price, output and employment) (equations (A6.4), (A6.5), and (A6.6)) and in particular employment can be solved as:

$$(1-u)N = m^2Fc/Hv \tag{A6.8}$$

(and this is Weitzman's equation (22) re-written as the solution for employment, rather than the number of firms). Since there are no profits even in the short-run in this model, it is not in fact possible to treat the number of firms as endogenous. Whatever the number of firms there will be zero profits in this model, simply because there is zero non-wage expenditure.

From the absence of any autonomous component of aggregate demand, it follows that it is not possible to model the impact of an aggregate demand shock. Thus, the conclusion that '[t]he profit maximising short term reaction to aggregate demand shocks is a pure quantity adjustment, which creates volatile pro-cyclical fluctuations of productivity and profits' (Weitzman, 1982) cannot be sustained from the original model, though the modification given below does support that conclusion.

The simplest way of modifying this model is to introduce an autonomous component of aggregate demand, so that the demand function is modified to:

$$d(p) = a(1/p) + b(1/p).\{(1/p) - (1/\overline{p})\} \tag{A6.2'}$$

where now $a = \{(1-u)Nw + Xw\}/m$, $b = \{(1-u)Nw + Xw\}.w/Hv$ where X is the autonomous component of demand in real terms (measured in wage units). The elasticity of demand is the same as before and hence so will the profit maximising price. So again $p = w/c[1 - Hv/cm]$, which gives the real wage:

$$w/p = c[1 - Hv/cm] \tag{A6.9}$$

In symmetric equilibrium $d = a(1/p)$ where $a = Z/m$ (having put $Z = (1-u)Nw + Xw$ for convenience).

Each firm is producing d using labour given by $c(L-F) = d$, hence employment is $mL = md/c + mF$ and then $(1-u)N = mL = md/c + mF$ which is equal to $Z/cp + mF = (1-u)Nw/cp + mF$. This is:

$$(1-u)N = (1-u)Nw/cp + mF \tag{A6.10}$$

The real wage is given by equation(A6.9) and the level of employment by:

$$(1-u)N = (cm/Hv)[mF + X(1 - Hv/cm)] \tag{A6.11}$$

It can be seen that a variation of autonomous demand would not affect the real wage, but would generate changes in employment etc. The profits in total are Xw, and hence profits per firm are Xw/m. The application of the zero profits condition would indicate the number of firms tending to infinity. However, it is more reasonable to think of firms continuing to enter provided that the rate of profit exceeds some minimum rate. To illustrate, suppose that a firm's capital requirement in real terms (wage units) is given by $K = h.L + i$ which is then equal to $h(1-u)N/m + i$. The rate of profit is then given by $Xw/\{h(1-u)N/m + i\}w$, and this would decline with the number of firms, and equating this with the minimum rate of profit would determine the number of firms. Substituting from equation (A6.11) would give $1/\{(hcmF/HvX) + (hc/Hv) - (h/m) + i\} = r_{min}$ and a quadratic equation for m (number of firms).

From equation (A6.11), it can be seen that employment and number of firms are positively related, with the basic mechanism that the greater the number of firms, the lower the employment per firm and the lower the productivity. Hence more employees are required for a given level of output.

7. Keynes's macroeconomic analysis and theories of imperfect competition

INTRODUCTION

Whilst Keynes' *General Theory* and most of Keynesian economics have been based on some form of atomistic competition, there have often been suggestions for the involvement of imperfect competition. These suggestions have ranged from the use of some aspects of imperfect competition to justify an assumption of price rigidity through to the argument that the economics of Keynes requires imperfect competition as part of its microeconomic foundations. This paper specifically addresses the questions of whether the macroeconomic analysis of Keynes requires imperfect competition as part of its microeconomic foundations and whether Keynes would have been well advised to have used imperfect competition rather than atomistic competition as the industrial structure. The term 'imperfect competition' will be used to signify those theories that conclude that price diverges from marginal cost, whether for reasons of fewness of numbers and/or from product differentiation. The term perfect competition is used to signify the case where there are a large number of firms which are essentially price-takers. The industrial structure assumed by Keynes is described as polypolistic or atomistic competition. This has some but not all of the features of perfect competition for as Chick (1983) argues 'Keynes's representative firm is an anomaly from the point of view of established thinking: it is a small "polypolistic" or atomistic firm which operates under uncertainty and therefore is not a price taker'. Robinson (1976) also argued that 'Keynes did not accept the "perfect competition" of the textbooks, but some vague old-fashioned notion of competition that he never formulated explicitly.'

KEYNES AND THEORIES OF IMPERFECT COMPETITION

It is clear that the *General Theory* (Keynes, 1936) did not draw upon any notions of imperfect competition in the sense defined above. There is reference to the degree of competition (but not degree of monopoly) being taken as given (Keynes,1936), which contains the suggestions that it is not necessarily atomistic competition that is assumed. However, the equality of price and marginal cost and of real wage and marginal productivity of labour strongly suggests that atomistic competition is assumed.

From the perspective of this chapter, there are two crucial aspects of the way in which Keynes modelled the production side of the economy. First, production and prices adjust rapidly to changes in demand for 'the degree of competition' which Keynes took for granted approximated Marshallian assumptions of sufficient competition in most markets to guarantee quick responses by sellers to shifts in the demand for their products' (Lekachman, 1977). The second is that there is a positive relationship between price and output produced (and the obverse of that is a negative relationship between real wage and employment). In effect, a situation of monopoly in which production adjusts rapidly to changes in demand (which is the way monopoly is generally modelled) and where prices and production were positively related (which is not necessarily the case) would mimic the situation of polypolistic competition as portrayed by Keynes.

At much the same time as Keynes was developing the *General Theory*, there was much activity on theories of imperfect competition, to some degree in response to the difficulties over perfect competition raised by Sraffa (1926). Keynes began work on what become the *General Theory* soon after completion of *A Treatise on Money*, so the first half of the 1930s can be seen as the period of development of the *General Theory*. Chamberlin submitted his thesis in April 1927, and it was published in 1933 (as Chamberlin, 1933). Joan Robinson also published her *Economics of Imperfect Competition* in 1933, and she was a key member of the famous 'circus' who were closely involved in debates with Keynes over the *General Theory*. Richard Kahn's fellowship dissertation (submitted in 1929, and now published as Kahn, 1989) had been concerned with the role of imperfect competition. Kahn is often given a particularly important role in the development of the *General Theory*, and Schumpeter suggested that his 'share in the historic achievement cannot have fallen very far short of co-authorship' (Schumpeter, 1954). Kahn dismissed that suggestion as 'clearly absurd', and described his role as 'I relieved the solitude and provided, by being on the spot, a more rapid method of discussion than correspondence by post' (Kahn, 1984).

The intellectual environment against which Keynes was working would suggest at a minimum that the retention of an atomistic competitive framework was a deliberate decision by Keynes and generally thought by him and the members of the circus (especially Kahn and Robinson) to be unnecessary for his key propositions.[1] Collard (1990) notes that 'neither of the main progenitors of the "revolutions" in macroeconomics and microeconomics in the 1930s,

---

1. Harcourt (1987) describes this as '[a] mystery which perhaps will never be completely solved is why, Keynes, who knew so much about the imperfect competition revolution, nevertheless chose to use the short-period Marshallian pricing model for his chapter on prices.' Further, 'Harrod ... had pointed out to Keynes in the 1920s the advantage of having imperfectly competitive microeconomic foundations (as we would say now) for the theory lying behind the policies of public works then being advocated. For if expansion of output were to be accompanied by either decreasing or at least constant costs, the fear of the inflationists' opposition to public works expenditure with respect to the generation of a wage-price spiral could be shown to be groundless.'

Robinson (1933) and Keynes (1936), had any doubt that the revolutions were totally separate ones'. The broad line of argument of this paper is that the revolutions were indeed quite separate, but that whilst the crucial propositions of Keynes did not require imperfect competition, his arguments could have been strengthened by its use.

Ohlin (in Keynes, 1973) provided an early statement of the view that Keynes should have used imperfect competition rather than atomistic competition in his analysis. He was concerned with an issue to which we return below, namely the relationship between real wages and employment, and argued that employment could increase without any reduction in real wages. He identified the contrary view with 'perfect' competition (inverted commas as used by Ohlin), and continued by saying that '[i]n this as in some other respects Keynes does not seem to me to have been radical enough in freeing himself from the conventional assumptions. When reading his book one sometimes wonders whether he never discussed imperfect competition with Mrs Robinson'. Keynes replied in some puzzlement to this, when he wrote that he had 'not been able to make out here what you [Ohlin] are driving at. The reference to imperfect competition is very perplexing. I cannot see how on earth it comes in. Mrs. Robinson, I may mention, read my proofs without discovering any connection' (Keynes, 1973). A few years earlier, Robinson had argued that '[t]here is no natural tendency even under competition to maintain full employment, which depends upon the level of saving and of investment. We are here only concerned to discuss an economic system in equilibrium, and we must suppose that both under competition and under monopoly the conditions necessary to full employment are maintained' and in a footnote that 'if there was full employment under competition, in equilibrium conditions, there will be full employment under the monopolists' (Robinson, 1933).

There did appear to be a potential complementarity between imperfect competition (most clearly in Chamberlin's *Theory of Monopolistic Competition*) and Keynes's *General Theory*. The theory of monopolistic competition predicted excess capacity as a long-term feature and that firms were essentially demand-constrained rather than cost-constrained (in the sense that each firm would willingly produce more if they could sell at the prevailing price). These features find echoes in Keynes's analysis where the level of economic activity is constrained by the level of aggregate demand rather than by aggregate supply. However, at another level there is a conflict. In the analysis of Chamberlin, it is the actions of the firms (and in particular entrants in each industry) in pursuit of profits which lead to the tangency solution between the perceived demand curve and the average cost curve. There is no particular reason to think that the wages and profits that arise would lead to expenditure which would be equal to the output produced (at the ruling prices). This can also be expressed as saying that the extent of excess capacity cannot be determined by both the level of aggregate demand and the interaction of firms. Further, a permanent increase in aggregate demand would lead to entry rather than a fall in the degree of capacity under-utilisation in the approach of Chamberlin.

The interchange between Keynes (as editor of the *Economic Journal*) and Joan Robinson (Keynes, 1983) over a paper submitted by Kalecki (which was rejected by Keynes but published as Kalecki (1941)) illustrates that the central ideas of imperfect competition had not become ingrained in the thinking of Keynes. Kalecki had assumed that firms operated subject to excess capacity in the long period, to which Keynes reacted by asking '[i]s it not rather odd when dealing with "long-run problems" to start with the assumption that all firms are always working below capacity' (Keynes, 1983). Joan Robinson replied to the effect that under-capacity working was 'part of the usual bag of tricks of Imperfect Competition theory' and produced the now standard diagram for the 'tangency solution' of imperfect competition with free entry exhibiting excess capacity in equilibrium. Keynes's response was to claim to be 'still innocent enough to be bewildered by the idea that the assumption of all firms always working below capacity is consistent with 'a long run problem''.

The original formulation of theories of imperfect competition[2] focused on questions such as product differentiation, excess capacity (notably in Chamberlin (1933)) and exploitation (payment to a factor below marginal product, which featured particularly in Robinson (1933)). Whilst the relationship between price and marginal cost was explored there was no suggestion of price rigidity (see, for example, Robinson 1933, ch. 4), though there was recognition that a decrease in the level of demand could lead to a rise in price (Robinson, 1933). The treatment of imperfect competition took on a rather different perspective in the second half of the thirties as compared with the first half, and price rigidity came to the fore. This change of direction can be identified with Means (1935, 1936). The celebrated kinked demand curve approach (Sweezy, 1939) was explicitly concerned with explaining price rigidity in the context of differentiated oligopoly. Hall and Hitch (1939) was distinct in many respects, such as being built on empirical observation and generally rejecting profit maximisation, and bringing arguments which would now be recognised as based on satisficing behaviour. For our purposes, the important aspect is that prices were seen as a (relatively) constant mark-up over average direct costs. With average direct costs viewed as approximately constant with respect to output, this suggests that price is constant (relative to average costs) in the face of variations in demand. By a different route, Kalecki (1938) arrived at a similar conclusion (for further discussion see Sawyer, 1991c).

However, most theorising in macroeconomics continued to assume (at least implicitly) atomistic competition, but departing from Keynes by assuming price rigidity. This came to the fore with the re-interpretation of Keynesian econom-

---

2. Chamberlin and Robinson are regarded here as the originators of theories of imperfect competition. Cournot, Bertrand and others pre-date them, particular in discussion of oligopoly. However, for our purposes, it is the interest generated by Chamberlin, Robinson et alia in the early thirties which is particularly relevant.

ics and the temporary equilibrium school. In the context of atomistic competition, they are correct to argue that there will be elements of trading out of equilibrium (simply because prices cannot adjust instantaneously in an economy without a Walrasian auctioneer), but the general assumption that there is rapid quantity adjustment is unappealing when applied to a production (rather than an exchange) economy. Our argument is that the causes and implications of price inflexibility are quite different under imperfect competition as compared with perfect competition. Under the latter, price inflexibility is either imposed or arises as an approximation to incomplete price adjustment (cf. Leijonhufvud, 1968), whereas in the former it arises either from the deliberate decisions of producers or from a delay in adjusting prices because of the costs of doing so. In a situation of perfect competition, price inflexibility is generally associated with a difference between (notional) demand and supply, with the actual trade being set by the short side of the market. In contrast, under imperfect competition (as argued below) the producers generally supply whatever is demanded at the price that they have set (or at least not changed), and there is an adjustment of supply to demand.

INTERPRETATION OF THE GENERAL THEORY

This section outlines an interpretation of the parts of Keynes's *General Theory* relevant for this chapter. Although our main concern is with the output side, we begin on the labour side. A major aspect of the approach of Keynes is that the determination of real wages does not occur in the way envisaged by a neo-classical labour market analysis (cf. Davidson, 1983a, 1983b). Specifically, real wages are *not* viewed as determined by the interaction of demand and supply of labour. It will be seen below that this point is reinforced when imperfect competition is used to characterise the output side.

In Chapter 2 of the *General Theory*, Keynes argued for the rejection of the 'second classical postulate', namely that real wage is equated with marginal disutility of labour: in other words some workers are forced off their supply curve. But he argued for the continued acceptance of the first postulate, namely the equality between real wage and the marginal product of labour. This implies, in the context of atomistic competition, a negative relationship between real wage and employment. Keynes's response to the empirical doubts cast on the negative sign of that relationship by Dunlop and Tarshis is discussed below. Keynes clearly argued that workers cannot set real wages, as indicated in the discussion in Chapter 3. In Chapter 21, Keynes clearly postulated flexible prices, and indeed in some respects prices that adjust instantaneously. Firms equate price with marginal cost by adjustment of price. 'Keynes' treatment of the labor demand function implies that the market for current output is clearing. The *General Theory* seems perfectly consistent on this point. Keynes implies throughout that prices, as contrasted with wages, adjust instantaneously, to bring the quantity demanded into line with the quantity supplied, the latter being fixed in the short run' (Grossman, 1972).

'Indeed there is little doubt that Keynes regarded product prices as highly flexible – he frequently insisted in the *General Theory* that the real wage varied inversely with the level of employment in the short-run (which, given the assumption of a relatively stable *money* wage, implies flexible product prices)' (Brothwell, 1975).

The equality of the real product wage and the marginal productivity of labour clearly imply that price equals wage divided by marginal product of labour. The money wage *w* is set by bargaining (individual or collective) by workers and employers. The marginal product of labour (*mpl*) depends on the volume of employment, which itself is set by the level of aggregate demand. The setting of price leads to the equality between real wage and mpl, though this equality has a quite different interpretation from the equality of neo-classical economics between the same variables. The direction of causation in the neo-classical analysis runs (at the level of the firm) from real wage (which is externally set so far as the firm is concerned) to the level of employment, whilst in the analysis of Keynes the direction of causation is essentially reversed (cf. Brothwell, 1988). Further, in the analysis of Keynes, the real wage is effectively set by the producers through their setting of price, and not set in the labour market by the interaction of the demand and supply of labour.

This view of Keynes (1936) can be portrayed as follows. Money wages are set in the labour sector, but the level of money wages is of little direct relevance for the level of employment (reflected in the use of the wage unit as the *numeraire*). Keynes (1936, ch. 19) analyses the effects of a change in money wages which work through the level of aggregate demand and expectations. The level of employment is closely based on the level of economic activity, which itself is set by the level of aggregate demand. The level of employment determines the marginal productivity of labour, and the equality between real wage and marginal productivity of labour is brought about by price changes. The labour sector is unable to influence the real wage, and in a number of respects is irrelevant for the macro economy.

In his review of Keynes (1936), Kalecki gave his own presentation of what he saw to be its key ideas.[3] From the perspective of this paper, two elements of presentation are particularly relevant, though much of Kalecki's review was a critique of Keynes's approach to investment. The first notable element was the use of a monopoly model where the equilibrium position for the representative firm of marginal value added curve had to be such as to ensure that the volume of profits forthcoming (at the output where marginal value added and marginal cost were equal) matched the volume of capitalists' expenditure (assuming that workers spent all their wage income).

The second element was Kalecki's focus on Keynes's use of the wage-unit as the *numeraire*. 'This way of accounting for the value of commodities has a deeper significance, because Keynes, in a subsequent part of his theory, shows

---

3. Kalecki's review of Keynes (1936) has been translated into English with a commentary as Targetti and Kinda-Hass (1982).

that a movement of wages induces a proportional movement of prices.' Further, despite some deficiencies in his argument, 'Keynes's statements, that the nominal wage magnitude does not influence, at least directly, the determination of short-period equilibrium, seems correct' (Targetti and Kinda-Hass,1982). In a footnote Kalecki added that he had also shown the independence of production from the movement of nominal wages in Kalecki (1933).

IMPERFECT COMPETITION

There are numerous theories of imperfect competition, incorporating different views on the underlying industrial structure and on the objectives of the firms involved. However, there is the common feature that it is possible to derive a non-causal relationship between real wage and employment (though this relationship cannot be unambiguously signed). A firm faces demand and cost conditions, and is envisaged as making interrelated decisions on price, quantity of output and on use of inputs. As a result of those decisions, a real product wage is offered by the firm along with a particular volume of employment, with the expectation of making a particular level of sales. As the level of demand facing a firm is varied, its decisions on price (and thereby on real product wage) and employment (in addition to output of course) vary in response. Thus a relationship between real product wage and employment can be mapped out, and one such has been given as the p-curve in Figure 6.1. Variations in non-labour costs would shift the curve (e.g. higher non-labour costs would shift the curve downwards). Movements along the curve would be generated by variations in the level of demand facing the firm (whether brought about by variations in aggregate demand or by changes in the prices of other products). The slope of the p-curve is not restricted to being negative. A positive slope could occur, for example, under profit-maximising oligopoly from either increasing marginal product of labour or from the degree of monopoly varying negatively with the level of demand. A formal derivation for the case of a monopolist has been given in Chapter 6.

The status of the relationship between real wage and employment under imperfect competition is essentially the same as that derived by Keynes under atomistic competition. In both cases, there is no implication that the relationship corresponds to a demand for labour function, in the sense that the real product wage is not parametric and to which the firm responds in terms of its employment decision. Firms respond to the demand that they face by deciding price and output (and thereby employment). Movements along the real wage/employment relationship occur through variations in the level of demand facing the firm. A firm could only move along the curve in the absence of the relevant demand variation at the expense of their own objectives such as profits.

It should be noted that most models of imperfect competition do not involve any notion of price rigidity. Indeed, in most respects the situation is the exact opposite, namely that it is (implicitly) assumed that prices are speedily adjusted as required. Any constancy of price in the face of demand changes arises from the decisions of firms as to what is in their best interests. This constancy is endogenous rather than exogenous, and particularly important is the intention of firms to meet the demand forthcoming at any price set. There will generally be mistakes over the expectations of demand and difficulties of adjusting production to meet demand, which are assumed to be absorbed by stock changes.

The key feature of imperfect competition in the context of macroeconomic analysis is not that prices are rigid (or even constant), but rather that the pricing decisions of firms set the real product wage. This exactly parallels the approach of Keynes in our interpretation above. In both cases, money wages are used as a key element on which prices are based. In effect, producers have the last call in the determination of the real (product) wage. Clearly, Keynes felt that he did not need any assumption of imperfect competition to derive this result, though he did require that output prices adjust rapidly. Keynes did not discuss the process by which prices change though it is implicit that producers (and not a Walrasian auctioneer) vary prices in line with marginal costs, and that producers have no significant market power.

In many representations of Keynesian economics, perfect competition is used, and as such presents continuing difficulties. The first is that at the level of the individual firm, a variation in the level of aggregate demand can only be exhibited as a variation in price. Simply, when the demand curve facing a firm is horizontal, changes in the level of aggregate demand cannot be represented by other than a vertical shift which is identical with the effect of a price variation. In contrast, in the case of imperfect competition, the demand curve facing a firm has to be positioned by reference to the general level of demand (as well as factors such as other prices), and variations in that level of demand cause the demand curve facing the firm to shift.

The second (and related) difficulty is that the marginal product-of-labour curve (which is mapped into the demand-for-labour curve) has an unchanging position (with respect to aggregate demand changes). A variation in the level of aggregate demand has to be shown as leading to a variation in output and employment, and then a move along the marginal product-of-labour curve through a variation in the real wage to maintain its equality with the marginal product of labour. Thus there is no simple way to represent aggregate demand changes in perfect competition at the level of the firm. The route developed by Patinkin (1965) was for firms to be forced off their (notional) demand-for-labour curves by an inability to sell the output which would be produced by the employment of labour as indicated by the demand-for-labour curve. In contrast, in the representation of imperfect competition above, firms are not forced off the p-curve but rather move along the p-curve as the level of aggregate demand varies. The difficulties of portraying aggregate demand effects on the perfectly competitive firm have added to the apparent problems of deriving a Keynesian macroeconomics with microeconomic foundations.

There are a number of interrelated features of the approach of Keynes derived in the circumstances of polypolistic competition, which are in our view misunderstood when placed in the context of perfect competition and which could be more readily derived from considerations of imperfect competition. The first of these features is that the labour sector and production sector (and, though outside of the scope of this paper, also the financial sector) operate in different ways. Specifically, that the labour sector is able to set money wages but that the production sector sets relative prices and real wages.

The second feature is that the relationship between the real wage and employment is a non-causal one, with the real wage set by producers. There is, though, the difference, further explored below, that under imperfect competition that relationship may be positive or negative.

The early writing of Kahn on imperfect competition (now published as Kahn, 1989) is significant since, as indicated, above Kahn was a major influence on Keynes. There are two aspects of Kahn (1989) which are particularly relevant for our discussion. The first is that his analysis of imperfect competition was set against the background of a general depression and he argued that '[i]t is however just when the theory of perfect competition appears to break down, namely during a period of slump, that a slight degree of imperfection may have far-reaching effects. Short-time working is no longer the mystery that it was before .... A substantial improvement in the perfection of the market, while of little consequence to a prosperous industry, would often be devastating in its effects on a depressed industry' (Kahn, 1989). The second is that the cost curves which producers typically face are of an inverted L-shape, i.e. constant variable costs up to full capacity. Cost curves of this form clearly pose considerable difficulties for the sustainability of perfect competition. Further, such cost curves would ease the problems (discussed below) of explaining the cyclical movements of real wages, since they do not create any presumption that real wages move counter-cyclically.

An important, though little discussed, point arising from Kahn (1989), is that perfect competition is incompatible with the general excess capacity observed in a depression. Under perfect competition, the level of output of a firm is such that marginal cost is equal to price, provided that price is above average variable cost. Thus in a depression (reflected in a low price), firms where price is below minimum average variable cost close down whilst the remainder produce with marginal cost above average variable cost, and hence it should be observed that some firms close down and the remainder operate without excess capacity (and with rising average costs).[4] Clearly, this assumes that there are variations in the cost conditions of firms, and it also undermines

---

4. 'The importance of the dissertation rests largely on the analysis of the influence of imperfection of the market on the manner in which, at a time of depression, an industry's output is distributed between the individual firms. I opened Chapter 7 by asking why most of the firms in the cotton-spinning industry, in which the degree of competition was regarded as high, work short-time, instead of those enjoying the lowest prime costs working to capacity. While the obvious answer is "imperfection of the market", until 1930 it was seldom given' (Kahn, 1989).

the usefulness of the use of the 'representative' firm. In contrast, under imperfect competition, firms suffer from a fall in demand during a depression but generally remain in business operating with excess capacity (though some may go out of business).

REAL WAGES AND EMPLOYMENT

The relationship between real wages and employment suggested by Keynes (1936) can be summarised by his conjecture that

in the case of changes in the general level of wages, it will be found, I think, that the change in real wages associated with a change in money wages, so far from being usually in the same direction, is almost always in the opposite direction .... This is because, in the short period, falling money wages and rising real wages are each, for independent reasons, likely to accompany decreasing employment; labour being readier to accept wage cuts when employment is falling off, yet real wages inevitably rising in the same circumstances on account of the increasing marginal return to a given capital equipment when output is diminished.

The empirical work of Dunlop (1938) and Tarshis (1939) casts doubt on Keynes's proposition.[5] Dunlop (1938) suggested that the English experience was that '[i]ncreases in wage rates have usually been associated with increased real wage rates, while decreases in wage rates have equally often been associated with a rise or fall in real wage rates'. Also 'wage rates have risen or fallen (almost equally often) at relatively low levels of unemployment. While *changes* in employment are more closely associated with changes in wage rates, important deviations remain. There seems to be no simple relation – and especially of a causal nature – adequate to summarize the two movements without very wide margins of error'. He gave a number of reasons as to why Keynes's expectations had not been fulfilled, of which two are notable for our purposes. The first was that '[t]he extent to which cost curves are rising, except at the very peak of the boom, has probably been over-emphasised'. The second was '[r]emoving Mr. Keynes' assumption of perfect competition [which] is more significant' and argued that the degree of monopoly tends to rise in the slump thereby reducing real wages.

Tarshis (1939) concluded that empirically 'there is a rather high direct or positive association between changes in money wages and changes in real wages'. It is interesting to note that he argued that Keynes's contrary predictions were based on three assumptions which were not realistic, of which the two relevant here are rising marginal costs and the constancy of degree of competition over the trade cycle. But these arguments were directed towards the relationship between the movements of real wages and those of money wages. Similar findings have been subsequently found, and many would regard the absence of a negative real wage/employment relationship as a stylised fact (see Michie, 1987, especially ch. 3).

---

5. For discussion between Dunlop and Keynes see Keynes (1979), and for a recent discussion see Michie (1987).

Whilst Keynes had 'always regarded decreasing physical returns in the short period as one of the very few incontrovertible propositions of our miserable subject!' (Keynes, 1973), there is a sense in which diminishing returns were not an integral part of the *General Theory*. Indeed, it could be argued that a rejection of diminishing returns and the associated negative relationship between real wages and employment would have enhanced his approach, though in order to do so he would have had to invoke imperfect competition. The derivation of a non-negative relationship between real wages and employment would surely have helped to reinforce the rejection of the real wage/employment relationship as a demand-for-labour curve. If we follow Brothwell (1988) in seeing Keynes's acceptance of the first classical postulate (equality between marginal product of labour and the real wage) as opening the way for the neo-classical synthesis, then the use by Keynes of imperfect competition rather than perfect competition might have had a profound effect on the evolution of macroeconomic analysis.

Keynes (1939) indicated that the generally positive relationship between real wages and output/employment found by Dunlop, Tarshis and others would have strengthened rather than weakened his argument, and 'it would be possible to simplify considerably the more complicated version of my fundamental explanation which I have expounded in my *General Theory*', and in a footnote indicates that Chapter 2 would be in most need of revision (a task which was not carried through as far as we are aware). Keynes argued that a positive relationship between real wages and employment strengthens the case for effective demand being the cause of employment variations, and considerably weakens the case for those who argue that public investment and similar policies 'produced their effects by deceiving, so to speak, the working class into accepting a lower real wage, effecting by this means the same favourable influence on employment which ... would have resulted from a more direct attack on real wages' (Keynes, 1939). Finally, Keynes said that he was 'comforted by the fact that their [Dunlop, Tarshis and Kalecki] conclusions tend to confirm the idea that the causes of short-period fluctuations are to be found in changes in the demand for labour, and not in changes in its real-supply price'.

The use of imperfect competition in the product market undermines the notion of the real wages and employment being determined by a labour market operating according to Walrasian principles. The real wage/employment relationship (the p-curve in Figure 6.1) derived from producers' decision-making does not have the status of a demand-for-labour curve. If, as many have erroneously done, the p-curve is given the status of a demand-for-labour curve, then there are possibilities of instability in the labour market. The aggregate real wage/employment relationship, based on the corresponding firm-level relationship would have the same status but there is little we can say about its shape. For simplicity, its shape is taken to be an inverted U-shape, though more complex shapes would tend to reinforce our conclusions. In Figure 7.1, an aggregate p-curve is combined with a supply-of-labour curve, and it can be seen that at a real wage of $(w/p)_a$, there may be excess supply of labour but the real wage is below the 'equilibrium' level. The use of imperfect competition strengthens the view that the labour sector cannot be treated like a market with well-defined demand and supply schedules, with real wages responding to excess demand. It can be noted as an aside that the inverted U-shaped 'demand' schedule is not restricted to labour but could apply to any input.

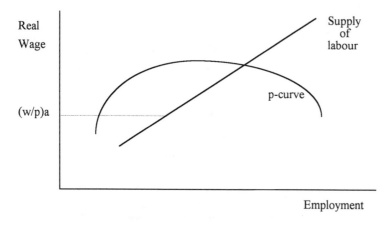

Figure 7.1 Interaction of supply of labour and p-curve

In this approach the level of employment in equilibrium would depend on the industrial structure through the influence of the latter on the position of the p-curve.[6] In each such equilibrium, unemployment would appear to be voluntary though the degree of employment and unemployment would depend on the industrial structure. This analysis, of course, ignores any role for aggregate demand, and there is no reason to think that the 'equilibrium' levels of employment real wages could be sustained in aggregate demand terms.

Keynes raised some questions on the strength of the statistical conclusions of Dunlop and Tarshis, and suggested that a suitable generalisation would be that 'for fluctuations within the range which has been usual in the periods investigated which seldom approach conditions of full employment, short-period changes in real wages are usually so small compared with the changes in other factors that we shall not often go far wrong if we treat real wages as substantially constant in the short period'. Further, Keynes pointed out that the

---

6. The usual static analysis would suggest that the p-curve shifts to the left as the degree of monopoly rises, leading to lower real wages and employment. But such analysis assumes that the cost and demand conditions facing the producers are unchanged, whereas it is expected that both cost and demand conditions depend on the industrial structure.

sign of the relationship between real wages and employment (as that between average cost and output) is likely to depend on the average level of employment and output over the relevant data period. However, this was rather different in tone from his earlier view, expressed in an interchange with Ohlin, that 'employment never did fall materially without a rise in the real hourly wage. Is not this one of the best established of statistical conclusions?' (Keynes, 1973) Ohlin responded by saying that he had 'talked this matter over with some Americans who know a lot about facts and they agree that in a recovery from a severe depression employment often grows without any fall in the real wage' (Keynes, 1973).

Thus, in response to the empirical work on real and money wages mentioned above, Keynes acknowledged the possible role of imperfect competition. Further, there is some indication (for example, in the quotes used above), that Keynes saw imperfect competition as strengthening his approach, but not fundamental to it.

SHOULD KEYNES HAVE USED IMPERFECT COMPETITION ?

It is well known that Walrasian general equilibrium analysis rests on perfect competitive assumptions and leads to an outcome of full employment. The 'imperfectionist' approach (Eatwell and Milgate, 1983) seeks to identify some features of the real world which are absent from general equilibrium analysis and argue that such features are the cause of unemployment in the real world. A particular example of this is the case of imperfect competition, where the terminology rather suggests an imperfectionist interpretation.

Keynes was quite explicit about all of these [Keynesian market failures] except the fifth [imperfections of competition]. Kaldor makes that last one, imperfect competition, the sole genesis of macroeconomic difficulties. Pure competition implies full employment equilibrium, he says, while imperfect competition implies Keynesian macroeconomics. He therefore blames Keynes for failing to see, or at least to say clearly, that his General Theory requires micro foundations encompassing increasing returns to scale and consequently monopoly, oligopoly, or monopolistic competition' (Tobin, 1983).

Weitzman (1982) sought to argue that imperfect competition (arising from the presence of increasing returns to scale) was the underlying reason for the occurrence of unemployment, and his contribution was discussed in the previous chapter. There was no suggestion in the original article that his analysis was closely linked with that of Keynes. Nevertheless some have seen his analysis as providing important microeconomic underpinnings for Keynes. '[T]hat 'money wage flexibility is not capable of maintaining full employment' [Keynes, 1936]. However the argument leading up to this conclusion is by no means as decisive and clear-cut as the conclusion itself and no doubt Keynes would have been very grateful for Mr Weitzman's support had it been available to him – the more so since the latter's argument (unlike Keynes's) relates to *real* wages and not merely to money wages' (Kaldor,1983).[7]

When seeking to answer the question of whether Keynes would have been well advised to have used imperfect competition rather than perfect competition, it is necessary to ask what Keynes's purpose was. It can be argued that Keynes sought to show that unemployment would arise even with atomistic competition.

Even though the small firm is no longer the dominant market form, it is well that Keynes took it as his model, for in doing so he met the neo-classical theory on its own ground. Only the assumption of perfect knowledge was changed. Those who wish to claim greater realism for the theory by introducing monopolistic elements into it do not seem to recognise that by doing so they undermine the power of Keynes's argument: Keynes showed that, even taking *the assumption* of neo-classical analysis, he could produce non-neo-classical results. Monopoly elements then strengthen the argument but the argument does not depend on them' (Chick, 1983).

This line of argument suggests that Keynes did not think that imperfect competition was in any sense intrinsic to his explanation of unemployment. But, further, that Keynes was concerned with establishing some theoretical proposition (i.e. that unemployment can occur under atomistic competition) rather than with the development of an analysis based on realistic assumptions.

It can be further argued that the essence of Keynes's 'message' for economic policy was the role of aggregate demand in the determination of the level of economic activity. There are, of course, many other themes in Keynes (1936). The role of aggregate demand, the focus on quantity adjustment to bring planned savings and planned investment into equality etc. arise in a monetary/financial economy but not in a barter economy. Thus it is important whether an economy is a monetary or a barter one but for some purposes it may not matter whether the economy is atomistic or imperfectly competitive. However, as indicated above, the nature of the industrial structure is of relevance for issues such as the sign of the real wage/employment relation, and the distribution of output between firms. Industrial structure, including that of the financial sector, would also be seen to be relevant for the determination of investment and savings.

The approach of Keynes was subject to considerable simplification and misrepresentation; in connection with this chapter the misrepresentation of particular relevance concerns price and wage rigidity. In the second half of the 1930s theories of imperfect competition were relatively novel, and there is clearly a strong possibility that Keynes's underemployment equilibrium would have been represented as arising from imperfect competition, rather than from a lack of effective demand.

Why did Keynes not exploit the microeconomic revolution fomented in this very town [Cambridge] by his own colleagues and disciples in the same years he was revolutionizing

---

7. See *Journal of Post Keynesian Economics*, 1983 for a critical symposium on Weitzman(1982); also see previous chapter.

macroeconomics. That certainly is a puzzle, as Kaldor says. To try to win the game on the other side's home field and with their book of rules was a mistake. But faithful neoclassicals on both sides of the Atlantic had no compunctions dismissing imperfect competition from microeconomic theory, as a trivial exception proving the rule of pure competition. They probably would not have found Keynes's macroeconomics any more appealing if he had based it on imperfect competition (Tobin, 1983).

The way in which Kalecki's macroeconomic analysis which was firmly based on imperfect competition was ignored by the mainstream economists would provide some support for the view of Tobin.

CONCLUDING REMARK

The general line of argument of this chapter has been that Keynes did not use and did not need to use any notions of imperfect competition to derive his major conclusions on the causes of unemployment. We have argued that some of his conclusions can be more easily derived in the context of imperfect competition than in that of atomistic competition. In particular, the idea that there are significant differences between the output sector and the labour sector, with the output price effectively settling the real wage can now be seen as readily derived from theories of imperfect competition, whereas the corresponding derivation for perfect competition has not found widespread appeal. Further, as suggested by Kahn, imperfect competition is required to explain why firms work with excess capacity during recession (rather than the reduction in output being met by some firms closing and others operating above capacity). Finally, as indicated above, when the levels of output and employment are viewed as essentially determined by the equality between *ex ante* savings and investment, then the industrial structure is relevant (for the levels of employment) only insofar as it influences savings and investment. A recent statement of an emerging conventional wisdom is that 'it has come to be accepted that it is impossible to explain the constraints that give rise to Keynesian macro results without recourse to theories of imperfect or monopolistic competition' (Collard, 1990). The line of argument of this chapter is to reject that conventional wisdom, but to suggest that Keynes's theory would have been much enhanced by the use of imperfect competition.

8. On the origins of post Keynesian pricing theory and macroeconomics

INTRODUCTION

The second half of the 1930s saw the publication of a series of seminal contributions on pricing, many of which can now be seen to have provided the foundations for post Keynesian pricing theories. Many of these contributions have entered the mainstream of microeconomics in the sense that they are often taught, even though they do not fit in easily with neo-classical economics. Whilst the mark-up pricing elements of these approaches play some role in macroeconomics, it is generally a rather marginal and misunderstood one (as argued below). The major purpose of this chapter is to review these contributions, and to indicate the important differences between them as well as the significant similarities.

The contributions discussed here were initially published within three years of the publication of Keynes (1936). Keynesian economics has often been associated with price rigidity and the view that malfunctioning of the economy arises from such rigidity. It is clear that Keynes did not appeal to either (product) price rigidity or imperfect competition in order to explain unemployment (for further discussion see Chapter 7). Chapter 21 of Keynes (1936) indicated considerable price flexibility, with prices changing with (a) costs, generally to maintain the relationship between prices and wages for a given level of demand (i.e. a constant real wage) or (b) with changes in demand, for a given schedule of costs. Keynes treated the nominal wage as the *numeraire*, which has often been confused with an assumption of rigidity of money wage (and which is in effect just the opposite in that this allows the money wage to take any value). However, it soon became accepted that '[a]t the core of the Keynesian polemics of the past ten years and more is the relationship between price flexibility and full employment'. Further, '[t]here always exists a sufficiently low price level such that, if expected to continue indefinitely, it will generate full employment' (all in italics in original) and 'in a static world with a constant stock of money, price flexibility assures full employment' (Patinkin, 1951).

The approaches to pricing considered here interact with such a view, as they appeared to provide explanations for price rigidity so that a Keynesian economics could proceed on the assumption of price rigidity, irrespective of Keynes's own assumptions. The interaction was reinforced by the publication of the works considered here about the same time as the *General Theory* (Keynes, 1936). It is argued here that, at most, these contributions only involve price rigidity with respect to changes in demand conditions and that any such rigidity results from the decisions of the producers; it is not imposed by some external agency. In the neo-classical approach, price changes arise only in response to excess demand, and a denial of the impact of demand on price appears superficially to exclude the possibility of price adjustments. It will become evident below that much confusion arises from introducing arguments from one framework (e.g. price constancy with respect to demand from imperfect competition) into another (e.g. price rigidity imposed on atomistic competition). It is argued that any constancy of price has quite different origins and different consequences in the context of price-setting firms than the imposition of price rigidity has in the atomistic competitive context.

The previous chapter has discussed the relationship between imperfect competition and the analysis of Keynes, and came to the conclusion that his conclusions can be derived without recourse to the assumption of imperfect competition (though we did argue that Keynes's analysis may have been strengthened by the use of imperfect competition microeconomic foundations). This chapter has a related purpose, namely to consider whether the post Keynesian theories of pricing developed within a few years of the publication of *The General Theory* could be seen to have contributed to the linkage between Keynesian economics and price rigidity. It is argued (with one partial exception) that they did not. Instead a major part of their contribution is seen to be the nature and role of price which they envisage through shifting the role of price away from being solely an allocative one.

The four contributions from the 1930s discussed here are Means (1933, 1935, 1936), Kalecki (1938, 1943b), Hall and Hitch (1939) and Sweezy (1939). The common features of these contributions include a focus on the setting of prices in an environment which does not involve atomistic competition and some (in varying degrees) attention to the imperfect information. This chapter has four main sections. The first section provides a consideration of the nature of the contributions of the above mentioned authors.[1] The second section discusses the relationship between approaches to pricing and macroeconomic analysis. The third section considers some of the differences between the four approaches, with an emphasis on the objectives of firms and their time-horizons for decision-making purposes. The fourth section reflects on the nature of prices as encapsulated in these approaches with contrasts drawn with the Walrasian general equilibrium view of prices.

---

1. Our coverage does not claim to be comprehensive. In particular, the work of authors such as Andrews (e.g. 1949) have not been included. For discussion of the approach of Andrews, see Lee et alia (1986).

APPROACHES TO PRICING

Means

We begin with the contribution of Means, which for our purposes contains three important ideas.[2] The first could be summarised as the consequences of the absence of a Walrasian auctioneer, whose role is the continual adjustment of price to reach equilibrium between demand and supply. This was not a contrast between a mythical auctioneer and the real world but rather between markets where prices are settled by haggling between buyers and sellers and those where prices are set by the seller. 'Means considered erroneous the assumptions that prices are always determined by the interaction of buyers and sellers and that they change in a highly flexible manner' (Samuels and Medema 1989). In some situations, of which the oriental bazaar is an example, price is set in the process of trade by haggling. In these cases, '[p]rice does not *precede* a trade, but is determined *in* trade and therefore flexibility of price can be assumed to exist' (Means, 1933), as a result of the haggling which leads to a sale. In contrast, 'prices are fixed by administrative action for periods of time' (Means 1933) prior to trade, and the price set would not usually lead to an equilibrium between supply and demand. These administered prices would be seen as a characteristic of most markets in an industrialised economy.

The second (and related) feature was the contrast drawn between 'market-dominated price' (prices made by interaction of a large number of buyers and sellers *and* administered prices in which one or more market-priced raw material constitutes a substantial part of the product's costs) and 'administration-dominated price' (all other prices). The 'market-dominated' prices would be expected to change more frequently than the 'administration-dominated' ones, and this was the original basis for Means's classification of industries in terms of one of the types of price regimes (e.g. Means, 1936).

This leads into the third feature, namely that 'market-dominated' prices were more responsive to demand than 'administration-dominated' ones, so that the former rose (relative to the latter) during the upswing of the business cycles and fell during the downswing. (This idea was later to form the starting point of Eichner's approach, as indicated in Eichner (1973)).

[The administered price thesis] specifically held that in business recessions administered prices showed a tendency not to fall as much as market prices while the recession fall in demand worked itself out primarily through a fall in sales, production, and employment. Similarly, since administered prices tended not to fall as much in a recession, they tended not to rise as much in recovery while rising demand worked itself out primarily in a rising volume of sales, production, and employment (Means (1972)).

Thus Means linked changes in price with changes in output, and the implication would appear to be that variations of output will be much greater when

---

2. See also Samuels and Medema (1989) especially sections III and IV. Our information on Means's doctoral dissertation (1933) is drawn from that paper.

administered prices apply than otherwise for a particular variation in demand. This implication arises, though, only from consideration of price and output decisions, which in turn have implications for the level of aggregate demand. There may be many other differences between sectors, notably over investment behaviour. It would appear that variations in output and employment over the business cycle would be more severe under a regime of administered prices than under market-dominated prices, but this says nothing about the average level of output and employment. Thus, as with a number of recent approaches (e.g. Okun 1981), that of Means would appear to leave the average level of economic activity unexplained.

Means (1936) argued that 'an administered price and a monopoly price are quite different aspects of price'. Administered prices were seen as both inevitable and impeding the functioning of the economy. '[I]inflexible, administered prices have acted as an impediment to that automatic readjustment which is supposed to occur through price changes and which is supposed to keep an economy in approximate balance with full use of our economic resources' (Means, 1936).

However, inflexible prices were inherent in modern technology so that questions of whether administered prices were right or wrong were irrelevant. Further, '[a]ccording to the rules of the laissez faire game, they [administered prices] could not be expected to come down [in a depression]. I am only saying that inflexible administered prices are incompatible with automatic economic adjustment'. (Means 1936)

Means does not provide any clear account of why inflexible prices would have these undesirable effects, though it can be inferred that inflexibility would clearly create problems in an atomistic competitive economy. In a number of respects, Means comes closest of the authors considered in this chapter to the later caricature of Keynesian economics as Walrasian general equilibrium with rigid prices.

Kalecki

Kalecki's approach to pricing went through a number of versions, which have been fully discussed in Kriesler (1987). Our remarks here particularly relate to the earlier versions, though most would apply more generally. Kalecki retained the pursuit of profits and a loose form of profit maximisation as firms' objectives, though the working assumption of constant average direct costs was reinforced by difficulties of exact calculation by firms (Kalecki, 1940). Kalecki's approach can be summarised as follows: prices are set as a mark-up over average direct costs (which include the costs of materials and manual labour) where the size of the mark-up depends on the 'degree of monopoly'. As first approximations, both the mark-up and average direct costs are taken as constant with respect to output, but that is not an integral part of the theory. However, those approximations do have the effect of providing a sharp distinction between micro- and macro-effects. The share of profits in national income becomes a microeconomic effect, derived as a summation over the pricing decisions of firms, whilst the volume of profits is a macroeconomic effect, determined by the aggregate level of expenditure but which cannot be determined by any appropriate summation over firms.

Of the four approaches considered here, Kalecki's approach could be considered the closest to a neo-classical approach. It retains profit maximisation (though subject to certain caveats), and has a strong affinity with the view that industrial structure (varying from monopoly through to perfect competition) has an impact on profitability, which many view as the basis of the neo-classical approach to industrial economics. Further, Kalecki was more concerned with the factors external to the firm determining price in relation to average direct costs. He was little concerned (at least in his writings) with the process by which prices were decided upon.

Kalecki (1943b) introduced the distinction between cost-determined and demand-determined prices. Some (notably Robinson, 1977) have seen this as paralleling the flexprice/fixprice distinction made by Hicks, Okun and others. But there are some important differences between the two dichotomies, notably that Kalecki indicates that cost-determined prices whilst unresponsive to demand changes do respond to cost changes, whilst the forces which might move fixprices are left unspecified. There is some parallel between this dichotomy and that of Means indicated above, with both indicating that the way prices are set and behave varies across different sectors of the economy.

It is argued here that Kalecki's main contribution in respect of price is the idea that the setting of product prices has implications for the distribution of income and the level of real wages. This could be seen from Kalecki (1938) where price determination was directly linked with the distribution of income between wages and profits.

In his review of *The General Theory* Kalecki highlighted Keynes's use of the wage unit as the *numeraire* and the demonstration that 'a movement of wages induces a proportional movement of prices .... If the fall in nominal wages due to unemployment leads to an equi-proportional fall in prices, there is no tendency to absorb unemployment' (Kalecki, as translated in Targetti and Kinda-Hass, 1982).

Further, there is the independence of production and employment from movements in nominal wages. The idea that price movements offset any nominal wage movements, which can be described as real wages being determined in the product market, has become a major feature of the post Keynesian approach. But it is not generally realised that such a view is a feature of (virtually) all theories of imperfect competition where the price set depends on money wages (and other costs) and the level of demand as was argued in Chapter 6 above (and in more detail in Sawyer, 1983).

Sweezy

Sweezy (1939) is best known for the kinked demand curve as an explanation of price inflexibility (which also appears in Hall and Hitch (1939), discussed below). The appearance of this article illustrates the perception in the 1930s of rigidity of price and the search for an explanation. '[T]he theory was advanced that there exists a kink in the demand curve for the product of an oligopolist and that this kink goes far to explain price rigidities in oligopolistic industries. [Further], the theory is an ingenious rationalisation of the price rigidities that were reported in many statistical studies of prices during the thirties, and no doubt this explains its popularity' (Stigler, 1947).

Sweezy's approach was intended to be a generalisation of how business people behaved. It retained the assumption of profit maximisation with the focus on the equality between marginal cost and marginal revenue, though there was an emphasis on 'a systematic inquiry into the nature of imagined demand curve' (Sweezy, 1939). The kink in the imagined demand curve (which would now more usually be called the perceived demand curve) arose, of course, from the perception by the firm that a price rise would not be followed by rivals whereas a price reduction would be so followed. The resulting gap in the marginal revenue curve (at the prevailing level of output) generates a degree of price inflexibility in the face of both demand and cost changes. As Sweezy noted, 'any disturbance which affects only the position of the marginal cost curve may leave short-run equilibrium of price and output entirely unaffected' (Sweezy, 1939).

A change in demand feeds through into mainly quantity changes rather than price changes. 'It seems clear that any such shift [in the perceived demand curve] will first make itself felt in a change in the quantity sold at the current price' (Sweezy, 1939). But there are also changes in perceptions associated with shifts in demand – when demand rises, the gap between the two marginal reve-nue curves is diminished as the upward elasticity is lower and the downward elasticity is higher than before. Conversely, when demand declines, the gap opens up. The argument is then that price tends to be relatively rigid for low levels of demand but can rise for high levels of demand. Sweezy suggested that his analysis could be developed to throw light on the issue of rigid prices.

Sweezy's approach has been criticised for only analysing movements in price relative to an initial situation. This criticism arises from a neo-classical perspective where the relevance of history is denied and where equilibrium is unaffected by the disequilibrium path. In contrast, Sweezy stressed that imag-ined demand curves 'can only be thought of with reference to a given starting point' (Sweezy,1939), so that the history of prices in an industry is relevant for the current level. There can be a large number of price/output combinations which, if reached, would constitute equilibrium in that there are no endogenous forces making for a change. The influence of the previous history of an industry on the prices set in that industry is a common theme in the contributions being discussed here.

Some elements of kinked demand type arguments have surfaced in recent years (e.g. Hahn, 1978) to seek to explain price stickiness. The conjectures which firms hold are then such as to make them reluctant to change price. How-ever, Hahn's models relate to situations of atomistic competition in which firms encounter quantity constraints, with the essential feature that the conjectures held by the firms mean that it is perceived not to be worthwhile to vary price. This is rather different from the position of Sweezy that firms are prepared to meet the demand which arises at the price that they set.

Hall and Hitch

In a number of respects, the paper of Hall and Hitch (1939) represented a more radical approach than the others considered in this chapter, with a departure from profit maximisation as the objective of a firm. In particular, it cast 'doubt on the general applicability of the conventional analysis of price and output policy in terms of marginal cost and marginal revenue, and suggests a mode of entrepreneurial behaviour which current economic doctrine tends to ignore' (Hall and Hitch, 1939), whereas both Kalecki and Sweezy retained profit maximisation as a working assumption. In their paper, Hall and Hitch questioned the meaning of marginal revenue and marginal cost (e.g. to what time span do they relate) and the nature of demand-curve (actual, perceived). However, one of the reasons they give for firms following the full cost approach to pricing is a kinked-demand-curve argument, parallel to that of Sweezy, which clearly makes use of the marginal revenue and cost concepts.

They argued that the majority of firms do not aim for the maximisation of profits through the equalisation of marginal revenue and marginal cost. Instead, in the determination of prices, firms 'try to apply a rule of thumb which we shall call "full cost", and that maximum profits, if they result at all from the application of this rule, do so as an accidental (or possibly evolutionary) by-product' (Hall and Hitch, 1939).

Much of the attention of Hall and Hitch was on the procedure for setting price. They provided a generalisation for the setting of the full cost price, namely 'prime (or direct) cost per unit is taken as the base, a percentage addition is made to cover overheads ... and a further conventional addition ... is made for profit' (Hall and Hitch, 1939). However, they thought that it was impossible to deduce the full cost price from 'the technical conditions of production and the supply prices of the factors' (Hall and Hitch, 1939). Thus while it is possible to portray price as a mark-up over average costs, it is not possible to formulate the precise factors that determine the extent of the mark-up. There is a degree of stability in pricing policies of firms, though '[p]rices in an industry become "unstable" as soon as any of the competitors form an idea of a profitable price which is markedly different from the existing prices' (Hall and Hitch, 1939).

Hall and Hitch argued that a full understanding of prices at any particular time can only be reached by allowance for the history of the industry concerned. They conclude that prices have a tendency to be stable, and 'will be changed if there is a significant change in wage or raw material costs, but not in response to moderate or temporary shifts in demand' (Hall and Hitch 1939).

Although it is not stated explicitly, it would appear that firms are viewed as generally satisfying the demand which is forthcoming at the full cost price. In periods of high demand, it is acknowledged that price may be moved up when firms find it difficult to satisfy demand.

PRICING AND MACROECONOMICS

The four approaches briefly surveyed above share a number of common features. The first is that they all refer to situations of imperfect competition in the general sense that some of the key attributes of perfect competition are absent. The situation of imperfect competition may involve fewness of numbers and/or product differentiation. The crucial point, which is explored below, is that any conclusion (especially on any notion of inflexibility of prices) cannot be readily translated over into atomistic competition.

The second common feature is that the Walrasian auctioneer is absent: rather, prices are set by producers in pursuit of their own objectives and changed when the producers think fit. Those who set the price do so in their own interests; similarly if prices do not change then it is presumed that it is in the producers' interests to hold prices constant.

The third feature (though this may be absent from Means's work) is that suppliers do intend to supply the demand which is forthcoming at the price that they set. This intention may be aided by the perception that average costs are approximately constant with respect to output. Firms may, of course, make mistakes and actual demand diverge from that expected. Mistakes are generally absorbed by stock changes, but that does mean that subsequent output decisions are influenced by those mistakes and stock changes. It is assumed for our purposes that mistakes over the level of demand are sufficiently small to be ignored, though it is recognised that any discussion of the movement of the economy through time would need to pay due attention to the impact of stock changes.

Keynesian economics has often been associated with notions of price and/or wage rigidity. In the context of the Keynesian IS–LM approach, price flexibility was seen to lead back to full employment through the operation of the Pigou effect, so unemployment was associated with price inflexibility. In the literature associated with the so-called re-appraisal of Keynesian economics and the temporary equilibrium approach, the absence of the Walrasian auctioneer is said to lead to some price and wage inflexibility, rationing by the short side of the market etc. The question arises then as to how to characterise markets in which there is no such auctioneer. One route would be to follow Means and others and characterise such markets as quite different from atomistic competition. In particular, in product markets prices are seen as set by the producers. Another route, which has generally been followed in the temporary equilibrium literature, is to retain most elements of atomistic competition other than complete price flexibility.

These two routes are often inappropriately mixed. Malinvaud (1977), for example, argues that '[t]he classical [*sic*] teaching, according to which prices quickly react to excess supplies or demand, is more and more inadequate for short-run macroeconomic analysis as we move into an ever-higher degree of organization of society'. He proceeds to argue that '[t]he conclusion therefore emerges that short-term quantitative adjustments are much more apparent and influential than short-term price adjustments' (Malinvaud, 1977).

It is clear that the authors considered in this chapter were not discussing fix-prices since price changes are explored within their model (and hence not autonomous). Further, whether or not prices remain unchanged, the producers intend to supply whatever is demanded at the ruling price. Therefore, there is no excess demand or supply, and hence no route by which the quantity traded is determined by the short side of the market.

The theories presented above differ to some degree over the responsiveness of price to costs. In the context of the 1930s this may not have been a crucial issue and so is not always explicitly dealt with. In the case of Sweezy, movement of the marginal cost curve within the gap in the marginal revenue curve would not lead to any price (or output) adjustment. Thus, over a range, profits absorb the effects of cost changes. For Hall and Hitch and for Kalecki, a cost change could be expected to lead to a proportionate price change. For Means, it could be inferred that large cost changes would lead to price changes but perhaps small cost changes would be absorbed.

It may be interesting to ask how a firm would alter price and output in response to variations in the demand that it faces. However, the answer to such a question can only be partial, for it does not address either the question of the origin of demand variation or that of the further repercussions of the price and output decisions. Those decisions will clearly have implications for income, wages, profits etc. At the aggregate level, there is then the question as to whether the wages and profits that result from a specific level of aggregate demand would themselves generate that level of demand. If it does, then there is macroeconomic equilibrium; if not, then there will be further changes to output and price.

The importance of the dichotomy drawn by Means between market prices and administered prices is that they arise from different market structures. This dichotomy is richer than the flexprice/fixprice one.[3] In particular, contemporary users of the flexprice/fixprice dichotomy have not drawn a sharp distinction between the differences in market structure for which the two types of price are relevant, but rather applied both types to essentially atomistically competitive markets. The dichotomy drawn by Means (and also that made by Kalecki) includes not only differences of the responsiveness of price to demand but also differences of market structure.

---

3. Hicks linked the fixprice case with markets where prices were set by producers and the flexprice with 'speculative markets, in which prices are still determined by supply and demand' (Hicks, 1974). He argued that a theory was needed which took account of both types of markets. He saw the major difference between these markets as '[i]n the fixprice market ... actual stocks may be greater, or may be less, than desired stocks; in the flexprice market ... actual stocks are always equal to desired stocks – when the stocks of the traders are taken into account' (Hicks, 1974).

The price-inflexibility arguments have been illegitimately carried over from imperfect competition to a form of perfect competition. Price inflexibility in the face of demand change may arise with administered prices, i.e. with the firms as price-setters. This is translated over into a market form in which firms are supposed to be price takers. The question is not whether price-setters exist but rather who plays that role. The difficulty in identifying a price-setter in perfect competition results in falling back on the device of an auctioneer. Imperfect competition clearly identifies the seller as the price-setter (though there may be situations where that may not be so). The disinterested auctioneer is thereby replaced by price-setters with specific interests, which will be pursued through the setting of prices (and other routes).

DIFFERENCES BETWEEN THE POST KEYNESIAN APPROACHES

There has been a tendency to conflate the different post Keynesian approaches to pricing. The reasons for this are understandable. For macroeconomic analysis, it is often sufficient to portray price as a mark-up over costs, without needing to specify the determinants of the mark-up or the precise definition of costs. The theories have the common elements of stressing the limited impact of demand (level or changes) on prices, and, as we have argued above, the adjustment of output to satisfy demand. However, in other respects, there are some significant differences which we briefly explore in this section.

The major difference concerns the usefulness or otherwise of portraying firms as profit maximisers. This difference has two aspects. The first is whether the optimisation concept is useful in the context of price setting. Although Kalecki retained profit maximisation, he did argue that firms could not achieve maximisation with any degree of precision. Hall and Hitch did not specify the motivation of firms and, as indicated above, they argued against the equality of marginal cost and marginal revenue. This division between those finding profit maximisation a useful device for modelling firm behaviour and those who reject (for a variety of reasons) notions of optimisation as useful in the understanding of human decision-making still continues.

The second aspect is less evident in the discussion above and relates to the relationship between short-term and long-term considerations. Hall and Hitch draw some attention to this, and argue that orthodox treatment had played down, if not ignored, the relationship between demand in different time periods. Besides that consideration, the price set may influence the level of profits and thereby the finance available for investment and the growth of future demand. These linkages have been extensively explored by Eichner (1987), Harcourt and Kenyon (1976), Shapiro (1981), Wood (1975) and others (for further discussion see Chapters 9 and 10 below). Amongst the authors considered here, Kalecki viewed the long period as a collection of successive short periods, and did not discuss the conflict between the short term and the long term. His approach could be summarised by saying that firms seek to maximise short-term profits, with investment decisions influenced by factors such as profits, output, capacity utilisation.

Means was more of a forerunner of those cited above, who view the management of firms as concerned with growth and the financing of investment. Barriers to entry provide some protection for incumbent firms and as a consequence

management did not have to be primarily concerned with making the maximum amount of profit on each transaction or for the current pricing period (which covered a number of sequential transactions). Moreover, because the managers had no legal claim over corporate profits, they had no reason to try to maximise the corporation's profits in the 'long period' .... To carry out their growth strategy for the corporation, management adopted, Means argued, an administered price policy' (Lee, 1990).

The above discussion can be briefly summarised by saying that Kalecki viewed producers as seeking as high a level of profits as possible in the short term, and then basing investment decisions on the profits generated. Means, in contrast, viewed pricing policy as being based on the growth requirements of the company.

THE NATURE OF PRICES

There are a number of implicit, but nevertheless important, features of price in the Walrasian general equilibrium approach. Prices have an allocative function, and resources are only allocated by the price mechanism. Prices respond to excess demand or supply. In the Walrasian tatonnement story, time is in effect suspended until the equilibrium price vector is discovered and then trading takes place. In much of Keynesian economics, the price response to excess supply has clearly been retained, whilst the allocative function of price has remained in the background. The importance of the post Keynesian approaches to pricing is that each of the features of Walrasian general equilibrium mentioned above are denied.

The concept of excess demand was introduced in the context of perfect competition with economic agents facing parametric prices. The supply function does not have the same meaning under imperfect competition as under perfect competition. However, our interpretation of imperfect competition above is that producers will seek to operate on the demand curve facing them, and in that sense there is zero excess demand. Under perfect competition, the presence of excess supply or demand is clear evidence of disequilibrium in the sense that at least one side of the market is dissatisfied with that outcome. Under imperfect competition, the presence of excess capacity does not necessarily indicate disequilibrium so far as price and output decisions are concerned in that there may be no forces at work at that level to reduce the extent of excess capacity. Producers have made decisions on prices and output (and thereby on capacity utilisation) which leads to the best outcome that they can achieve in the circumstances that they face (and in doing so collectively cause the economic environment to change). The level of capacity utilisation may be unsatisfactory but the producers can only respond to that by investment decisions (which is likely to introduce elements of instability in that high levels of capacity utilisation generate investment, thereby raising aggregate demand further). For a variety of reasons, producers may wish to have some degree of excess capacity (whether as a barrier against entry, insurance against demand fluctuations etc.). This suggests that the presence of excess capacity may not generate pressures to lower prices (relative to costs). At a particular level of output, there would be no tendency for prices to fall (relative to costs).

The movement of money wages is not a direct concern of this chapter, but let us assume that money wages fall under the impact of unemployment. Any impact on the real wage would depend on the firms' responses to the decline in labour costs: in the context of a closed economy, with a given level of demand, it would be expected that prices fall in line with wages, leaving the real wage unchanged.

Price changes may be associated with output changes, both resulting from changes in demand. In the approaches discussed above, the general expectation is that the major change will be in output with price change playing a minor role (from a given change in demand). As Robinson (1933) pointed out, under imperfect competition it is even possible for prices to rise in the face of a decline in demand. Kalecki similarly noted that there were reasons for a rise in the price–cost margin as demand declined.

When producers (rather than a disinterested auctioneer) set prices then it would be expected that those prices would be set in the interests of the producers themselves. Thus the immediate function of price is to satisfy the objectives of the producers. Gerrard (1989) lists five roles of price, namely the conductive, positional, strategic, financial and the allocative. With the exception of the allocative function, these functions are derived from the use that the producers seek to make of price. For example, the financing role is derived from the producers seeking to set prices to generate finance for investment purposes. In contrast, the allocative role is only a by-product of price determination. In the Walrasian general equilibrium approach, the role of the auctioneer could be said to be dedicated to resource allocation and co-ordination of economic activity. The other side of this is that in the post Keynesian approaches economic co-ordination is undertaken in a variety of ways. This does not arise explicitly in the approaches to pricing discussed above, though

[i]n conceiving of the corporate economy as a continuous monetary flow of economic activity that was co-ordinated by market and administered prices, by administrative co-ordination, and by rules and goals, Means sought to dispel the notion that the American economy operated as a cybernetic mechanism which automatically tended to eliminate underutilization of all economic resources, including labour, productive plant and natural resources (Lee, 1990).

CONCLUDING REMARKS

The four approaches to pricing originating from the 1930s discussed in this chapter should be seen as quite distinct contributions since there are significant differences between them. However, they do share a number of common features. They indicate an insensitivity of price to demand and demand changes, which may sometimes be usefully represented as a constancy of price. Since these approaches relate to conditions of imperfect competition, the consequences of any price constancy are quite different from those that arise from imposing price rigidity in the context of atomistic competition. Simply, the latter involves excess supply or demand, whereas the former results from the producers' decisions and with output adjusting to meet demand. More generally, these (and other) post Keynesian approaches to pricing should be viewed as part of a quite separate paradigm of price determination and resource allocation.

9. Post Keynesian analysis and industrial economics

INTRODUCTION

Although post Keynesian economics is often linked with demand-side macroeconomic considerations, it has always involved a strong microeconomic supply-side analysis. Indeed, it should be said that the post Keynesian analysis does not draw any sharp distinction between demand-side and supply-side. The components of the overall analysis that could be viewed as supply-side and microeconomic have generally focused on pricing and investment decisions which are, of course, also particularly relevant for macroeconomic analysis. This chapter explores the nature of post Keynesian approaches to price setting, objectives of the firms and the nature of competition, which could be put under the general heading of industrial economics.

This chapter has some links with the next one in two particular respects. The first is the differing views between post Keynesian economists on the links between price, profits and investment, which are discussed in this chapter and then more formally modelled in the next chapter. The second respect is that whilst firms set prices in their own interests, there are systemic effects of those pricing decisions and also systemic requirements for the overall configuration of prices. This chapter (as some previous chapters have also done) discusses the influences on the setting of prices by firms, whilst the next chapter presents a model in which the systemic requirements can be explored.

The post Keynesian tradition has often involved discussion of matters such as pricing and investment which could be seen as part of industrial economics, but there is not a fully developed post Keynesian approach to industrial economics as such. Indeed, as will be argued below, there are a number of approaches to industrial economics which have been labelled post Keynesian, but which are by no means consistent with one another. The underlying purpose is to try to sketch out a sensible approach to industrial economics, which does not operate in isolation from macroeconomic considerations nor from broader issues in economic analysis. The term post Keynesian is broadly interpreted and traditions such as theories of monopoly capital, which has links with Marxian analysis, are drawn upon.

The first main section of this chapter provides a discussion of the relationship between industrial economics and neo-classical economics. The purpose of this section is to indicate the uneasy relationship between them and indeed some significant inconsistencies between the two, and provide a basis for later discussions in which the influence of orthodox industrial economics on post Keynesian analysis will become evident. Differing views on the motivation and objectives of firms (e.g. profit maximisation or not) within post Keynesian approaches are then considered, where it is argued that there are some deep-seated differences between post Keynesian economists on this subject. It also emerges that these differences spill over into the question of the relationship between prices and investment, and the determination of the level of capacity utilisation. The nature of competition is the subject of the next section, where it is argued that post Keynesian approaches have tended to understate the role of competition and rivalry between firms. This leads onto the question of what are the relevant institutional assumptions for the late 20th century. It is argued that the post Keynesian emphasis on the importance of the institutional arrange-ments of an economy is relevant but also impels some consideration of what those arrangements are. It is then argued that orthodox industrial economics has retained the neo-classical neglect of the production process and the assumption of technologically determined relationships between inputs and outputs. There would appear to be much to be gained from an injection into the study of industrial economics of the insights of post Keynesians and others on the organisation of production and the causes of variations in labour productivity.

INDUSTRIAL ECONOMICS AND NEO-CLASSICAL ECONOMICS

One difficulty in discussing the relationship between industrial economics and neo-classical economics is that the former is an area of study whereas the latter is a school of thought, and each school of thought could be expected to have industrial economics as a particular area of study. However, industrial econo-mists share a sufficiently common approach and language to be able to converse with one another, which allows comparisons to be made between neo-classical economics and industrial economics. Particularly in its general equilibrium form, neo-classical economics is general in the sense of dealing with the common properties of inputs and outputs. This would apply both to inputs such as labour services, capital equipment (whose common property is that they contribute to production) as well as to outputs such as consumer goods and services (whose common property is that they generate utility for consumers). Although general equilibrium theory does not mention activities such as advertising, research and development, in so far as they can be considered to be included in general equilibrium theory they would share the common characteristics of other activities (as inputs or outputs). In some contrast, analysis within industrial economics is concerned with the specific properties of certain activities. For example, the specific properties of advertising are discussed (e.g. whether it is to be considered informative or persuasive) and the difficulties of firms determining the level of advertising (e.g. because of problems of forecasting the effect of advertising) are considered. Similar remarks would apply to research and development activities, where, since research is to find new ideas, perfect information (or the equivalent) cannot be assumed.

It is argued here that industrial economics as practised in what would be regarded as mainstream textbooks is at considerable variance with neo-classical economics.[1] It could be argued that some mix of perfect competition and monopoly with adaptations to deal with topics such as advertising, research and development, would be neo-classical industrial economics. Indeed, some have seen the structure-conduct-performance (SCP) paradigm as part of neo-classical economics,[2] it is argued here that the SCP paradigm is in substantial conflict with neo-classical economics, though it has retained the 'black box' view of the firm.

Whilst the previously dominant SCP paradigm has come under increasing criticism in the last decade or so, it still retains a considerable influence, at least as an organising idea for much empirical work in industrial economics. It is then useful to take the SCP paradigm as an example of mainstream industrial economics in order to illustrate the line of argument. Since the SCP paradigm can be viewed as strongly influenced by neo-classical economics, many of the arguments are that the SCP approach and neo-classical conflict should apply *a fortiori* to other approaches to industrial economics.

The first aspect of our argument of the differences between neo-classical economics and the SCP approach (and industrial economics more generally) is that the SCP approach heavily involves the notion that industrial structure moulds conduct and thereby industrial performance. At a minimum, this could be interpreted as saying that the structural conditions (in this case number of firms, ease of entry) are relevant for behaviour and performance. Some of these structural conditions may be seen as technologically determined, whilst others are strongly influenced by (past and present) behaviour of the existing firms. This stands in contrast with the usual neo-classical position, yet fits with the general post Keynesian position of the relevance of institutions and of history.

The second aspect draws on the income distribution considerations of firms' pricing policies. Cowling (1982) and Sawyer (1983), building on the insight of Kalecki (1938), have illustrated the simple point that the pricing policies of firms influence the price–cost margin, which in turn has implications for the distribution of income between profits and wages. The approach of Kalecki indicates that the market power of firms (based on variables such as industrial concentration, ease of entry) sets the price-cost margins and thereby the distribution between wages and profits. But whatever theory of firm behaviour is adopted (other than perfect competition), the view is derived that the distribution of income is dependent on pricing decisions. The neo-classical theory of

---

1. Books such as Scherer (1980), Hay and Morris (1991), Clarke (1985) and Sawyer (1985b) provide textbook accounts of the prevailing orthodoxy in industrial economics.

2. Ferguson (1988), for example, argues that '[t]he SCP approach involves the logical application of neo-classical models to draw deductions about the performance of markets'.

income distribution is, of course, the marginal productivity theory, and that it is not consistent with theories of firm behaviour other than perfect competition. Once it is acknowledged that firms (whether individually or collectively) can effectively set prices in a particular industry, then the profit margin (and thereby profit and wage shares in value added) in that industry has no connection with the marginal productivity of 'capital' (even if that latter concept could be defined).

The third aspect of the argument is that topics such as advertising, research and development form a major part of the study of industrial economics, and yet they expose many weaknesses in the neo-classical approach. In the case of advertising, it is difficult, if not impossible, for the neo-classical approach to admit that advertising may be persuasive for that would open the Pandora's box that tastes can be moulded. In such cases, it would not be possible to maintain the assumption of a utility function that does not evolve in response to advertising and other pressures. Yet, the notion that advertising raises profitability (which has been subject to considerable testing in industrial economics) generally relies on precisely that possibility.[3]

Research and development, invention and innovation (as well as advertising to a lesser degree) pose in a sharp form the difficulties of modelling decision-making as though the decision-maker is fully informed and capable of processing all relevant information. The essential difficulty was expressed by Arrow when he wrote that 'there is a fundamental paradox in the determination of demand for information; its value for the purchaser is not known until he has the information, but then he has in effect acquired it without cost' (Arrow, 1962). Kay (1989) argues further that 'it is difficult to consider problems of innovation without questioning the relevance of maximising behaviour (though some neo-classical theorists somehow manage this)' for this involves the 'abandonment of the strict knowledge conditions usually associated with optimising behaviour'.

The fourth aspect concerns methodology, bearing in mind that much of the debate over methodology in economics (particularly in the first two decades after the war) was intertwined with different approaches to topics within industrial economics. It is perhaps not surprising that much of the debate over realism of assumptions and the use of deductive or inductive reasoning has been conducted in the context of industrial economics. Hall and Hitch (1939) and the full-cost pricing approach was based on a deductive approach, and appeared to contrast with the inductive profit maximising approach. Lester (1946) and Machlup (1946) provide the classic references for the intellectual clash over the applicability of marginalism in the context of price and employment decisions. Within these debates are clear attempts to narrow economic

---

3. The argument is that advertising as information raises the effective elasticity of demand facing firms, thereby generally lowering profitability. Conversely, advertising as persuasion lowers the elasticity of demand, thereby raising profitability. Further, the persuasive aspect is likely to raise barriers to entry in that consumers will prefer the products of existing producers to those of new firms, again aiding profitability.

analysis down to neo-classical economics, as for example in the following quotation. 'Economics in a narrow sense is confined to such aspects of conduct as can be explained with reference to the principles of maximising satisfaction, income, or profit. Under definitions of this sort any deviations from the marginal principle would be extra-economic' (Machlup, 1946). Within the study of industrial economics, departures from profit maximisation and marginalism are frequently considered and there has been (albeit a diminishing) influence of case studies and empirical evidence. In each of these regards, post Keynesian economics shares features with industrial economics.

OBJECTIVES OF FIRMS

Within the broad post Keynesian tradition, it is useful to distinguish a number of distinct approaches. The first can be generally associated with the theories of monopoly capitalism (e.g. Baran and Sweezy, 1966, Cowling, 1982), and the work of Kalecki in particular. The features of this approach which are particularly important for our discussion are the integration of microeconomic and macroeconomic analyses, and the retention of profit maximisation as a working assumption. The second, which has sometimes been called the post Keynesian approach, is particularly linked with the work of Eichner (but also authors such as Harcourt and Kenyon (1976), Shapiro (1981) and Wood (1975)). This approach emphasises the operation of large corporations which are to a significant degree managerially controlled and which operate in oligopolistic environments with strong elements of price leadership. Price decisions are closely linked with investment requirements, and growth is emphasised as an objective of the corporation, so that pricing, investment, growth and income distribution are closely linked. These two approaches have links with much of conventional industrial economics, in that the objectives of the firm can be summarised in terms of optimisation, though there is discussion of the problems of decision-making. Further, both approaches provide views on the determination of prices and investment which are particularly relevant in a macroeconomic context. It is these two approaches that are the centre of our attention in this chapter, in particular because of their implications for macroeconomic aggregates.

The third approach is more concerned with the internal organisation of firms and the analysis of the decision-making process. One convenient description would be that this approach is concerned with the 'knowledge, ignorance and surprise in economic organisation' (to use the subtitle of Kay, 1984). In contrast to the two approaches outlined above, this approach is much more concerned with the theory of the firm, and much less concerned with the economic analysis of industry. Because of the focus of this chapter on the industry rather than the firm, this approach will receive relatively little attention in this chapter, except in the discussion of the objectives of firms. For a discussion of the relationship between this general approach and post Keynesian economics, see Kay (1989).

There has been a strong tradition within post Keynesian economics for the rejection of unbounded rationality and of the notion of a 'single-brain' firm. However, within those general rejections, there has been a wide variety of specific responses. The differences between the responses may be more apparent than real in the sense that some of the differences may be attributable to the different purposes to which the resulting theories are to be put. For example, it may be useful (for reasons of simplicity) to assume a single well-defined objective of a firm in the context of a macroeconomic analysis, but for a more detailed examination of decisions on research programmes such an assumption may be inadequate for the purpose at hand. One response is to follow authors such as Kalecki who argued that firms are primarily interested in profits but because of uncertainties it could not be assumed that firms are able to actually maximise profits (cf. Kalecki, 1971a) and that precise calculations of marginal costs etc. are not possible. But this leads to pricing based on an approximation of marginal cost (in Kalecki's case taken as average variable costs with the perception of constant marginal cost arising in part through firms' inability to estimate marginal cost more precisely). Hence as far as pricing decisions are concerned profit seeking is the objective. For longer term decisions, specifically investment, Kalecki did not attempt any precise formulation, but rather saw factors such as actual and expected profitability as influencing those decisions.

Some authors (including the present one) within the broadly defined post Keynesian tradition would to a greater or lesser extent adhere to some form of profit maximisation by firms. This may take the form of saying that firms seek to make profits as great as possible (which appears to avoid identification with a neo-classical view) with overtones of bounded rationality and incomplete information. Baran and Sweezy (1966), for example, argue that

[t]he firm ... always finds itself in a given historical situation, with limited knowledge of changing conditions. In this context it can never do more than improve its profit position. In practice, the search for 'maximum' profits can only be the search for the greatest *increase* in profits which is possible in the given situation, subject of course to the elementary proviso that the exploitation of today's profit opportunities must not ruin tomorrow's. This is all there is to the profit maximisation principle, but it also happens to be all that is necessary to validate the 'economising' behaviour patterns which have been the backbone of all serious economic theory for the last two centuries.

Nevertheless, within the constraints of information and computational ability, the outcome as modelled within the theory will still be that of the equalisation of marginal cost and marginal revenue.

There have been a variety of other views advanced which share the common feature of the rejection of profit maximisation in any form. These views would include full-cost pricing (Hall and Hitch, 1939) through target rate of return pricing to investment requirement pricing (Wood, 1975, Eichner, 1973). These share the common feature of basing price on some notion of average costs, with the mark-up set to meet some other objective (achievement of satisfactory results, sufficient funds for investment etc.). There is a focus below on the view that links pricing with investment, specifically the work of Eichner.

As long as some notion of profit maximisation is maintained, it is clearly inevitable that notions of marginal cost and marginal revenue are involved, at least in the formal expression of the theory. In that sense subjective elements are involved in price formation, and fit uneasily with the general (but not universal) post Keynesian rejection of the subjectivist approach to price formation. This is a difficulty which is also shared by the neo-Sraffian approach in the sense that the driving force behind firms is taken to be profit-seeking, so that such firms are trying to equate marginal costs and revenues. Bradley and Howard (1982) note that in Sraffa (1960) there is 'no assumption pertaining to economic agents. In particular, there is no specification that producers maximise profits.' Since the Sraffian approach analyses the long-run outcomes with a uniform rate of profit, it has been possible to remain silent on the motivation and objectives of firms. However, it is difficult to see how such a position of a uniform rate of profit would be achieved other than through the pursuit of profits by firms and the mobility of capital in pursuit of profits. In the next chapter, a model is outlined in which it is possible to combine profit maximisation under conditions of oligopoly (i.e. a Kaleckian approach) with a long-run uniform rate of profit. Such a model can be seen to share the features of a Sraffian approach in the sense that short-run behaviour is set by profit considerations but the rate of profit is determined by the over-all requirements of the economic system.

In contrast, some of the range of views that reject profit maximisation appear to offer an objective basis for prices. For example, a cost-plus pricing view portrays price as a mark-up over average direct costs. The investment financing view would suggest that the size of the mark-up was closely linked to the firm's financing requirements (e.g. Eichner, 1973), which appears to fit more easily with the search for an objective rather than a subjective basis for price formation. However, that would seem to be to a large extent illusory since pricing decisions are based on a variety of expectations, whether of output, costs or future growth prospects.

The differences between the two views are not as sharp as they have been drawn above. Both marginal costs and average variable costs are forecasts (perceptions) made for decision-making purposes and in that sense subjective. However, the accuracy or otherwise of forecast average variable costs can be verified but not for marginal costs (since marginal costs are the difference between two levels of output, only one of which can be observed).

These differences have some important implications for the relationship between profits and investment. On the one side, a Kaleckian view would be that firms seek to gain as much profit as possible, and based on those actual profits along with factors such as prospective profits and capacity utilisation, firms make their investment decisions. At the firm level, profits are one of the determinants of investment expenditure decisions, though at the aggregate level, additionally, investment decisions largely determine profits. This can be expressed as $I(\Pi^*) = s.\Pi^*$ where Π^* is maximised profits, I investment which depends on profits and s propensity to save out of profits.

This raises the question of whether the firm would forego profits, other than for reasons of protecting its long-term profits prospects (e.g. through limit pricing, avoidance of upsetting customers etc.). The Eichnerian approach would appear to be that firms forego profits if they do not have a growth outlet for them. For '[c]ontinuous and accelerating growth is the overriding goal of a capitalist enterprise. This goal pushes the firm toward a long-run perspective in its pricing decisions' (Shapiro, 1981). Further, '[t]he central principle of the present theory, therefore, is that the amount of profits which the firm sets out to earn is determined by the amount of investment that it plans to undertake' (Wood, 1975).

There are three significant differences between a Kaleckian approach and the Eichnerian approach. Before discussing those differences, a significant area of agreement should be noted, namely that internal finance (savings out of profits) is the largest form of finance for investment, and that over the long term at least investment requirements will have a strong influence over the level of profits. The financial markets are viewed as imperfect in the technical sense that a firm cannot borrow as much as it wishes at the prevailing market rate of interest, but that the cost of borrowing depends on the amount to be borrowed, credit worthiness etc. (which Kalecki analysed under the heading of the principle of increasing risk).

The first difference has been indicated above, namely the objectives of firms. The Kaleckian approach adheres to a loose form of profit maximisation, whereas the Eichnerian approach stresses growth as an (if not the) objective of the firm. In the Kaleckian approach, growth occurs as a consequence of the pursuit of profits. At the aggregate level, the pace of growth through its connections with investment is a major determinant of profits. In the Eichnerian approach, it would appear that firms are prepared to forego profits if the growth prospects that it faces are poor and thereby it has a low demand for investment. This may be an unlikely occurrence, and a reduction in profits in circumstances of low investment would help maintain the level of aggregate demand. In effect, the 'megacorp' has restricted itself to investment in productive assets, and is assumed not to undertake financial investment (for such investments could absorb any 'excess' profits).

The second difference concerns the status of the relationship between profits and investment. In the Kaleckian approach, the demand for investment is influenced by profits and the prospects of profits, whilst at the aggregate level:

$$s_p.\Pi = I - s_w.W \qquad (9.1)$$

where I is investment expenditure, Π profits and W wages and s_p, s_w the propensity to save out of profits and wages respectively. This is extended by Steindl (1952) to the industry (not the firm) level, where he argues that 'in *equilibrium* the rate of internal accumulation is largely determined by the rate of expansion of the industry'. This conclusion depends on entry into the industry under 'ideal forms' of competition. In those industries where entry is difficult, the forces of competition are muted. Then '[t]he internal accumulation [retained profits] therefore tends to exceed the amount required for expansion of capital equipment in these industries. The flow of the 'surplus" funds into other industries is impeded by the additional effort required for entering new lines .... The automatic limitation of the rate of internal accumulation, and this of the profit margins at given levels of utilisation of capacity by the rate of investment is seriously disturbed' (Steindl, 1952).

In the Eichnerian approach, there is a corresponding relationship but it applies initially at the level of the firm with the aggregate relationship derived from summation. In contrast the Kaleckian relationship only holds at the aggregate level (and for the Steindl relationship as a result of competition). This can be seen most clearly in the approach of Wood (1975), in the derivation of a financing curve. The profit margin for the firm is related to the retention ratio, external finance ratio, growth rate and (incremental) capital–output ratio. It is (after eliminating liquid assets):

$$\pi = (1-x).g.k/r \qquad (9.2)$$

where π is profit share, g growth rate, k investment/increase in output ratio, x external finance ratio and r retention ratio, and this can simply be re-written as:

$$r.\Pi = I - E \qquad (9.3)$$

where E is external finance. This equation applies at the firm level, with a corresponding relationship derived for the aggregate level through summation. However, at the aggregate level, the total of external finance has to equal the savings of workers and rentiers.

The third difference is related to the second, and this is the question of how the equilibrium condition is reached. In the Kaleckian case, this comes from the active nature of investment which forces savings and thereby profits to adjust, though as has been noted elsewhere, Kalecki paid little attention to equilibrium requirements. In the Eichnerian approach the adjustment would appear to come through the adjustment of profit margins in the short run. However, in the longer run, there has to be some mechanism by which the firms' desires on external finance are reconciled with the willingness of workers and rentiers to save.

The view of a range of post Keynesian authors such as Eichner (1973,1976), Wood (1975) is that firms have investment requirements (linked to the prospective rate of growth of demand) and set their profit margins accordingly to generate finance for that investment. For example,

the firm (which we take to be the price leader for the current pricing period) makes a decision on future investment plans on the basis of the relation between the trend in actual rates of capacity utilisation, and some desired rate of plant utilisation, given its expectations about the future growth of market demand and the expected profitability of various alternative investment projects. It then chooses a mark- up that will produce the required level of retained profits with which to finance the desired investment expenditure, and persist with the implied price, allowing capacity utilisation to vary with the level of demand, around some average expected level associated with the chosen mark-up (Harcourt and Kenyon, 1976).

In the simple case of internal finance only, the relationship would again read as $s.\Pi = I$. However, this relationship holds at the level of the firm, and comes about through the adjustment by the firm of s and Π to ensure that its investment programme can be financed.

It has been argued that the Kaleckian degree of monopoly approach is based on a concept of profit maximisation (albeit of a rather imprecise form). But this is to a large degree short-run profit maximisation (though there is some regard paid to the longer-term consequences of pricing). This leaves open then the question of the longer-term influences on prices, whether there are long-run equilibrium prices towards which market prices move, and if so the nature of the adjustment process. Kalecki (1942) can be seen to suggest that firms may continue to invest in industries with a high rate of profit. The increase in the capital stock may not have any impact on the degree of monopoly, but it affects the rate of profit through its affect on capacity utilisation. The arguments of Steindl (1952) are that in the long term the profit rate in an industry has to be brought into line with the growth rate of the industry so that savings out of profits are sufficient to finance the required investment (taking into account the debt ratio).

These arguments can be brought together by the use of a modified version of the model presented by Dutt (1988). The intention is to derive a model which is sufficiently general so that the differences between the approaches of Kalecki, Steindl and Eichner can be highlighted.

THE NATURE OF COMPETITION

Much of the post Keynesian pricing and investment literature has foregone any investigation of the interdependence between firms, whether that takes the form of rivalry or of tacit collusion. Some form of price leadership has often been assumed, explicitly in the case of, for example, Eichner (1973, 1987), so that competition between firms is muted. Theories such as full-cost pricing, target rate of return pricing etc., as well as managerial theories of Baumol (1959), Marris (1964), Williamson (1964), have treated the firm in isolation as pursuing its own objectives largely unhindered by its rivals (except in so far as its rivals' position is reflected in the demand curve facing the firm in question). The influence of the 1930s is much in evidence both in terms of the theories that date from that period and from the influence of the extensive collusive understandings between firms which become apparent at that time.

A Kaleckian approach based on the degree of monopoly does make some acknowledgement of the impact of varying intensities of rivalry on the profit margin, though it has to be said that the analysis is not a deep one. It can also be argued that the Kaleckian approach is to a large extent the SCP one in which structural features such as number of firms and ease or otherwise of entry largely determine the profit margin.

The monopoly capitalism tradition[4] (which is to be seen as being influenced by both Marxian and traditional industrial economics) has to some degree counterpoised competition and monopoly. It is particularly the case with the structure-conduct-performance (SCP) approach where perfect (atomistic) competition and monopoly are viewed as polar opposites. One point to be made here is that within the general post Keynesian approach there should be no presumption that competition is either beneficial or sustainable. The modelling of firm behaviour has to take account of competitive pressures, interdependence between firms and the macroeconomic aspects.

The view expressed here is that an unsatisfactory feature of much of the post Keynesian literature is that insufficient attention is paid to competition and rivalry. It has to be recognised that modern capitalism has at least the structure of oligopoly (i.e. industries typically dominated by a few large firms), so that any competition is not of the atomistic variety. However, rivalry can and does exist within an oligopolistic structure, and indeed some would argue that the intensity of rivalry does not depend on the number of firms involved and can on occasions be particularly intense amongst two or three firms. There will clearly be limits on how far firms will pursue their rivalry since it is generally destructive of profits over-all if not of the profits of some of the individual firms. Further, there are a variety of understandings between firms, and mergers are one route through which the extent and impact of rivalry can be held in check. Competition and rivalry in circumstances of oligopoly have not been extensively analysed. The propositions that perfect competition may have some desirable properties are subject to well-known difficulties such as the restrictiveness of the assumptions under which the propositions hold and the narrowness of the Pareto welfare criteria. But there is no reason to think that any proposition (whatever its limitation) that is established for perfect competition would carry over to rivalrous competition under oligopoly. In other words, there is no reason at present to believe that such oligopolistic competition will be beneficial for the economy as a whole.

It would be entirely within the post Keynesian tradition to argue that the way in which rivalry and competition operate will be different in different economies and different eras of history. Further, whilst the 19th century atomistic competition gave way to 20th century oligopoly there have been waves of collusion and of degrees of competition, the timing of which will be different in different economies. Most theorising in industrial economics has not generally considered the expansion of firms into new geographical territory. There is, of course, some reference made to multinational enterprises, but they are generally viewed as enterprises writ large. The tendency of firms and of

---

4. For a survey of theories of monopoly capitalism see Sawyer(1988b), and for discussion of the relationship between the post Keynesian and Marxian approaches to competition see Sawyer (1994a).

capitalism to expand is largely overlooked. But the search for growth and for the use of profits involves firms in expansion into new products and into new geographical areas.

There is some force to the argument that the inter-war years and the early post-war period were the high-water mark for collusion between independent firms. The decline in formal collusion was aided by some legislative changes, the growth of international trade and the growth of industrial concentration. The legislative changes may reflect some change in 'informed opinion' on the relative benefits of the use of the market and of planning but also may be a reflection that larger firms felt constrained by these restrictive practice agreement. Resale price maintenance (RPM), whereby a producer could enforce retailers selling its product at a particular price, is an example here. The growth of supermarkets was inhibited by RPM which served to protect the interests of the small, high-cost distributors rather than those of the large, low-cost distributors. The growth of international trade should not be seen as synonymous with increased competition, for as Cowling (1982) and others have pointed out a great deal of international trade takes the form of exchange between different branches of a multinational enterprise. Nevertheless there may, at least initially, be difficulties of arriving at implicit understandings between firms coming from different countries and perhaps more importantly different social and economic cultures. The growth of industrial concentration means, of course, that the necessity for inter-firm agreement is diminished.

The argument here is then for a restoration of a view which sees elements of rivalry and collusion within virtually every industry. The approach of Eichner and some other post Keynesians has (at least implicitly) assumed the absence of price competition between firms with a dominant firm able to exercise price leadership. Similarly, Baran and Sweezy (1966) postulate that 'the appropriate general price theory for an economy dominated by such corporations is the traditional monopoly price theory of classical and neo-classical economics'. But to argue for an element of competition and rivalry within an oligopolistic environment is not to argue that there is extensive or atomistic competition nor is it to argue that competition brings economic benefits. Thus, approaches such as the theory of contestable markets would be rejected for adopting a quite unrealistic view of the degree of competition and of its potential for the public good.

Competition and rivalry, as has been emphasised by economists in the Austrian tradition, is a process rather than a state. Perfect competition does not involve competition in any meaningful sense. Atomistic competition is not a stable position in general since relatively strong firms drive out and take over relatively weak firms, and there is a process of concentration and centralisation. Competition is generally destructive of profits, and there is always the paradox of why profit-seeking firms compete. 'The system of free competition is a rather peculiar one. Its mechanism is one of *fooling* entrepreneurs. It requires the pursuit of maximum profit in order to function, but it destroys profits when they are actually pursued by a large number of people' (Lange,1937). There are obviously explanations of why some competition persists between firms which arise from the difficulties which independent firms have in making and maintaining agreements (implicit or expicit) over price and output levels, and over the division of the profits of any collusion. Further, new firms may see opportunities for profit and enter an industry. But the point here is that there will be an inbuilt tendency for the degree of rivalry to be diminished (e.g. by firms merging together) as rivalry and competition limit profits. Competition between firms arises from their pursuit of profits, but that competition limits their ability to gain profits. When the pressure on profits from competition become particularly intense, firms can be expected to take actions to limit those pressures. The actions can range from seeking out agreements with other firms, mergers and acquisitions through to lobbying for regulation and protection. Competition will, of course, favour the strong and harm the weak (which is not meant to be a tautology under which the strong are defined as those favoured by the market). Thus the outbreak of competition will arise when some firms feel relatively strong and wish to promote their own position. The outcome of that would be expected to be fewer firms and a diminution of rivalry when the strong firms have asserted their strength.

Many of the post Keynesian approaches have been rather static in the sense of taking the industrial structure (whether in terms of the degree of industrial concentration or in terms of an established price leader) as given and paying little regard to the process of change and in some versions appearing to ignore the pressures of competition on firms. But the Kaleckian degree of monopoly approach (e.g. Kalecki, 1971a, Cowling, 1982), whilst stressing the role of monopoly and oligopoly, has also seen competition and rivalry as being involved. Indeed Cowling (1982) argues that 'rivalrous behaviour and collusion coexist and result from a high degree of concentration within a specific market'. However he does argue (Cowling 1992) that, on the basis of recent theoretical work, co-operation is the norm between firms which is not undermined by potential entry. For '[t]he typical flexibility of the modern corporation, which allows it to move in any of a large number of directions, which in turn provides the basis of the symmetry assumption. The deterrent to entry is the immediacy of expected retaliation'. A particularly important element of the dynamic nature of competition is the operation of the forces of cumulative causation whereby the strong become stronger and the weak weaker (as has been argued in earlier chapters).

INSTITUTIONAL REALITIES

The development of post Keynesian ideas in general and those in the sphere of industrial economics as a particular example has to proceed at two levels. One level is the general features of such an approach which would span a variety of time periods and societies. The other level is the analysis of a specific economy in a particular era. The institutional details change over time and differ between societies, necessitating some differences in the analysis. The purpose of this analysis is to consider the specific features of late 20th century industrialised capitalist economies.

How the structural realities of the late 20th century capitalist economies are to be characterised are a matter of debate and considerable dispute. This section should be considered as a provisional attempt to indicate some of features that I see as significant. The first one is the observation that in most industries, high levels of industrial concentration have been established, and that whilst there may be declines in concentration in some industries at some times, the extent of these declines are generally not large relative to the levels of concentration. Large firms are diversified, spreading themselves across many, usually related, sectors, with a firm undertaking production and distribution in several countries. Most industrialised capitalist economies are relatively open, and, in particular, governments often encourage the entry of foreign multinational corporations. But whilst large firms are economically important, firms of all sizes survive, which raises the question of the nature of the relationship between large and small firms. Small firms are often suppliers of inputs to large firms (and vice versa) but the economic power generally lies with the larger firms. The economic influence of large firms may well be understated by their relative size when they are surrounded by small firms that are dependent upon them. In effect, large firms may seek to deal with the problems of control in a large organisation by sub-contracting out work. Finally, there are considerable elements of managerial control within large corporations, though the relationship is not well represented by managerial theories such as those of Baumol (1959) and Marris (1964) in which the interests of owners and managers are portrayed as in conflict. There is often a considerable overlap of interests (see e.g. Francis, 1980) but managers are typically in effective control of decision-making.

If these characterisations are accepted, then what is the significance for a post Keynesian industrial economics? I would argue that there are three elements. First, firms are much more complex than the representation of owner-controlled or manager-controlled would suggest. In particular, there are likely to be conflicts of interest between different groups of shareholders and between managers, and the possibility of coalition of interests between some managers and some owners. Corporations are large organisations with varying histories and differing power structures which will be reflected in the objectives currently being pursued.

Second, whilst firms seek to grow (whether as an objective in itself or as a by-product of the pursuit of profits), the consequences of the pursuit and achievement of such growth and expansion have to be considered. The process of growth will usually involve the development of new products and movements into new market areas. There will be the consequent geographical expansion of firms and the evolution of multinational operation. The striving for growth and profits brings firms into conflict with one another, at least initially.

Competition and rivalry arise from this conflict between firms over profits, but the pursuit of profits leads firms to look for ways to reduce competition since it threatens profits.

Third, industrialised economies are currently passing through an era in which there is more rivalry and competition than in many previous decades (and I hazard the guess than in future decades). If that is so, there is something of a paradox in that over the past two decades an era of relatively intense rivalry and competition has been associated (at least in Europe and the United States) with unemployment and sluggish growth of output and of productivity. The emergence of Japan as a major economic power with strong firms has posed considerable problems for the established American and European firms. The growth of firms out of their national economies into multinational status brings those firms into conflict with one another and with national firms. There has also been a general shift of political opinion in favour of competition (though with varying definitions of the term competition), as is particularly evident when contrasting current debates over competition with those that occurred in the 1930s and 1940s. Rivalry and competition are inherently dynamic and involve winners and losers. Intense competition is then seen as unsustainable for it will generate losers and will threaten profitability. Hence, it would be expected that any upsurge of competition and rivalry is a temporary phenomenon, after which market control would be re-instated but at the international rather than the national level. It is clearly the case, as authors such as Clifton (1977), Auerbach and Skott (1988) have argued, that the mobility of capital on a global basis is much greater than hitherto. This is reflected in the inter-penetration of markets that were previously largely supplied by domestic firms only. The mobility of capital arises through the enhanced ability of capitalist firms to perform accurate calculations and to monitor opportunities and the reduction in transport and communications costs. These changes may have initially brought a degree of rivalry, but at the same time they permit firms to collude more effectively if they wish to do so.

The size of firms and the question of managerial control both point to the relevance of the internal structures of firms for the operation of firms and then more generally of industries. Drawing on the distinction drawn by Coase (1937) between allocation by market and allocation by administrative decision, the increasing size of firms points towards some elimination of the role of market transactions. Thus it can be argued that it is not only competition that has a tendency to self-destruct but also that markets tend to be replaced by administrative decisions. For example, any merger between firms represents not only an elimination of a degree of competition but also the replacement of a market relationship by a non-market in that the transactions that had been conducted between the firms via the market are now made by administrative actions within firms.

The evidence of the past 150 years or so is that there is a strong tendency in capitalist economies for the absolute and relative size of large firms to increase.

This would appear to be strong evidence that a market system based on atomistic competition is unstable. Atomistic competition appears to dissolve into oligopoly. The growth of large firms would be explained by many (especially Williamson, 1975) 'because the managerial guidance or internal planning they provide is more efficient than the price adjustment process the market provides' (Dugger, 1983). This would suggest (leaving aside questions of efficiency) that a post Keynesian industrial economics should address two questions. First, why is there some tendency for the market to be replaced by internal planning? Second, an understanding of the allocation of resources which only deals with the external relations between firms is likely to be seriously incomplete, in light of the extent to which decisions on resource allocation and usage are taken within firms.

ASPECTS OF PRODUCTION

In much of economic analysis, the relationship between inputs and outputs is summarised by some form of production function. In neo-classical economics, the production function permits the substitution of inputs for each other, whilst others often postulate fixed factor proportions (particularly *ex post*). Some post Keynesian macroeconomic analysis (as will be seen in the next chapter) makes the assumption of fixed proportions between inputs and outputs without enquiring into the determinants of those proportions. However, such an assumption should be seen as a simplifying device for a particular mode of analysis. The fixed factor proportions assumption has two features which should be not only noted but then contrasted with other work in the post Keynesian tradition.[5] The first is that labour productivity appears to be taken as a technologically determined given, whereas there is much evidence that productivity is influenced by many features internal and external to the firm. The second feature is that production is undertaken subject to constant returns to scale, so that increasing costs do not put a brake on expansion, but there is no more general influence of the mode of production on economic activity and relationships. In contrast, a range of writers, often writing on Fordism and post Fordism, have seen the mode of production has having many implications for economic, social and political relationships. Although we cannot hope to do justice to these two lines of thought, it is worthwhile to indicate their significance for our general line of argument.

Post Keynesians have rightly questioned the usefulness of production functions, especially when some notion of aggregate capital is used[6] and where *ex*

---

5. In describing these works as being in the post Keynesian tradition, the scope of post Keynesian is being very broadly defined, and some would see work on, for example, Fordism and post Fordism as in the radical political economy tradition.

6. This is particularly so in the context of the use of aggregate production function in connection with marginal productivity theory of income distribution. But this has not prevented the use of measures of aggregate capital by post Keynesians in the context of, for example, the measurement of productive capacity. In those areas, there are still measurement problems but not the logical

post substitution between labour and capital equipment is assumed. Instead, there has often been a view that production is subject to fixed factor proportions, which helps to discredit marginal productivity notions (since the marginal product of one factor can no longer be defined) and which is thought to have some empirical basis. There has, however, been a general neglect of the variations in labour productivity between firms and between countries, not all of which can be explained by differences in the amount of capital equipment per employee.

The observed variations in productivity (and presumed variations in efficiency) have numerous implications. Apart from the obvious point that this observation reinforces the general view that productivity is not technologically determined, there are two implications to be noted.

First, productivity differences will to some degree translate into cost and profit differences. Cost differences inject a dynamic element into the situation in that those firms with cost and profit advantage will be looking to expand their market shares at the expense of the high-cost producers. For reasons discussed above, higher profits will enhance the ability to expand, and lower costs will make the achievement of any kind of equilibrium difficult (and for which Steindl 1952 provided a detailed analysis where the cost differences were related to size of firm).

Second, the productivity differences between firms requires some explanation. The X-inefficiency view of Leibenstein (1966) may help understand why technical efficiency is not achieved but is of less help in explaining the extent of the differences of productivity. It is also difficult to explain how those differences of productivity persist within an industry. For all the firms within an industry are presumably subject to the same external environment. This suggests that the internal structures of the firms are relevant, where structure would be taken to include the hierarchical nature of the firm, the relationship between managers and workers etc. It also suggests that whatever the pressures on firms are, they are not so strong and so homogeneous that all firms have to conform. A range of outcomes (here in terms of productivity levels) are clearly possible, which contrasts with most (perhaps all) theorising in neo-classical and classical economics, which strongly point towards a single unique outcome.

The concepts of Fordism and post Fordism include not only characterisations of the predominant mode of production but also postulates economic, social and political implications which flow from the nature of the mode of production.[7] The Fordist mode of production features mass production, whereas the post Fordism mode is associated with flexible specialisation. Fordism is also seen to be associated with a stable mode of economic growth, and of

---

difficulties which arise in measuring aggregate capital for use with the marginal productivity theory.

7. For recent reviews of the concepts of Fordism and post Fordism see entries under that heading by Klaus Nielsen in Hodgson, Samuels and Tool (1994) and by Peter Nolan in Arestis and Sawyer (1994)

'*social and economic regulation* involving a set of specific institutions such as large, hierarchical corporations, mark-up pricing, wage formation via collective bargaining and indexation, and monetary emission and credit policies oriented to secure effective aggregate demand' (Nielsen, 1994). Fordism would also involve consumption of standardised, mass commodities (to match with mass production). Post Fordism is a more elusive concept, and 'most writers that invoke the term do so in order to record a radical departure from Fordist patterns of economic and social organization' (Nolan, 1994).

It could be said that most (perhaps all) post Keynesian macroeconomic analysis has, in effect, made assumptions much in line with the characterisation of Fordism (though there are obviously aspects of Fordism to which macroeconomic analysis does not refer).

THE FINANCIAL SECTOR AND THE INDUSTRIAL SECTOR

Post Keynesian economics has often stressed that a monetary economy operates in a way that is essentially different from a barter economy. But much post Keynesian analysis does not make explicit reference to monetary and financial aspects. This is evident in, for example, the preceding discussion in this chapter and in the model developed in the next chapter. But money and finance is always there in the background: any expansion of economic activity has to be financed (as discussed in Chapters 3 and 4), and a higher level of economic activity involves a greater transactions demand for money and hence some combination of increased stock of money and velocity of circulation has to be forthcoming. The model discussed in the next chapter has to be understood as assuming that the stock of money will be permitted by the banking system to expand as required by the 'needs of trade'.

The source of finance (whether internal or external) may influence the level and form of investment expenditure for, as is often argued, internal finance is generally less costly than external finance and may allow more scope for enterprises to undertake risky ventures. The relationship between the financial sector and the industrial sector may be a relatively passive one on the financial side in the sense that the necessary finance may generally be supplied as required by the industrial sector. But even then there may be many routes through which the financial sector has an impact on the industrial sector: for example the interests of the two sectors over the appropriate level of the exchange rate and interest rates may often conflict and the political strength of the two sectors may influence the setting of those key rates.

It is useful to distinguish three roles of the financial sector. First, the financial sector channels funds from savers (surplus units) to investors (deficit units). It is, of course, the case that some of that channelling of funds takes place outside the formal financial system through, for example, direct personal contact and more importantly much of investment is directly financed by the internal finance of the firm concerned (see below). A significant change in the

British economy (and some others) over the past 40 years (as suggested by figures quoted below) has been the rise of savings by the personal sector which have to be channelled to the corporate and government sector to finance investment expenditure and the public sector budget deficit.[8] The nature of the financial system influences the efficiency with which these funds are transferred (e.g. the administrative costs involved) but also will influence the direction in which the funds flow.

Second, the financial sector (and specifically the stock exchange) provides a forum in which existing financial assets are traded. The provision of the ability to readily trade shares provides, it is argued, the individual (though not society) with liquidity in that the individual may sell her shares at the going market price whenever she wishes. However, it can be observed that such markets (i.e. stock and currency markets) display considerable volatility, which reduces the liquidity of the corresponding financial assets in the following way. The ability to sell the asset at the market price remains, but the market price fluctuates over time so that there is no assurance as to the level of price when the asset is to be sold. This role of the financial sector is of significance in (at least) two ways. The first is that resources are used in providing the facilities for the exchange of existing financial assets, and the question arises as to whether the benefits of liquidity thereby provided outweigh the costs of the resources used. The second is that the nominal value of wealth based on share ownership obviously depends on the level of share prices. The volatility of those prices generates a corresponding volatility in nominal wealth, which may have effects on decisions in the real economy.[9]

It can be remarked as something of an aside here that volatility of prices tends to reduce the usefulness of price as a co-ordinating device. It has been seen in other chapters that the neo-classical concept of the role of price is the allocative co-ordinating one. The paradox involved here is that volatility of price may well be greater in those markets that come closer to the perfectly competitive ideal. In a perfectly competitive market, prices would perform only the allocative role; but the very volatility of price thereby engendered would mean that decision-making would be made more difficult. Thus prices in a

---

8. This relates to the net savings of the personal sector. The savings of some individuals will be used to finance the spending of other individuals, a notable example being the inflow of funds into building society deposit accounts which are recycled as mortgages for house purchase.

9. This effect of nominal wealth on spending decisions is likely to be extenuated, particularly in the short run, in that a large proportion of shares are owned by pension funds to underpin the commitment of those funds to provide pensions. A change in nominal wealth held by pension funds would only effect spending decisions in so far as it lead to changes in pensions being paid. See Toporowski (1993) for some discussion on the effects of nominal wealth on spending decisions, particularly in the light of the apparently negligible effect of the stock market crash of October 1987 on expenditure.

perfectly competitive market may well be highly volatile and hence not perform the allocative function very well.[10]

Third, the financial sector, particularly the banks, provides credit which enables spending decisions to be carried through. This credit provision overlaps with the first role identified above, as a substantial part of credit provided is in effect the recycling of savings from surplus to deficit units. But net credit creation by banks results in the creation of money: the banks would have the ability if they so wished to cut off any intended expansion in expenditure.

[T]he possibility of stimulating the business upswing is based on the assumption that the banking system, especially the central bank, will be able to expand credits without such a considerable increase in the rate of interest [to a level at which present investments would be displaced by the same amount as credits raised by governments]. If the banking system reacted so inflexibly to every increase in the demand for credit, then no boom would be possible on account of a new invention, nor any automatic upswing in the business cycle. For then there would be a change only in the structure of investments made, not in their volume. Investments would cease to be the channel through which additional purchasing power, unquestionably the *primus movens* of the business upswing, flows into the economy (Kalecki, 1990, as quoted in Toporowski, 1993 with his addition).

This quote indicates the potential power of the banking system over whether any incipient expansion in economic activity can occur: hence, for example, if banks respond to an increased demand for loans by raising the interest rate on loans substantially then the volume of loans taken out may not rise and expenditure not increase.

The neo-classical view on this would appear to be that the relationship between financial and non-financial sectors is akin to the relationship between any other two sets of sectors. Demand and supply schedules for funds can be derived and an equilibrium price and quantity of funds derived, corresponding to the loanable funds approach. Underlying the demand for funds is the investment expenditure for which firms seek finance, whereas underlying the supply of funds are the savings made by households and others. For the industrial companies, any quantity of funds are readily available at the going rate of interest (in a perfect capital market) and the cost of finance is independent of its source and of the financial structure of the corporation: the theorem of Modigliani–Miller (1958)[11]. However, as Stiglitz and Weiss (1981) and Stiglitz (1985), amongst others, have argued, there are particular features of credit that lead to forms of credit rationing. This was recognised in an informal manner by Kalecki, with his discussion of the 'principle of increasing risk'. However, in the hands of Kalecki, it points to the importance of (retained) profits as a source of internal finance and the limits on expansion that are placed on firms by the requirement that expansion is financed.

10. In one sense, many of the markets in which prices are highly volatile are not undertaking an allocative role in that those markets are trading existing assets (e.g. shares, currency) and not thereby allocating the use of new resources.

11. For a detailed discussion of the Modigliani–Miller theorem see Milgrom and Roberts (1992) chs. 14 and 15. For a critique drawing on theoretical and empirical arguments see Gordon (1993).

When the relationship between the financial and industrial sectors is summarised by the interaction of the demand for and supply of funds (as in the simple neo-classical approach), then the cost of capital is determined by that interaction. Consequently, the cost of capital reflects the productivity of capital (underlining the demand for funds) and thriftiness (the supply of funds). From that perspective, the financial market could not be accused of imposing a short-term perspective on the industrial sector, in part because the financial sector is merely acting as a conduit for the funds flowing from one part of the real sector to another part. The post Keynesian approach would be rather different in a number of ways. First, the relationship between borrower and lender is not necessarily the arms-length parametric price one envisaged in the neo-classical analysis (as further discussed in general terms in Sawyer 1992a). Indeed, it could be said that it is very difficult to envisage a purely arms-length parametric price relationship in the case of finance, simply because the credit-worthiness of the borrower is always relevant to the lender. Second, the financial sector does not merely act as a conduit, but rather has its own views on the (relative) desirability of different types of projects. This may mean, for example, that small to medium sized firms or those involved in high-risk activities find some difficulties in securing finance. Third, the rate of interest is seen as a monetary rather than a real phenomenon. In other words, rather than the rate of interest balancing the demand for and supply of funds (the loanable fund view), it is seen as balancing the demand for and supply of money (the liquidity preference view).

Post Keynesians have advanced (sometimes implicitly) a range of views on the nature of the relationship between the financial and the industrial sectors. It may, of course, be the case that the nature of the relationship changes over time, and the differing views may be a reflection of that. Before discussing the different views, one common theme can be identified. In a monetary economy, expenditure has to be financed, and the willingness or otherwise of the financial sector to provide finance for those seeking to spend ahead of receipts from sales that will justify the initial expenditure influences the evolution of the economy. Specifically, the available finance for investment in terms of both volume and composition will influence the nature and rate of growth.

A first view, associated here particularly with the work of Kalecki, portrays the financial sector as to a large degree passive, in supplying finance as required especially as far as the banks are concerned, which leads to the view that money and credit are created as required. The interest rate on credit is set by the banks as a mark-up over the minimum lending rate set by the Central Bank, and the banks are seen as willing to provide credit at that interest rate. However, the financial sector does place some restrictions on the industrial sector: for example, each firm faces a limit on the degree to which it can borrow. An individual's or a firm's access to finance is heavily conditioned by their initial wealth and profits. Both Kalecki and Steindl argued that the overall ratio between internal finance (retained profits) and external finance (savings of rentiers and workers) has an impact on investment decisions within the economy. The ability of firms to change the balance between internal and external finance is limited as they cannot change profits (already at a maximum) nor the savings of rentiers and workers. However, the financial sector may retain political power, and use that power to further their own interests (which can conflict with those of the industrial sector). Bhaduri and Steindl (1983) have viewed the rise of monetarism as a 'social doctrine' in this light. Further, it is evident to many that the political influence of the financial sector has grown in many countries (including the UK, USA and Australia) over the past decade or more.

The second view, which is related to the first and can be associated with authors such as Galbraith, Eichner and Wood, views the industrial sector as having largely freed itself of any control by the financial sector. The preference by industrial firms for internal finance is associated with a desire to avoid any interference by the financial sector which would arise from the use of external finance. Insofar as firms are successful in using only internal finance, there would appear to be no outlet for the savings of workers and rentiers.

The first and second approaches identified here continue the Keynesian identification of firms as deficit units and households as surplus units (though when firms successfully internally finance their investment programme they are clearly neither deficit nor surplus units). How far that is a correct characterisation is an important question in the understanding of the relationship between firms and households, and also in the interpretation of economic events.

The personal sector has tended to increase its savings rate. In the UK in the first half of the 1950s, the savings ratio (as a proportion of disposable income) averaged 3.5 per cent, and this gradually rose to reach an average of 11.3 per cent in the second half of the 1970s (peaking in 1979 at 13.4 per cent). The ratio declined somewhat in the 1980s, especially in the second half of that decade under the impact of financial liberalisation and an explosion in personal debt. The early 1990s saw a recovery in the ratio to over 10 per cent. The significant element in these figures is the volume of savings generated by the personal sector, though with much of the savings accounted for by contributions to pension funds and to life assurance policies. The significant element for the argument here is that these savings are undertaken outside of the corporate sector and represent external finance for that sector. The corporate sector may be unable or unwilling to absorb those savings through borrowing to finance investment: in such a case those savings act as a deflationary force on the economy.

Table 9.1 provides some indication of the source of capital funds for industrial and commercial companies in the UK in the late 1980s and early 1990s. It is noticeable that internal sources of finance generally provided less than half of the capital funds (with the higher figure in 1992 more a reflection of the recession and decline in the over-all use of capital funds than any upswing in the use of internal finance). Whilst internal finance is an important source of finance (and market capital issues a much less significant one), it is clearly not the case that large corporations avoid external finance. This observation casts doubt on the idea that corporations adjust profit margins to secure sufficient internal finance for their investment programme, and indeed in the face of extensive savings by the personal sector, the corporate sector has to absorb some of such savings through external finance.[12]

Table 9.1 Sources of capital funds: industrial and commercial companies, UK (percentage from identified sources)

Year	Internal funds	Bank and other loans	Market Capital Issues	Other
1988	40.1	38.4	8.8	12.6
1989	33.1	40.8	7.5	18.7
1990	35.3	32.6	7.3	24.8
1991	49.8	4.8	21.7	23.7
1992	62.2	-1.2	13.6	25.5

Source: Calculated from *Financial Statistics*, March 1994

The two views briefly discussed understate the significance of the financial sector for economic activity in at least two respects: the volatility of prices for existing financial assets and credit pyramiding. Before discussing these two aspects, it should be noted that their significance has probably increased considerably in the past two decades, in part as the result of financial deregulation. One aspect of the volatility of the prices of financial assets is the consequent ability of some to make (and for others to lose) considerable amounts of money on changes in prices. For our discussion here of more significance is the impact of those volatile prices on decision-making in the industrial sector. The fluctuations in prices such as interest rate and exchange rate, which are relevant for decision-making in the industrial sector, are likely to be detrimental to well-informed decisions.

The credit pyramid arises when the liabilities of one financial institution become the assets of another. In turn, this can mean that the failure of one financial institution can have severe knock-on effects on other financial institutions as well as on non-financial ones.

The third one, which can be particularly associated with Hilferding and Lenin, views the financial sector in a dominant role vis-à-vis the industrial sector. Lenin (1936) saw that the operation of banks had helped to promote the

---

12. It is not an absolute necessity that the corporate sector absorbs such savings since the government budget deficit could absorb them.

formation of trusts and monopolies and '[t]he merging of bank capital with industrial capital, and the creation, on the basis of 'finance capital', of a financial oligarchy'. As a result '[f]inance capital, concentrated in a few hands and exercising a virtual monopoly, exacts enormous and ever-increasing profits from the floating of companies, issue of stock, state loans, etc., tightens the grip of the financial oligarchies and levies tribute upon the whole of society for the benefit of the monopolies'. Hilferding (1981) argued that growth of a small number of banks particularly as owners of industrial firms means that one bank can have an ownership interest in a wide range of firms including firms potentially in competition with one another. Thus the bank would have an interest in reducing competition between the firms in which it has an ownership stake in order to increase profits. Hilferding argued that banks would then strive to reduce competition, by encouraging cartels, mergers etc., and the firms themselves would welcome a reduction in competition. Hence, there would be strong forces at work fostering the growth of monopoly.

CONCLUDING REMARKS

Keynesian economics was often accused of lacking microeconomic foundations. Whatever the validity of such an accusation for Keynesian economics, it was clearly not the case either for Keynes or for post Keynesian economics. This chapter has been concerned with the latter and in part with showing that there have always been firm foundations in terms of firm behaviour. This chapter has also been concerned to argue that a post Keynesian approach to industrial economics should be embedded in an appreciation of the macroeconomic environment within which firms operate and with full account taken of the relationship between the industrial sector and the financial sector.

10. Prices, pricing, capacity utilisation and unemployment in the post Keynesian traditions

INTRODUCTION

This chapter considers a range of non-neo-classical approaches to issues of pricing, investment, capacity utilisation and unemployment. By seeking to use a common framework, the intention is to explore the differences between these approaches with a view to seeking a degree of synthesis. In doing so, two issues come to the fore, namely the conceptualisation of the long term and the role of aggregate demand in the determination of the level of economic activity, and particularly the rate of capacity utilisation. In the non-neo-classical tradition there are strong links between prices, growth, income distribution and capacity utilisation, so it is inevitable that the discussion must pay some regard to those matters as well. Indeed, much of the chapter is devoted to trying to deal with some difficulties with the formulation of models which incorporate all of these factors.

In making comparisons between different approaches, there are clear dangers of forcing a common framework onto them which does an injustice to at least some of the approaches. In the particular case of price, it has to be acknowledged that the various approaches operate on different levels. It is useful to draw on the distinction made by Eichner (1987) between theories of pricing and theories of prices. Much of the post Keynesian literature has been concerned with the former, that is with theories of how prices are set at the level of the firm or industry. Consideration of the setting of prices may involve some generalisation of the procedures used for pricing, or theorising at the level of the firm or industry. These theories are microeconomic in orientation, though most post Keynesian authors have been aware of the macroeconomic implications of and impact on pricing. When the configuration of prices which satisfy some economy-level steady-state condition (perhaps based on a theory of pricing) is derived, then such a theory of price has been generated. Theories of price, of which the Sraffian approach is the most relevant for our discussion, are not concerned with the process of price formation but rather with a configuration of prices which conforms to some system-level requirement (e.g. of an equalised rate of profit). In that dichotomy, the Walrasian general equilibrium analysis provides only a theory of prices, but not of pricing since there are no mechanisms of price setting (unless the auctioneer is so considered). However, the non-neo-classical approach is able to generate both a theory of pricing and of price, as will become apparent below.

Carvalho (1984/5) has highlighted the wide range of post Keynesian views on historical time versus logical time and the use of long-period analysis. The term 'long period' is often used to denote a steady-state position which the economy may eventually reach (and generally around which the economy would tend to fluctuate). In discussion below, the expression long-term is used without any connotation that it is a position that is eventually reached nor that it is unaffected by what happens in the short term. The long term may be interpreted in the spirit of Kalecki when he wrote that 'the long-run trend is but a slowly changing component of a chain of short-period situations; it has no independent entity' (Kalecki, 1971a). However, the long term may be given the interpretation of being the end of a process. The approach adopted here for comparisons is the use of a two-sector model of a capitalist economy in first the short term and then the long term.

Whilst there have been a variety of approaches to price setting within the post Keynesian and Kaleckian traditions, two approaches have come to the fore. One has stressed the links between prices and investment (specifically that prices are set so as to generate profits to help finance investment). The other has focused on price as a mark-up over costs where the mark-up is set in an effort to fulfil short-run objectives: in particular to maximise short-run profits. It would then appear that the former stresses the long-term influences on price whilst the latter stresses the short-term influences. The main purpose of this chapter is to discuss these approaches to price setting with particular emphasis on the relationship between the short term and the long term.

Post Keynesian authors have frequently emphasised the problems surrounding the notion of optimisation, whether through lack of relevant information and/or limited computational abilities. Yet, as Reynolds (1989) has argued, most post Keynesian models of pricing do not incorporate uncertainty in any fundamental way, and that is reflected here. The use of algebraic formulation to explore the interrelationships leads inevitably to a downgrading of the emphasis on uncertainty. At the level of individual enterprise, the algebraic formulation suggests a spurious precision, whereas the over-all model generally builds in some element of the fulfilment of expectations (which is particularly evident in, though not confined to, the long-term models discussed below). Further, in constructing such a model assumptions have to be made over, for example, the determinants of aggregate demand. It will be seen below that there are differences of view over the influences on investment behaviour and the role of aggregate demand in the long term.

There is a sense in which decisions on price, investment, output etc. can be treated independently in neo-classical economics. The elementary treatment does indeed do that: for example, the demand for labour is based on the marginal product of labour and equated with the real wage. There are, of course, more sophisticated treatments in which a variety of decisions are integrated. But it is still the case that a firm's operations in one market are not severely restricted by its operations in other markets. In post Keynesian and Kaleckian approaches, firms have to acquire finance for the purchase of factors of production (especially of capital equipment) and finance may come from internal or external sources. External finance has often been viewed as more expensive than internal finance, and a preference for internal finance leads to a link between profits and investment. But finance can come from borrowing from banks, which would lead to some initial increase in the stock of money, with the eventual impact on the stock of money depending on the reactions of those to whom the money is paid. Although it may well be the case that banks are willing to extend further loans when the demand for loans is forthcoming, nevertheless some individual firms may be constrained from further borrowing when banks regard them as bad risks.

The next section provides a brief discussion on theories of prices and of pricing.[1] In the following section, a general model of the capitalist economy is introduced within which a number of approaches appear as special cases. Some of the properties of this model are then briefly examined. The fourth section contains a brief discussion on the role of capacity utilisation. In the fifth section some of the problems associated with the long-term version of the model advanced in the third section are considered. The sixth section introduces considerations arising from the labour sector, whilst the seventh section discusses external finance. The chapter is completed by some concluding remarks.

THEORIES OF PRICING AND PRICE

It is convenient to discuss post Keynesian (broadly defined) theories of pricing by means of a three-way classification. The first group, which is particularly represented by the work of Kalecki (and the monopoly capitalism approach), retains a simplified view of the firm and the pursuit of profit maximisation as the central objective. The second group, represented by the work of authors such as Eichner (1973, 1987), Harcourt and Kenyon (1976) and Wood (1975), emphasises the influence of growth and investment on the profit margin. Although authors vary somewhat, in general large corporations are treated as managerially controlled and concerned with growth, with profits viewed as a means (to growth) rather than as an end in itself. The third group, represented by authors such as Hall and Hitch (1939), Coutts, Godley and Nordhaus (1978) is a departure from optimisation, and for our current purposes can be represented as saying that price is a (often constant) mark-up over average direct costs. In terms of the representation used below, this third group generates a particularly simple case where the mark-up of price over costs is unaffected by the other variables of the model (which include capacity utilisation). This

---

1. For a broader discussion of pricing within the post Keynesian tradition see Sawyer (1992b) and chapter 3 above.

approach is not further discussed as its algebraic representation would be a special case of the Kaleckian pricing equation even though the two approaches differ in a number of other respects.

Most post Keynesian theories of pricing in effect assume that expectations over price and output are fulfilled, following Keynes (1973) when he wrote that 'the theory of effective demand is substantially the same if we assume that short-period expectations are always fulfilled'. When producers are price-makers, then firms charge the prices they wish to charge even if those prices may not be the ones they would have wished to charge had they been fully informed. Further, producers may miscalculate the demand forthcoming at the prices set, and it is asserted here that differences between actual demand and production will be largely absorbed by stock changes. Whilst the particular course of a business cycle will be influenced by these expectational mistakes, there is a sense in which enterprises are assumed to be well-informed over demand conditions. On investment, there has been emphasis on the role of 'animal spirits' and the essential uncertainty of the future. Nevertheless, investment expenditure has sometimes been modelled within the post Keynesian approach as though expectations about the future were firmly based (e.g. the approach of Eichner in which enterprises are well informed on the underlying growth prospects for the economy).[2] However, the approaches of Kalecki and Steindl could be seen as involving firms with imprecise expectations on the future since they are concerned with the broad influences on investment without any precise modelling of future expectations, and views on future profitability are strongly influenced by the current levels.

A notable feature of Kalecki's approach (as compared with many other post Keynesian approaches) is the separation between pricing and investment decisions, in the sense that prices are set without any direct regard to the financing of investment. Investment decisions depend on pricing decisions in the sense that the profits and output (and changes in output) that arise as a consequence of pricing are important influences on investment. The second (and related) feature is the short-term orientation of pricing decisions. In some formulations of his approach (and particularly as formalised in Cowling and Waterson, 1976) the objective of enterprises is taken as short-term profit maximisation, even though 'in view of the uncertainties faced in the process of price fixing it will not be assumed that the firm attempts to maximise its profits in any precise sort of manner' (Kalecki, 1971a), which is interpreted from the context to mean that firms do pursue profits maximisation, though imperfectly.

Kalecki (1971a) considered the impact of the level of overhead costs (relative to prime costs) on the degree of monopoly. It is a well-known conclusion from short-run profit maximisation that fixed costs do not influence price decisions. Kalecki suggests that 'there may arise a tacit agreement among the

---

2. 'the megacorp-price leader and the other firms in the industry must be able to discern what the industry's rate of expansion is likely to be and then translate that perceived secular growth rate into plans for adding to their productive capacity' (Eichner, 1987, p.375).

firms of an industry to 'protect" profits, and consequently to increase prices in relation to unit prime costs' which can be interpreted to mean that the relationships between firms change so as to lead to an increase in price–cost margins.

The second approach to pricing considered here is represented by the work of authors such as Eichner (1973,1987), Wood (1975), Harcourt and Kenyon (1976), who emphasise the role in the pricing decisions of profit margins required to meet growth targets. Large corporations are generally treated as managerially controlled and concerned with growth. The level of profit is viewed as a means to growth rather than as an end in itself.

The approach of Eichner is illustrative of those approaches that suggest that profit margins are to some degree adjusted in light of the financing requirements for investment. It is important to note that the adjustment of profit margins is undertaken at the level of the enterprise to achieve the required amount of internal finance. An apparently similar conclusion was drawn by Steindl (1952): 'the rate of internal accumulation is determined largely by the rate of expansion of the industry'. For Steindl, however, this result was brought about by competitive pressures and holds only in equilibrium and at the level of the industry.

Eichner's approach centres on the enterprise bringing its demand for investment finance into equality with its supply of investment finance. The demand for finance depends inversely on its cost, presumably for the usual reasons associated with the ranking of investment projects in order of their expected profitability. The supply of finance is drawn from internal and external sources. The effective price-setter in an industry is the price-leader; it is assumed that the leader's price permits the follower firms to finance their investment. Internal finance can always be augmented by raising price, since the demand curve facing a typical industry is taken to be inelastic, and the elasticity facing the price leader is also perceived to be less than unity. In contrast Kalecki and others (cf. Cowling and Waterson, 1976) have assumed that the perceived elasticity of demand facing an individual enterprise is greater than unity, and is higher at the firm level than at the industry level. In Eichner's approach, higher profit margins would encourage entry by other enterprises and substitution by consumers and thus higher profits can only be achieved at some long-term cost. These future costs are expressed as an implicit rate of interest on internal finance.

There are three possible outcomes in connection with the intersection of the demand for and the supply of investment finance, as compared with the initial position. The first would mean a reduction in the profit margin and therefore in the use of internal finance as compared with the previous period. This case would involve a clear departure from profit maximisation (whether interpreted as short-term or long-term), and arises when the enterprise has limited profitable investment outlets. This case could be ruled out if non-financial enterprises acted as financial institutions lending out funds. The firm could acquire finance at a negative (implicit) rate of interest, and lend it out at a positive rate. The second possible outcome would involve internal finance only, whilst the third outcome would be that the enterprise made use of both external and internal finance.

The interaction between microeconomic level and macroeconomic phenomena raises certain difficulties for theories of pricing based on investment requirements. The first difficulty is that firms are often portrayed as deciding upon price and investment expenditure on the basis of expectations of future growth and a target rate of capacity utilisation. In general, the rate of growth, which comes about as a result of the price (and thereby real wage) and investment decisions of firms, will not be equal to the firms' expected growth rate, nor will the rates of capacity utilisation be equal to their target rates.

The second difficulty relates to the equality between the demand for and supply of investment funds at the level of the firm. The price set by the price leader to secure adequate finance (possibly including some external finance) may not generate sufficient finance for the other firms. A more important issue concerns the equilibrium requirement of *ex ante* equality between savings and investment. If all enterprises are able to finance investment out of their own savings, and there are no savings by households, then the equality between saving and investment would hold at the microeconomic level, and this equality would also hold (by summation) at the macroeconomic level. On the other hand, if enterprises resort to external finance, rentiers and/or workers must generate sufficient saving in order to match that demand for external finance, a point to which we shall return below.

In so far as price leadership is successful, Eichner's approach implies a high 'degree of monopoly'. The number of enterprises in the industry is not directly relevant here, though it could well be argued that price leadership is easier to achieve, when the number of enterprises is small. Price leadership also means that the industry elasticity of demand is relevant for calculations of joint profit maximisation, thus reinforcing the assumption of low elasticity of demand. However if price set by the price leader is not exactly matched by all other firms in the industry the profit margin–profits function would have a more substantial curvature. Alternatively, as suggested by Reynolds (1989), 'the additional risk that other firms may not follow [the price-leader] will provide an additional constraint on the mark-up. Analytically, ... it may be ... converted to an implicit interest rate'. Similarly, a higher degree of monopoly may arise from a lower risk of entry: in that sense a higher degree of monopoly would lead to a lower implicit cost of raising profit margins. Thus, the degree of monopoly might influence the mark-up, in Eichner's approach as well as in Kalecki's, and this is taken into account below.

The two assumptions of inelastic demand and interdependence between periods raise difficulties for the postulate of short-term profit maximisation. The former assumption could lead to an infinite price in the short-term, whilst the latter would indicate that short-term profit maximisation may harm long-term profitability. Shapiro (1981), drawing on Steindl (1952), postulates the dependence of the growth rate of sales on the (current) profit margin. A strong interdependence of demand between periods would then arise. In contrast, Kaleckian and similar formulations do not take explicit account of interdependence between periods. This lack of interdependence requires two assumptions. The first is that the firm approaches profit maximisation by considering the long-run elasticity of demand, rather than the short-run elasticity (or equivalently that the elasticity of demand does not change with the length of the time period of adjustment). The second assumption arises from taking barriers to entry into account. It could be assumed, following Cowling(1982) and others, that entry is effectively blocked or, alternatively, that firms follow a limit pricing strategy to prevent entry.

Shapiro (1981) notes that 'if the price of a commodity is to promote the growth of the firm, pricing has to be based on the principles of the maintenance and augmentation of (1) profit margins and (2) markets' (cf. also Levine 1981, Steindl, 1952). If, for convenience, investment and profits are expressed net of depreciation, the argument can be stated as follows. The finance available for investment is derived from internal finance of $t.(p-c).q$ (where t is the proportion of profits saved, p is price, c is unit costs and q is output); and external finance which is taken to be a proportion z of internal finance. Growth of capital stock, g, is then given by:

$$g = (1+z).t.(p-c).q/p_K.K = (1+z).t\big[(p-c)/p\big].(q/q^*).(q^*/K).(p/p_K)$$
$$= (1+z).t.(m/1+m).(u/v).(p/p_K)$$

$$(10.1)$$

where p_K is the price of capital goods and q^* is full capacity output. This provides a relationship between the growth of capital and the profit margin (g,m) given: the dividend policy (reflected in t); the debt-equity policy (reflected in z); the level of capacity utilisation (u); and the capital–output ratio (v). Decisions by the enterprise concerning, for example, dividend policy (t) and debt-equity policy (z) are likely to be interdependent.

The variables g, m and u in equation (10.1) can be regarded as unknowns, and we will leave t, z and v to one side for the moment. The focus is on the determination of the first group of variables. The growth performance of any single firm will be heavily constrained by the growth prospects of the industry to which it belongs. Faster growth is possible by price reductions and appropriation of market shares of other firms. Following Shapiro (1981), the growth rate and the profit margin are set by the interaction of equation (10.1) with the dependence of the growth of sales on price, assuming that firms aim for and achieve a normal level of capacity utilisation.

Equation (10.1) is capable of a number of interpretations. The work of Eichner would suggest that enterprises have expectations about growth and targets for the rate of capacity utilisation, so that equation (10.1) determines the mark-up when the enterprises have calculated the desired mix between internal and external finance (i.e. the value of z). Steindl (1952) distinguishes between the cases of competition and oligopoly. Under strong competition, capacity utilisation will be pushed towards full capacity and the profit margin will be driven towards that which would yield a 'normal' rate of profit. However, under conditions of oligopoly, this pressure on capacity utilisation is not present; Steindl and others have elaborated on the reasons why enterprises will accept spare capacity (e.g. to inhibit new entry, to be able to meet upsurges in demand). When the profit margin is set by the 'degree of monopoly', equation (10.1) serves to determine the degree of capacity utilisation for a given growth rate.

The Sraffian approach provides the example of a theory of price (as opposed to pricing). For our purposes the key features of this approach are firstly the focus on long-period equilibrium prices, which may be viewed as centres of gravity around which actual market prices fluctuate. There is no concern with the way by which prices are set in the short term nor with the process by which the long-period equilibrium is reached. Secondly, there is mobility of capital generating a tendency towards the equalisation of the rate of profit across sectors. Although it is not generally specified, this would appear to assume that the objective of firms is profit maximisation in some sense.

DIFFICULTIES WITH PROFIT MAXIMISATION

There are at least two significant shortcomings in the neo-classical approach to pricing based on short-term profit maximisation. Similar problems, moreover, are faced by the Kaleckian approach. The first is that there is no allowance for the impact of the short term on the long term or vice versa. The second is that the theory is vacuous unless the nature of the short term is defined; i.e. unless, for example, the theory specifies which costs can be varied in the short term. It has become conventional to identify short-term variable costs with labour and material costs, though it is clear that some capital inputs can be more easily varied than some labour inputs. The difficulties of pinning down marginal cost have been discussed in connection with some economists' advocacy of marginal cost pricing for public enterprises. Many of these difficulties would also arise if attempts were made to test the prediction of price as a mark-up over marginal cost. Kalecki also faced the problem of identifying which labour costs should be included in direct costs for the purposes of price formation (Sawyer 1985a, pp.271–7). He appears to have distinguished between wages (paid to manual workers) and salaries (non-manual workers) on the basis of the variable nature of the former and the fixed nature of the latter.

The Kaleckian approach will now be modified by formalising the Baran and Sweezy proposition quoted in the previous chapter in order to avoid the first of these difficulties. The starting point is a notion of the maximisation of sustainable profits. An enterprise which contemplates long-term operation will not wish to charge a high price in the short run if by doing so it adversely affects profits in the longer run. But it may be postulated that an enterprise aims to set a price that would yield the highest level of profits that could be maintained over time (provided that all other factors were held constant). This would mean, for example, that an enterprise that was not threatened by entry would use long-run elasticity of demand rather than short-run elasticity in its calculations. This does not mean, of course, that an enterprise would ever face an unchanging situation from period to period.

The maximisation of sustainable profits is an artificial construction. Consider a firm with a given stock of capital equipment (which it will augment through investment), which is facing given demand conditions. It would then be possible to calculate for this situation the price and the level of output as well as the size of the labour force, etc. which the firm would choose, under the assumption that the initial conditions will continue indefinitely. This would mean, for example, that the firm uses a long-term elasticity of demand in its calculations. The variety of ways in which demand in different periods of time can be related would also be taken into account. The use of inputs other than the capital stock would be adjusted so as to generate maximum profits. This does not imply that all types of labour, for example, are variable inputs: in practice it may be easier for a firm to vary its use of some capital equipment (e.g. vehicles) than to vary the use of some types of labour (e.g. skilled labour with long-term contracts).

For any set of demand conditions, there would be a sustainable profit-maximising price, output and input usage. The firm could set that price and output, though in general the actual use of inputs would differ from the sustainable profit-maximising levels. Employment of inputs will be heavily conditioned by past employment of inputs and by expectations of future employment since there are hiring and firing costs etc. The price and the output derived from sustainable profit maximisation does not necessarily lie on the short-run demand curve facing the firm. In such circumstances, the firm may maintain price at its long-term level and allow output to deviate from the chosen level in the short run. This has strong similarities with the normal cost-pricing view of Coutts, Godley and Nordhaus (1978). The use of inputs will be varied somewhat, but in general not to the same extent as output.

When the notion of sustainable profit maximisation is adopted, enterprises would base their pricing decisions on non-capital costs, and would seek to adjust prices in response to changes in those costs. A long-term perspective on pricing suggests that the appropriate costs should be more broadly defined than that usually signified by the expression 'variable costs'. Indeed, the possibility of variation in the use of inputs is not relevant to whether the costs of those inputs are also included in the cost calculations of the enterprise. Furthermore, growth and investment requirements influence prices even if firms do not explicitly take such requirements into account when setting price. The long-term viability of a firm will require that it is able to finance most of its investment out of profits.

The notion of sustainable profit maximisation is an attempt to overcome the clearly myopic nature of short-run profit maximisation. It suggests that pricing can be viewed as a decision with long-term implications without making it dependent on the growth prospects of the enterprise. However, it retains the separation of the price decision from the investment decision.

A GENERAL MODEL

The initial purpose of this section is to construct a general (though still relatively simple) model that can encompass the ideas expressed above in a way that permits some comparisons to be made. A one-sector model is not adequate to allow for ideas such as the mobility of capital and the equalisation of the rates of profit, and the simplest model able to do so is a two-sector model. The model abstracts from technical change, which is rather unsatisfactory as positive investment through time generally requires the stimulus of technical change. However, it would appear that the basic arguments of this section would not be altered by allowing for exogenous technical change, the introduction of which would further complicate the presentation. The rate of depreciation of existing capital equipment is assumed to be a constant proportion of the existing capital stock. The model developed here is rather in the spirit of Dutt (1988).

In this two-sector model, sector 1 produces consumer goods and sector 2 investment goods. Output of sector i is X_i, with a price of p_i. The employment coefficients are a_i in sector i (i=1,2) so that total labour employed is $a_1.X_1 + a_2.X_2$. For simplicity, the coefficients a_i are treated as constants, and a fuller treatment would allow for their value being influenced by relative costs of labour and capital equipment and to reflect the intensity of labour which itself is likely to be influenced by the rate of unemployment and the structure and level of real wages. The uniform money wage is w, K_i is an index of capital equipment available in sector i with monetary value of $p_2.K_i$ on which the rate of profit is r_i with a rate of depreciation h_i. The proportion of gross profits in sector i which are spent on consumer goods is taken as $1 - s_i$, leaving a proportion s_i as gross savings. For convenience, savings out of wages are assumed to be zero (though the role of savings external to enterprises is discussed further below).

The first set of equations relate to the short-term in the sense that the two sectors grow at different rates (g_i, $i = 1,2$), and there is no presumption that growth rates are constant over time. The capital stock in each sector and the balance between sectors (reflected in $k = K_2/K_1$) are given in the short-term. Prices are re-evaluated each period, including the price of the existing capital equipment. The equality between output of consumer goods and the demand for them is given by:

$$X_1 = (w/p_1).(a_1.X_1 + a_2.X_2) + (1-s_1).r_1.(p_2/p_1).K_1 + (1-s_2).r_2.(p_2/p_1).K_2 \quad (10.2)$$

Output of investment goods is equal to gross investment expenditure, i.e.:

$$X_2 = (g_1 + h_1).K_1 + (g_2 + h_2).K_2 \quad (10.3)$$

where $g_i + h_i \leq 0$ ($i = 1,2$) on the basis that gross investment cannot be negative.

An accounting relationship between price and the rate of profit for each sector is given by:

$$p_1 = p_2.(K_1/X_1).r_1 + w.a_1 \tag{10.4}$$

$$p_2 = p_2.(K_2/X_2).r_2 + w.a_2 \tag{10.5}$$

A slightly modified scale-free form of these equations is:

$$u_1/v_1 = (w/p_1).(a_1.u_1/v_1 + a_2.(u_2/v_2).k) + (p_2/p_1).[(1-s_1).r_1 + (1-s_2).r_2.k] \tag{10.2'}$$

$$u_2/v_2 = (g_1 + h_1)/k + g_2 + h_2 \tag{10.3'}$$

$$1 = (p_2/p_1).(v_1/u_1).r_1 + (w/p_1).a_1 \tag{10.4'}$$

$$p_2/p_1 = (p_2/p_1).(v_2/u_2).r_2 + (w/p_1).a_2 \tag{10.5'}$$

where u_i is a measure of capacity utilisation in sector i, v_i is the stock of capital to capacity output ratio and k is K_2/K_1.

In the short-term model, the growth of the economy is driven by the growth of the capital stock and hence by the demand for investment goods, which in turn is likely to be heavily influenced by expectations of growth. A major ingredient of Kalecki's investment theory was the influence of the change of economic activity on investment, and the role of investment in the generation of economic cycles. However, the concern here is with the steady-state and not with cyclical movements. The important ingredient of Kalecki's investment theory is seen to be the influence of profitability, internal finance (also linked to profitability), and capacity utilisation on investment decisions, which are assumed to be carried through and thereby determine the growth of capital equipment (and Harcourt and Kenyon (1976) provide a similar list of influences). However, Bhaduri and Marglin (1990) argue for a formulation of investment as a function of profit margin, rather than the profit rate, and capacity utilisation on the grounds that this clearly separates the two influences at work whereas the rate of profit reflects the dual influences of profit margin and capacity utilisation. Further, they argue that the use of profit rate and capacity utilisation in the investment generates a stagnationist view that higher real wages stimulate economic activity. In light of that argument, the investment functions here read:

$$g_1 = f_1(g_1^{se}, m_1, u_1/u_1^*) \tag{10.6}$$

$$g_2 = f_2(g_2^{se}, m_2, u_2/u_2^*) \tag{10.7}$$

where g_i^{se} is expected growth of sales, m_i is mark-up and u_i^* is the target level of capacity utilisation ($i = 1,2$). The target level of capacity utilisation may be regarded as the one desired by the enterprises.

Much post Keynesian writing in this area has argued that 'there is no force pushing the firm to full-capacity utilisation of plant. The actual rate of capacity utilisation will depend on the level of demand; however, it is likely that the firm will *attempt* to operate at less than full capacity' (Harcourt and Kenyon, 1976). Further, and particularly relevant here, 'the capacity utilisation rate becomes a decision-variable' (ibid). For the present, the target level of capacity utilisation is taken as given, though further discussed below. The implication which is picked up here is that investment will be influenced by the difference between actual rate of capacity utilisation and the target rate.

It can be argued that an investment function in the post Keynesian tradition should not directly include the rates of profit, and this would appear to conform to the approach of Eichner. The essence of the argument, particularly in the context of the long-run, is that the profit in its role as source of internal finance is a permissive factor for investment but, provided that the rate of profit exceeds some minimum acceptable level, then investment will eventually proceed in accordance with the requirements of production. In the post Keynesian approach substitution between factors of production on the basis of relative factor prices is usually regarded as unimportant. If such arguments are accepted then the investment functions would not only take the form:

$$g_1 = f_1(g_1^{se}, u_1/u_2^*) \qquad (10.6')$$

$$g_2 = f_2(g_2^{se}, u_2/u_2^*) \qquad (10.7')$$

but also certain conditions would need to be imposed on the function. When enterprises are in steady state, then expected growth (of output) will be in line with growth of capital stock, and capacity utilisation will be at its target level. In this case, the investment function would be of a form such that $g_i^{se} = g_i$ would imply $u_i = u_i^*$, the significance of which will become apparent below.

The financing of investment in each sector requires that:

$$(g_1 + h_1).K_1 = s_1.\Pi_1 + E \qquad (10.8a)$$

$$(g_2 + h_2).K_2 = s_2.\Pi_2 - E \qquad (10.8b)$$

where Π_i are profits in sector i ($i=1,2$) and E is the transfer of funds between sectors (with no requirement that E is positive). These equations can be seen as accounting identities only. However, within the view that pricing is geared to investment finance requirements, the firms' choice of s_i, Π_i and E could be seen as derived from of optimising calculations based on the perceived relative costs of internal and external finance. Eqn.(10.8b) is derivable from the preceding equations, and so does not constitute an independent equation. These equations can be re-written as:

$$g_1 + h_1 = s_1.r_1 + e \tag{10.8a'}$$

$$g_2 + h_2 = s_2.r_2 - e/k \tag{10.8b'}$$

where $e = E/K_1$. The price–variable cost relationships are given by:

$$p_1 = (1 + m_1).w.a_1 \tag{10.9}$$

$$p_2 = (1 + m_2).w.a_2 \tag{10.10}$$

where m_i is the profit margin in sector i. These equations could be considered as accounting identities which would calculate m_i, given a_i, p_i and w. This will be the case in a Sraffian approach where in the long-period the profit margins arise as a result of the equalisation of the rates of profit.

A Kaleckian view would see the profit margin as dependent on the degree of monopoly, i.e. :

$$m_1 = m_1(d_1, u_1) \tag{10.11a}$$

$$m_2 = m_2(d_2, u_2) \tag{10.12a}$$

where d_i is the degree of monopoly in sector i and the mark-up may also depend on capacity utilisation (u_i). The profit margin is the one which as far as possible maximises profits in the short term (subject to allowance for impact on long-term profits). In the approach of Eichner, the perceived impact of the current profit margin on long-term growth prospects serves to limit the margin set. Eichner's approach (cf. Eichner, 1987, p.392) can be generalised to allow the influence of market power on the mark-up to give:

$$m_1 = m_1(d_1, g_1.v_1) \tag{10.11b}$$

$$m_2 = m_2(d_2, g_2.v_2) \tag{10.12b}$$

A synthesis of the approaches of Kalecki and Eichner would be:

$$m_1 = m_1(d_1, u_1, g_1.v_1, h_1.v_1) \tag{10.11c}$$

$$m_2 = m_2(d_2, u_2, g_2.v_2, h_2.v_2) \tag{10.12c}$$

which clearly combines variables included above and introduces depreciation. The inclusion of depreciation would reflect the argument of Kalecki above concerning the impact of overheads on profit margins and that gross profits have to finance depreciation as well as growth. For generality we allow that net growth and depreciation have possibly differential effects on profit margins.

These equations constitute 11 independent equations with 11 unknowns, namely u_i, m_i, g_i, r_i, w/p_i ($i = 1,2$) and e. The system of equations can in principle be solved. This model is short term in the sense that the capital stock in each sector is taken as given and there is no requirement that the growth rates of the two sectors are equal. There is a financial transfer from one sector to another, which has to occur to balance finance and investment expenditure in each sector. The levels of capacity utilisation are endogenously determined, and there is no requirement here that they are equal to the target levels of utilisation.

This model can be used for at least three distinct purposes. First, the model incorporates, albeit in a very simple form, a theory of pricing and a theory of price determination. Equations (10.9, 10.10, 10.10c, 10.10d) reflect the way in which prices are set. But prices also have to conform to the equilibrium requirements of the overall economic system. In effect, variables such as the level of capacity utilisation and the growth rate vary until the mark-up established by firms in the light of the prevailing circumstances produces prices which conform to the system requirements. In particular, finance must be available to meet the investment requirements. The model is Kaleckian in spirit in that the level of capacity utilisation is not constrained to be that of full capacity or some target level (a point which we return to below).

Second, we are in a position to explore the predicted impact of the degree of monopoly and other exogenous factors on the endogenous variables. It is not possible to establish unambiguously the sign of the effects of a variation in the degree of monopoly, though the impact on capacity utilisation, the growth rate and the rate of profit would be negative unless the partial derivative of the growth function with respect to capacity utilisation is, in some sense, large. The inclusion of the effect of growth on the mark-up reinforces the likely negative effects. A positive relationship between capacity utilisation and the mark-up operates in the same manner. The expectation of the post Keynesian and Kaleckian approaches is that under-utilisation of capacity would generally result, although the forces that lead in general towards such an outcome have been little discussed. With a linearised one-sector equivalent of the model given here (and discussed in Sawyer, 1992b), a solution can be obtained. We have experimented with ranges of parameter values thought to be reasonable. The model provides two values for capacity utilisation, though it is always the case that one of the values is strongly negative. The positive solution for capacity utilisation (relative to the desired level) is often less than unity and generally does not exceed 1.5 which could be considered reasonable as actual capacity utilisation may well exceed that desired by the enterprises especially in the short run. As would be expected, high growth expectations (and relatively large parameter values in the investment equation) tends to generate high values of capacity utilisation. This model operates under the assumption that the levels of capacity utilisation indicated as the equilibrium ones could be actually achieved. But clearly if the endogenously determined levels of capacity utilisation exceeded those that are physically possible, then a different model (or at least a different version of the underlying model) would be required which incorporated such limitations (and this line of argument has been pursued in the context of socialist economies viewed as resource-constrained in Sawyer (1991a)). Similarly, a different version would be required if the level of employment implied by the model exceeded the available labour supply.

Third, the model can be used to illustrate some problems which arise in the post Keynesian approaches to pricing and growth. There is first of all no particular reason to think that the expected rate of growth and the target rate of capacity utilisation will be achieved. This however does not seem to raise any particular difficulties in a Kaleckian approach. In the short run, expectations and intentions may well be frustrated. (In this model, expectations over price and output are fulfilled though output may not yield the target rate of capacity utilisation). For Kalecki, the long run is a sequence of short runs and over the course of time, firms may find that their long run expectations and objectives are disappointed.

The investment-requirements approach to pricing implies that expectations regarding growth and capacity utilisation targets would, at least on average, be realised. There remains the question of how expectations about the growth rate are formed; and it may be reasonable to postulate that expectations are based on experience so that expected growth rates converge on actual growth rates. However, the target rate of capacity utilisation is based on considerations of cost and strategic advantage.

There are at least two sets of factors not included in the above model which may tend to push the level of capacity utilisation towards the target range. The first is the savings and investment behaviour. The propensity to save out of profits is treated here (as is the usual case) as independent of the investment behaviour. In the one-sector model at least, capacity utilisation is negatively associated with the difference between propensity to save and to invest out of profits, and those decisions are linked since they are taken by the same corporations. It can be postulated that persistent low levels of capacity utilisation would tend to reduce the difference between the propensity to save out of profits and the propensity to invest. Further, there is a lower limit to gross investment of zero.

The second is the impact of low capacity utilisation on the degree of monopoly and thereby the mark-up. If low capacity generates low mark-ups and the resulting shift from profits to wages has an expansionary effect on demand, there is thereby a route to limit how low capacity utilisation can fall. This implies, of course, that higher real wages (resulting from lower profit margins) prevent low levels of capacity utilisation and corresponding high levels of unemployment.

In the short term, employment is given by:

$$L = a.(u_1/v_1).K_1 + b.(u_2/v_2).K_2 = (a_1u_1/v_1 + a_2ku_2/v_2).K_1 \quad (10.13)$$

and hence unemployment (as a proportion of the full employment level L_f) by:

$$U = 1 - (a_1X_1 + a_2X_2)/L_f \quad (10.14)$$

This general approach would serve to determine, *inter alia*, real wages and employment levels. There is, of course, no reason to think that the employment and real wage levels thereby determined would be compatible with full employment of labour.

There is often an interest in the sign of the relationship between a number of the variables which are endogenously determined within a model such as the one discussed here, as between, for example, the rate of profit and the real wage. In particular, there is often seen to be a negative relationship between the rate of profit and the real wage (e.g. Marglin, 1984) though this can be transformed into a positive one when capacity utilisation is allowed to vary (Dutt, 1987). In the model discussed here, any relationship between say real wage and the rate of profit was be non-causal since both are endogenously determined. Further, it turns out that the sign of the relationship between the rate of profit and the real wage depends on the particular exogenous change that is being investigated. It would also follow that other relationships (such as that between rate of growth and the real wage) would also vary in sign depending on the particular exogenous variation.

ON CAPACITY UTILISATION

The target levels of capacity utilisation enter in two ways. The first was seen above in the investment equations, and the second in the price equation. The level of capacity utilisation which is accepted by enterprises (and in some cases labelled desired) has been postulated to depend on a variety of factors. The view of Harcourt and Kenyon (1976) that 'operating at less than full capacity gives the firm a safety margin with which to accommodate sudden swings in demand'. Cowling (1982) and Spence (1977) portray the holding of excess capacity as a means of inhibiting entry on the basis that an expansion of output (and thereby reduction of price) could be made by existing firms in response to entry. Potential entrants, concerned with post-entry profits, are thereby deterred from entering the industry. The incumbents in an industry with higher profitability will need higher barriers to entry to deter entrants, and hence more spare capacity. Steindl (1952) brings in the idea of firms accepting some level of under-utilisation of capacity, though in his case it is related to economies of scale in the presence of growth of demand. Capacity is built ahead of demand, and the lumpiness of investment (due to economies of scale) means that when a new factory is brought on stream it generates excess capacity until demand grows sufficiently to absorb the extra production. Each of these arguments suggests that the desired level of capacity utilisation will be less than that which is physically possible. But equation (10.3') indicates the relationship between capacity utilisation in sector 2 and growth rates and ratio of capital in the two sectors. Thus, in general, it is not possible for both the growth rate to be at its expected level and capacity utilisation to be at its target level. This clearly means that firms will not usually find their capacity utilisation target achieved and their expectations on growth fulfilled.

The specific formulation used is influenced by Skott (1989b), reflecting the idea that firms will adopt more excess capacity when profit rates are high in order to deter entry and is:

$$u_1^* = z_1(r_1) \qquad\qquad (10.15)$$

$$u_2^* = z_2(r_2) \qquad\qquad (10.16)$$

Clearly more complex formulations are possible, but here it is sufficient to note that the target level of capacity utilisation can be modelled. Capacity is measured such that the physical limit on capacity corresponds to a value of u of unity, and hence $u_i^* \leq 1$ but u_i/u_i^* can fall either side of unity. One general implication of this line of argument is that capacity utilisation is determined by the decisions made by firms rather than by the level of aggregate demand, and we return to the question of the role of demand below.

LONG TERM CONSIDERATIONS

The long term may be considered in the spirit of Kalecki as an entity without any separate existence and based on the average of a series of short-term situations. An alternative and more wide-spread view is that the long term is the end of a process and represents some kind of equilibrium towards which the economy will tend, although some would see the long term as a position around which the economy will fluctuate in the short term.

The absolute size of the two sectors was taken as given in the short-term model considered above, though only the relative size of the two sectors (reflected in k) was directly reflected in the model. Over time the absolute and relative size of the two sectors changes and these changes could be tracked through the additions to the capital stock arising from the investment functions.

When the long term is seen as the end of a process, the allocation of capital equipment between the two sectors (k) becomes a variable, and an equilibrium value for k implies that the growth rates of the two sectors are equal ($g_1 = g_2$). The inclusion of k as a variable in the set of 11 equations used above presents no problem in that its inclusion implies the replacement of g_1, g_2 by a single growth rate g. Thus in effect two variables (k and g) replace two others (g_1, g_2), and the model remains determinate. When the long term is seen as a series of short terms, this could be the end of the discussion, for any difference between, for example, the expected and actual growth rates would be of no particular significance.

However, the long term is often associated with the fulfilment of expectations and in particular here that would mean that both growth expectations and the desired levels of capacity utilisation were achieved. Hence, $u_i = u_i^*$ and $g_i^{se} = g_i$ (i=1,2). The investment functions from equations (10.6) and (10.7) under these long-term conditions simplify to $g_i = f_i(g_i, r_i)$, which can be solved to give $g_i = h_i(r_i)$, where the relationship between growth rate and profit rate is expected to be positive.[3] Clearly the conditions $g_i^{se} = g_i$ do not involve problems of over-determinacy unless equations specifying the formation of growth expectations are introduced (a notable example of which would be for expectations on growth to be set by reference to the growth of the labour force).

However, the imposition of the condition $u_i = u_i^*$ means that the system of equations is now over-determined, as clearly capacity utilisation cannot be determined both by firms' own decisions and the level of aggregate demand. But this over-determinacy depends on the postulated form of the investment function for the long term. It could be argued that the influence of the rate of profit on investment is a short-term phenomenon (e.g. arising from financing considerations), and that the long-term investment function onto which the short-term investment function converges is solely concerned with growth prospects. In this case, the investment function collapses to take the form of $g_i = g_i^{se}$. The problem of over-determinacy is thereby avoided but at the expense of in effect removing the role of investment and aggregate demand in the determination of the level of economic activity.

Even when the problem of over-determinacy is averted it is still the case that capacity utilisation levels are set by the decisions of the enterprises, and this raises the question of what role is left for aggregate demand. In the context of the model discussed here, the role of aggregate demand can be seen as twofold. First, aggregate demand remains part of the model, and thereby determines the value of the endogenous variables. However, insofar as a high level of demand generates a high rate of profit that would be associated with a low target rate of utilisation (and thereby a low actual rate of utilisation). Thus there is an indirect influence of aggregate demand through the influence of the rate of profit on target rate of utilisation, though the sign of the influence is opposite to the one usually assumed (since here high demand would be associated with a low rate of capacity utilisation).

Second, aggregate demand remains significant for the determination of the scale of the operation of an economy including the level of unemployment. The equations above are all scale-free, and thus relate to the levels of output *relative* to capacity. Investment expenditure would add to the capital stock, and the cumulative investment expenditure in conjunction with capacity utilisation would set the absolute scale of economic activity, and this is clear from equation (10.14) in the case of unemployment. The relative aspects of long-term equilibrium are generated by the equations given above. But the absolute level is left under-determined within the model. However, the absolute levels depend as indicated on cumulative investment and in that way the long-term position can be described as path-dependent where the relevant aspect of the path is the investment expenditure. On the basis that investment expenditure is a key

---

3. $dr_i/dg_i = (1 - f_{i1})/f_{i2}$ (where f_{ik} is the first derivative of f_i with respect to the kth argument), which is positive provided that $f_{i1} < 1$.

element of aggregate demand, it can be said that the absolute scale in the long term is influenced by (short-term) aggregate demand.

The mobility of capital which occurs as capital is created (and is reflected in movements in k) may be seen to lead in the long term to the equalisation of the rate of profit ($r_1 = r_2$). But in the Kaleckian approach, a tendency towards the equalisation of the rate of profit operates through variations in capacity utilisation (Kalecki, 1942) rather than through changes in the price–cost margin. Thus even if there is equalisation of the rate of profit, there remain disagreements over the mechanisms by which it occurs: and this is related to the question as to whether the long term can be characterised by excess capacity (or perhaps more accurately a divergence between actual and target rates of capacity utilisation).

The imposition of the condition of the equalisation of the rate of profit once again leads to a problem of over-determinacy. This could be overcome if one is prepared to assume that there is a single equation governing investment so that equation (10.6) and (10.7) are replaced by a single equation which in the long term (with the imposition of the condition $u_i = u_i^*$) takes the form:

$$g = f(g^{se}, r) \qquad (10.6a)$$

where r is the single rate of profit. In our approach at least, the equalisation of the rate of profit also requires a conformity of investment behaviour between sectors.

The conclusion that can be drawn from this section is that the role of aggregate demand in the determination of the level of economic activity in the long term depends on the interpretation given to the long term. A Kaleckian view under which the long term is the collection of short terms would clearly give aggregate demand the same role in the long term as in the short term. When the long term is seen as the end of a process, the impact of aggregate demand is on the path to the long term and particularly thereby on the size of the capital stock and employment level.

THE LABOUR SECTOR: SOME CONSIDERATIONS

The discussion above has ignored the labour sector of the economy, with the presumption that the real wage and employment were determined on the product side of the economy (where there are both demand and supply influences at work). This is rather in line with the traditions of Kalecki and Keynes within which the labour sector sets the money wage, but the real wage is set through pricing decisions (cf. equations (10.9) and (10.11)). But this implies that in effect the labour force is prepared to accept whatever real wages are offered, whereas workers have notions of what constitutes acceptable levels of real wages and press for higher wages. The ability of workers to obtain high real wages will be constrained by, *inter alia*, levels of unemployment. Whilst retaining the idea that the money wage is set on the labour side of the economy, the ideas just mentioned can be represented by the following formulation for money wage changes $\dot{w}$ (for an elaboration of this formulation see Sawyer (1982a, 1982b); a dot above a variable signifies the proportionate rate of change of that variable):

$$\dot{w} = w_1 + w_2.\dot{p}_1^e + w_3.U + w_4.(w/p_1 - T) \qquad (10.17)$$

where $\dot{p}_1^e$ is the expected rate of inflation for consumer goods and T is the

target real wage representing the notion of an acceptable level of real wages. In the short term, this equation sets wage inflation (for given expected price inflation) with unemployment and the real wage determined in the model discussed above. This equation sets the rate of wage inflation, and inflation can be seen to act as a safety-valve to release the tension between the actual and the target real wage.

The long term is assumed to be characterised by an equality between money wage changes, price changes and expected price changes, and an absence of money illusion so that $w_2 = 1$.[4] Thus in the long-term :

$$U = -\{w_1/w_3 + w_4/w_3(w/p_1 - T)\} \qquad (10.18)$$

and this equation could be used to effectively determine the level of unemployment in the long term, given the real wage set in the model above. It can also be seen by reference back to equation (10.14) that the scale of operation of the economy would thereby also be determined. The level of unemployment as determined in equation (10.18) will be labelled U_A. When the level of unemployment as determined from equation (10.14) is less than the level of unemployment as determined in equation (10.18) then wage inflation would be increasing (relative to the expected rate of inflation). The target real wage is likely to be conditioned by the actual experience of real wages, and in that way to depend on the path taken to long-term equilibrium. In consequence the long-term level of unemployment could to that degree be viewed as path-dependent. However, it would have to be noted that the absolute scale of the economy is set in this approach by labour sector considerations and the role of aggregate demand is once again displaced.

However, a constant rate of unemployment as a long-term characteristic clearly implies growth of employment (here equal to the growth of the capital stock g) equal to growth of the labour force. There are at least two possibilities to be considered here. The first is that firms' investment behaviour conforms to the growth of the labour force: in other words firms realise that the growth of

---

4 . It may be argued (e.g. Epstein and Schor, 1990) that there are different eras so far as wage inflation is concerned. For example, $w_2 < 1$ may correspond to the early post-war years, whereas $w_2 = 1$ may characterise more recent years even in the short term.

the economy is constrained by the growth of the labour force and invest accordingly. The second is the flexibility of the growth of the labour supply through variations in the average age of people joining and leaving the labour force, movements into or out of the household, and migration. Thus, at least over some range, the growth of the labour force is able to adjust to the growth of t capital stock.

There need not be any requirement that the same model applies to all situations. Thus in terms of the two possibilities advanced in the previous paragraph, it can be argued that there are eras when an economy becomes constrained by the growth of the labour force, and others when the growth of the labour force is pliable enough to accommodate to the growth of output and the capital stock.

EXTERNAL FINANCE AND WORKERS' SAVINGS

In the discussion so far external financing has been treated in a rather summary way, and in particular nothing has been said as to how the balance between the external financing of the two sectors is secured. In this section we briefly consider the consequences of removing the assumption of zero workers' savings, and in doing so discuss the role of external finance further.

The supply of funds (from savings) from workers to enterprises raises a number of issues. First, the external and internal finance have different costs, and the relative costs and availability of the two types of finance may influence investment decisions (in the Kaleckian approach) and financing decisions (as in the approach of Eichner).

Second, there is now a requirement that enterprises' use of external finance must equal the savings by workers (in addition to the overall equality of savings and investment). In other words, '[h]ow are the relative rates of outside and internal accumulation brought into adjustment with the decisions of entrepreneurs with regard to the gearing ratio' (Steindl, 1952). Clearly this means that the sole use of internal finance by enterprises is inconsistent with any savings by workers. Further, there is 'a question of adjusting the *proportions* in which savings are contributed by the two groups of savers, entrepreneurs and outside savers, to the proportion in which entrepreneurs wish to finance their total investment by own capital and debt' (Steindl, 1952 emphasis in original).

Third, interest is assumed to be payable by enterprises on borrowing from workers. Following Pasinetti (1962), interest payments are added to workers income and subject to consumption/savings decisions in the same way as wages are, and for simplicity it is assumed that workers' savings decisions are not influenced by the general level of interest rates. Profits relevant for savings decisions are taken to be net of interest payments, though it is assumed that costs for pricing purposes remain as labour costs only and do not include interest charges. It is assumed, following Kalecki and others, that in general the average rate of profit is considerably in excess of the average rate of interest.

The financing equations for the two sectors now read:

$$g_i + h_i = (s_i + e_i).(r_i - j_i.b_i) \quad i = 1,2 \tag{10.19}$$

where e_i is the ratio of external borrowing to profits net of interest, b_i the ratio of external debt to capital stock and j_i the average rate of interest on borrowing paid by sector. In the short-term, b_i is taken as predetermined by previous borrowing, and it is assumed that all borrowing is undertaken on a variable interest rate basis so that interest rates are in effect renegotiated each period.

The savings and external borrowing decisions of the enterprises can be viewed as influenced by the average rate of interest charged. The demand for external finance by the enterprises is $e_i.(r_i - j_i.b_i)$. External finance is obtained in the first instance from financial institutions, and the average interest rate will arise from the interaction between the enterprises and the financial institutions. But any requirement for external finance in excess of previous levels of workers' savings would necessitate credit creation by the financial institutions. We first look at the terms under which the financial institutions grant loans and then the implications for the stock of money.

Following the general notion behind Kalecki's principle of increasing risk, the average rate of interest charged can be taken to depend on the external finance ratio. For our purposes we focus on the relationship between e_i and j_i, and argue that (in the short term) the banks/financial institutions will in effect present the enterprises with a positive relationship between e_i and j_i, summarised as $j_i(e_i)$ ($i = 1,2$). The external finance ratios and the average rates of interest are then seen to be determined by the interaction between enterprises and the financial institutions.

When the banks are 'horizonalists' (Moore, 1989) and set an interest rate at which they are willing to meet the demand for loans, j_i's are thereby determined.

Combining equation (10.19) with equations (10.2') to (10.5') above yields:

$$\begin{aligned} e_1.(r_1 - j_1.b_1).p_2/p_1 &+ e_2.(r_2 - j_2.b_2).p_2/p_1.k \\ &= t.\{w/p_1.[a.u_1/v_1 + b.(u_2/v_2).k] + p_2/p_1.[j_1.b_1 + j_2.b_2.k]\} \end{aligned} \tag{10.20}$$

which is the equality between workers' savings and external finance.

Thus the terms on which banks are prepared to supply finance, summarised by the expression $j_i(e_i)$, forms a part of the over-all model, and thereby will influence variables such as capacity utilisation, real wages and the rates of profit.

The provision of loans by the banks will, of course, also involve additions to the stock of money. However, whether money thereby created remains in existence depends on the willingness of enterprises and workers to hold the money, i.e. it will depend on the demand for money. Following Kaldor and Trevithick (1981), we argue that any excess of the stock of money over the demand for money (for given interest rates, income etc.) will lead to the repayment of loans and thereby the extinction of the 'excess' money.

The implications of this exercise are two-fold. First, although the mix of internal and external finance may be an enterprise decision, nevertheless the over-all external finance ratio has to conform to systemic requirements on the equality of external finance and workers savings. Second, the interest rates are viewed as set by real rather than monetary factors.

CONCLUDING REMARKS

The macroeconomic models examined in this chapter have the general feature of being based on the decisions of enterprises over prices and financing which nevertheless have to conform to over-all systemic requirements. The role of aggregate demand (as reflected in an independent investment function and the equality between savings and investment) depends on the conceptualisation of the long term that is used. It has been argued that when the long term is viewed as a succession of short terms, no particular difficulties arise and aggregate demand retains its influence. But when the long term is seen as the end of a process (and in particular that expectations are fulfilled) the role of aggregate demand lies in determining the size of the economy (and in particular the levels of output and employment) though not the rate of capacity utilisation.

References

Abernathy, W., Clark, K., and Kantrow, A.M. (1991), *Industrial Renaissance: Producing a Competitive Future for America*, New York: Basic Books.

Amable, B. (1993), 'Catch-up and convergence: a model of cumulative growth', *International Review of Applied Economics*, vol. 7.

Appelbaum, E. (1979), 'The labor market', in A. Eichner (ed.) *A Guide to Post-Keynesian Economics*, London: Macmillan.

Arestis, P. (1986), 'Wages and prices in the UK: the post-Keynesian view', *Journal of Post Keynesian Economics*, vol. 8. Reprinted in Sawyer, M. (ed.) *Post-Keynesian Economics*, Aldershot: Edward Elgar, 1988.

Arestis, P. (1991), *The Post Keynesian Approach to Economics*, Aldershot: Edward Elgar.

Arestis, P. and Kitromilides,Y. (eds) (1989), *Theory and Policy in Political Economy*, Aldershot: Edward Elgar.

Arestis, P. and Sawyer, M. (eds) (1992), *A Biographical Dictionary of Dissenting Economists*, Aldershot: Edward Elgar.

Arestis, P. and Sawyer, M. (eds) (1994), *The Elgar Companion to Radical Political Economy*, Aldershot: Edward Elgar.

Arrow, K.J. (1959), 'Towards a theory of price adjustment' in M. Abramovitsz (ed.) *The Allocation of Economic Resurces*, Standford: Stanford University Press.

Arrow, K.J. (1962), 'Economic welfare and the allocation of resources for invention', in National Bureau for Economic Research, *The Rate and Direction of Inventive Activity: Economic and Social Aspects* Princeton, NJ: Princeton University Press.

Auerbach, P. (1988), *Competition: the Economics of Industrial Change*, Oxford: Blackwell.

Auerbach, P. (1992), 'Vertical integration, planning and the market' in P. Arestis and V. Chick (eds), *Recent Developments in Post Keynesian Economics*, Aldershot: Edward Elgar.

Auerbach, P. and Skott, P. (1988), 'Concentration, competition and distribution: a critique of theories of monopoly capitalism', *International Review of Applied Economics* vol. 2.

Baran, P. and Sweezy, P. (1966), *Monopoly Capital*, New York: Monthly Review Press.

Baranzini, M. and Scazzieri, R. (eds) (1986), *Foundations of Economics: Structure of Inquiry and Economic Theory*, Oxford: Blackwell.

Basile, L. and Salvadori, N. (1984–5), 'Kalecki's pricing theory', *Journal of Post Keynesian Economics* vol. 7.

Battalio, R.C., Kagel, J.H. and McDonald, D.N. (1985), 'Animals' choices over uncertain outcomes: some initial experimental results', *American Economic Review*, vol. 75.

Baumol, W.J. (1959), *Business Behaviour, Value and Growth*. London: Macmillan.

Baumol, W. (1986), 'Productivity growth, convergence and welfare: what the long-run data show', *American Economic Review*, vol. 76.

Bausor, R. (1983) 'The rational expectations hypothesis and the epistemics of time', *Cambridge Journal of Economics* vol. 7.

Becker, G. (1957), *The Economics of Discrimination*, Chicago: University of Chicago Press.

Becker, G. (1966), 'Crime and punishment: an economic analysis', *Journal of Political Economy*, vol. 74.

Becker, G. (1973), 'The theory of marriage, part 1', *Journal of Political Economy*, vol. 81.

Bergstrom, A.R., Catt, A.J.L., Peston, M.H. and Silverstone, B.D.J. (eds.) (1978), *Stability and Inflation*, Chichester:Wiley.

Berle, A.A. and Means, G.C.,(1932), *The Modern Corporation and Private Property*, London: Macmillan.

Bhaduri, A. and Steindl, J. (1983), 'The rise of monetarism as a social doctrine' *Thames Papers in Political Economy*, Autumn, 1–18.

Bhaduri, A. and Marglin, S. (1990), 'Unemployment and the real wage: the economic basis for contesting political ideologies', *Cambridge Journal of Economics*, vol. 14.

Boltho, A. (1982), 'Growth' in A. Boltho (ed.), *The European Economy: Growth and Crisis*, Oxford: Oxford University Press.

Bowles, S. (1985),'The production proess in a competitive economy: Walrasian, neoHobbesian and Marxian models', *American Economic Review*, vol. 75.

Bradley, I. and Howard, M. (1982), 'Piero Sraffa's 'Production of commodities by means of commodities" and the rehabilitation of classical and Marxian political economy' in I. Bradley and M. Howard (eds), *Classical and Marxian Political Economy* London:: Macmillan.

Brenner, H. (1979), 'Influence of social environment on social pathology: the historical perspective' in James E. Barrett et alia (eds), *Stress and Mental Disorder*, New York:Raven Press.

Brothwell, J.F. (1975), 'A simple Keynesian response to Leijonhufvud', *Bulletin of Economic Research*, vol. 27.

Brothwell, J.F. (1988), 'The *General Theory* after fifty years why are we not all Keynesians now?' in J. Hillard (ed.), *J.M. Keynes in Retrospect*, Aldershot: Edward Elgar

Brown, A.J. (1955), *The Great Inflation, 1939–1951*, Oxford: Oxford University Press.

Burchell, B. (1992), 'Changes in the labour market and the psychological health of the nation', in J. Michie (ed.), *The Economic Legacy, 1979-1992*, London: Academic Press.

Calmfors, L. and Drifill, J. (1988), 'Bargaining structure, corporatism and macroeconomic performance', *Economic Policy*, no. 6.

Carabelli, A. M. (1988), *On Keynes's Method*, London: Macmillan.

Carlyle, T. (1849), 'The nigger question', *Miscellaneous Essays*, vol. 7.

Carlyle, T. (1850), *Latter Day Pamphlets*, London: Chapman and Hall.

Carvalho, F. (1984–5), 'Alternative analyses of short and long run in Post Keynesian economics', *Journal of Post Keynesian Economics*, vol. 7.

Chamberlin, E. (1933), *The Theory of Monopolistic Competition*, Cambridge, Mass. : Harvard University Press.

Chang, W. W. and Smyth, D.J. (1971), 'The existence and persistence of cycles in a non-linear model: Kaldor's 1940 model re-examined', *Review of Economic Studies*, vol. 38.

Chick,V. (1983), *Macroeconomics After Keynes*, Deddington: Philip Allan.

Chick,V. (1986),'The evolution of the banking system and the theory of saving, investment and interest', *Economies et Societes* (Cahiers de l'ISMEA Serie Monnaie et Production, no.3).

Clark, A.E. and Oswald, A.J. (1994), 'Unhappiness and unemployment', *Economic Journal*, vol. 104.

Clarke, R. (1985), *Industrial Economics* Oxford: Basil Blackwell.

Clifton, J. (1977), 'Competition and the evolution of the capitalist mode of production', *Cambridge Journal of Economics*, vol. 1.

Clower, R. (1965), 'The Keynesian counter revolution' in F.Hahn and F.Brechling (eds), *The Theory of Interest Rates* , London: Macmillian.

Coase, R. (1937), 'The nature of the firm', *Economica*, vol. 4.

Coase, R. (1992), 'The institutional structure of production', *American Economic Review*, vol. 82, no. 4.

Coddington, A.(1983), *Keynesian Economics: The Search for First Principles*, London: Allen and Unwin.

Colander, D.C. and Guthrie, R.C. (1980–1), 'Great expectations: what the Dickens do 'rational expectations" mean', *Journal of Post Keynesian Economics*, vol. 3.

Collard, D. (1990), 'Unemployment', in J. Creedy (ed.), *Foundations of Economic Thought*, Oxford: Blackwell.

Coutts, K., Godley,W. and Nordhaus, W. (1978), *Industrial Pricing in the United Kingdom*, Cambridge: Cambridge University Press.

Cowling, K. (1982), *Monopoly Capitalism*, London: Macmillan.

Cowling, K. (1985), 'Economic obstacles to democracy', in R.C.O. Matthews (ed.) *Economy and Democracy*, London: Macmillan.

Cowling, K. (1987), 'An industrial strategy for Britain', *International Review of Applied Economics*, vol. 1.

Cowling, K. (1990), 'The strategic approach to economic and industrial policy' in K. Cowling and R. Sugden (eds), *A New Economic Policy for Britain*, Manchester: Manchester University Press.

Cowling, K. (1992), 'Monopoly capitalism revisited', in A. del Monte (ed.), *Recent Developments in the Theory of Industrial Organization*, London: Macmillan.

Cowling, K. and Sugden, R. (eds) (1990), *A New Economic Policy for Britain: Essays on the Development of Industry*, Manchester: Manchester University Press.

Cowling, K. and Sugden, R. (1993a), 'A strategy for industrial development as a basis for regulation', in R. Sugden (ed.) *Industrial Economic Regulation: A Framework and Exploration*, London: Routledge.

Cowling, K. and Sugden, R. (1993b), 'Industrial strategy: a missing link in British economic policy', *Oxford Review of Economic Policy*, vol. 9.

Cowling, K. and Waterson, M. (1976), 'Price cost margins and market structure', *Economica*, vol. 43.

Crosland, C.A.R. (1956), *The Future of Socialism*, London: Jonathan Cape.

Cutler, T. (1992), 'Vocational training and British economic performance: a further instalment of the "British labour problem"', *Work, Employment and Society*, vol. 6.

Davidson, P. (1977), 'Money and general equilibrium', *Economie Appliquee*, vol. 4 (reprinted in P. Davidson, *Money and Employment* (edited by Louise Davidson), London: Macmillan, 1992).

Davidson, P. (1982–3), 'Rational expectations: a fallacious foundation for studying crucial decison-making', *Journal of Post Keynesian Economics* vol. 5.

Davidson, P. (1983a), 'The dubious labor market analysis in Meltzer's restatement', *Journal of Economic Literature*, vol. 21.

Davidson, P. (1983b), 'The marginal product curve is not the demand for labor curve and Lucas's labor supply function is not the supply curve for labor in the real world', *Journal of Post Keynesian Economics*, vol. 6.

Davidson, P. (1991), 'Is probability theory relevant for uncertainty? A post Keynesian perspective', *Journal of Economic Perspectives*, vol. 5.

Davidson, P. (1993), 'Would Keynes be a new Keynesian?', *Eastern Economic Journal*, vol. 18.

Desai, M. (1973) 'Growth cycles and inflation in a model of class struggle', *Journal of Economic Theory*, vol. 6.

Dow, S. (1985), *Macroeconomic Thought: A Methodological Approach*, Oxford: Basil Blackwell.

Drazen, A. (1980), 'Recent developments in macroeconomics disequilibrium theory', *Econometrica*, vol. 48.

Dugger, W.M. (1983), 'The transactions cost analysis of Oliver E. Williamson: a new synthesis?' *Journal of Economic Issues* vol. 17.

Dunlop, J. (1938), 'The movement of real and money wage rates', *Economic Journal* vol. 48.

Dutt, A.K. (1987), 'Alternative closures again: comment on "Growth, distribution and inflation"', *Cambridge Journal of Economics*, vol. 11.

Dutt, A.K. (1988), 'Competition, monopoly power and the prices of production', *Thames Papers in Political Economy*, Autumn 1988 (reprinted in Arestis and Kitromilides, 1989)

Earl, P.E. and Kay, N. (1985) 'How economists can accept Shackle's critique of economic doctrine without arguing themselves out of their jobs', *Journal of Economic Studies*, vol. 12.

Easton, B.H. (1978), 'Price formation, the Phillips curve, and factor shares', in Bergstrom et alia (1978)

Eatwell, J. and Milgate, M. (eds) (1983), *Keynes's Economics and the Theory of Value and Distribution*, London: Duckworth.

Edwards, R. (1979), *Contested Terrain*, London: Heinneman.

Edwards, R., Reich,M. and Gordon, D. (eds) (1973), *Labour Market Segmentation*, Lexington: Lexington Books.

Eichner, A.S. (1973), 'A theory of the determination of the markup under oligopoly', *Economic Journal*, vol. 83 (reprinted in Sawyer, 1988).

Eichner, A.S. (1976), *The Megacorp and Oligopoly, Micro-foundations of Macro Dynamics* Cambridge: Cambridge University Press.

Eichner, A.S. (ed.) (1983), *Why Economics is Not Yet a Science* , New York: M.E. Sharpe.

Eichner, A.S. (1985a), *Towards a New Economics*. New York: M.E. Sharpe.

Eichner, A.S. (1985b), 'Preface', in P. Arestis and T. Skouras (eds) *Post Keynesian Economic Theory*, Brighton: Wheatsheaf.

Eichner, A.S. (1987), *The Macrodynamics of Advanced Market Economies* New York: M.E.Sharpe.

Eichner, A.S. and Kregel, J. (1975), 'An essay on post Keynesian theory: a new paradigm in economics', *Journal of Economic Literature*, vol. 13.

Epstein, G.A. and J.B. Schor (1990), 'Profit squeeze and Keynesian theory' in S.A. Marglin and J.B. Schor (eds), *The Golden Age of Capitalism*, Oxford: Clarendon Press.

Evans, P. (1985), 'Do large deficits produce high interest rates ?', *American Economic Review*, vol. 75.

Ferguson, P. (1988) *Industrial Economics: Issues and Perspectives*. London: Macmillan.

Findlay, D.W. and Parker, D. (1992), 'Military spending and interest rates', *Defence Economics*, vol. 3.

Flanagan, R.J.(1992), 'Wages and wage policies in market economies: lessons for central and Eastern Europe', *OECD Economic Studies*, no. 18, Spring.

Francis, A. (1980), 'Company objectives, managerial motivations and the behaviour of large firms: an empirical test of the theory of "managerial" capitalism', *Cambridge Journal of Economics*, vol. 4.

Frank, J.F. (1986), *The New Keynesian Economics*, Brighton: Harvester Wheatsheaf.

Friedman, M. (1968), 'The role of monetary policy', *American Economic Review*, vol. 58.

Friedman, M. (1982), *Capitalism and Freedom*, Chicago: Chicago University Press.

Galbraith, J.K. (1967), *The New Industrial State*, Harmondsworth: Penguin Books.

Gerrard, W. (1989), *Theory of the Capitalist Economy: Towards a Post Classical Synthesis*, Oxford: Blackwell.

Gerrard, W. (1990), 'On matters methodological in economics', *Journal of Economic Surveys*, vol. 4.

Gerrard, W. (1994), 'Probability, uncertainty and behaviour: a Keynesian perspective', in J. Hillard and S. Dow (eds), *Keynes, Knowledge and Uncertainty*, Aldershot: Edward Elgar.

Godley, W. and Nordhaus, W. (1972), 'Pricing in the trade cycle', *Economic Journal*, vol. 82.

Gomes, G.M. (1982), 'The irrationality of rational expectations', *Journal of Post Keynesian Economics*, vol. 5.

Goodhart, C. (1989), 'The conduct on monetary policy', *Economic Journal*, vol. 99.

Goodwin, R.M. (1967), 'A growth cycle', in C.H. Feinstein (ed.) *Socialism, Capitalism and Growth*, Cambridge: Cambridge University Press.

Gordon, D.M., Edwards, R. and Reich, M. (1982), *Segmented Work, Divided Workers*, Cambridge: Cambridge University Press.

Gordon, M.J. (1993), *Finance, Investment and Macroeconomics*, Aldershot: Edward Elgar.

Grossman, H. (1972), 'Was Keynes a Keynesian?', *Journal of Economic Literature*, vol. 10.

Hahn, F. (1978), 'On nonWalrasian equilibria', *Review of Economic Studies*, vol. 45.

Hall, R. and Hitch, C. (1939), 'Price theory and business behaviour', *Oxford Economic Papers*, no.2 (reprinted in Sawyer, 1988).

Hamouda, O. and Harcourt, G. (1988), 'Post Keynesianism: from criticism to coherence?', *Bulletin of Economic Research*, vol. 40 (reprinted in Pheby, 1989).

Harcourt, G.C. (1982), *The Social Science Imperialists*, London: Routledge.

Harcourt, G.C. (1987), 'The legacy of Keynes : theoretical methods and unfinished business', in David A. Reese (ed.) *The Legacy of Keynes, Nobel*

Conference XXII, San Francisco: Harper & Row (reprinted in C. Sardoni (ed.), *On Political Economists and Modern Political Economy: Selected Essays of G.C. Harcourt,* London: Routledge).

Harcourt, G.C. (1992a), *On Political Economists and Modern Political Economy,* edited by Claudio Sardoni, London: Routledge.

Harcourt, G.C. (1992b), 'Markets, madness and a middle way', *The Second Donald Horne Address,* National Centre for Australian Studies, Monash University.

Harcourt, G.C. and Kenyon, P. (1976), 'Pricing and the investment decision', *Kyklos,* vol. 29 (reprinted in Sawyer, 1988).

Hart, O. (1982), 'A model of imperfect competition with Keynesian features', *Quarterly Journal of Economics,* vol. 97.

Hay, D. and Morris, D. (1991), *Industrial Economics and Organization,* Oxford: Oxford University Press.

Hayek, F.A. (1988), *The Fatal Conceit,* London: Routledge.

Henderson, W., Dudley-Evans, T. and Backhouse, R. (eds) (1993), *Economics and Language,* London: Routledge.

Henry, S.G.B., Sawyer, M. and Smith, P. (1976), 'Models of inflation in the U.K.: an evaluation', *National Institute Economic Review,* no. 76.

Hicks, J. (1974), *The Crisis in Keynesian Economics,* Blackwell, Oxford.

Hilferding, R. (1981), *Finance Capital.* Based on translations by Watnick, M. and Gordan, S., edited with an introduction by Bottomore, T. London: Routledge & Kegan Paul. Original published in German 1910.

Hirschman, A.O. (1971), *Exit, Voice and Loyalty,* Cambridge, Mass.: Harvard University Press.

Hirschman, A.O. (1985), 'Against parsimony: three ways of complicating some categories of economic discourse', *Economics and Philosophy,* vol. 1.

Hodgson, G. (1988), *Economics and Institutions,* Oxford: Polity Press.

Hodgson, G. (1989), 'Post Keynesianism and institutionalism: the missing link' in Pheby (1989).

Hodgson, G. (1994), 'Corporate culture and evolving competences', *Research Papers in Management Studies, University of Cambridge,* no. 14.

Hodgson, G, Samuels,W. and Tool,M. (eds) (1994), *The Elgar Companion to Institutional and Evolutionary Economics,* Aldershot: Edward Elgar.

Jorgenson, D. (1967), 'The theory of investment', in R. Ferber (ed.) *Determinants of Investment Behaviour,* New York: National Bureau of Economic Research.

Kahn, R. (1984), *The Making of Keynes' General Theory,* Cambridge: Cambridge University Press.

Kahn, R. (1989), *The Economics of the Short Period,* London: Macmillan (originally submitted as fellowship dissertation, King's College Cambridge, 1929).

Kaldor, N. (1940), 'A model of the trade cycle', *Economic Journal,* vol.50.

Kaldor, N. (1955), 'Alternative theories of distribution', *Review of Economic Studies*, vol. 23.

Kaldor, N. (1957), 'A model of economic growth', *Economy Journal*, vol. 67.

Kaldor, N. (1961), 'Capital accumulation and economic growth', in F. Lutz (ed.), *The Theory of Capital*, London: Macmillan.

Kaldor, N. (1970) 'The new monetarism', *Lloyds Bank Review*, no.97.

Kaldor, N. (1972), 'The irrelevance of equilibrium economics', *Economic Journal*, vol. 82.

Kaldor, N. (1978), *Further Essays in Economic Theory*, London: Duckworth.

Kaldor, N.(1983) 'Keynesian economics after fifty years' in Worswick and Trevithick (1983).

Kaldor, N. (1985), *Economics without Equilibrium*, Cardiff: University College Cardiff Press.

Kaldor, N. and Trevithick, J. (1981), 'A Keynesian perspective on money', *Lloyds Bank Review*, no. 139, Spring (reprinted in Sawyer, 1988).

Kalecki, M. (1933), *Proba teorii koniunktury*, Institute of Research on Business Cycles and Prices, Warsaw. (English version appears as Chapter 1 of Kalecki, 1971a).

Kalecki, M. (1935), 'A macrodynamic theory of business cycles', *Econometrica*, vol. 3

Kalecki, M. (1937a), 'A theory of the business cycle', *Review of Economic Studies*, vol. 4.

Kalecki, M. (1937b), 'Principle of increasing risk', *Economica*, vol. 4.

Kalecki, M. (1938), 'The determinants of distribution of the national income', *Econometrica*, vol. 6.

Kalecki, M. (1940), 'The supply curve of an industry under imperfect competition', *Review of Economic Studies*, vol. 7.

Kalecki, M. (1941), 'A theorem on technical progress', *Review of Economic Studies*, vol. 8.

Kalecki, M. (1942), 'Mr. Whitman on the concept of "degree of monopoly"', *Economic Journal*, vol. 52.

Kalecki, M. (1943a), 'Political aspects of full employment', *Political Quarterly*, vol. 14.

Kalecki, M. (1943b), *Studies in Economic Dynamics*, London: Allen & Unwin.

Kalecki, M. (1944a), 'Full employment by stimulating private investment?', *Oxford Economic Papers*, no. 7.

Kalecki, M. (1944b), 'Professor Pigou on "The classical stationary state": A Comment', *Economic Journal*, vol. 54.

Kalecki, M. (1970), 'Theories of growth in different social systems', *Scientia*, no. 56.

Kalecki, M. (1971a), *Selected Essays on the Dynamics of the Capitalist Economy* Cambridge: Cambridge University Press.

Kalecki, M. (1971b), 'The class struggle and the distribution of national income', *Kyklos*, vol. 24.

Kalecki, M. (1990), *Collected Works of Michal Kalecki,* vol. 1 (ed. J. Osiantynski), Oxford: Clarendon Press.

Kay, N.M. (1984), *The Emergent Firm.* London: Macmillan.

Kay, N.M. (1989), 'Post-Keynesian economics and new approaches to industrial economics', in J.Pheby, (ed.) *New Directions in Post-Keynesian Economics,* Aldershot: Edward Elgar.

Kennedy, P. (1988), *The Rise and Fall of Nations,* New York: Vintage

Keynes, J.M. (1930), *A Treatise on Money,* London: Macmillan.

Keynes, J.M. (1936), *The General Theory of Employment, Interest and Money,* London:Macmillian.

Keynes, J.M. (1937), 'The general theory of employment', *Quarterly Journal of Economics,* vol. 51.

Keynes, J.M. (1939), 'Relative movements of real wages and output', *Economic Journal,* vol. 49.

Keynes, J.M. (1971), *The General Theory of Employment, Interest and Money: The Collected Writings of J.M. Keynes,* vol. 7, London: Macmillan.

Keynes, J.M. (1972), *Essays in Biography: The Collected Writings of J.M. Keynes,* vol. 10, London: Macmillan.

Keynes,J.M.(1973), *The General Theory and After: Part II Defence and development: Collected Writings,* vol. 14, London: Macmillan.

Keynes,J.M.(1979), *The General Theory and After: A Supplement: Collected Writings,* vol. 29, London: Macmillan

Keynes, J.M. (1983), *Economic Articles and Correspondence: Investment and Editorial: Collected Writings,* vol. 12, London: Macmillan.

Kriesler, P. (1987), *Kalecki's Microanalysis: The Development of Kalecki's Analysis of Pricing and Distribution,* Cambridge: Cambridge University Press.

Kriesler, P. (1989), 'Kalecki's pricing theory revisited', *Journal of Post Keynesian Economics,* vol. 11

Lange, O. (1937), 'On the economic theory of socialism', *Review of Economic Studies,* vol. 4.

Lavoie, M. (1992), *Foundations of Post Keynesian Economics,* Aldershot: Edward Elgar.

Lawson, T. (1988), 'Probability and uncertainty in economic analysis', *Journal of Post Keynesian Economics,* vol. 11.

Lawson,T. (1989), 'Abstraction, tendencies and stylised facts: a realist approach to economic analysis', *Cambridge Journal of Economics,* vol. 13.

Layard, R. and Nickell, S. (1985), 'The causes of British unemployment', *National Institute Economic Review,* no. 110.

Layard, R. and Nickell, S. (1986), 'Unemployment in Britain', *Economica,* vol. 53 (Supplement).

Lee, F.S. (1986), 'Kalecki's pricing theory: two comments', *Journal of Post Keynesian Economics,* vol. 8.

Lee, F.S. (1990), 'G.C. Means's doctrine of adminstered prices' in P. Arestis and Y. Kitromilides (eds), *Theory and Policy in Political Economy*, Aldershot: Edward Elgar.

Lee, F.S. *et alia* (1986), 'P.W.S. Andrews's theory of competitive oligopoly: a new interpretation', *British Review of Economic Issues*, vol. 8

Leibenstein, H. (1966), 'Allocative efficiency vs X-efficiency' *American Economic Review*, vol. 56.

Leijonhufvud, A. (1968), *On Keynesian Economics and the Economics of Keynes*, Oxford: Oxford University Press.

Lekachman, R. (1977), 'The radical Keynes', in R. Skidelsky (ed.), *The End of the Keynesian Era*, London: Macmillan.

Lenin, V.I. (1936), *Imperialism: the Highest State of Capitalism*, in V.I. Lenin, *Selected Works*, vol. 5, London: Lawrence & Wishart. First published in 1916.

Lester, R.A. (1946), 'Shortcomings of marginal analysis for wage-employment problems', *American Economic Review* vol. 36.

Levine,D.(1981), *Economic Theory*, Vol II, London: Routledge & Kegan Paul.

Lindbeck, A. and Snower, D. (1988), *The Insider Outsider Theory of Employment and Unemployment*, Cambridge Mass.: MIT Press.

Loomes, G. and Taylor, C. (1992), 'Nontransitive preferences over gains and losses', *Economic Journal*, vol. 102.

Machlup, F. (1946), 'Marginal analysis and empirical research', *American Economic Review*, vol. 36.

MacKay, R. Ross (1993),'Local labour markets, regional development, capital and human capital', *University College of North Wales, Bangor, School of Accounting, Banking and Economics Research Papers Series RP93/35*

McCloskey, D.N. (1986), *The Rhetoric of Economics*, Brighton: Harvester Press.

McDonald, I. (1985), 'Market power and unemployment', *International Journal of Industrial Organisation*, vol 3.

Malinvaud, E. (1977), *The Theory of Unemployment Reconsidered*, Oxford: Basil Blackwell.

Malinvaud, E. (1984), *Mass Unemployment*, Oxford: Basil Blackwell.

Mandel, E. (1964), 'The economics of neocapitalism', *Socialist Register*

Marglin,S. (1984), 'Growth, distribution, and inflation: a centennial synthesis', *Cambridge Journal of Economics*, vol. 8.

Marris, R. (1964), *The Economic Theory of 'Managerial' Capitalism*, London: Macmillan.

Marsden, D. (1986), *The End of Economic Man?: Custom and Competition in Labour Markets*, Wheatsheaf Books, Brighton.

Marx, K. (1976), *Capital*, vol. 1 (translated by Ben Fowkes), Harmondsworth: Penguin Books: first published 1867.

Matthews, R. (1968), 'Why has Britain had full employment since the war?', *Economic Journal*, vol. 78.

Means, G.C. (1933), 'The corporate revolution', manuscript of doctoral dissertation, Harvard University, Gardiner C. Means Papers, series I, Franklin D. Roosevelt Library.

Means, G.C. (1935), 'Industrial prices and their relative flexibility', US Senate Document 13, 74th Congress, 1st Session, Washington.

Means, G.C. (1936), 'Notes on inflexible prices', *American Economic Review*, vol. 26, Supplement.

Means, G.C. (1972), 'The administered-price thesis reconfirmed', *American Economic Review*, vol. 62.

Michie, J. (1987), *Wages in the Business Cycle: An Empirical and Methodological Analysis*, London: Frances Pinter.

Milgate, M. (1987), 'Thomas Carlyle', in J. Eatwell, M. Milgate and J. Newman (eds) *The New Palgrave*, London: Macmillan.

Milgrom, P. and Roberts, J. (1992), *Economics, Organization and Management*, New York: Prentice-Hall.

Minsky, H.P. (1975), *John Maynard Keynes*, New York: Columbia University Press.

Minsky, H.P. (1978), 'The financial instability hypothesis: a restatement', *Thames Papers in Political Economy*, Autumn.

Minsky, H.P. (1982), *Can 'It' Happen Again*, New York: M.E. Sharpe.

Modigliani, F. and Miller, M.H. (1958), 'The cost of capital, corporation finance and the theory of investment', *American Economic Review*, vol. 48.

Moore, B. (1979), 'The endogenous money stock', *Journal of Post Keynesian Economics*, vol. 2.

Moore, B. (1983), 'Unpacking the post Keynesian black box: bank lending and the money supply', *Journal of Post Keynesian Economics*, vol. 5.

Moore, B. (1984), 'Keynes and the endogeneity of the money stock', *Studi Economici*, vol. 22.

Moore, B. (1988), *Horizontalist and Verticalists*, Cambridge: Cambridge University Press.

Moore, B. (1989), 'The endogeneity of credit money', *Review of Political Economy*, vol. 1

Morgan, P.B. and Tustin, D. (1992), 'The perception and efficiency of labour supply choices by pigeons', *Economic Journal*, vol. 102.

Myrdal, G. (1944), *The American Dilemma: The Negro Problem and Modern Democracy*, New York: Harper & Row.

Myrdal, G. (1957), *Economic Theory and Underdeveloped Regions*, London: Duckworth.

Ng,Y.K. (1986), *Mesoeconomics*, Brighton: Wheatsheaf Books.

Nielsen, K. (1994), 'Fordism and Post-Fordism', in Hodgson, Samuels and Tool (1994).

Nolan, P. (1994), 'Fordism and Post-Fordism', in Arestis and Sawyer (1994).

O'Donnell, R.M. (1989), *Keynes: Philosophy, Economics and Politics*, London: Macmillan.

OECD (1977), *Towards Full Employment and Price Stability*, Paris, 1977 (the McCracken Report).

Okun, A.(1981), *Prices and Quantities: A Macroeconomic Analysis*, London: Blackwell.

Ong, N.-P. (1981), 'Target pricing, competition and growth', *Journal of Post Keynesian Economics* vol. 4.

Panico, C. and Salvadori, N. (eds) (1993), *Post Keynesian Theory of Growth and Distribution*, Aldershot: Edward Elgar.

Pasinetti, L. (1962), 'Rate of profit and income distribution in relation to the rate of economic growth', *Review of Economic Studies*, vol. 29 (reprinted in Sawyer, 1988).

Pasinetti, L. (1974), *Growth and Income Distribution*, Cambridge: Cambridge University Press.

Pasinetti, L. (1981), *Structural Change and Economic Growth*, Cambridge: Cambridge University Press.

Patinkin, D. (1951), 'Price flexibility and full employment' in *Readings in Monetary Theory*, selected by a Committee of the American Economic Association, Blakiston, New York.

Patinkin, D. (1965), *Money, Interest and Prices*, second edition, London: Harper & Row.

Patinkin, D. (1982), *Anticipation of the General Theory? And Other Essays on Keynes*, Oxford: Basil Blackwell.

Pheby, J. (ed.) (1989), *New Directions in Post Keynesian Economics*, Aldershot: Edward Elgar.

Phillips, A.W. (1958), 'The relation between unemployment and the rate of change of money wage rates in the United Kingdom, 1861–1957', *Economica*, vol. 25.

Pigou, A. (1943), 'The classical stationary state', *Economic Journal*, vol. 53.

Plosser, C. (1989), 'Understanding real business cycles', *Journal of Economic Perspectives*, vol. 3.

Pollin, R. (1991), 'Two theories of money supply endogeniety: some empirical evidence', *Journal of Post Keynesian Economics*, vol. 13

Porter, M. (1990), *The Competitive Advantage of Nations*, London: Macmillan.

Radcliffe Report (1959), *The Committee on the Workings of the Monetary System*, London: HMSO, Cmnd 827.

Reich, M. (1984), 'Segmented labour: time series hypothesis and evidence', *Cambridge Journal of Economics*, vol.8.

Reynolds, P. (1984), 'An empirical analysis of the degree of monopoly theory of distribution', *Bulletin of Economic Research*, vol. 36.

Reynolds, P. (1987), *Political Economy: A Synthesis of Kaleckian and Post Keyneisan Economics*, Brighton: Harvester-Wheatsheaf.

Reynolds, P. (1989), 'Kaleckian and Post-Keynesian theories of pricing: some extensions and implications' in Arestis and Kitromilides (1989).

Richardson, G.B. (1960), *Information and Investment*, Oxford: Oxford University Press.

Robbins, L. (1932), *An Essay on the Nature and Significance of Economic Science*. London: Macmillan.

Robinson, J. (1933), *The Economics of Imperfect Competition*, London: Macmillan.

Robinson, J. (1956), *The Accumulation of Capital*, London: Macmillan.

Robinson, J. (1972), 'The second crisis in economic theory', *American Economic Review*, vol. 62.

Robinson, J. (1976), 'Michal Kalecki: a neglected prophet', *New York Review of Books*, 4 March 1976.

Robinson, J. (1977), 'What are the questions?', *Journal of Economic Literature*, vol. 15.

Romer, D. (1993), 'The new Keynesian synthesis', *Journal of Economic Perspectives*, vol. 7.

Rothschild, K. (1978), 'Arbeitslose: Gibt's Die ?', *Kyklos*, vol. 31.

Routh, G. (1980), *Occupation and Pay in Great Britain, 1906–1979*, London: Macmillan.

Rowthorn, R. (1977), 'Conflict, inflation and money', *Cambridge Journal of Economics*, vol.1.

Rowthorn, R. (1992), 'Centralisation, employment and wage dispersion', *Economic Journal*, vol. 102.

Rutherford, M. (1984), 'Rational expectations and Keynesian uncertainty', *Journal of Post Keynesian Economics*, vol. 6

Samuels, W. (1987), 'Institutional economics', in J. Eatwell, M. Millgate and P. Newman (eds) *The New Palgrave*, London: Macmillan.

Samuels, W. and Medema, S.G. (1989), 'Gardiner C. Means's Institutional and Post-Keynesian Economics', *Review of Political Economy*, vol. 1.

Samuelson, P. (1939), 'Interaction between the multiplier analysis and the principle of acceleration', *Review of Economics and Statistics*, vol. 21.

Sargan, J.D. (1964),'Wages, prices in the United Kingdom' in P. Hart, G. Mills and J. Whittaker (eds), *Econometric Analysis for National Economic Planning*, London: Butterworth.

Sawyer, M. (1982a), *Macroeconomics in Question*, Brighton: Wheatsheaf Books.

Sawyer, M. (1982b), 'Collective bargaining, oligopoly and macro economics', *Oxford Economic Papers*, vol. 34.

Sawyer, M. (1983), *Business Pricing and Inflation*, London: Macmillan.

Sawyer, M. (1985a), *Economics of Michal Kalecki*, London: Macmillan.

Sawyer, M. (1985b), *Economics of Industries and Firms*, second edition, London: Croom Helm.

Sawyer, M. (1987), 'The political economy of the Phillips' curve', *Thames Papers in Political Economy*, Summer.

Sawyer, M. (ed.) (1988a), *Post Keynesian Economics*, Aldershot: Edward Elgar.

Sawyer, M. (1988b), 'Theories of monopoly capitalism', *Journal of Economic Surveys*, vol. 2.

Sawyer, M. (1988c), 'Introduction', in M. Sawyer (ed.) *Post Keynesian Economics* Aldershot: Edward Elgar.

Sawyer, M. (1988d), 'On the relationship between real wages and unemployment', *Cyprus Journal of Economics*, vol. 1.

Sawyer, M. (1989), *The Challenge of Radical Political Economy*, Hemel Hempstead: Harvester Wheatsheaf.

Sawyer, M. (1991a), 'Analysing the operation of market economies in the spirit of Kaldor and Kalecki', in J. Michie (ed.), *The Economics of Restructuring and Intervention*, Aldershot: Edward Elgar.

Sawyer, M. (1991b), 'Post Keynesian macroeconomics', in I. Stewart et alia (eds), *Economics in Perspective*, London: Routledge. (amended as Chapter 3 of this volume.)

Sawyer, M. (1991c), 'The economics of shortage', in J. Michie (ed.), *The Economics of Restructuring and Intervention*, Aldershot: Edward Elgar.

Sawyer, M. (1992a), 'The nature and role of the market', *Social Concept*, vol. 6, no. 2. (A slightly revised version appeared in C. Pitelis (ed.), *Transaction Costs, Markets and Hierarchies*, Oxford: Blackwell, 1993.)

Sawyer, M. (1992b), 'Prices and pricing in the post Keynesian and Kaleckian traditions', in G. Mongiovi and C. Ruhl (eds), *Alternative Traditions in Macroeconomics*, Aldershot: Edward Elgar.

Sawyer, M. (1992c), 'Reflections on the nature and role of industrial policy' *Metroeconomica*, vol. 43.

Sawyer, M. (1992d), 'On the relationship between the origins of Post Keynesian pricing theory and macroeconomics', in P. Arestis and V. Chick (eds), *Recent Developments in Post Keynesian Economics*, Aldershot: Edward Elgar. (Amended as Chapter 7 of this volume.)

Sawyer, M. (1994a) 'Post Keynesian and Marxist notions of competition: towards a synthesis', in M. Glick (ed.), *Competition, Technology and Money: Classical and Post-Keynesian Perspectives*, Aldershot: Edward Elgar.

Sawyer, M. (1994b), 'Industrial strategy and employment in Europe', in J. Grieve Smith and J. Michie (ed.), *Unemployment in Europe – Policies for Growth*, London: Academic Press.

Scherer, F. (1980), *Industrial Market Structure and Economic Performance*. Skokie, Illinois: Rand McNally.

Schettkat, R. (1992), *The Labor Market Dynamics of Economic Restructuring*, New York: Praeger.

Schumpeter, J. (1954), *History of Economic Analysis*, London: Allen & Unwin.

Shackle, G. (1972), *Epistemics and Economics,* Cambridge: Cambridge University Press.

Shackle, G. (1983–4) 'The romantic mountain and the classic lake: Alan Coddington's Keynesian economics', *Journal of Post Keynesian Economics,* vol. 6.

Shackle, G. (1989), 'What did the *General Theory* do?' in J. Pheby (ed.) *New Directions in Post-Keynesian Economics,* Aldershot: Edward Elgar.

Shah, A. and Desai, M. (1981), 'Growth cycles with induced technical change' *Economic Journal,* vol. 91.

Shapiro, A. (1992), *We're Number One! Where America Stands and Falls in the New World Order,* New York.

Shapiro, C. and Stiglitz, J.E. (1984), 'Involuntary unemployment as a worker discipline device', *American Economic Review,* vol. 74.

Shapiro, M. and Ahlburg, D. (1983), 'Suicide: the ultimate cost of unemployment', *Journal of Post Keynesian Economics,* vol. 5.

Shapiro, N. (1981), 'Pricing and the growth of the firm', *Journal of Post Keynesian Economics,* vol. 4.

Silvestre, J. (1990), 'There may be unemployment when the labour market is competitive and the output market is not', *Economic Journal,* vol. 100.

Skott, P. (1985), 'Vicious circles and cumulative causation', *Thames Papers in Political Economy,* Summer.

Skott, P. (1989a), 'Effective demand, class struggle and cyclical growth', *International Economic Review,* vol. 30.

Skott, P. (1989b), *Conflict and Aggregate Demand,* Cambridge: Cambridge University Press.

Solow, R. (1956), 'A contribution to the theory of economic growth', *Quarterly Journal of Economics,* vol. 70.

Solow, R. (1979), 'Alternative approaches to macroeconomic theory: a partial view', *Canadian Journal of Economics,* vol. 12.

Solow, R. (1986), 'Unemployment: getting the questions right', *Economica,* vol. 53.

Spence, A.M. (1977), 'Entry, capacity, investment and oligopolistic pricing', *Bell Journal of Economics,* vol. 8.

Sraffa, P. (1926), 'The laws of return under competitive conditions', *Economic Journal,* vol. 36.

Sraffa, P. (1960), *Production of Commodities by Means of Commodities,* Cambridge: Cambridge University Press.

Stafford, G.B.S. (1970), 'Full employment since the war: a comment', *Economic Journal,* vol. 80.

Steindl, J.(1952), *Maturity and Stagnation in American Capitalism,* Oxford: Blackwell (reissued with new introduction by Monthly Review Press, 1976).

Steindl, J. (1979), 'Stagnation theory and stagnation policy', *Cambridge Journal of Economics,* vol. 3.

Stewart, M. (1972), *Keynes and After*, Harmondsworth: Penguin

Stigler, G. (1947), 'The kinky oligopoly demand curve and rigid prices', *Journal of Political Economy*, vol. 55. (Reprinted in American Economic Association, *Readings in Price Theory*, London: Allen & Unwin, 1953.)

Stiglitz, J. (1985), 'Credit markets and the control of capital', *Journal of Money, Credit and Banking*, vol. 17.

Stiglitz, J. and Weiss, A. (1981), 'Credit rationing in markets with imperfect information', *American Economic Review*, vol. 71.

Sweezy, P. (1939), 'Conditions of demand under oligopoly', *Journal of Political Economy*, vol. 47. (Reprinted in American Economic Association, *Readings in Price Theory*, London: Allen & Unwin, 1953.)

Sylos Labini, P. (1984), 'On the concept of the optimum rate of profit' in *The Forces of Economic Growth and Decline*, Cambridge, Mass.: MIT Press.

Symons, J. and Layard, R. (1984), 'Neoclassical demand for labour functions for six major economies', *Economic Journal*, vol. 94.

Targetti, F. and B. Kinda-Hass, (1982), 'Kalecki's review of Keynes' *General Theory'*, *Australian Economic Papers*, vol. 21 (reprinted in Kalecki, 1990).

Tarshis, L. (1939), 'Changes in real and money wages', *Economic Journal*, vol. 49.

Thirlwall, A. (1972), 'The Phillips curve: a historical note', *Economica*, vol. 39.

Thirlwall, A. (1983), 'Comment' in Worswick and Trevithick (1983).

Thirlwall, A. (1987), *Nicholas Kaldor*, Brighton: Wheatsheaf Books.

Tobin, J. (1983), 'Comment' on Kaldor (1983) in Worswick and Trevithick (1983).

Toporowski, J. (1993), *The Economics Financial Markets and the 1987 Crash*, Aldershot: Edward Elgar.

Velupillai, K. (1983), 'A neoCambridge Model of income distribution and unemployment', *Journal of Post Keynesian Economics*, vol. 5.

Weiss, A. (1990), *Efficiency Wages*, Princeton: Princeton University Press.

Weitzman, M. (1982), 'Increasing returns and the foundations of unemployment Theory', *Economic Journal*, vol. 92.

Wible, J. R. (1984–5), 'An epistemic critique of rational expectations and the neoclassical macroeconomic research program', *Journal of Post Keynesian Economics*, vol. 7.

Williamson, O.E. (1964), *Economics of Discretionary Behaviour*, London: Kershaw.

Williamson, O.E. (1975), *Markets and Hierarchies*, New York: Free Press.

Williamson, O.E. (1986), *Economic Organisation: Firms, Markets and Policy Controls*, Brighton: Wheatsheaf.

Wood, A. (1975), *A Theory of Profits*, Cambridge: Cambridge University Press.

World Bank (1993), *World Development Report, 1993*, Oxford: Oxford University Press.

Worswick, D. and Trevithick, J. (eds) (1983), *Keynes and the Modern World*, Cambridge: Cambridge University Press.

Wray, R. (1990), *Money and Credit in Capitalist Economies: The Endogenous Money Approach*, Aldershot: Edward Elgar.

Wulwick, N. (1987), 'The Radcliffe central bankers', *Journal of Economic Studies*, vol. 14.

Index

References to post Keynesian economics are not specifically indexed

Abernathy, W. 27
AD-curve 81, 91,100, 101, 108, 111
adjustment mechanisms 112–3
administered prices 92, 104, 135–6, 141
aggregate demand 4, 43, 44, 56, 70, 74, 75–6, 79–80, 81, 87, 100–1, 105, 108–9, 113, 114, 120, 123,125, 131
Ahlburg, D. 6
allocative role of markets 4
allocative role of price 54–5, 56
Amable, B. 22
Andrews, P.W.S. 134
Appelbaum, E. 41
Arestis, P. 6, 42, 51, 163
Arrow, K. 102, 149
atomistic competition 31
auctioneer, Walrasian 54, 96, 102, 125, 135, 140
Auerbach, P. 19, 65, 160
Austrian approach 19

Backhouse, R. 67
balance of trade 25
Baran, P. 150, 151, 157, 177
Baranzini, M. 9
Basile, L. 38
Battalio, R.C. 12
Baumol, W. 22, 155, 159
Bausor, R. 46
Becker, G. 12
Bhaduri, A. 167, 180
Boltho, A. 7
bounded rationality 59, 151
Bowles, S. 15
Bowley's Law 89–90

Bradley, I. 58, 152
Brenner, H. 6
Brothwell, J. 123, 128
Brown, A. 9
budget deficit 23
Burchell, B. 6
business cycles 45, 48–9

Calmfors, L. 25
capacity utilisation 73–4, 75–6, 82, 88-9, 107–8, 181
Carabelli, A.M. 16
Carlyle, T. 8, 12
Carvalho, F. 52, 59, 171
centrapetalism 21, 64
Chamberlin, E. H. 11, 119, 120, 121
Chang, W.W. 48
Chick, V. 16, 33, 37, 45, 53, 109, 119, 131
Clark, A.E. 13
Clark, K. 27
Clarke, R. 38, 148
Clifton, J. 65, 160
Clower, R. 37, 109, 111
Coase, R. 20, 62, 160
Coddington, A. 47, 60
Colander, D.C. 46
Collard, D. 132
competition 63–4, 118, 155–158
competitive advantage 21
constraints on full employment 22
consumer behaviour 60
cost-determined prices 97, 138
costs of unemployment 6, 11, 13
Coutts, K. 40, 172, 178
Cowling, K. 21, 26, 38, 64, 148, 150, 158, 173, 174, 185

credit money 33–7 *passim*, 53-4
Crosland, C.A.R. 106
cumulative causation 21–2, 63–4
Cutler, T. 26

Davidson, P. 16, 18, 32, 46, 56, 122
demand-determined prices 97, 137
demand-side 3–5 *passim*, 53, 70,
    146
demand and supply analysis 15–20
demand deficiency 1
demand for labour 72–3, 94, 97,
    125, 171
demand management 84
Desai, M. 49
diminishing returns 128
dismal science 2, 8–10, 27
Dow, S. 51, 66
Drazen, A. 107, 111
Drifill, J. 25
Dudley–Evans, T. 67
Dugger, W.M. 161
Duhem–Quinne thesis 67
Dunlop, J. 127, 128, 130
Dutt, A.K. 155, 179, 185

Earl, P. 47
Easton, B.H. 89
Eatwell, J. 58, 130
economic policy implications 87–91
economics as a science 6, 8–10
    passim, 66–9 *passim*
education and training 26–7
Edwards,R. 64
Eichner, A. 10, 30, 39, 40, 48, 50,
    51, 65, 66, 67, 135, 143, 150,
    152, 154, 155, 157, 167, 170,
    172, 174, 176, 181, 182, 190
employment 79–80
Epstein, G.A. 189
equilibrium analysis 32, 51, 63, 71
equilibrium approach 63, 113
Evans, P. 23
excess capacity 11, 56

expectations 32, 45, 46–7, 57–61,
    112–3, 173

Ferguson, P. 148
finance 45-6
    external 189–2
    sources of 168
financial instability hypothesis 36
financial sector 27–8, 163–9
financing requirements 152, 153,
    175, 181
Findlay, D.W. 23
first classical postulate 128
fixprice 92, 103, 104, 137, 141
Flanagan, R.J. 17
flexprice 92, 103, 104, 137, 143
Fordism 161, 163
Francis,A. 159
Frank, J. 56, 72
Friedman, M. 8, 32, 41, 67
full cost pricing 139–0, 151, 155
full employment 14, 16, 23–9, 130
functional role of unemployment
    14–15

Galbraith , J.K. 167
general equilibrium analysis 32, 66,
    130, 143, 170
General Theory 13, 37, 47, 60,
    112,118, 119, 120, 122–4, 128,
    134, 137
Gerrard, W. 37, 47, 54, 68, 144
Godley, W. 40, 103, 172, 178
Gomes, G.M. 46
Goodhart, C. 54
Goodwin, R. 44, 48
Gordon, D. 64
Gordon M.J. 166
Grossman, H. 123
growth 40, 180-6 *passim*
growth of firms 150, 153, 160, 177
Guthrie, R.C. 46

Hahn, F. 106, 139

Hall, R. 3, 40, 59, 66, 92, 107, 121, 134, 139, 141, 143, 149, 151, 172
Hamouda, O. 50, 51
Harcourt, G. C. 6, 12, 28, 39, 50, 51, 119, 150, 155, 172, 175, 180, 185
Harrod, R. 119
Harrod–Domar model 13
Hay, D. 148
Hayek, F. 19, 28
Henderson, W. 67
Henry, S.G.B. 24, 42, 74
Hicks, J. 92, 103
Hilferding, R. 169
Hirschman, A.O. 11, 19, 55
Hitch, C. 3, 40, 59, 66, 92, 107, 121, 134, 139, 141, 143, 149, 151, 172
Hodgson, G. 11, 19, 47, 53, 57, 58, 61, 64, 66, 111, 163
Howard, M. 58, 152
human behaviour 57–61, 66

imperfect competition 3, 72, 75, 91–133 *passim*
imperfections 18
increasing returns 161
increasing risk, principle of 45
industrial economics 4, 137, 146–69 *passim*
industrial reserve army 14-15
industrial sector 163–69 *passim*
industrial strategy 26
inflation 6, 9, 15, 24, 35, 43, 81-83 *passim*
information 149
institutional change 2
institutional realities 159–62
institutions 61–3
internal finance 39, 45, 174
interest rates 23, 188–90
investment 32, 34, 44–6, 47, 60, 75–6, 108–09, 152, 180–1, 184

investment funds 175
investment requirements approach to pricing 183
IS–LM analysis 53, 55, 70, 92, 140

Jorgenson, D. 44, 108

Kagel, J.H.12
Kahn, R. 121, 128, 129
Kaldor, N. 21, 30, 34, 39, 48, 53, 63, 67, 93, 101, 130, 131, 192
Kalecki, M. 1, 3, 11, 14, 15, 16, 22, 23, 30, 31, 32, 35, 38, 40, 44, 48, 50, 51, 52, 53, 59, 65, 75, 78, 86, 96, 101, 105, 107, 108, 121, 123, 124, 128, 134, 136, 137, 141, 142, 143, 148, 151, 153, 155, 158, 165, 166, 167, 171, 173, 174, 177, 180, 182,188, 191
Kantrow, A.M. 27
Kay, N. 47, 149, 151
Kenyon, P. 39, 143, 150, 155, 172, 174,180,185
Keynes, J.M. 1, 8, 10, 11, 12, 16, 18, 28, 30, 31, 32, 37, 41, 44, 44, 46, 47, 50, 52, 60, 70, 78, 86, 92, 100, 103, 112, 118, 119, 120, 121, 122, 123, 125, 127, 128, 130, 131, 132, 133, 137, 169, 173, 188
Keynesian economics 10, 16, 111, 125, 130, 133, 143
Kinda–Hass, B. 31,123, 124, 137
kinked demand curve theory 92, 104, 106, 121, 138–39
Kregel, J. 30, 51
Kriesler, P. 38, 136

labour market: see labour sector
labour sector 1, 41–4, 64, 97–100, 123, 188–90
Lange, O. 158
Lavoie,M. 51

Lawson, T. 16, 67
Layard, R. 14, 79, 80, 97
Lee, F. 38, 143, 145
Lee, F. et alia 134
Leibenstein, H. 162
Leijonhufvud, A. 37, 122
Lenin, V.I. 169
Lester, R.A. 149
Levine, D. 176
Lindbeck, A. 13, 56, 72
long term 186–88
Loomes, G. 12

Machlup, F. 150
MacKay, R. 17
macroeconomics 2–3, 4, 12, 35, 37,
    40, 52–3, 92, 96, 109–12, 120,
    140, 142, 161, 170, 175
Malinvaud, E. 6, 37, 93, 103, 141
managerial control 160
Mandel, E. 8
marginal costs 31, 177
marginal product of labour 125, 128
Marglin, S. 71, 82, 85, 86, 90, 180,
    185
market
  definition of 18
  metaphor 18, 20
  operations of 2, 63–6
  power 65, 182
mark-up pricing 38
Marris, R. 155, 159
Marx, K. 14, 15
Marxian approach 30, 50, 55, 63–4,
    146
Marxian view of competition 108
Matthews, R. 7
McCloskey, D. 20, 67
McDonald, D.N. 12
McDonald, I. 101
Means, G. C. 3, 37, 92, 121, 134,
    135, 136, 140
Medema, S.G. 135
megacorp 39

methodological individualism 12
methodology 51–3, 66–9
Michie, J. 128
microeconomic foundations of
    macroeconomics 114
microeconomics 4, 120, 175
Milgate, M. 12, 58, 130
Milgrom, P. 166
Minsky, H. 36
Modigliani–Miller theorem 166
monetarism 70, 78, 167
monetary economy, nature of 32
money 163
  endogenous 33–7 *passim*
  exogenous 33
  nature of 31, 32–37 *passim*, 53–5
  stock of 24
money wages 123
monopoly, degree of 37–8, 82, 85,
    136, 173, 175, 182
monopoly capitalism 62, 156, 172
monopoly model 72–3
Moore, B 34, 53, 191
Morgan, P.B. 12
Morris, D. 148
Myrdal, G. 21, 22, 63

NAIRU (Non–accelerating inflation
    rate of unemployment) 43–4, 55
'natural' rate of unemployment 16,
89
neo-classical economics 10, 13, 19,
    50, 54, 147–0, 157, 177
neo-classical/Keynesian synthesis
56
neo-Keynesian approach 56
new classical macroeconomics 1
Ng, Y-K, 99
Nickell, S. 79, 80
Nielsen, K. 163
Nolan, P. 163
Nordhaus, W. 40, 103, 172, 178

O'Donnell, R. 16

objective approach to pricing 152
objectives of firms 150–5 *passim*
OECD 8, 14
Ohlin, B. 120, 130
Okun, A. 92, 104, 105, 136
Ong, N-P. 39
optimisation 172
organisations 61–3
Oswald, A. 13
over–determinacy 3, 70–91 *passim*
overhead costs 173

p–curve 81, 95, 96, 101, 124, 129
Panglossian approach 9–10
Panico, C. 30
Parker, D. 23
Pasinetti, L. 30, 52, 191
path–dependency 189
Patinkin, D. 33, 126, 133
perfect competition 72, 94, 118, 126
Phillips, A.W. 41
Phillips' curve 9, 41, 75, 78, 83–4,
    87, 89
Pigou, A. 53
Pigou effect 53, 105
Plosser, C. 1
Pollin, R. 36, 53
polypolistic competition 118, 119,
    126
Post Fordism 161, 163
power 62, 65
predictability of future 32, 46–7
price
  adjustment 37, 102, 103
  decisions on 150
  determination of 25
  inflexibility of 65, 107, 140, 142
  leader 39, 174, 175
  rigidities 37, 55, 103, 104–8
    passim, 111, 121
  setter 103, 107, 174
prices, nature of 143–5
  roles of 54–5, 144–5
  stickiness of 92

theories of 170, 172–77, 183
pricing, theories of 3, 37–40, 66–7,
    133– 45, 170, 172–77, 183
production 161–3
productivity differences 162
profit margin 174
  maximisation 44, 136, 138, 149,
    151–3 *passim*, 173, 175, 177–9
  rate of 82
  share 38–9
profits 38, 40, 59, 76–7, 153, 158,
    181
profits and investment 153

quantity adjustment 102, 103, 105

Radcliffe Report 34
rational behaviour 12, 114
rational expectations 46, 58, 112
re–appraisal of Keynesian
    economics 92, 102–4
real balance effect 35, 105
real business cycles 1
real wage/employment relationship
    80–1, 95–7, 124–5, 127–30
real wages 16, 38–9, 41, 42, 55,
    72–4 *passim*, 79, 82, 84, 85, 90,
    123, 126, 127–30, 137
reflux, law of 35
Reich, M. 64
resale price maintenance 157
research and development 147, 149
Reynolds, P. 38, 51, 171, 175
Robbins, L. 11, 13
Roberts, J. 166
Robinson, J. 11, 30, 118, 119, 120,
    121, 137, 144
Romer, D. 1
Rothschild, K. 17
Routh, G. 42
Rowthorn, R. 25, 43, 78
Rutherford, M. 46

Salvadori, N. 30, 38

Samuels, W. 65, 134, 163
Samuelson, P. 48
Sargan, D. 74
satisficing behaviour 60–1
savings 32, 39, 45, 184
Sawyer, M. 2, 6, 9, 10, 15, 17, 21, 23, 24, 26, 31, 38, 42, 43, 48, 51, 62, 63, 64, 67, 71, 72, 74, 82, 85, 137, 148, 156, 163, 166, 183, 184, 189
Say's Law 31, 56, 99, 100
scarcity of resources 11
Scazzieri, R. 9
Scherer, F. 148
Schettkat, R. 17
Schor, J. 189
Schumpeter, J. 119
segmented labour markets 64
Shackle, G. 47, 58, 61
Shah, A. 49
Shapiro, A. 26
Shapiro, C. 15
Shapiro, M. 6
Shapiro, N. 39, 143, 150, 153, 176
Silvestre, J. 99
Simon, H. 60
Skott, P. 21, 49, 63, 160, 161
Smith, P. 24, 42, 74
Smyth, D.J. 48
Snower, D. 13, 56, 72
Solow, R. 7, 16, 107
sound finance, doctrine of 23
Spence, A.M. 185
Sraffa, P. 30, 58, 119, 152
Sraffian approach 30, 50, 58, 59, 65, 152,170, 177, 182
Stafford, G. 7
stages of development of banking system 33
stagnation 62
stagnationist approach 180
Steindl, J. 39, 62, 75, 76, 78, 109, 154, 162, 167, 174, 176, 177, 185, 190

Stewart, M. 7
Stigler, G. 67, 138
Stiglitz, J. 15, 166
structure–conduct–performance paradigm 108, 148, 156
subjective approach to pricing 152
Sugden, R. 26
supply–of–labour curve 128
supply–side 2–5 *passim*, 53, 55, 70, 114, 146
sustainability 99
sustainable profit maximisation 176–9
Sweezy, P. 3, 92, 106, 107, 121, 134, 138, 139, 150, 151, 157, 177
Sylos–Labini, P. 101
Symons, J. 97

target rate of capacity utilisation 181
target real wage 42, 74, 85, 189
Targetti, F. 31, 123, 124, 137
Tarshis, L. 127, 128, 130
Taylor, C. 12
Thirlwall, A. 9, 63, 93
time, historical 171
time, logical 171
Tobin, J. 130, 131
Tooke,T. 35
Tool, M. 163
Toporowski, J. 164, 165
trade cycles, see business cycles
trade unions 19
training 26
transnational corporations 62
Trevithick, J. 34, 53, 93, 192
two-sector model 179–85
Tustin, D. 12

uncertainty 32, 52, 58, 171, 173
unemployment 1–5 *passim*, 6–29 *passim*, 55, 74–5, 88–9, 92, 93, 111, 187, 189

unemployment, causes of 20–2
unemployment and economic
    analysis 10–5
utility maximisation 60

variable costs 178
Velupillai, K. 78

w-curve 81
wage determination 25, 41–3, 74,
    189
Walras' Law 109, 114
Walrasian auctioneer see
    auctioneer
Waterson, M. 38, 174
Weiss, A. 13, 42, 56, 72, 166
Weitzman, M. 93, 95, 99, 101, 102,
    115,116, 131
Wible, J.R. 46
Williamson, O.E. 19, 155, 161
Wood, A. 39, 143, 150, 152, 153,
    154, 167, 172, 174
worker involvement 27
workers' savings 190–2
World Bank 22
Worswick, D. 93
Wray, R. 32, 34, 35, 37, 53
Wulwick, N. 34

X–inefficiency 162

ELECTRIC

KILNS

Bowl and tea caddy by Katie Kazan, 1973. Cone 6 procelain and colored oxides. Photo by Alida Conin.

ELECTRIC
KILNS

BY HARRY FRASER

AMERICAN EDITION EDITED BY SARAH BODINE

WATSON-GUPTILL PUBLICATIONS, NEW YORK

Library of Congress Cataloging in Publication Data
Fraser, Harry, 1937–
    Electric kilns.
    London ed. published in 1969 under title: Kilns
and kiln firing for the craft potter.
    1. Electric kilns. 2. Pottery. I. Title.
TP841.F7 1974   738.1'3   73-22046
ISBN 0-8230-1610-2

First Printing, 1974

Designed by Robert Fillie
Set in 10 point Melior by Publishers Graphics, Inc.
Printed and bound in U.S.A. by Halliday Lithograph Corporation

Endpaper drawing by L.A. Fisher
Engineering Experiment Station
University of New Hampshire

To Jill

CONTENTS

Preface to the American Edition, 8

Foreword, 9

Preface, 10

Acknowledgments, 11

1. Evolution of the Kiln, 12
First Kilns, 14
Downdraft Kilns, 14
Vertical Intermittent Kilns, 14
Bottle Kilns, 19
Advent of the Tunnel Kiln, 23
Top-hat Kiln, 25
Primitive Firing Methods–Aali, 25
Modern Studio Kilns, 29

2. Choosing Your Kiln, 30
Size and Capacity, 30
Kiln Site and Access, 32
Electrical Requirements, 34
Firing Cost, 35
Firing Temperature, 35
Shipping and Delivery, 37

3. Design, Construction, and Repair, 38
Framework, 38
Brickwork, 40
Electrical Wiring and Fittings, 41
Elements, 42
Element Regulation, 42
Element Repair and Replacement, 46
First Firing, 47

4. Making Studio Electric Kilns, 50

5. Accessories and Instrumentation, 72
Rotary Switch, 72
Kiln Sitter, 72
Time Switch, 73
Energy Regulator, 76
Door Switch, 77

PREFACE

There has been a tremendous upsurge in do-it-yourself pottery in the last few years. This coming winter, hundreds of evening institutes in towns and villages all over the country will introduce pottery-making into their curriculum and by so doing will swell the ranks of the thousands whose courses are already well established. The following winter hundreds more will be following in their wake. This increasing interest in pottery making is not confined to any one country but is characteristic of all countries where progressive improvements in the standard of living have provided people with a greater amount of leisure time and a desire to use it more constructively. However, the explosive interest in the ancient craft of potting is also largely attributable to the development of a range of studio electric kilns which fire to high temperatures but are priced to suit all pockets, considerably easing the problems of pottery firing.

Despite the tremendous success with which the long-awaited arrival of the modern studio kiln has been received it still tends to remain something of a mystery to many pupils and teachers—a mysterious magical box of tricks of immense complexity and uncertain operation, seemingly demanding years of experience before satisfactory operation can be achieved. Every kiln firing is viewed with awe, every kiln fireman with wonderment. Many pupils would dearly like to purchase their own kilns to produce pottery in their own homes, but they do not because they dare not, believing as they do that kiln firing is so dreadfully complicated. Nothing could be further from the truth. Kiln firing merely demands a working knowledge of what each switch or knob is for—and these are few in number—coupled with a very basic knowledge of what happens to pottery at each stage of a kiln firing.

This book has been written to supply this knowledge and to enable the complete novice to select the right kiln and to fire his pottery with complete assurance and satisfaction.

There will be much here, too, for the teacher or advanced studio potter, who may find those chapters on kiln instrumentation or kiln evolution of particular interest.

FOREWORD

Most potters are highly skilled in the art of shaping and decorating their particular products, but unfortunately there are many who fail to obtain optimum results from the last, and in some ways the most important, of the series of processes involved—namely, the firing of the finished article.

The correct firing of pottery is not quite so simple as beginners in the craft often believe, but on the other hand, there is no "black magic" in the process. Success in firing mainly comes from an understanding of what happens when ceramic materials are heated, the specific firing requirements of the products and an ability to control the temperature/time cycle and atmosphere of the kiln. Hence the author has wisely concentrated on these fundamental aspects.

The book does, however, cover a large number of related subjects such as the historical development of the kiln, kiln design and construction, accessories and instrumentation, kiln placing and a very useful chapter entitled "Some faults and how to overcome them." The book can,

therefore, fairly claim to be comprehensive and as such will not only prove of inestimable value to the craft potter and the pottery teacher, but will also find a useful place on the shelf of the student, the research worker, and the industrial ceramist.

The author studied ceramics at the North Staffordshire College of Technology and afterwards spent several years in the pottery industry as a technical manager before becoming captivated by the craft potter's art.

During more recent years he has had much experience in pottery and also in the design and production of small electric pottery kilns. Henry Fraser is, therefore, well qualified in his subject and without doubt has succeeded in producing an interesting and informative book that will certainly fill a long-felt need.

Henry L. Podmore, B.Sc.,F.R.I.C., F.I. Ceram.
Podmore & Sons Ltd.
Stoke-on-Trent

PREFACE TO THE AMERICAN EDITION

The ability to adjust to environmental and procedural requirements is an asset to the craftsman and the opportunities offered by new situations often lead to discovery and innovation. With the increasing concern about the availability of natural fuel in the United States and the ongoing evolution of techniques, potters are beginning to consider electricity as an alternative method to gas and oil firing.

The electric kiln, which at present has had more widespread use in Europe than in the United States, is a largely unexplored medium for the craft potter. The evolution of electrical firing equipment has been directed towards commercial use and the expedient firing of large loads of ware. As a result the studio potter tends to regard the electric kiln as a production device rather than a tool for achieving the most desirable relationship between form and surface in the glazing and firing of clay.

Traditionally, one of the most exciting things in the firing process is the uncertainty of the outcome. No matter how precise the formula or detailed the instructions, each kilnload, each group of pots, has its own characteristics and oddities, successes and disappointments.

Electric kilns have been subject to the criticism of their not being capable of producing startling or unexpected results from the glaze firing. In the neutral, oxidizing atmosphere, and without the variations of flame-produced heat, the interaction of clay body and glaze coating is not as great as when a gas or wood kiln is heavily reduced, drawing oxygen from both body and glaze. Yet implicit in these drawbacks of the electric kiln is the advantage of a more precise degree of color, form, and texture control. This context suggests a new kind of challenge for the potter, and the work illustrated in this book is exemplary of a response to this challenge.

This book is a pioneering effort in acquainting the American studio potter with the workings of electric kilns. Its purpose is to expand the context and unravel technical aspects of the electric kiln while demonstrating its innovative potential.

S.B.

6. Temperature Control, 78
Pyrometers, 80
Potentiometers, 81
Thermocouples, 81
Thermolimit (Pyrolimit), 83
Controlling Pyrometer, 83
Temperature Regulator, 84
Program Controller, 85
Inaccurate Pyrometer Readings, 87
Pyrometric Cones, 87

7. Difference in Firing Technique Between Studio and Industrial Potters, 90
Earthenware and Porous Clays, 90
Stoneware and Porcelain, 93

8. Kiln Furniture and Stacking the Kiln, 94
Shelves, 94
Supports, 97
Stacking the Biscuit, 97
Stacking the Glaze, 99

9. Firing the Kiln, 102
Clay Firing Temperatures, 104
Biscuit Firing, 104
Cooling, 105
Inspection, 105
Glaze Firing, 106
Cooling, 107

10. Basic Effects of Heat on Clay and Glazes, 108
Vitrification and Porosity, 110
Importance of Silica, 110
Modifications of Silica, 111
Stages in the Biscuit Firing, 111
Matching Glazes, 113
Eutectics, 113
Interface, 114
Bubbles and Craters, 114
Effects of Cooling, 114

11. Some Pottery Faults and How to Overcome Them, 116
Crazing, 116
Shivering, 119
Crawling, 119
Cut Glaze, 120
Scumming, 120
Dunting, 120
Cracking, 121
Pinholed Glaze, 122
Devitrification, 122
Glossy and Matt Glazes, 123
Blow-out, 123
Sulphuring, 123
Bloating, 124
Blistering, 124
Dull Underglaze Colors, 125
Dull Overglaze Colors, 125

12. Experimental Glazing and Multiple Firing, 126
Reduction, 126
Effect of Reduction, 128
Effect on Elements, 128
Formation of Reducing Atmosphere, 130
Raku, 131
Clay Body Variation, 132
Luster, 132
Underglaze and Overglaze Colors, 132
Multiple Firings, 137

Tables, 138

Bibliography, 140

Suppliers List, 141

Index, 142

ACKNOWLEDGMENTS

My thanks are due to the following companies who have so kindly provided information or photographs used in the compilation of this book:
Podmore & Sons Ltd., Kilns & Furnaces Ltd., Ether Instruments Ltd., Bernard W. E. Webber Ltd., The Metallic Tile Co. (Rowley Bros.) Ltd., A Meakin Ltd., The Carborundum Co. Ltd., British Ceramic Services Co. Ltd., Gibbons Bros. Ltd., Sangamo Weston Ltd., W. T. Copeland & Sons Ltd., Doulton Fine China Ltd., Harrison & Sons Ltd.

Also to the Editors of *A History of Technology* published by the Clarendon Press, Oxford, for permission to reproduce Figures 1, 2 and 3 and for information about primitive firing methods; to Mr. A. R. Mountford, Director of the City Museum, Hanley, for much information and assistance on the subject of Roman and Medieval kilns; to the North Staffordshire College of Technology for assistance with photographs; and to the College of Earth and Mineral Sciences, Pennsylvania State University for permission to reproduce material from *Fundamentals of Ceramics*. For the American edition, thanks go to: Amaco (American Art Clay Company, Inc.), A.D. Alpine, Inc., Evenheat Kiln, Inc., L. and L. Manufacturing Company, Skutt Ceramic Products, and Unique Kilns for supplying photographs of kilns and accessories, and to the Edward Orton Jr. Ceramic Foundation for permission to reproduce their pyrometric cone conversion chart.

Special thanks are also extended to Laurance E. Webber, P.E., former Director of the Engineering Experiment Station of the University of New Hampshire, who kindly allowed his booklet, "Making Studio Electric Kilns," originally published in 1947, to be reprinted here. I am grateful to the potters represented in the chapter on experimental glazing in electric kilns for providing photographs of their work and comments on special techniques and processes.

1
EVOLUTION
OF THE KILN

Pottery is possibly man's oldest industry. Its origins are probably closely connected with the time thousands upon thousands of years ago, when primeval man observed that footprints or other depressions made in clayey soil had hardened in the sun. He could also have noticed that depressions in the shade were often softer and cooler than those exposed to the rays of the sun.

When man mastered fire, he began to make environments in which to use it. For example, at Jarno in the Kurdish foothills, Neolithic hearths have been found which were scooped out of the floor and hardened by fire. There is probably some link between the fortuitous hardening of these hearths and the purposeful firing of clay objects in the open fire because even during the last ice age, we know that the mammouth-hunters of Vestonice in Moravia constructed hearths in which they hardened images of animals.

We also know, by excavational discoveries, that clay products which had been burned in a fire were made in Britain and other parts of Europe 15,000 years ago and in the Nile valley some 13,000 years ago.

Pottery firing in those days could have consisted of little more than placing the clay pots on the ground and building an open fire around them. By packing fuel on and around the ware and damping it, the fire could be made to burn longer. Perhaps the first ovens evolved from these preliminary attempts at enclosing the fire.

It must not be assumed, however, that the advent of the kiln marked the demise of the open fire. Open firing is quite effective up to about 750° C. (1382° F.) and fuels such as brushwood, grass, and dung could be used which were cheaper than the wood or charcoal necessary for stoking a kiln. It was partly such economic considerations that made it necessary to fire pottery by the open-hearth method as late as

1. *An Egyptian pottery in the Middle Kingdom, c. 1900 B.C., using characteristic narrow vertical kilns; from a tomb at Beni Hasan.*

2. *Egyptian pottery of Dynasty V, c. 2500 B.C.; the small kiln appears to be closed at the top with a layer of vegetable matter.*

3. *New-Kingdom Egyptian pottery, c. 1450 B.C.; the kiln is of the same type as in Figure 2; from a tomb at Thebes.*

1863 A.D. in Lewes. In a kiln, however, the improved draft control gives better results, there is better heat conservation, and higher temperatures can be maintained than with the open fire.

First Kilns

It is, of course, impossible to give precise dates at which processes were invented as the history of pottery is anything but one of constant development. By studying actual discoveries at the sites of ancient temples, tombs, and so on, we have however, been able to learn much about the ancient potter's craft. From pictures on the walls of tombs of the Theban period (300 B.C. to 1700 B.C.), for example, we can see how the Egyptian potter modeled his vases by hand from clay which had been worked to a homogeneous consistency by constant treading and kneading with the bare feet (the same process, done by hand we now refer to as "wedging"). The pottery was then placed in the narrow vertical kilns which were loaded from the top, as shown in Figures 1, 2, and 3, and closed with vegetable matter.

These simple vertical kilns were of the updraft type, as were the horizontal kilns also in use at this time primarily in the Far East.

The Far-Eastern kilns were generally larger than those of other areas and therefore required firing less frequently. The early ones were normally horizontal or slanted operating on a through draft rather than on the direct updraft principle. One of the big disadvantages of through draft and updraft kilns is that it is very difficult to baffle back the heat—the flames tend to rush unimpeded through the firing chamber and this is largely responsible for their poor efficiency. Therefore, the downdraft principle was developed which resulted in considerable fuel savings while allowing higher temperatures to be reached and maintained.

Downdraft Kilns

The typical Far-Eastern climbing downdraft kiln, illustrated in Figure 4, consisted of a series of downdraft chambers joined together. The lowest one was fired first, producing exhaust gases which passed through and preheated each subsequent chamber and emerged from the short chimney or stack located on the highest one. Additional firemouths set in the side of each chamber assisted the firing but the last two or three chambers required very little extra heat to reach normal firing temperatures since the kiln structure and the enclosed pottery would be preheated from the firing of the earlier chambers.

The downdraft principle which was later adapted to the European vertical updraft kiln allows the exhaust gases to remain in the kiln for a longer period of time than in the vertical system thereby spreading the heat more evenly to the kiln and the ware and requiring less fuel.

Vertical Intermittent Kilns

A kiln which is heated and then cooled down so that the ware can be removed is called an "intermittent" or "periodic" kiln as distinct from a "continuous" kiln, from which fired pottery emerges in a steady flow. All the early kilns, and indeed kilns up to comparatively recent times, were of the intermittent variety.

Generally, vertical kilns were used more often than the horizontal type, particularly in Western Europe where several very good examples of the Roman vertical intermittent kiln have been excavated. As shown in Figures 7 and 8, the kiln is of simple construction consisting basically of a stokehole dug out of the ground and a

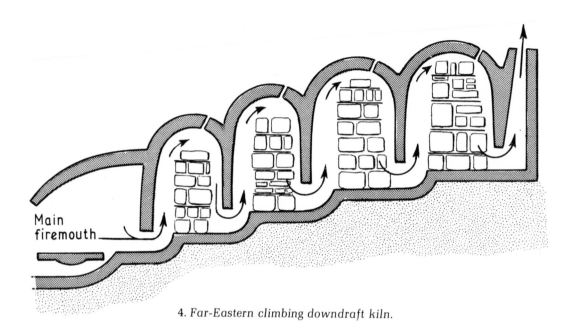

4. Far-Eastern climbing downdraft kiln.

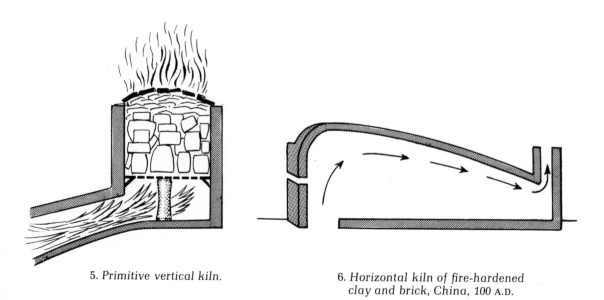

5. Primitive vertical kiln.

6. Horizontal kiln of fire-hardened
clay and brick, China, 100 A.D.

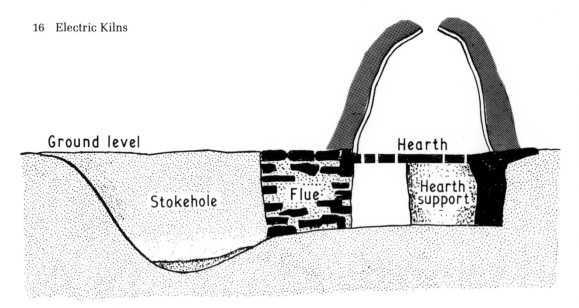

7. Roman vertical kiln: vertical section.

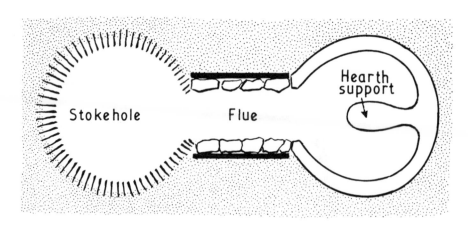

8. Roman vertical kiln: plan.

9. View of Roman kiln excavated at Trent Vale, Stoke-on-Trent.

10. Perforated Roman kiln floor excavated at Trent Vale, 1st century A.D.

flue dug under the ground to a firing chamber. A central support in this chamber supported the radiant clay firebars, that served as the hearth of the kiln. The pots were loaded carefully onto the hearth and a domed roof of clay and grass or straw with an aperture left in the top for the escape of smoke, steam, and gases was built around them. The fuel was loaded from the stokehole into the firemouth, the flames sweeping up the flue, through the hearth, through the load of ware, and out through the hole or holes in the roof.

Figure 9, a photograph of a kiln excavated at Trent Vale, Stoke-on-Trent (England), outlines the layout of a typical Roman vertical kiln. The domed roof is not shown as this would probably have been destroyed after each firing. Figure 10 shows the area where the clay bars or perforated clay floor which held the ware was located.

There were many Roman variations of this type of kiln: sometimes a pair of kilns were built radiating from the same stokehole; sometimes the hearth support was permanent, sometimes temporary.

About two tons of wood would have been needed to fire such a kiln and the maximum temperature it could attain would be about 960° to 1000°C. (1760° to 1832°F.). There would, however, have been a considerable temperature variation; while certain parts of the kiln might reach 1000°C. (1832°F.), other parts would probably not rise about 850°C. (1562°F.) or so.

It would have been far easier for the Romans to transport the fuel rather than the clay or the fired pots. Consequently, they often built their kilns near a source of clay or near a roadway or navigable river rather than near a source of fuel.

In England this type of kiln continued virtually unchanged for centuries. It should not, however, be assumed that in England and Western Europe at this time *all* pottery kilns were of the simple updraft type built mainly below ground level. This type certainly appears to have been the most popular—probably because of economic considerations—but there were several variations on this theme such as the tenth-century derivitives of the Roman design where several firemouths fed one firing chamber filled with pots.

There is little doubt that the Romans also built more permanent kilns above ground with bricks and other hard materials, although such kilns do not appear to have been in general use in Europe until medieval times.

In the sixteenth century an Italian named Piccolpasso set down in considerable detail the manner in which pottery was produced. He described not only the processes and the tools used but also included sketches of the kilns. Other sources from that time refer to kilns having a "round copped form," marking the similarity, at least in roof structure, to the Roman ones. The sixteenth-century woodcut in Figure 11 illustrates a kiln (in the bottom right-hand corner) which appears to have preheating or drying chambers underneath the actual firing chambers.

In the City Museum in Hanley, Stoke-on-Trent, the base structure of a kiln that was in use about 1700 A.D. can be seen. This particular kiln, shown in Figure 12, which was located on the grounds of what is now the Albion Hotel in Hanley, was carefully uncovered and removed brick by brick and stone by stone and resited in the Museum ground by the Stoke-on-Trent Archaeological Society. Each piece was put together *exactly* as it was found; the angle at which each brick was set was very carefully reproduced, the kiln was built facing exactly the same direction and even

11. *16th-century woodcut depicting pottery production. Courtesy of City Museum, Hanley.*

the thickness of the cement and the positions of the broken shards, and so on, found around the kiln were carefully copied. The kiln is therefore not a replica but a true original uncovered and preserved after being hidden for so many generations.

The kiln consists of a central chamber about 8′ in diameter with a single entrance. Seven firemouths are arranged around its periphery. It is interesting to note that saggars were in use, as is evidenced by those found actually inside the kiln. Saggars are refractory boxes made of a clay which normally contains a lot of grog. The saggars are biscuit fired so that they are strong enough to be stacked one above the other. Saggars are still in use today but by no means as extensively as they were some fifty years ago largely as a result of the use of clean fuels and electricity for firing.

Above the kiln base was built a brick dome which was about 8′ high and probably had a single exhaust hole in the top. The pottery to be fired was carried into the kiln inside saggars which were stacked one above the other until the kiln was filled. Then the entrance was tightly bricked up and the fires were started.

The Hanley kiln, which has several firemouths radiating from a central firing chamber, is a logical development from the primitive Roman type, the main difference is that the Hanley kiln was constructed above ground level with a more permanent domed roof.

Bottle Kilns

The Roman updraft kiln was also the forerunner of the "bottle" oven which gave such character to the skyline of the Potteries area of North Staffordshire. Bottle ovens of the updraft type were probably first built around 1700 A.D. Since then many different types have been produced and used extensively.

The bottle oven was a very important factor in the development of Stoke-on-Trent as the major pottery-producing area of Great Britain, although increasing amounts of pottery were being made in the

12. *Base structure of kiln in use about 1700* A.D. *at Hanley, Stoke-on-Trent. Courtesy of City Museum, Hanley.*

13. *18th-century woodcut showing ware in saggars being carried into a bottle oven.*

Stoke-on-Trent area well before the advent of the bottle oven, for many local clays were excellent for pottery production. A good-quality coal is needed to obtain the best results from a bottle kiln—a coal that burns with a long flame that can lick up into the kiln and give better heat distribution. There are abundant supplies of such coal in the North Staffordshire area and this fact must have considerably enhanced the appeal of Stoke-on-Trent as an advantageous site for the production of pottery. Eventually, literally thousands of bottle kilns were built and operated in the Potteries.

Most bottle ovens consisted basically of two virtually separate structures; the domed roof oven into which the saggars of ware were placed and an outer wall surrounding this and tapering to a hole, 2' to 5' in diameter, at the top. The domed roof

oven, referred to as the "Hovel," was built with several firemouths arranged around its periphery—much like the Hanley kiln. The floor of the hovel was raised 2' or so above ground level and had a firehole made in the center so that the heat and flames from each of the firemouths could pass under the floor and into the hovel through the firehold. Much of the heat from the firemouths, however, escaped upwards between the tightly packed saggars and the inside wall of the hovel. To protect the saggars immediately in front of the firemouths from becoming overheated, a protective wall known as a "bag" wall was built, which deflected the heat upwards into the hovel. The hot gases then passed out of the hovel either through a hole in the center of the domed roof or through vent holes which were arranged around the lower parts of the roof structure. All these exhaust holes were equipped with covers or dampers, which the kiln operator manipulated during the firing to reduce the rate of temperature increase in certain parts of the kiln while increasing it in other parts to obtain a more even temperature distribution. Spy holes were spaced evenly around the kiln so that the fireman could check the color of the glow and use this to estimate the temperature. The outer wall served to protect the hovel and the firemen from bad weather, and also created the necessary draft to pull the exhaust gases from the hovel, upwards and out of the kiln.

At the famous Spode bone china factory of Copelands Ltd. in Stoke-on-Trent a bottle oven dating back to 1800 A.D. like the one shown in Figure 15, is preserved

which was in use up to 1963.

In the nineteenth century, downdraft versions of the bottle kiln were produced. In these kilns the heat from the firemouths generally passed vertically upwards to the crown of the kiln and was there drawn down, passing through holes in the floor of the kiln connected to a flue or flues. These either led to a separate chimney or were continued up through the brickwork of the kiln and out through the hole at the top. Several kilns of this type are still in use today.

The downdraft principle is now extensively in the firing of the intermittent solid-fueled kilns commonly used by many tile-manufacturing and brick-making companies—particularly were a reduction atmosphere is required.

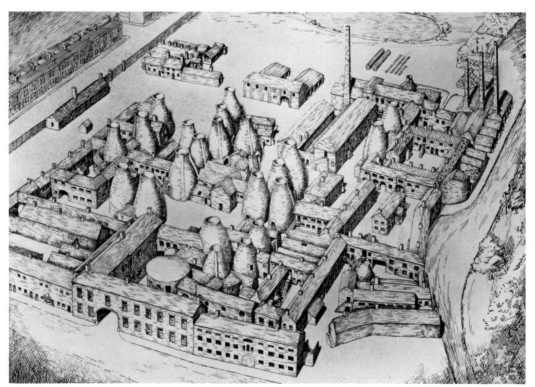

14. *Illustration of the "Spode" factory of Copelands Ltd. in 1820. Courtesy of Messrs. Copeland*

15. *Bottle oven built at the Copeland factory about 1800. Courtesy of Messrs. Copeland Ltd.*

Advent of the Tunnel Kiln

Advances in science and engineering have revolutionized the ceramic industry, introducing new kiln designs such as the tunnel kiln that afford more efficient and economic production of ware with greater consistency. Up to this time pottery had always been fired in intermittent kilns—the ware was placed in them when they were cold, the kiln was fired and then allowed to cool down again in order to remove the fired ware. This meant that large amounts of fuel had to be used at great expense to heat up the kiln and its contents and this fuel was wasted in the cooling.

In addition, production was delayed by the fact that the ware could not be taken from the kiln until it had cooled sufficiently for its contents to be handled.

The "tunnel kiln" was invented to avoid this waste of heat energy. The ware is carried through a tunnel on a suitable vehicle—a truck covered with a refractory lining, a moving refractory belt, or possibly a heat-resisting metal conveyor if the maximum temperature is below 1100°C. (2012°F.). At the entrance of the tunnel the temperature is comparatively low, building up gradually to a maximum in the center of the kiln, and then progressively dropping until the temperature is about 50° to 200° C. (122° to 392°F.) at the kiln exit. A variation in firing the tunnel kilns is the "counterflow system" in which the ware fed into the kiln is preheated by exhaust air as it travels to the firing zone. Subsequently, secondary air obtained by passing cool air over the hot trucks leaving the firing zone is used in fuel combustion.

The basic counterflow system has been refined in modern tunnel kilns. Kilns are often built as two tunnels in the cooling sector: the tunnel through which the ware passes and an outer tunnel or jacket through which air is circulated. The hot air obtained from cooling the ware is piped away to be used as central heating for other departments of the factory or for drying greenware.

The modern tunnel kiln may be gas, oil, or electrically fired, muffle (or baffle—a refractory internal shell which protects ware from contact with the combustion gasses) or open flame, large or small, straight or curved.

The tunnel kiln is filled with a continuous column of trucks of ware which is pushed down the tunnel by the action of a slowly moving ram. The ram pushes the column one truck length down the kiln and then automatically retracts. The exit doors are opened, a truck full of fired ware is pulled out of the kiln, and the exit doors are closed again. The entrance doors are then opened and another truck of green ware is pushed into position between the ram and the previous truck. The entrance doors are then closed and the ram-pusher started. The speed of the ram-pusher can be varied in order to regulate the output of the kiln to conform to the rate of production.

Once a tunnel kiln has been heated to its desired temperature, it can be kept at this point by comparatively small additions of fuel. Therefore tunnel kilns are kept in constant operation—particularly the bigger kilns where just cooling down may take several days, wasting a considerable amount of heat. When I joined Armitage Ware in 1963, a 300′ long tunnel kiln was shut down for an overhaul after thirteen years' continuous operation, although at many factories kilns are shut down regularly once a year for inspection and overhaul.

The number of burners and the total length of a tunnel kiln can vary widely. Some kilns—particularly those for com-

16. *Modern intermittent kiln used for reduction firing of tile and bricks. Courtesy of Metallic Tile Company.*

paratively low temperatures—may be very small, only 15' to 20' in length, and may have only one burner on each side. On the other hand, the 431' biscuit kiln used by Alfred Meakin Ltd. has over 300 burners.

The first tunnel kiln, built at Vincennes, France, in 1751 and operating until 1802, was constructed for firing enameled ware. Another French kiln was erected in 1809 for firing decorated earthenware. The ware was placed in iron cages that were pulled through the kiln by a chain. In the late nineteenth century the first tunnel kiln for firing bricks was built by a Swede named Bock. He used rails, trucks, and a sand seal to prevent the heat built up around the ware from leaking down past the sides of the trucks thereby overheating the wheel bearings. The kiln was fired with coal fed in at the top. Hot air was pumped away from the firing zone and fed back into the kiln entrance to complete the drying of the unfired bricks. American brick factories built tunnel kilns in the early 1890s and in Europe a number of kilns were installed by Dinz between 1900 and 1910, but the producer-gas-fired model developed about 1910 by Faugeron, a Frenchman, was probably the first commercially successful tunnel kiln. At about this time Conrad Dressler (whose firm was taken over by Gibbons Brothers in 1927) began designing tunnel kilns in Britain on a muffle (baffle) principle. In 1926 he introduced the multiburner kiln, many examples of which are still in operation. There are many different tunnel kilns manufactured today. Muffle types for the gas and oil-fired versions with a comparatively small cross-sectional area allowing rapid firing schedules with even temperature distribution are increasingly more common.

There is also a trend towards smaller continuous kilns, such as the "Trent" gas-fired kiln which uses refractory shelves as trucks for transporting ware. The comparatively small roller conveyor kiln illustrated in Figure 20 is also becoming increasingly popular.

Top-Hat Kiln

Tunnel kilns lend themselves well to flow-line production methods but they are generally large and cost a lot of money to install; consequently, they may be unsuitable or too expensive for a small company. In this case, the intermittent top-hat kiln can be used successfully.

The top-hat kiln shown in Figure 21 is electrically fired. The ware is stacked, usually on shelves, in a refractory base. The kiln is then lifted up by crane, gantry (a framework supported at each end), or pneumatic device and lowered over the base. After firing, instead of allowing the kiln to cool completely, the shell is lifted up and moved a few yards away where it is lowered into position over another base stacked with pots. The heat retained by the kiln shell is thereby utilized in the next firing.

Intermittently operated truck kilns illustrated in Figure 22 are also used extensively. A truck full of ware is pushed into position inside the kiln and the doors closed. After firing, the truck of ware is removed and immediately replace by another truck and the process is repeated.

Primitive Firing Methods— Aali

The progression from primitive kilns to modern tunnel kilns has taken place primarily in those areas of the world associated with a reasonable standard of living—Europe, Scandanavia, America, Australasia, and so on. In many parts of the world, pottery is still fired in primitive kilns.

The village of Aali in Bahrain in the Per-

17. Truck tunnel kiln. Courtesy of Gibbons Brothers Ltd.

18. Internal view of truck tunnel kiln structure. Courtesy of the Carborundum Company Ltd.

19. Rolling a truck of ware into a tunnel kiln. Courtesy of Gibbons Brothers Ltd.

20. Gas-fired roller hearth kiln at A. Meakin Ltd. Courtesy of Gibbons Brothers Ltd.

21. Top-hat kiln in raised position (above), in lowered position (below).
Courtesy of Podmore and Sons Ltd.

22. *Intermittent truck kiln. Courtesy of Kilns and Furnaces Ltd.*

sian Gulf for example, contains many kilns made from local burial tombs. The tombs are dug out more or less in two separate chambers, one above the other. The clay pots are placed in the upper chamber, which is about 7′ in diameter, and the bottom chamber, about 9′in diameter, serves as the firemouth. The two chambers are connected by a hold of about 22″ diameter. These kilns are similar to the simple updraft types used by the Romans, except that the Aali potters also build four exhaust passages of about 9″ diameter on the outside of the upper chamber and use a lid to seal off the 22″ exhaust hole when necessary. This enable the fires to be kept roaring and provides better temperature distribution. Palm fronds inserted into the firemouth through a 15″ hole are used for fuel.

The village community produces some excellent wheel-thrown pottery—particularly jugs and pitchers, which are simply biscuit fired and used. Biscuit-fired pots are used as water containers because the contents stay quite cool. This happens because the water seeps very slowly through the pot and vaporizes on reaching the out-side, dispelling the latent heat inside. The coolness of the water is often surprising to European visitors who expect the water to be at room temperature which in the tropics may be 120°F. or higher.

Modern Studio Kilns

In the past fifteen to twenty years, kilns made for the studio pottery market were scaled-down versions of small industrial kilns, or kilns designed for use in laboratories, pilot plants, and test situations. They were often equipped with sophisticated instrumentation and accompanied by complex technical handbooks that were beyond the comprehension of the studio potter. The kilns were also very expensive and only when it became obvious that there was a rapidly increasing demand for smaller and simpler kilns was serious thought given to producing kilns specifically for studio potters—kilns that were built to much simpler and therefore cheaper specifications.

Suppliers of pottery tools and equipment now offer a wide range of kilns to accommodate studio, school, and professional potters and ceramic sculptors.

2
CHOOSING
YOUR KILN

The electric kiln provides a clean, safe vehicle for firing ware at moderate cost; the biggest expense may prove to be the initial purchase of the kiln itself. Therefore you must consider all the circumstances surrounding your particular working and producing situation before deciding on the right kiln for you. Here are the major factors which should enter into this consideration:

The approximate size of the kiln and the number of people using it.

The space in which the kiln is to be situated and difficulty of access to the kiln site.

The electricity consumption of the kiln in relationship to the existing electricity supply.

The maximum temperature to which the kiln will be fired—that is the type of pottery you want to produce.

Size and Capacity

The approximate size of the kiln required can only be determined by you, the prospective buyer. You alone know the size and quantity of pots that you want to produce and fire. A pottery teacher, however, has a particularly difficult decision to make in estimating the output of a class rather than that of an individual. In general, the best policy is to select the kiln that is likely to be too large rather than one which is likely to be too small. There can be nothing more distressing for the pottery student than finding that the ware he has taken perhaps days or weeks to produce to the firing stage cannot be fired immediately because the kiln is too small, resulting in a build-up of ware to be fired. It may be of some help to know that the most popular size of kiln for use in schools is one with interior dimensions of 15″ x 15″ x 18″. This is a reasonably sized kiln, large

23. *Pasco model P-10, top-loading sectional electric kiln, firing chamber 23″ diameter by 27″ deep, maximum temperature 2250°F., cone 6. Courtesy of the American Art Clay Company, Inc.*

24. *Amaco model EC-55, top-loading electric kiln, firing chamber 18″ by 18″ by 18″, maximum temperature 2000°F., about cone 01. Courtesy of American Art Clay Company, Inc.*

25. *Skutt model 231-18, top-loading ten-sided sectional electric kiln, firing chamber 23⅜″ diameter by 18″ deep, maximum temperature, cone 6. Courtesy of Skutt Ceramic Products.*

enough to cope with the largest pieces likely to be produced by pottery students. The decision on the correct size of kiln does, however, have to be tempered by common sense: a large pottery class of, say, forty or fifty students will need a considerably larger kiln than a small one of perhaps ten or twenty students. The more ambitious studio potter and the larger pottery classes will need kilns that are considerably larger than 15″ x 15″ x 18″. Kilns with interior dimensions of 18″ x 18″ x 24″ and even larger, are quite commonly used. On the other hand, there are also very small pottery kilns with internal dimensions of 6″ x 6″ x 6″ or less. Most of these kilns were originally designed as test kilns and as such have been invaluable to many ceramic laboratories both in industry and in educational establishments. They are,

however, also used by studio potters for firing small items such as ceramic beads for jewelry. Such kilns will usually heat up very quickly at their maximum setting—many of them are capable of attaining 1300°C. (2372°F., cone 10) in as little as 3½ to 4 hours. Therefore, to obtain a good glaze finish, it is usually necessary to keep the kiln at a comparatively low setting during most of the firing.

Kiln Site and Access

A major factor to be taken into consideration when choosing your kiln is the space in which the kiln will be situated. There should be at least enough space to allow the sides of the kiln to be 8″ away from any wall with enough space between the back of the kiln and the wall for loading and for any overhauls or element replacement

26. Skutt model 231, top loading ten-sided sectional electric kiln, firing chamber 23⅜" diameter by 27" deep, maximum temperature 2300°F., cone 8. Courtesy of Skutt Ceramic Products.

27. Econo-Kiln model K-14, top-loading sectional electric kiln, firing chamber 14⅜" diameter by 13¼" deep, maximum temperature 2300°F., cone 8. Courtesy of L & L Manufacturing Company.

which you might need to do. In actual practice, the rear of the kiln is often pushed within 8" to 12" of a wall but provision is made for the kiln to be moved forward again if access to the rear is required. Front-loading kilns demand a little more floor space than top-loading kilns for the door to swing open and for loading the kiln from the front. If floor space is very limited, a top-loading kiln such as the one shown in Figure 24 may be the only answer. Top-loading kilns have their advantages—they provide easy access to all interior areas for stacking the ware or when elements or bricks need repair, and they afford a good vantage point to see that pieces are not touching, particularly in the glaze fire; they also fire more economically, requiring less fuel. But top-loading kilns also have some important disadvan-

tages—when placing a shelf above a layer of pots there is a risk of particles of grit or kiln wash falling or rubbing onto the pots below which can't be seen; the upward-lifting door can also prove heavy to handle, so it must be secured open properly to avoid accidental slippage.

The larger electric kilns are generally supplied in one complete unit rather than in prefabricated form. Pottery kilns are comparatively heavy pieces of equipment (for example, a kiln with internal dimensions 15" x 15" x 18" is likely to weigh between 280 lbs. and 500 lbs.) and care should be taken to ensure that the kiln required can be easily moved from the delivery point to the actual site where it is to be installed. The author knows of instances where kilns have been purchased and delivered to schools and studio potteries and

28. Alpine model EF-10, front-loading electric kiln, firing chamber 24" wide by 21" deep by 35" high, maximum temperature 2350°F., cone 10. Courtesy of A.D. Alpine, Inc.

then it has been found that the kilns were too large to pass through doorways or to be negotiated down flights of steps. If access to the kiln site is only possible by a very difficult approach, then the only alternative may be for the kiln to be supplied in prefabricated form. Most kiln suppliers would be only too pleased to offer a quotation for doing this, but as can be appreciated the cost of supplying the kiln in this form is considerably higher than the cost of a kiln supplied as one complete unit. Not only is the cost of building the kiln in prefabricated form greater, but it's necessary for the kiln manufacturer to send engineers with the kiln to build it on the site. One solution to this problem is the top-loading sectional kiln which is lightweight and can be easily assembled on the site. Sectional kilns (such as the ten-sided Skutt kilns shown in Figures 25 and 26) have the added convenience of versatility of size, being easily made larger or smaller by the addition or subtraction of a section. Each extension often includes its own multiple-element wiring system. The largest model of these sectional kilns offered by kiln manufacturers for studio use has a firing chamber of about 23" diameter by 27" high.

The floor under your kiln ideally should be made of cement or concrete. If you place the kiln on any other floor, such as tile or wood, it is best to protect it with an asbestos sheet because the heat from the kiln can discolor the tile or the wood finish. You can also place the kiln on cinder block or bricks to raise it for easier loading. Set the kiln on the stand provided by the manufacturer and place it on the floor or blocks, making sure that it is level. If it is not level, the kiln will undergo unnecessary stresses and the balancing of supports and shelves will be more difficult.

The ceiling of the kiln room, especially if it is made of wood, should be several feet above the kiln. Electric kilns do not constitute a fire hazard but common sense dictates that it is best not to have inflammable materials immediately on top of the kiln or hanging nearby. Never fire a kiln in an area, such as a closet or cabinet, where four sides are tightly enclosed. Air should be allowed to circulate around the kiln to prevent exterior overheating. Most kilns, incidentally, do not attain an external temperature greater than 120° to 140°C. (248° to 284°F.) during normal pottery firings, the hottest point usually being at the kiln door and the coolest at the rear of the kiln at the top and the coolest at the bottom of the firing chamber).

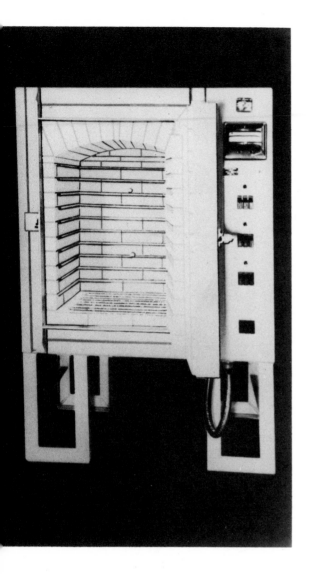

Electrical Requirements

Another major factor to be taken into consideration is the electrical supply to which the kiln will be connected. Most kilns, like electric stoves, have to be specially wired into the electricity supply. A seven-sided sectional kiln such as the L and L "Econo-Kiln," shown in Figure 27, which is 14⅜" in diameter by 13¼" deep and fires to 1260°C. (2300°F., cone 8), draws 12 amperes on a standard 220/110 volt supply on a single-phase circuit. The wiring requirement may be different if an extension is added to a sectional kiln. This should be taken into consideration at the outset of the kiln installation. It may be cheaper in the long run to get the adequate wiring for both units installed at the outset.

Larger kilns take considerably more current—for example, an Alpine EF-10 front loader shown in Figure 28 with interior dimensions of 24" x 23" x 35" that fires to 1300°C. (2372°F., cone 10) draws 85 amperes on a single phase, 240 volt supply line. Most utility poles have three-phase electricity cables from which single-phase lines are taken and fed into each house. Industrial plants often have a three-phase supply passed directly into the factory to a substation from which emanate the single-phase lines to each department and many new schools and public buildings are being wired for three-phase operation. The single phase kiln has two power leads and one ground, and the three phase kiln has three power leads and one ground. A three-phase kiln needs the four wires of a three-phase power source to operate properly, safely, and efficiently.

Incorrect wiring can be very dangerous, therefore electrical requirements and installation should be discussed with a qualified electrician who will be able to tell whether the kiln under consideration can be wired into the existing electricity supply. Putting in additional cable can be fairly expensive if it is a long way from the electrical supply to the kiln outlet.

As an extra precaution, when installing the kiln, connect it to a conducting ground such as a metal cold water pipe. Connect all sections of the container together with a copper wire (which may be bare). Be sure that the plug-in wire does not touch any part of the kiln when connected.

Firing Cost

Firing cost can be estimated by multiplying the kilowatt rating by the cost of one unit of electricity and then multiplying this by the length of time required to fire

Dyna-Kiln model H1824,
18" x 18" x 24", 2300°F.
Courtesy of L & L Manufacturing Co

Unique Kilns "Pro" serious,
average size 20" x 20" x 20", 2600°F.
Courtesy of Hed Industries, Inc.

Amaco table model EC-36,
10" x 9" x 10", 2000°F.
Courtesy of American Art Clay Co, Inc.

Alpine model EFG-2,
16" x 16" x 15", 2800°F.
Courtesy of A.D. Alpine, Inc.

29. Electric kilns.

the kiln. According to Amaco, the American Art Clay Company, firing costs for most electric kilns are 3¢ for each K.W.H. (kilowatt hour). Therefore, for a glaze firing, that takes an average time of six hours to complete, the cost would range somewhere between $1.00 and $2.00. The cost of electrical power, however, varies to a large extent. In the Scandanavian countries, for example, electricity is cheaper than oil or gas energy. Check with the local power company to determine the cost of electrical units for your studio.

Firing Temperature

The temperature at which the kiln will be fired is also an important consideration. This is determined by the type of ware, that is low-fire earthenware or high-fire stoneware or porcelain and the temperature at which these clay bodies and their proper glazes mature. When working with high-fire clay (clays which mature at cone 8 to cone 10 or above), the kiln must be equipped with high-temperature elements. Most small and medium-size ready-made kilns can fire to cone 6 or cone 8 maximum, although the elements will last longer if they are not continually fired to capacity.

There are several different types of elements that can be used for electric kilns. Generally speaking, the higher the temperature to which the kiln will have to be fired the more expensive the elements become. If the kiln is not likely to be fired to a temperature higher than 1000°C. (1832°F., cone 06) then Nichrome elements can be used. These are considerably cheaper than the Kanthal A elements that are used in kilns having a maximum firing temperature of 1200°C. (2192°F., cone 5). If higher temperatures than these are required for stoneware work, then Kanthal A1 elements will be necessary—these are more

expensive than the Kanthal A type. There are other grades of Kanthal wire which are sometimes used for pottery kiln elements, but the A and A1 grades seem to be the most popular.

In addition to the more expensive elements required for higher temperatures, more expensive refractory bricks have to be used. For this reason, the low-temperature kilns fitted with Nichrome elements cannot be converted to high-temperature ones merely by changing the type of elements because the kiln brickwork would not be capable of withstanding the increased temperature. Kilns fitted with Kanthal A elements, however, often have bricks that can withstand temperatures well over 1300°C. (2372°F., cone 10). Therefore, it is usually possible to change to Kanthal A1 elements and convert the kiln for higher temperatures. Elements are discussed in the following chapter.

Shipping and Delivery

As previously mentioned, kilns are normally delivered as one complete unit and they would normally be transported from the manufacturer by truck or by a railroad freight company. Arrangements for shipment and delivery can be made with the supplier, who often will provide an estimate on shipping cost before the order is placed for the kiln.

As soon as the kiln is delivered, be sure to check the packaging immediately to see that nothing is missing. A damaged crate can often indicate damaged goods. Refuse any obviously damaged cartons before signing for them. In that way the damages will be charged to the transport company. Inspect the kiln thoroughly while unpacking it and report any damages right away. Usually a company will accept damage claims within 15 days of receipt of merchandise.

3
DESIGN, CONSTRUCTION, AND REPAIR

A great deal of thought, calculation, and research, as well as a considerable amount of trial and error, have gone into the construction of the modern efficient electric pottery kiln and it is this careful attention to detail that has produced kilns that provide efficiency and long life with freedom from continual maintenance.

The basic structure of the kiln is designed to give adequate strength to withstand movement and knocks without being clumsy and excessively heavy. The refractory insulation brickwork used in kiln construction may vary from one size of kiln to another, depending on the acceptable heat-loss limit and the proposed firing temperature. The bricks themselves have to be well fitted together if the kiln is to give long service, and carefully shaped around the door so that it will close snugly to prevent excessive heat loss. The position and size of spyholes are determined to provide the optimum firing performance while affording enough room to view the cones and the kiln interior while firing. Choice of elements, design, and layout are likewise very much a part of the technology of kiln construction.

Framework

In kiln construction the framework is built first and then the brickwork is built within the frame, the electrical fittings and elements being added afterwards.

The framework, as shown in Figure 31, is normally built of angle-section steel, although in smaller kilns the framework may be made from strip steel. Angle-section steel is, however, particularly useful for building in the brickwork because it provides support on two sides. All joints are normally welded together although the sheet paneling can be attached with screws or bolts.

After extensive use, rust may form

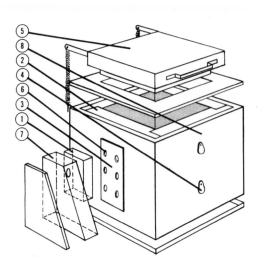

30. General Key for Parts
1. Switch box or electrical outlet
2. Firebrick
3. Transite
4. Peephole
5. Door or lid
6. Element terminals
7. Terminal guard or terminal guard cover
8. Kiln shell

Courtesy of American Art Clay Company, Inc.

31. *Typical steel framework for studio electric kilns. Courtesy of Kilns and Furnaces Ltd.*

around the door and spy hole of the kiln from the steam and vapors generated during the firing process. Although this is not especially detrimental, Unique Kilns advises occasional removal of the rust with a wire brush and sand paper followed by a retouch of the area with heat-resistant paint. It is important, however, to be careful when removing the rust to avoid contamination of the heating elements.

Brickwork

The two types of bricks generally used for the construction of kilns are refractory bricks and refractory insulation bricks. Refractory bricks are usually fairly dense and comparatively heavy in weight, some of them being heavier than the common house-brick. The fireclay brickwork used at the backs of fireplaces is a refractory brickwork. Refractory bricks absorb heat comparatively quickly; if one face of the brick is exposed to heat the other side of the brick will quickly become warm as the heat is conducted through the brick. Refractory bricks, therefore, tend to be used in those positions where heat loss is not quite so important—for example, in building chimneys or for the exterior brickwork of kilns. This type of brick is seldom used in the manufacture of electric kilns, for although they're quite capable of withstanding the heat generated inside the kiln, this heat would very easily be conducted away if the bricks were used for the interior lining. Also the use of these bricks would, of course, considerably increase the weight of the kiln. This would make shipping charges more expensive and moving kilns generally more difficult. The bricks used for the manufacture of electric kilns are normally of the refractory insulation type (K-16 to K-28, depending on the temperature at which the kiln is to be fired). These have all the heat-resist-

ing qualities of refractory bricks but are very porous. Since air is a good insulator, the large number of air pockets inside these bricks prevents heat from traveling very quickly through the brick to the opposite face. The pore structure also makes the bricks very light in weight; often workmen in kiln manufacturing workshops carry around huge stacks of bricks. This can be quite an awe-inspiring sight if the weight of a brick is estimated in terms of common house bricks. An ordinary house brick weighs about eight pounds, but a typical refractory insulation brick of the same size would weigh about two and one half pounds.

The high porosity (pore structure) also makes these bricks comparatively soft and easy to cut with a normal hacksaw. They can therefore be easily shaped for kiln doors, for elements grooves, or for spy holes.

The brickwork is built into the frame using a heat-resisting compound of a similar composition to the bricks themselves, or a fireproof mortar (a slurry of fireclay and sodium silicate). Care is taken to make the joints as fine as possible as large gaps between bricks filled with jointing compound are unsightly in appearance and a possible source of weakness. The refractory brick insulation in the kiln wall is usually 4″ to 5″ thick and is surrounded by a non-refractory wall made from other brick, transite or asbestos sheet, or similar material. Walls do not have to be thicker than this. Some loss of heat is even desirable near the end of the firing cycle.

If the bricks inside the kiln chip or crack, they can often be patched with kiln cement, available from a kiln supplier. Pre-moistion the area to be repaired and use as much cement as required. If the brick is badly damaged, you should replace it. Unique Kilns suggests that a sketch showing the dimensions and position of the damaged area will assist the factory in providing replacement brick.

Electrical Wiring and Fittings

In most kiln designs, the "works" such as junction boxes, terminals, and so on, are installed at the back or front of the kiln and access to them can normally be gained by removing a panel from the kiln. Electric kilns, especially the larger sizes require a lot of current and the switching device must be rugged to withstand the sparking which may occur when the kiln is switched on and off. The switching is therefore often done through a contactor, a robust relay that allows the kiln to be switched on and off without burning out any of the connections. (Smaller kilns may not be equipped with a contactor and this is why one is normally required if any

form of energy regulator is subsequently installed on the kiln, for these energy regulators operate by continually switching the kiln on and off.)

The electricity supply to each element is normally carried through a small brass connector shown in Figure 32. Steel connectors tend to oxidize too readily.

An energy regulator complete with a pilot light which is switched automatically on and off as the energy regulator switches the current to the elements on and off is standard on some kilns. A few kilns are equipped with a door switch as a standard item—particularly where the kiln is to be used for metal enameling. However, the majority of kilns used by the studio and school potter have a rotary switch with four settings: "Off," "Low," "Medium," and "High." These settings refer to the amount of current that is allowed to flow

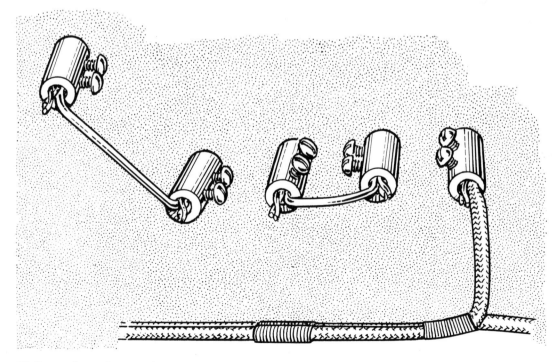

32. *Brass element connectors.*

to the elements, thereby indicating the rate at which the kiln increases its temperature.

Usually the kiln is equipped with a control panel—rather like the dashboard of an automobile—where the electrical accessories are installed. Some kilns, however, are supplied with a separate control panel which has to be mounted on an adjacent wall or other convenient surface.

Most kiln manufacturers build the door-closing device so that a padlock can be installed to lock the door.

Elements

There are several types of elements that can be installed on kilns, including Nichrome, Super Kanthal or silicon carbide, but the most popular are the Kanthal A and Kanthal A1 elements.

Nichrome elements, as the name implies, are made basically from an alloy of nickel and chromium and are used in kilns which are not required to operate at temperatures above about 1050°C. (1915°F., cone 05). When installed, these elements may enable a kiln to attain temperatures up to 1150°C. (2109°F., cone 1), but at temperatures as high as this the elements would burn away very quickly and so for all practical purposes, the maximum temperature is normally kept down to 1000°C. (1830°F., cone 06). This temperature, however, is sufficient for enameling, for overglaze decorating, and for low-temperature glazing. Nichrome wire is comparatively cheap but does not have the durability of higher temperature alloys.

Kanthal A and A1 elements are made from alloys of iron, aluminum, chromium, and cobalt. It is claimed that elements made from these alloys will give three times the life of the Nichrome types at similar temperatures. These alloys do not contain nickel and the great disadvantage is that once they have been fired they become very brittle and have to be well supported in the kiln. Any knocks or shaking can easily break them at this stage. Kanthal A elements will allow the kiln to reach maximum temperatures of about 1200°C. (2200°F., cone 6) and Kanthal A1 elements will allow a maximum operating temperature of 1300°C. (2372°F., cone 10). These are the two types of elements most commonly used in electric kilns. An important feature of Kanthal wire is that after firing, the wire becomes coated with aluminium oxide, which protects the wire from attack by most of the harmful gases. Exposure to reducing atmospheres however, will remove this coating very quickly and the elements will rapidly deteriorate unless the coating is restored by an oxidizing fire, (see Chapter 12 for a discussion of reduction firing in electric kilns). Alkali vapors and halogen vapors, for example, fluorine and iodine, are harmful to elements and so is lead vapor. However, Kanthal wire is not attacked by sulphur compounds as is Nichrome wire.

Super Kanthal and silicon carbide elements are used only for very high-temperature work beyond the temperatures used in pottery production. Temperatures of 1600°C. (2912°F., cone 24) can be attained with Super Kanthal and 1500°C. (2732°F., cone 18) with silicon carbide. Both types of elements are very expensive and as the resistance of the silicon carbide elements increases with each firing, voltage regulators have to be installed. Both types are normally used only in industry.

Element Regulation

Nichrome and Kanthal elements are wound into a continuous spiral which is usually formed into a hairpin shape, that is

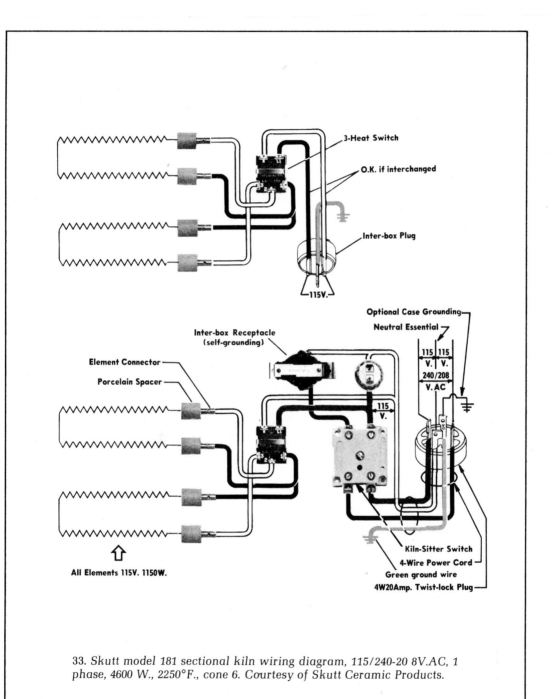

33. *Skutt model 181 sectional kiln wiring diagram, 115/240-20 8V.AC, 1 phase, 4600 W., 2250°F., cone 6. Courtesy of Skutt Ceramic Products.*

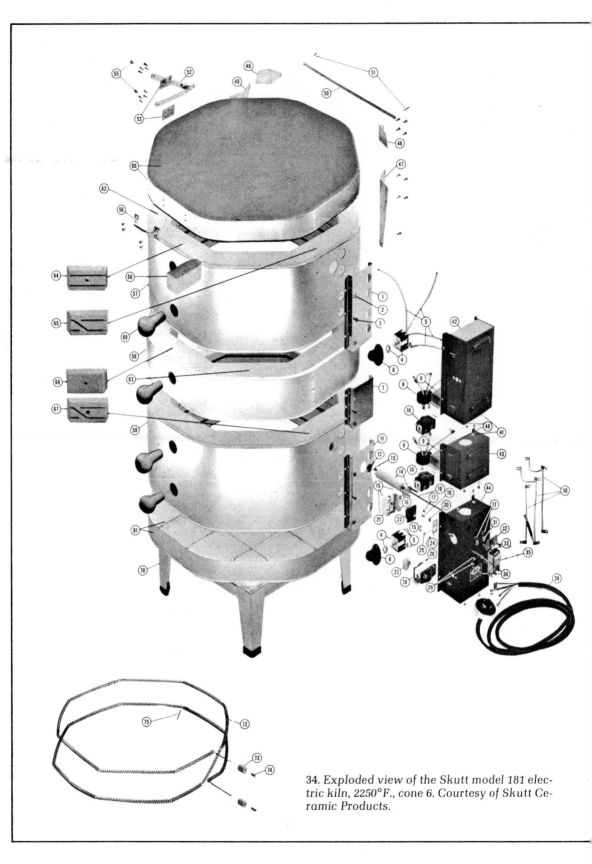

34. Exploded view of the Skutt model 181 electric kiln, 2250°F., cone 6. Courtesy of Skutt Ceramic Products.

two rows of elements coils joined at one end. The last 6" to 9" of each end of the element is not coiled but is left as a straight wire, called a "tail," that can be pushed through the rear wall of the kiln and linked up with the brass connectors.

The determination of the correct amount of wire to use for the elements, the calculation of how much wire of a certain grade is needed to supply the necessary amount of heat for a given kiln size, the adjustment of data to conform to different voltages, and the calculation of the number of coils into which the elements must be made—which must be within certain limits if optimum element life is to be obtained, is part of the science of kiln technology.

Most high-temperature kilns are designed to give a very even temperature distribution at around 1100°C. (2012°F., cone 03). At temperatures above and below this point there tends to be an increasing degree of temperature variation. In an attempt to obtain the least possible variation over a wide range of temperature, some kiln manufacturers install graded elements in their kilns. This does have the slight disadvantage that it is not possible to keep one spare element to guard against a risk of element failure since it is hard to know which element will fail first, but this disadvantage is more than compensated by the more even firing characteristics.

An alternative way of obtaining an even temperature distribution over the complete firing cycle is to wire the elements into groups or "banks" and to install an independent energy regulator to control each bank of elements. Two or three thermocouples are then installed on the kiln, so that if the temperature in one part of the kiln shows signs of lagging behind the rest of the kiln the energy regulator controlling the elements in that region can be turned to a higher setting so that more heat is introduced. This system is often used with large studio and semi-industrial kilns but is not usual with the kilns more commonly used by studio and school potters because of the expense involved.

The vast majority of craft pottery kilns are of the exposed element type. This means that the elements are supported in grooves or channels cut into the walls of the kiln leaving the elements clearly visible. This method is much cheaper, more efficient, and lends itself to easier maintenance than the alternative muffle type of kiln in which the elements are completely hidden from sight behind a thin wall of refractory material through which the heat has to pass to reach the ware.

Element Repair and Replacement

The elements in most studio electric kilns are easy to repair and replace. If a grooved brick which holds the element becomes damaged in handling or transporting or if after some use the elements, which have a tendency to expand, disengage from their grooves, and as a result the element sags, it is possible to hold it in position with unpointed 1½" Kanthal pins which are available from a kiln supplier and are sometimes furnished with the new kiln. Remember that Kanthal elements are brittle after the initial firings, so it is advisable to heat them electrically to a visible redness before trying to bend them onto the pins.

Important: turn off and unplug the kiln before working with the elements. And use a wooden tool or other nonconductor to push the elements into place. The elements can be "skewered" by inserting the pins straight in with pliers or they can be hung on the pins by pushing them in at a slight angle toward the back of the kiln.

When the kiln does not heat properly

Ref. No.	Part No.	Description	Ref. No.	Part No.	Description
1	101	Radiation shield for upper ring	39	S239	Power cord with 4-blade plug
2	102	Spacing washers	40	140	6-32 x ¼" Pan head screws
3	103	½" #6 sheet metal screws	41	141	Grounding lock washers
4	104	3-heat switch & nut	42	S142	Upper switch box
5	S105	Element feeder wires, set	43	S143	Blank ring jumper box
6	106	Knob for 3-heat switch	44	S144	Master switch box
7	107	Radiation shield for blank ring	46	146B	Lid hinge leaf, right hand
8	S108	Interbox plug w/wires	47	147B	Body hinge leaf, right hand
9	S109	Retaining straps for interbox plugs	48	148B	Lid hinge leaf, left hand
10	110	Interbox receptacle	49	149B	Body hinge, leaf, left hand
11	111	Radiation shield, master ring	50	250	Lid hinge rod
12	112	Kiln-Sitter gauge washer	51	151	Cotter pin
13	113	Kiln-Sitter Kanthal tips	52	252	Latching lid brace
14	S114	Kiln-Sitter porcelain tube in holder	53	S153	Lid brace anchor pad
15	115	4-40 hex nuts	55	155	6-32 v ¼" thumb screw
16	116	Kiln-Sitter contact-opening spring	56	156	Lid handle
17	117	6-32 x 3/16" Rd. Hd. Screw	57	S257	Upper ring stainless jacket
18	118	Kiln-Sitter sensing rod	58	S258	Blank ring stainless jacket
19	119	6-32 x 5/16" Rd. Hd. Screw	59	S259	Master ring stainless jacket
20	120	Latch plate retaining washer	60	S260	Lid with stainless band
21	S121	Kiln-Sitter switchbody w/contacts	61	S261	Bottom slab with stainless band
22	122	Kiln-Sitter shunt block w/plunger	62	262	Straight grooved brick
23	223	Pilot light	63	263	Blank ring brick
24	124	Kiln-Sitter latch plate	64	264	Grooved peep-hole bricks
25	125	Latch plate return spring	65	265	Terminal brick
26	126	Return spring hub	66	266	Blank ring peep-hole brick
29	129	4-40 x ¼" Rd. Hd. Screw	67	267	Kiln-Sitter terminal brick
30	S130	Full set yel. wire harn's. for mstr. bx.	68	168	Venting prop
31	131	Guide plate spacer	69	169	Peep-hole plugs
32	S132	Kiln-Sitter guide plate &claw	70	S270	Kiln stand
33	133	6-32 x ½" Rd. Hd. Screw	72	272	Heating elements
34	134	4-40 x 1¼" Rd. Hd. Screw	73	173	Porcelain spacer tubes
35	S135	Kiln-Sitter falling weight in bracket	74	174	Element connectors
38	238	Power cord strain relief	75	175	Kanthal corner pins

and you think that the elements need to be replaced, first make sure that the problem actually does lie in the elements. This can be done by a number of methods. Check the fuse box and all connections for defective cords or receptacles. If the kiln is new, also make sure that the electrical output is adequate for the temperature to which it is being fired. You can also have the power company run a recorded volt test with the kiln on for a normal firing period and off over a 24 hour period. If the average voltage of the test is less than that rated on the kiln, you can expect a longer firing time.

Then check the elements by turning them on to high. Humming of the elements is normal in Kanthal types. The humming should stop at red heat. If only one element does not work, the defect may be in that element, in the switch box, or in a broken or disconnected wire from the switch to the element. You can run a test on the elements with a voltmeter or test lamp, shown in Figure 35. This gives a positive check because even a defective element may glow red in time. When using the test lamp, it is important to turn all kiln switches to off or disconnect the kiln at the wall plug. Plug the test lamp into a wall outlet. Touch each terminal of a single element wire with the wire ends of the test lamp. If the lamp fails to light, this is positive proof that the element wire should be replaced.

Also, you can check for breaks along the element connection particularly where it enters the brick. Remember to handle the elements gently as they are brittle. If you find no break, open the switch box and inspect for discolored components. If you are still unsure, replace parts beginning with the switch. When ordering the switch, be sure to give the model number of the kiln.

If a Kanthal element burns through at the connector, it is often possible to stretch the element a little in order to reconnect it. Again be sure that the kiln is off and unplugged. Heat the part of the element that is inside the kiln (close to the element tail) with a blow-torch flame, while pulling the wire gently from the rear connection chamber. Naturally, any attempt to do this while the element is cool would probably result in breakage, since Kanthal wires become brittle after a few firings, but at high temperatures they are always soft. According to Skutt, with normal use, elements last approximately 400 cone 3 to cone 6 firings, 1,000 cone 06 to cone 04 firings, or 2,000-plus overglaze or other low-temperature firings. But this varies widely depending on individual use. *Always unplug the kiln from the wall outlet when working with elements.* When you have determined the location of the defective element, unscrew the switch box and loosen the element connection board. Cut off the old element ends and remove the element. When ordering a new element, always quote the serial number of your kiln to the kiln manufacturer, indicating which element has failed, and always make certain that *every* trace of the burnt-out element has been removed from the element grooves before fitting the replacement. This is most important.

When installing new elements, work on only one element at a time to avoid confusion. Refer back to the wiring diagram for assistance. The procedure for changing elements varies somewhat from kiln to kiln. The instruction manual provided with the kiln will explain in detail how to proceed.

First Firing

After the kiln has been assembled and any brick chips or foreign matter around the elements have been cleaned out, brush the

Cut

1. An extension cord. Cut off socket with 3" or 4" of cord.

2. Separate insulated wires. Cut one segment of cord one foot from end. Strip off 1" of insulation from all cut ends.

3. Twist bare wires on socket with wires of break in cord. Wrap exposed wires with electrician's insulating tape.

4. Incorporate nails or single strand wire into the bare ends of the cord for contact points. Wrap connections with insulation tape.

5. Wrap separated wires together to within 10" of the nails.

35. *Test lamp. Courtesy of the American Art Clay Company, Inc.*

shelves and floor with a thin coating of kiln wash—a slurry of water mixed with ½ part kaolin or china clay and ½ part silica or flint. Kiln wash can be homemade or purchased ready-to-use from a ceramic supplier. Leave a 1″ margin around the floor area; alternatively you could spread a thin layer of beach sand on the floor of the kiln. The shelves probably will not need to be recovered completely again. When the kiln wash chips off or where glaze has run onto the shelf, just sand these areas and patch them. Do not apply kiln wash to the sides or lid of the kiln.

Before firing the kiln, be sure that you understand the operation of the switches and the Kiln Sitter (see Chapter 5 on accessories). Then set up some shelves on stands inside the kiln, put a small cone in the Kiln Sitter and a large cone of the same temperature at the spy hole in the empty kiln and test fire at biscuit temperature— 923° to 1046°C. (1693° to 1915°F., cone 09 to cone 05). Leave spy-hole plugs out and the door ajar or lid propped up. Follow a standard switching schedule—one hour on low, one' hour on medium, one hour on high—until the kiln shuts off or the cone falls. The large cone will indicate whether the Kiln Sitter and pyrometer, if installed, are functioning properly. Alternately, Unique Kilns suggests allowing the kiln to operate at 500°C. (900°F.) for at least eight hours to dry out the residual moisture in the kiln. This method necessitates the use of a pyrometer. The first firing, also known as "bake-out," drives away any moisture present in the brickwork, after which the kiln is ready to be put into full service.

After this first firing has taken place, it may be noticed that a few fine cracks have formed in the interior brickwork of the kiln. These cracks will close up when the kiln is next heated and they will open up again when the kiln is subsequently cooled. In this way they serve as expansion joints and are in no way detrimental to the operation of the kiln.

You may also notice odors during the first few firings which come from paint components and moisture from the refractory brick. During subsequent firing of ware, odors and sometimes smoke can also be caused by the melting wax, if you have applied it to the foot of your pots (the wax-burn-off smell is apparent in the very early stages of the firing), by the release of gasses in the interaction of the clays and glazes, and often from organic impurities in the clay body itself. Sometimes a particular strain of clay will give an especially heavy odor and smoke. The best remedy for this is good ventilation in the kiln room; either open windows or run an exhaust fan.

4
MAKING STUDIO ELECTRIC KILNS

If you want the satisfaction of making your own equipment, you can build an electric kiln somewhat cheaper, in terms of materials, than you can purchase one ready-made, disregarding the time you will put into the construction (probably about 60 or 70 hours).

The following chapter presents the publication, "Making Studio Electric Kilns" by Laurance E. Webber in its entirety.* Originally published in 1947, this manual gives detailed instructions and drawings for making electric kilns. Since prices are also from the original edition, allowance must be made for the general price increases which have occured, but the relative costs are generally accurate.

* *Reproduced courtesy of Laurance E. Webber, Center for Industrial and Institutional Development, University of New Hampshire.*

Errata. In the "Bill of Materials" on page 5, one line should be added in the carborundum slab section: 1 Carborundum slab 13½ in. by 13 in. by ⅝ in. Notice of Change of Address: The Philip Carey Manufacturing Company, 22 Moulton Street, Cambridge, Massachusetts 02138.

MAKING STUDIO ELECTRIC KILNS

By

Laurance E. Webber

ENGINEERING EXPERIMENT STATION
UNIVERSITY OF NEW HAMPSHIRE
DURHAM, NEW HAMPSHIRE

Foreword

THE TWO KILNS DESCRIBED in this bulletin are outgrowths of the one described in our previous publication.* The construction of the first kiln (which has a firing chamber 13″ wide by 13½″ deep by 13″ high) is completely described so that one can assemble it with no further information at hand. The larger kiln ware box is 22″ wide by 18″ deep by 27″ high. It is described sufficiently to permit its construction by using the description in conjunction with that of the smaller one. This is felt to be satisfactory because methods of grooving bricks, cutting insulation, etc., are the same for both kilns.

Electricity at 220-240 volts, either alternating or direct current, is required for both kilns. The smaller kiln draws approximately 20 amperes and the larger draws about 45 amperes. Regular dwellings are commonly serviced by electric power at 220-240 volts at the meter. Consequently, many home studios can accommodate the smaller kiln by merely running a single electrical circuit capable of carrying about 25 amperes from the meter to the kiln. Larger studios are usually so located as to have available power for the 45 ampere kiln.

Temperatures as high as 2350°F. can be attained in both kilns which are designed to give satisfactory performance and life up to such temperature. However, the life of the heating elements will be longer when operation is carried on at the lower temperatures usually used for pottery work. The higher temperatures are harder on the entire kiln constuction and such temperatures are not attained as quickly as the usual lower ones.

The kilns are relatively economical to operate, particularly when the uniformity of results obtainable with them is kept in mind. Based on an electricity cost of 2 cents per kilowatt hour, the smaller kiln can be fired 8 hours for approximately 75 cents and the larger kiln can be fired 8 hours for approximately $1.75. Even at 4 cents per kilowatt hour the cost of firing is small compared with the value of the ware.

The designs of these kilns have been thoroughly considered. The following warning should be heeded: *Do not alter the electrical characteristics of either of these kilns* unless you are completely familiar with the results to be expected from such changes.

Acknowledgments

Grateful acknowledgment is made to Edwin Scheier, Associate Professor of The Arts at the University of New Hampshire, for his enthusiastic cooperation in this work. His willingness to try out various arrangements has been most helpful. Several design difficulties in the larger kiln were worked out by Professor Scheier in a similiar kiln constructed under his direction at Puerto Rico. George S. Harker, Graduate Assistant, made the original drawings for the larger kiln and also made many valuable suggestions regarding details of construction. Mr. Harker's interest and able cooperation have been of great assistance in the successful completion of this project.

---

*"Making an Electric Kiln," Engineering Experiment Station Publication No. 1, January, 1943.

MAKING STUDIO ELECTRIC KILNS

By Laurance E. Webber[1]

Part I

Fig. 3 — Front view of the 13″ x 13½″ x 13″ electric kiln which usually can be built for about $100. When complete it weighs approximately 375 pounds.

13″ x 13½″ x 13″ Electric Pottery Kiln

THE KILN DESCRIBED HERE was designed at the suggestion of several people who felt that the internal size of the one previously designed (Publication No. 1) for 110-120 volts was inadequate for production firing. This kiln has an internal size of 13″ wide by 13″ high by 13½″ deep, a volume of

[1]Research Associate Professor, Assistant Director, Engineering Experiment Station.

2,280 cubic inches. (See Fig. I and Fig. II.) The temperature is very uniform because there are heating elements in all six walls of the kiln. A source of 220-240 volts, either alternating or direct current, is required. The electrical load is approximately 4.5 kilowatts since the kiln is designed to draw approximately 20 amperes at this voltage. Operation may be carried to a kiln temperature of 2350°F. with safety; however, longer life may be expected from the heating elements if operated at lower temperatures.

The total cost of materials usually runs above $100. All-day operation would cost only approximately 75 cents, computed at a cost of 2 cents per kilowatt hour. From 60 to 70 man hours are needed to build the kiln. The weight of the completed unit is approximately 375 pounds.

This design has been carefully tested, both mechanically and electrically: consequently, the following admonition is made: *Do not change dimensions or alter the electrical characteristics in any way* unless you are sure of the effects of such changes. Much time and money have been wasted by persons who have attempted to design electrically-fired kilns without sufficient recognition of the factors involved.

Details of Construction

The first thing to be ascertained by the prospective kiln builder is whether or not a source of 220-240 volts of electricity (A.C. or D.C.), from which approximately 20 amperes may be drawn, is available. This should be checked by a local electrician. A circuit made up of No. 10 B&S gauge wire should be

Fig. 4 — Rear view of 13" x 13½ x 13" kiln.

run directly from the fuse box to the kiln. The circuits should be protected by 25 ampere fuses. *No other electrical device or appliance should be used on the kiln circuit when the kiln is in operation.*

If it is found that a satisfactory electrical circuit can be obtained, the following bill of materials should be ordered. Sources from which purchases were made are indicated; however, except in the case of the Kanthal resistance ribbon, persons in parts of the country other than New England should use local distributors of the required materials. Various common supplies, such as No. 14 wire, screws, etc., may be secured from a local electrical or hardware supplier and are not listed.

Bill of Materials

3 cartons (75) Babcock & Wilcox Co. K-26 9-inch
   Straights Insulation Bricks   Approx. Cost $28.00
The B. F. Marsh Co., 19-29 Crescent St., Worcester, Mass.

2 Units Kanthal A-1 Resistance Ribbon .118 x .0118"   Approx. Cost $24.00
The Kanthal Corp., Amelia Place, Stamford, Conn.

Asbestos Sheathing ¼ in. thick, cut as listed later.
27 pieces of Hi-Temp No. 19 Insulation Blocks 6 in. by 2 in. by 36 in.
                                Approx. Cost $30.00
The Philip Carey Mfg. Co., 267 Melford St., Charlestown District, Boston,
   Mass.

32 ft. of 1 in. by 1 in. by ⅛ in. angle steel.
5 feet of ¼ in. diameter cold rolled steel.
6 feet of 1 in. by ⅛ in. hot rolled steel.
Source: Any local steel handler.   Approx. Cost $2.00

1 Enclosed-type safety switch suitable for 250 volts and 25 amperes, fused
   for 25 amperes.
2 Surface mounting toggle switches suitable for 250 volts and 10 amperes.
1 Package (50) 2-C-10 "Sta-Kon" (or equivalent) electrical connectors.
Source: Any local electrical supplies store.   Approx. Cost $7.00

2 or 3 Carborundum Slabs 13¼ in. by 12¾ in. by ⅝ in. Approx. Cost $15.00
The Carborundum Company, Perth Amboy, N. J.

Approximate total cost for these materials $106.00

The cost of the kiln will be increased or decreased from this figure according to how many or how few of the remaining parts may be on hand for the complete construction of the kiln. Unfortunately, standard cartons of the fire bricks make it necessary to purchase more than are required to build one kiln. Choice of switches depends upon who is going to use the kiln and where it is placed. If only one worker is to be around the kiln, cheaper, knife-type switches will work satisfactorily unless prohibited by local wiring rules. Enclosed switches of Underwriter Laboratories inspected grade should be used in studios in which several persons are working. A few feet of No. 14 B&S gauge asbestos covered wire, a few machine screws, wood screws, nuts, cap screws, and washers are also required. These may be purchased in local hardware and electrical supplies stores.

When the required parts have been received, they must have some work done on them. First to be considered is the cutting to length and coiling of the wire for the heating elements. The Kanthal A-1 resistance ribbon may be bent freely before it is heated, but after it has been heated it becomes brittle and will not stand bending. Therefore, do not apply heat to the ribbon until the kiln is completed. Carefully note the resistance marked on the tag on this wire as it is received.

The following table indicates the length of ribbon which should be used for the various coils, depending upon the specific resistance of the ribbon. A figure other than zero in the third decimal place of the resistance value takes the next lower resistance value length. For example, suppose that the tag shows the resistance to be .465 ohm per foot, the coil lengths will be the same as for .460 ohms per foot. The coils are formed on a board prepared by driving brads into it, spaced as shown on the detail sheet.

| | Length of Ribbon Required (Computed for 230 Volts) | | |
| | 6 coils | 4 coils | 5 coils |
Resistance of Ribbon Ohms per foot	Sides	Top and Bottom	Rear and Door
.450	12'-9"	19'-2"	15'-4"
.460	12'-6"	18'-9"	15'-0"
.470	12'-2¾"	18'-4¼"	14'-8¼"
.480	11'-11¾"	17'-11½"	14'-4½"
.490	11'-8¾"	17'-7¼"	14'1"
.500	11'-6"	17'-3"	13'-9½"
.510	11'-3¼"	16'-11"	13'-6½"
.520	11'-½"	16'-7"	13'-3¼"
.530	10'-10¼"	16'-3¼"	13'-2½"
.540	10'-7¾"	15'-11½"	12'-9¼"
.550	10'-5½"	15'-8¼"	12'-6½"

Now we come to the actual winding of the coils.[2] Six coils are required for the sides, 4 for the top and bottom, and 5 for the rear and door. For connections 8½ inches of wire should be left unformed on each end of each coil; that is, there should be 8½ inches on each end of the coils which are not wound over the brads. Figure I shows how a coil should look when completed. These coils are frequently referred to as "hairpins".

In winding all these coils, the wire is bent lightly around each brad until the entire winding is completed. Then the coil is lifted off the brads and each individual loop is pinched with the fingers to bring it together. Care should be exercised to see that no loop is pinched so as to bring the windings in too close contact; that is, there should be a minimum space of about ⅛ inch between the two sides of each "wave". This pinching operation will serve to make the coil more easily manageable and will compress it to fit into the space allowed.

---

[2]See Kanthal Catalogue for other methods of forming wire and shaping firebricks.

Cutting the Bricks

The grooves are cut in the bricks for the wires by the use of an easily constructed special tool made as follows: The point is cut or ground from a ¾ inch wood bit, after which a piece of steel ³⁄₁₆ inch thick, ½ inch wide. and 1¼ inches long is brazed to the bottom of the wood bit. This cutter is rotated at about 700 revolutions per minute in a drill press. The bricks are easily grooved by pushing them against the cutter. The grooves are made as shown in Fig. I, which also shows the number of each type required. A guide should be clamped to the drill press table in order to insure that the cuts in the bricks will be parallel.

Scraps of K-26 firebricks from cutting the odd sizes should be saved because small pieces can be used for shelf spacers in the kiln and spy-hole plugs can be filed from larger pieces. The necessary cuts to be made on bricks for the door are shown in Fig. I. Two or more spy holes should be cut in the door at different heights. Care must be exercised to see that the loops of the door heating elements are spread around the spy holes.

The hairpin coils should be slipped into the grooves in the K-26 firebricks as the kiln is assembled, and the ends of the coils bent back on themselves inside the kiln. A groove should be cut with a hacksaw blade to permit the wire to pass from one row to the next where necessary. After the kiln is assembled, holes through which the ends of the coils are passed should be drilled with a ³⁄₁₆-inch diameter rod, about 28 inches long, filed or ground to a diamond-shaped point. The holes are drilled from the front of the kiln, through the door. The ends of the rear coils must be bent at right angles to the coils so they will come out through the rear of the kiln. Care should be exercised to see that there is at least one inch between each coil end as it passes through the rear of the kiln. The coils expand laterally when they are heated; consequently, they should be so arranged that they cannot touch one another in their expanded condition.

Cutting the Hi-Temp No. 19 Insulation

The following table should be followed as a schedule in cutting the Hi-Temp No. 19 insulation. It is possible to do this cutting with a hand saw, but it is much quicker and easier to do it with an ordinary power saw. The saw will be dulled, but will not be permanently damaged.

Required Cuts for Hi-Temp No. 19

Twenty-seven pieces 2″ by 6″ by 36″ are all that are required since scrap may be utilized to make up the necessary pieces.

Material for Botton
8 pieces - 2″ x 6″ x 26½″   Should be whole.
2 pieces - 2″ x 2″ x 26½″*   Should be whole.
                                   Note: Order of Dimensions:
                                         Thickness, Width, Length.

Material for Top
4 pieces - 2″ x 6″ x 26½″
4 pieces - 2″ x 6″ x 22½″
1 piece - 2″ x 2″ x 26½″*   *Split one 2″ x 6″ x 36″ pieces for these.
1 piece - 2″ x 2″ x 22½″

Material for Back

8 pieces - 2" x 6" x 18"
2 pieces - 2" x 2" x 18"

Material for Front

2 pieces - 2" x 4½" x 26"   *Must* be whole
2 pieces - 2" x 2¼" x 13"
4 pieces - 2" x 6"   x 15½"
4 pieces - 2" x ½" x 15½"

Material for Sides

12 pieces - 2" x 6" x 18"
4 pieces - 2" x ½" x 18"

List of Cuts of Asbestos Board

The following list of pieces of ¼-inch thick asbestos board should be copied and sent to the Company supplying the board:

For top and bottom: 2 pieces 26½" (wide) x 27" (deep)
For sides: 2 pieces 26½" (deep) x 26" (high)
For back and front: 2 pieces 26" (wide) x 26" (high)

(In the center of one of these latter pieces cut an opening 13" x 13"

For back panel: 1 piece 18" x 18"
For placing under door: 1 piece 13" x 4"
For door panel: 1 piece 2" x 10"

Making the Steel Frame

Angle iron should be sawed and accurately filed to the size shown in Fig. I. The notches are cut at an angle of 45°. This steel can be bent cold in a vise. The frame is completed by bending the 1¼-inch end over and fastening it with two small screws (either 8-32 or 10-32). The end of the screw should be cut off flush with the inside of the frame with a cold chisel. If welding equipment is available, welding is, of course, a simpler method than using screws. The edges for the frame can be readily forged to the shape shown in Fig. I. The method of attaching the frame will be taken up in the discussion of the assembly of the kiln.

Detailed Assembly of the Kiln

Assembly is most readily carried out on six or seven common red bricks or 2-inch high blocks. Bricks or blocks should be placed on a sturdy table, accessible from all sides. A piece of asbestos board 26½" x 27" (which has been cut to size by the company supplying it) is placed on the bricks. Checking with Fig. II the insulation blocks for the kiln bottom should next be placed. They should be arranged so that the cracks do not line up. (See Fig. II.)

The bottom fire bricks which carry the bottom heating elements are now placed, followed by the sides and top. A small jack or wood frame may be used to support the roof bricks until the kiln is completed. The top bricks require a little support to defer sagging of the roof. The method to use follows. Cut the heads from $\frac{1}{4}$-inch diameter, 6-inch long spikes. Carefully drill holes $\frac{1}{2}$ inch from the upper edge of the top bricks and insert the spikes $\frac{1}{2}$ their length in each brick. Two spikes are required in the full bricks but one is sufficient in the $2\frac{1}{2}"$ x $2\frac{1}{2}"$ x $9"$ bricks. Spikes should also be used to tie the $4\frac{1}{2}"$ x $4\frac{1}{4}"$ x $2\frac{1}{2}"$ side bricks to the $4\frac{1}{2}"$ x $2\frac{1}{2}"$ x $8\frac{1}{4}"$ bricks. Stainless steel (18-8) rods are better than spikes but are more expensive and more difficult to obtain.

The back brick assembly is placed on a board and carefully lifted into position. The placement of the insulation blocks is the next step in the assembly of the kiln. To do this most easily use the table which shows the cuts required for the insulation in conjunction with Fig. II. The $13"$ x $4"$ piece of asbestos board is placed in front of the kiln opening for the door to rest on. This prevents the door from wearing down the insulation.

The factory precut asbestos board sides are placed on top of the insulation, after which the steel frame is put on. Putting the frame on is most readily accomplished by squeezing the unit together with large wood-gluing clamps before slipping the frames on front and back. The edges are laid in place and marked for $\frac{5}{16}$-inch holes through which the one- or $\frac{3}{4}$-inch long, $\frac{1}{4}$-20 cap screws pass. The corners under these holes are drilled and tapped $\frac{1}{4}$-20 to receive the cap screws.

The back panel, to which the electrical switches are bolted, is indicated in the asbestos board list. This panel should be bolted to the brackets of $\frac{1}{8}"$ x $1"$ steel shown in Fig. I. The brackets are attached to the kiln by 8-32 or 10-32 machine screws in holes drilled and tapped into the top and bottom rails of the kiln. No. 8 wood screws, 1 inch in length, are used to hold the brackets to the asbestos board rear of the kiln. It may be desirable to attach $\frac{1}{4}$-inch mesh hardware cloth to this switch panel in such a way as to prevent any possible contact with electrically-charged wires.

The ends of the coils protruding from the back of the kiln are slipped into the Sta-Kons or other electrical connectors and securely fastened. All coil connections are made on the back of the kiln, *outside* the firing chamber. The end of each hairpin to be joined to another should pass completely through the connector. This insures good tight joints as pressure is exerted in two places on the joint.

The side hairpins must be connected in series, as must the top and bottom hairpins and as must the rear and door hairpins. These three series circuits should be connected in parallel to the 220-240 volt source.

In Fig. 1 (see enclosed work sheet) observe the top row of points of the Rear Terminal Connections. The point next to extreme right, NOT the point below it, should be connected to the door coils in series. There should NOT be a connection between the second and third points from the right in the upper row. The point which is third from the right, upper row, should be connected to the left single pole switch.

The ends of the two hairpins which belong in the door should be pushed through holes drilled in the front of the door. The connection between the rear coils and the door coils can be readily made by the use of a piece of flexible approved heater cord which should be securely attached to the switch panel just as it is usual to attach it to a junction box, etc. The other end of the cable should have fitted to it a female electrical plug to carry 10

9

amperes at 250 volts. A male receptacle having an electrical rating equal to that of the plug should be attached to the door. The door coil ends are connected to this receptacle. The piece of 2″ x 10″ asbestos board should be spaced away from the face of the door as a guard against accidental contact with the terminals. A method of attaching such a guard is shown in Fig. I. The sketch in Fig. I also shows a method which has been used to attach rigidly an electrical receptacle to the door binders. The kiln should be given a coat of good grade aluminum paint to act both as a preservative of the metal and as a certain amount of heat insulation.

Details of Operation

The first firing of the kiln should be carried out slowly. The current flows in the side coils when the main switch is closed. This switch should be left closed, *without* the door in, for about an hour. The door should then be placed and the kiln temperature brought to 1000-1200°F.: the kiln should then be permitted to cool overnight from this temperature before further heating. A reasonable estimate of this temperature can be made by observing the inside of the kiln through the spy hole, with the current off. When color (dark red) is observed inside the kiln, the temperature is high enough.

Little experience is required to become familar with the operation of the kiln. Usually it is planned to fire in about 8 hours. Only the main switch is closed at the start of the run. This alone is left closed until the moisture has been driven from the ware, at which time the snap switch is closed. passing electricity through the top and bottom coils. When it is desired to increase the temperature. or the heating rate, the second snap switch may be closed, thus passing electricity through the back and door coils. Operation is continued with all coils in use until the desired temperature is reached. Two or three trials should suffice to establish the correct timing of switch closing.

Pyrometers

This kiln may have. a hole drilled through the back to receive a thermocouple which is attached to a milliammeter to continuously read the temperature of the kiln. Commercial pyrometers may be purchased. or the rare builder who has the facilities may construct his own. All electric kilns used by the University of New Hampshire are equipped with pyrometers which have been constructed for continuous temperature reading. The end point of a firing is always checked with pyrometric cones but the pyrometer is most useful to indicate when more coils should be placed in use to insure reaching the desired temperatures in a pre-determined time. The kiln should be placed on 6 or 7 common red bricks on a study table about 30 inches high.

10

PART II

Fig. 5 — Front view of 18″ x 22″ x 27″ electric
kiln, loaded for firing with Scheier pottery.

18″ x 22″ x 27″ Electric Pottery Kiln

THIS STUDIO KILN has a ware chamber 18 inches deep, 22 inches wide. and 27 inches high. With the door closed the kiln is 41½″ wide, 46½″ high, and 38″ deep. The weight is about 1500 pounds. It draws 45 amperes at 230 volts, A.C. or D.C. The heating elements are arranged to completely surround the ware box in five parallel circuits designed so as to keep the temperature inside the kiln as free from bothersome gradients as possible.

Many details of construction used for the smaller kiln apply to this one: therefore, it is necessary for prospective builders to thoroughly read all details of construction previously described in this publication.

The insulation used in this kiln differs somewhat from the method followed in our previous constructions. Here we are using an insulating firebrick (K-20) next to the firebricks (K-26) which hold the heating elements. A temperature of 2350°F. can be safely attained. A little experience in stacking and firing the ware will enable the operator to avoid uneven temperatures. Temperature rise in a particular zone may be halted by switching off the current in the electrical circuit of the zone.

The materials alone for this kiln usually can be obtained for about $300.00. At 2 cents per kwhr. an 8-hour run would cost only about $1.75. Records kept on one such kiln, when new, showed the consumption of 65 kwhrs. to attain a temperature of 2000°F.

11

Details of Construction

A source of 220-240 volts, alternating current or direct current, capable of delivering 45 amperes must be available. When the availability of power has been ascertained, the materials should be ordered.

Bill of Materials

Quantity	Material	Approx. Price
37	Pieces of Hi-Temp No. 19 Insulation blocks. 6″ by 2″ by 36″ Asbestos board (see cutting size list)	
	Source: Philip Carey Manufacturing Co. 267 Medford Street Charlestown District Boston, Mass.	$ 50.00
300	B & W K-20 9″ Insulation Straights	
100	B & W K-26 Insulation Straights	
	Source: B. F. Marsh Company 19-29 Crescent Street Worcester, Mass.	135.00
4	Bars Angle Steel 1½″ x 1½″ x ¼ x 22 feet	
1	Bar Flat Steel 1″ x ⅛″ x 20 feet	
1	Bar Round Steel ½″ diameter x 12 feet	
1	Bar Flat Steel, 1½″ x ½″ x 4 feet	
	Source: Local suppliers	20.00
2	Pounds Kanthal A-1 resistance ribbon. .118″ x .0118″	
	Source: The Kanthal Corp. Amelia Place Stamford, Conn.	25.00
150 ft.	No. 12 Asbestos covered wire	
5	10 ampere, 250 volt switches	
5	Screw bases for pilot bulbs	
10	6-8 volt base pilot bulbs (5 spares)	
5	Porcelain tubes approx. 3″ long	
100	Sta-Kon 2-C-10 pressure connectors	
	Source: Local electrical supplier	25.00
4	T-hinges, 10″	
50	Cap screws, ⅜″ diameter x ¾″	
50	Lock washers, ⅜″	
10 sq. ft.	Hardware cloth, ¾″ mesh	
	Source: Local hardware supplier	6.00
1	Kiln setter, 18″ x 22″ x ¾″	
3	Kiln setters, 17½″ x 21½″ x ¾″	
6	Kiln setters, 17¾″ x 10¾″ x ⅝″	
	Source: The Carborundum Company Perth Amboy, N. J.	60.00
		$321.00

The list of pieces of asbestos board in Table I should be ordered. cut to size.

Table I — Asbestos Board Cutting List

No. of Pieces	Material Size	Placement
2	40¾″ x 27″ x ½″	Top and Bottom
2	44¾″ x 27″ x ½″	Sides
2	44¾″ x 39¾″ x ½″	Back and Door
2	40¾″ x 9″ x ½″	Door Top and Bottom
2	44¾″ x 9″ x ½″	Door Sides
1	27″ x 32″ x ¼″	Rear Terminal Cover
1	27″ x 8″ x ¼″	Door Terminal Cover
1	6″ x 6″ x ¼″	Main Terminal Holder
1	12″ x 12″ x ¼″	Switch Panel

Since the completed kiln weighs about 1500 pounds a strong base must be provided. If a wooden table is used the kiln should rest on common bricks. If the kiln is to rest directly on the base, ¼″ thick asbestos board should be placed under the kiln so that the frame can later be slid under the ½-inch thick asbestos board bottom. In this latter case, the bottom side frames should be put in place at the beginning of assembly. If the suggested method of swinging the door is used. it is essential to securely fasten down the kiln so that it cannot be tipped over on the operator. Some rigid attachment to the floor should be made.

Table II — Materials Cutting List.

Item	Dimensions for: K-26 Insulation Brick	Number Required	Remarks
(Refer to (Fig. 1)			
	9″ x 4½″ x 2½″	96	See Fig. 1
F 1	4″ x 4½″ x 2½″	8	*Cut two per brick
	K-20 Insulation Brick		
	9″ x 4½″ x 2½″	224	See Fig. 1
1	5″ x 4½″ x 2½″	68	
2	4″ x 4½″ x 2½″	50	*Cut from Item 1
3	9″ x 4½″ x 2″	2	
4	5″ x 4½″ x 2″	1	
5	4″ x 4½″ x 2″	1	*Cut from Item 4
	Hi-temp No. 19 Insulation Block		
A	36″ x 6″ x 2″	15	See Fig. 1
B	36″ x 3″ x 2″	3	
C	27″ x 6″ x 2″	18	
D	27″ x 3″ x 2″	3	*Cut from Item C
E	36″ x 4½″ x 2″	2	
F	36″ x 4″ x 2″	1	
G	32″ x 4½″ x 2″	2	
H	9″ x 4″ x 2″	1	*Cut from Item C

*One-half the width of the saw blade will be lost from these items and from the pieces from which they are cut.

Tables II and III indicate how the insulation materials should be cut and where they should be placed. The first layer of insulation blocks should be laid to project ¼ inch ahead of the bottom piece of asbestos board so that the frame will fit in the groove around the insulation block and come flush with the face of the kiln. The groove in the insulation block should be hand cut after assembly to fit the frame snugly. The K-20 insulating firebricks may be cut with the same saw (preferably power saw) used to cut the Hi-Temp insulation. Grooving of K-26 bricks has been described in the description of the smaller kiln.

Table III — Placement of Cut Materials.

K-26 Insulation Bricks Required For:	Uncut	*Cut as F 1	Slotted
Top	3		12
Bottom	3		12
R. Side	0		12
L. Side	0		12
Back	0		18
Front	6	8	18

K-20 Insulation Brick Required For:	Uncut	*Cut as 1	2	3	4	5
Top	20	10	10			
Bottom	20	10	10			
R. Side	40	10				
L. Side	40	10				
Back	24	12	12	2	1	1
Front	80	16	18			

Hi-Temp No. 19 Insulation Block Required For:	A	B	C	*Cut as D	E	F	G	H
Top	4	1						
Bottom	4	1						
R. Side			7	1				
L. Side			7	1				
Back			4	1	2		2	
Front	7	1				1		1

*Refer to Fig. 1 for reference numbers and letters.

A wooden frame should be carefully and accurately constructed to fit inside the firing chamber during construction. It is easier to remove this frame by building it with screws so placed as to permit taking it apart from the inside when the kiln is completed.

Pieces of doubled Kanthal ribbon should be run through holes drilled in the upper sides of the K-26 firebricks to hold them in place on the top and in the door. The photograph indicates suggested bricks to carry the ties. Steel supporting rods and bars are located in the roof during assembly of the kiln as shown in Fig. I. Three peep holes in the door are helpful.

The entire kiln and the door are framed with angle steel. Material 1½″ x 1½″ x ¼″ is satisfactory; but, because of local conditions, it may be more convenient to accept any size near this, *e.g.* ³⁄₁₆″ thick material. The details of size and shape for the side frame pieces for both the kiln body and the door are shown in Fig. 2. It is best to heat the material before bending. Four frames must be cut and bent to shape; two for the body and two for the door. The construction procedure for these larger frames follows that used in making the smaller frames; however, bending in this case is made easier and better by the application of heat. A minimum allowance of ⅛″ is required in making each bend. These frames, when completed, should have inside measurements *not under* 41″ x 46″. It will be found much easier to put on the frames if they have inside measurements ⅛″ to ¼″ above the minimum size of 41″ x 46″. It is exceedingly difficult to put on undersize frames. Cap screws, ⅜″ in diameter, are used here in place of the ¼″ cap screws used to hold the side frames on the smaller kiln.

A method of fastening the door tightly shut is shown in Fig. 2. The grooves in the insulation blocks around the door and front of the kiln permit the steel frame to be recessed so there is a minimum of heat lost when the door latch is secured. This latch is designed to permit adjustment of the closing pressure.

Four 10″ T-hinges furnish the main door support. Figure 2 shows the details for two alternate methods of taking some strain off the hinges. Any commercially available system of fastenings, links, and turnbuckle may be used to support the door by attaching them with stranded steel cable or special high tensile strength steel wire. The former will likely be more easily obtainable.

If the caster method is used, the floor upon which it rolls must be smooth and level. It is advisable to use a strap of steel across the corners of the kiln as indicated in Fig. 2. This material may be of any convenient size, *e.g.* 1″ x ¼″.

The resistance ribbon should be wound on a board as previously described for the smaller kiln. Required lengths of resistance ribbon are shown in the following table:

Table IV — Hairpin Lengths for Various Resistances of Kanthal A-1 Ribbon.

Resistance of Wire	For 6 hair-pin circuit 12 required	For 5 hair-pin circuit 5 required	For 4 hair-pin circuit 4 required	For 9 hair-pin circuit 9 required
.450	9′-4″	11′-2″	14′-0″	6′-2½″
.460	9′-3″	11′-1½″	13′-11″	6′-2″
.470	9′-1″	10′-11″	13′-7″	6′-½″
.480	8′-11″	10′-8″	13′-4″	5′-11″
.490	8′-9″	10′-5½″	13′-1″	5′-10″
.500	8′-6″	10′-3″	12′-9½″	5′-8″
.510	8′-4″	10′-½″	12′-6″	5′-6½″
.520	8′-2″	9′-10″	12′-3½″	5′-5½″
.530	8′-1″	9′-9″	12′-1″	5′-4″
.540	7′-11″	9′-5½″	11′-10″	5′-3″
.550	7′-9″	9′-3½″	11′-7″	5′-2″

Table V indicates the number of hairpins used in each of the five parallel circuits, A, B, C, D, and E, Fig. 2. It is essential that Tables IV and V should be carefully followed so as to use the correct number of hairpins of the proper length in each circuit. This design has been painstakingly developed to keep temperature gradients at a minimum under normal stacking conditions. If unusual arrangements of ware cause hot zones to develop, the current can be turned off for a while in a particular section.

Table V — Number of Hairpins in Circuit

Circuit Letter	A	B	C	D	E
Number of hairpins in the circuits	5	6	4	6	9

The numbers below refer to hairpin slot numbers

A	B	C	D	E
1	6	8		22
2	7	9		23
3	11	12	16	24
4	10	13	17	25
	14			
5			18	26
	15			
			19	27
			20	28
			21	29
				30

Figure 2 and Table V show where each type of hairpin should be placed. All connections of one hairpin with another should be made *outside* the kiln firing chamber. The ends of both hairpins should pass completely through the connector. Some of the hairpins in circuit E will have to be stretched out so that they will be virtually straight wires resting in the bottom of the slots in which they belong. Furthermore, the cut made to permit such wires to pass from one slot to another in these cases must be made so the hairpin does not extend across the entire slot. Care should be exercised to see that the hairpin ends are not closer than 1½ inches as they pass through the rear of the kiln.

Only experience in firing can accurately indicate the sequence for switching circuits on and off; but generally a cycle is started by applying power to circuit A first, then to circuit B, D, and E in sequence. Circuit C is used to increase the speed of firing or to finish off a cycle. Liberal use of cones throughout the kiln is helpful in establishing the firing characteristics of the kiln with variously stacked loads.

The ends of the heating elements should be protected by the 27″ x 32″ x ¼″ sheet of asbestos board, spaced 3 inches away from the rear of the kiln on brackets. (See drawing Figure I.) The brackets may be fastened to the kiln by ¼″-20 cap screws in the frame at the top and bottom. Slots should be made in the brackets to permit easy removal of the panel for access to the ends of the heater wires where they protrude through the rear of the kiln. Two 2″ x ¼″ bolts to which the main power leads are connected should be mounted on the 6″ x 6″ x ¼″ asbestos board. This panel is in turn attached to the inside of the 27″ x 32″ x ¼″ asbestos board rear cover.

16

The terminal panel is spaced about 1½″ from the rear cover and held firmly in place by bolting to a suitably bent piece of 1″ x ⅛″ strap steel. The door heater terminals are protected by the 27″ x 8″ x ¼″ asbestos board. This cover can be attached to the door frame by small steel angles bolted in place. Hardware cloth of ¼″ mesh should be used as a guard around all covers.

The controlling switches may be placed almost anywhere on or near the kiln. Practically any convieniently available switches which have a capacity of 10 amperes at 250 volts can be used. The kiln constructed at the University of New Hampshire is controlled by the use of five flush-mounting toggle switches, capable of carrying the load.

An indicator light can be attached to each circuit to show whether or not current is on. A 6-8 volt bulb should be mounted in a small socket arranged to permit easy changing of bulbs. This latter may be accomplished by having the bulb project through the switch panel. The wiring diagram in Fig. 2 shows the proper circuits for these bulbs. The small resistor can be made by winding 10 inches of the Kanthal resistance ribbon around a porcelain tube of the type used in "knob and tube" electric wiring. The tube can be readily mounted on a small rod running through it and attached to the switch panel.

The entire assembly should be given a coat of aluminum paint of good grade. This will help to prevent the metal parts from rusting, will give some degree of heat insulation, and will greatly improve the appearance of the kiln.

The same recommendations given under the pyrometers section for the smaller kiln write-up apply here.

ENGINEERING EXPERIMENT STATION PUBLICATIONS

Making an Electric Kiln, by Laurance E. Webber and D. S. Eppelsheimer. 1943. 25 cents. *Engineering Publication No. 1.* Revised Aug., 1948.

Utilization of Lignin by Zinc Salt Treatment, by J. Seiberlich. Reprinted from January, 1945, issue of *Chemical Industries.*

Fundamentals of Lignin Chemistry as Applied to Fertilizers, by J. Seiberlich. Presented at the Quarterly Meeting of the Northeastern Wood Utilization Council at Orono, Maine, June 29, 1945.

Project for Utilization of Lignin — An Industrial Waste Product, by Dr. Stuart Dunn, Dr. Joseph Seiberlich, and Dr. D. S. Eppelsheimer. Presented at the Quarterly Meeting of the Northeastern Wood Utilization Council at Orono, Maine, June 29, 1945. Out of print.

Production of Wood Gas as a Domestic Fuel, Preliminary Report by R. A. Caughey, June 12, 1942.

Relative Adhesion of Mortars to New and Used Brick for Star Brick Yard, Epping, N. H. Reprinted March, 1943. Out of Print.

The Lamination of Cotton Fabrics, by Ralph N. Prince and Joseph Seiberlich. Reprint from *Rayon Textile Monthly,* September, 1944.

(over)

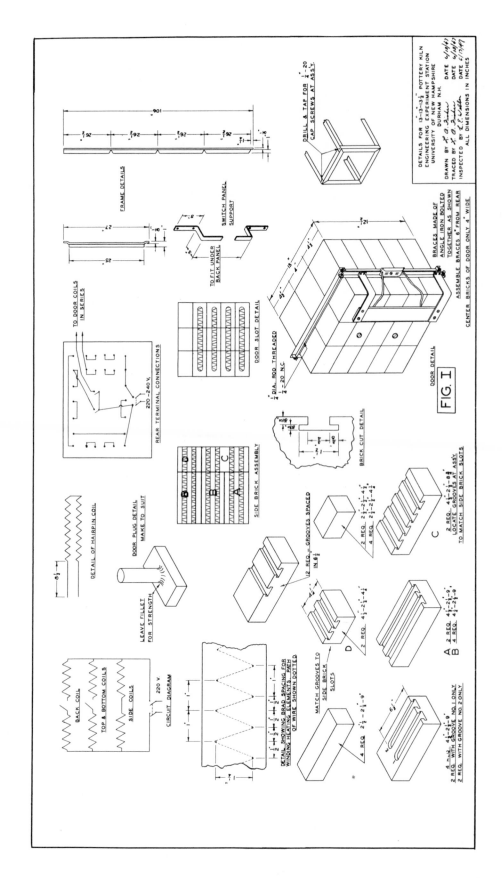

FIG. I

DETAILS FOR 13-13-13½ POTTERY KILN
ENGINEERING EXPERIMENT STATION
UNIVERSITY OF NEW HAMPSHIRE
DURHAM N.H.

DRAWN BY ___   DATE 6/14/47
TRACED BY ___   DATE 6/14/47
INSPECTED BY E.E. Watts   DATE 6/15/47
ALL DIMENSIONS IN INCHES

FRAME DETAILS

SWITCH PANEL SUPPORT

TO FIT UNDER BACK PANEL

DRILL & TAP FOR ¼-20 CAP SCREWS AT ASS'Y

REAR TERMINAL CONNECTIONS

TO DOOR COILS IN SERIES

220-240 V.

DOOR SLOT DETAIL

DOOR DETAIL

¼ DIA. ROD THREADED ¼-20 N.C.

BRACES MADE OF ANGLE IRON BOLTED TOGETHER AS SHOWN
ASSEMBLE BRACES 6" FROM REAR
CENTER BRICKS OF DOOR ONLY 4" WIDE

SIDE BRICK ASSEMBLY

BRICK CUT DETAIL

DETAIL OF HAIRPIN COIL

DOOR PLUG DETAIL MAKE TO SUIT

LEAVE FILLET FOR STRENGTH

C
2 REQ. GROOVES SPACED IN 8½"
2 REQ. 4¼-2-8½
LOCATE GROOVES AT ASS'Y
TO MATCH SIDE BRICK SLOTS

A   2 REQ. 4¼-2-9
B   4 REQ. 4¼-2½-9

D
2 REQ. 4¼-2½-4¼

BACK COIL
TOP & BOTTOM COILS
SIDE COILS
220 V.
CIRCUIT DIAGRAM

DETAIL SHOWING BRAD SPACING FOR WINDING HEATING ELEMENTS PATH OF WIRE SHOWN DOTTED

MATCH GROOVES TO SIDE BRICK SLOTS

4 REQ. 2½-2½-9

2 REQ. WITH GROOVE NO. 1 ONLY
2 REQ. WITH GROOVE NO. 2 ONLY

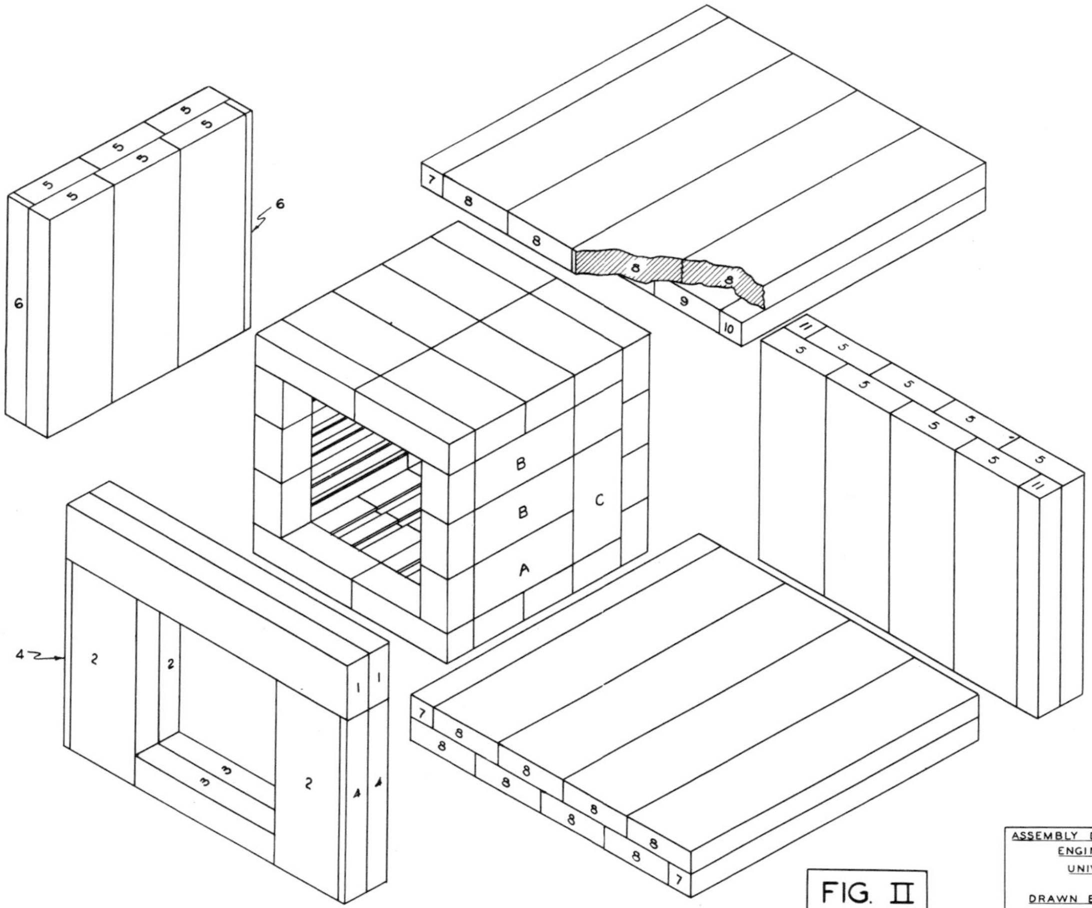

FIG. II

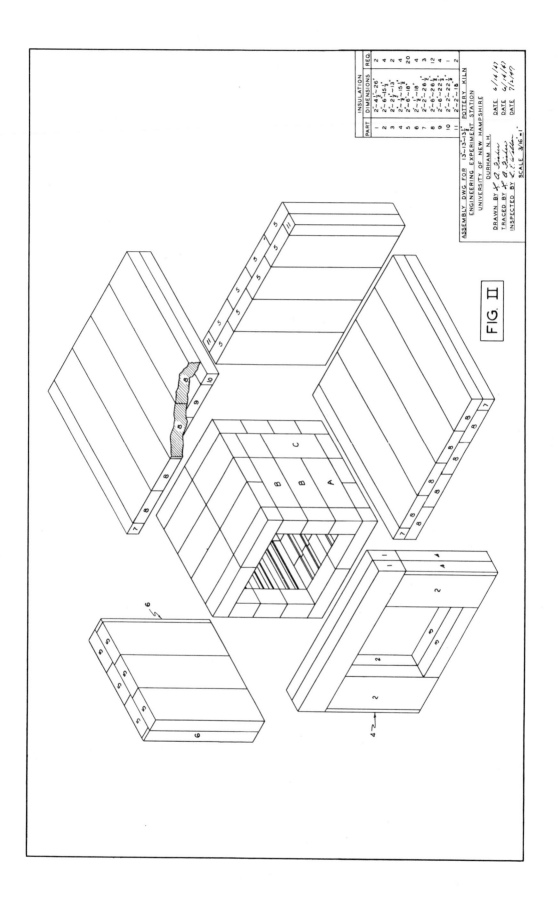

INSULATION		
PART	DIMENSIONS	REQ.
1	2"~4½"~26"	2
2	2"~6"~15½"	4
3	2"~2½"~13"	2
4	2"~½"~15½"	4
5	2"~6"~18"	20
6	2"~½"~18"	4
7	2"~2"~26½"	3
8	2"~6"~26½"	12
9	2"~6"~22½"	4
10	2"~2"~22½"	1
11	2"~2"~18"	2

ASSEMBLY DWG FOR 13"~13"~13½" POTTERY KILN
ENGINEERING EXPERIMENT STATION
UNIVERSITY OF NEW HAMPSHIRE
DURHAM N.H.

DRAWN BY L. A. Fisher DATE 6/14/47
TRACED BY L. A. Fisher DATE 6/14/47
INSPECTED BY L. E. Walker DATE 7/2/47
SCALE 3/16" = 1"

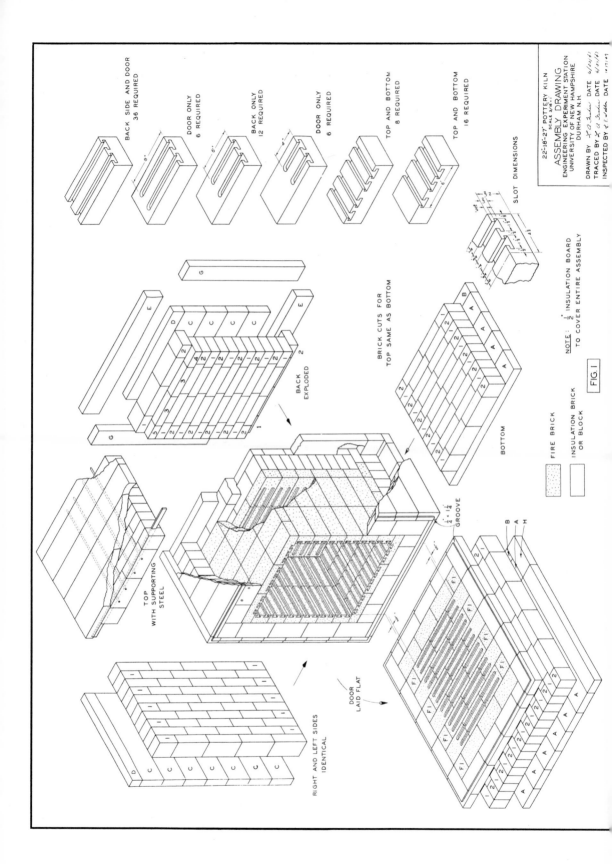

BACK SIDE AND DOOR
36 REQUIRED

DOOR ONLY
6 REQUIRED

BACK ONLY
12 REQUIRED

DOOR ONLY
6 REQUIRED

TOP AND BOTTOM
8 REQUIRED

TOP AND BOTTOM
16 REQUIRED

SLOT DIMENSIONS

BACK
EXPLODED

BRICK CUTS FOR
TOP SAME AS BOTTOM

BOTTOM

NOTE: $\frac{1}{2}$" INSULATION BOARD
TO COVER ENTIRE ASSEMBLY

FIRE BRICK

INSULATION BRICK
OR BLOCK

FIG. I

TOP
WITH SUPPORTING
STEEL

GROOVE

DOOR LAID FLAT

RIGHT AND LEFT SIDES
IDENTICAL

22"-18"-27" POTTERY KILN
SCALE 3/4"=1'
ASSEMBLY DRAWING
ENGINEERING EXPERIMENT STATION
UNIVERSITY OF NEW HAMPSHIRE
DURHAM N.H.

DRAWN BY _____ DATE _____
TRACED BY _____ DATE _____
INSPECTED BY _____ DATE _____

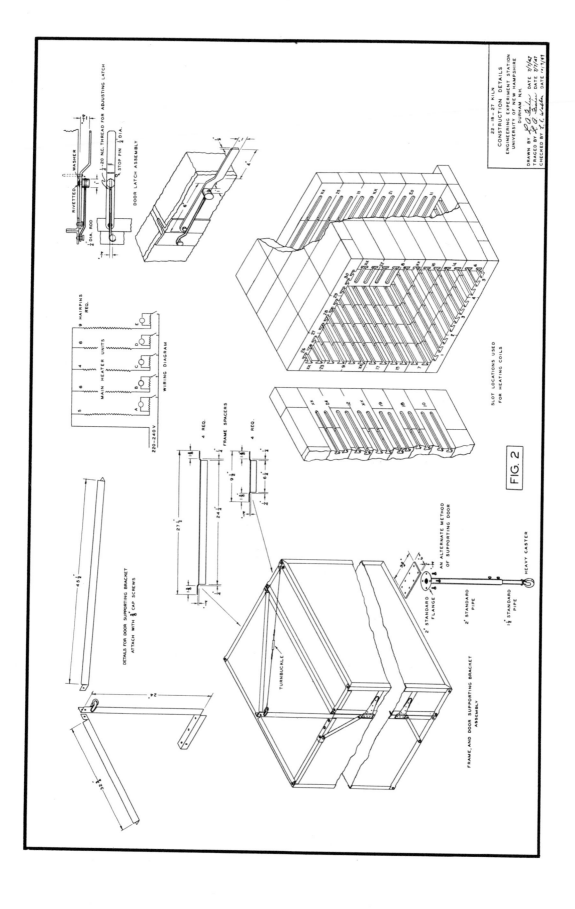

FIG. 2

5
ACCESSORIES AND INSTRUMENTATION

There are many different types of "extras" which can be fitted to pottery kilns, some of which are standard in certain models. The more popular ones are discussed below.

Rotary Switch

Some provision for varying the rate of temperature increase of a pottery kiln is more or less essential. The rotary switch, otherwise known as a three-position or four-position switch, is the simplest way of providing this service, and one of these is installed as standard equipment on most studio electric kilns.

The switch itself has only four positions at which it can be set. These positions are generally indicated by "Off," "Low," "Medium," and "High." These settings refer to the rate at which the kiln will increase in temperature.

The switch is usually wired in what is referred to as a "series/parallel" circuit, which is an electrical way of varying the manner in which the elements are wired into the main supply at each position of the switch. The amount of heat generated by the elements at each setting is thereby differentiated. With most kilns, when the switch is set at "low," the energized elements do not actually glow, as does an electric heater, but remain at "black heat."

Because the electricity supply is not switched on and off to retard the temperature rise, as is done with an energy regulator, a contactor is not required.

Since often sectional electric kilns fire hotter at the top than at the bottom, it is useful to have a three-temperature switch in each section to aid in regulating this temperature discrepancy.

Kiln Sitter

This is a device which can be installed by the kiln supplier when you buy the kiln or

36. *Kiln Sitter. Courtesy of Webbers Ltd.*

can be ordered from the same supplier to be attached later. The Kiln Sitter effects the collapse of a small Orton cone that operates a switching device to cut off the electrical supply to the kiln.

The Kiln-Sitter equipment, shown in Figure 36, comprises a metal box containing a heavy-duty mechanical switch. A heavy porcelain tube on the end of which the small cone is placed projects into the kiln. A high-temperature heat-resistant feeler rod lies on the cone and a claw installed on the feeler rod holds a counterweight in position.

To begin firing, press in the self-locking push-button. This completes the switch circuit. When the required temperature has been reached the cone bends, and the feeler rod drops. This motion lifts the claw which in turn releases the weight. In falling this weight releases the heavy-duty switch with a snap action and turns off the kiln.

If you want to "soak" the glaze firing when using a kiln sitter, Skutt advises using the following method:

1. Turn *all* switches to "medium."

2. Lift the Kiln Sitter falling weight half way.

3. Push the Kiln Sitter plunger in firmly, making sure it is well latched.

4. Gently lower the falling weight so as not to unlatch the plunger.

5. Leave in this position for 20 to 30 minutes.

6. Push the falling weight down to unlatch plunger in the Kiln Sitter, turn all switches to "off."

On "medium" this is a safe procedure since neither the ware nor the kiln can be harmed if you exceed the suggested 30 minutes. *Do not* put the switches on "high." Full instructions are usually provided with the Kiln Sitter.

This equipment is easily installed by drilling a 1″ hole through the kiln case and brickwork, inserting the ceramic tube, and screwing the metal case to the kiln framework with the screws provided. The price of the Kiln Sitter is similar to that of an indicating pyrometer (see Chapter 6 for a discussion of the comparative merits of pyrometers and Kiln Sitters.)

Time Switch

There are many different types of time switching devices varying in size and complexity. Those, such as the one shown in Figure 38, sometimes used in kiln circuits, generally have a 24 hour graduated time scale which is usually subdivided still further into portions of an hour. Two separate pointers alongside the scale, are movable so that they can be set to any point on the dial. When the electricity supply is switched on, the time switch begins to operate like a clock and will automatically operate a relay to switch on the kiln when the time indicated by one of the two pointers reaches the actual time of day. Subsequently, the kiln will be switched off when the dial reaches the second pointer. Certain models can be programmed to operate at the required times on a required day, that is they have day control in addition to hour control.

Time switches can be useful under certain circumstances but one must remember that the length of time taken for any firing will vary from one firing to the next depending for example upon the variation in the amount of ware inside the kiln or in the voltage of the electricity supply.

About ten years ago I carried out many firings at RAF Marham, in Norfolk, in a small kiln equipped with a time switch. I found the time switch very useful for auto-

Check these **every** time you set a cone.

Guide Plate: Grip Claw, push it down about 1/8″ and, at that level, move it left and right while you look directly down into firing chamber where Rod's excursion must be accurately centered between Cone Rests.
When your eye detects otherwise, don't procrastinate:

a—Loosen the two Guide Plate Screws with your Skutt screwdriver, then snug up lightly.

b—Resume the left-and-right business while with the other hand you employ the handle of our screwdriver (or a heavier one) to tap Guide Plate left or right until Rod's excursion is centered between Cone Rests.

c—Retighten screws firmly, *then confirm* that adjustment has held. If not, repeat the above but with screws snugged tighter in Step "a".

Keep Tongue adjusted so Falling Weight will be released at the proper time (when cone has sagged and lowered Rod to the position shown in Fig. A): Loosen set screw in Falling Weight and slide Tongue up or down until it barely escapes from Claw with Gauge in position. Retighten set-screw **firmly**.
—Or, with a sharp eye, make a quick and quite accurate check of the Tongue setting by letting the Weight come away from the switch box far enough that it will support the **tip** of the Claw. Then look inside the firing chamber: Sensing Rod should be exactly where shown in Fig C below.

Keep a light coating of HIGH FIRE kiln wash on those metal surfaces touching the Cone both before and after it sags. But accumulation of kiln wash here — or inside Porcelain Tube—will cause OVERFIRING. Let wash dry before placing cone.

Be sure all the kiln's switches are turned to OFF.

With Gauge removed, raise Falling Weight to its upright position (Fig. A), and capture it

there by light downward pressure on Claw. Maintain this light pressure while, with other hand, you place Jr. cone as shown in Figs. B and 6, with any flat side down except the numbered one (so number will still be readable after firing).

1. In the automatic shutoff, use only Junior cones (pressure-molded 1⅛″ long), not tips taken from the weaker hand-molded Seniors. But use only Full Seniors (2-9/16″ long) as visible check cones, and at the SAME level as the automatic cone. See Fig. 11.

2. To fire slightly hotter, slide Junior cone endwise to utilize its thicker end. Fig. D. The opposite for cooler. Fig. E. MAKE NO OTHER ADJUSTMENTS.

3. Fired automatic cones should be crescent-shaped like Fig. C, and IDENTICAL from all firings. If not, you're in trouble — **watch** Senior visual cones until cured.

4. Any cracks across lower face of fired Junior Cone? Deep ones weaken the cone so it bends prematurely. See Cracking Cones, P. 12.

5. BEWARE! Let nothing impede the free fall of the Weight. Let no foreign object get inside the Tube (remove such with wire hook and double check to be certain Rod's travel is without impediment).

6. Falling Weight has extra mass to insure reliable tripping. To test, set Plunger, then raise Weight to only the 2 o'clock position and release it cleanly. This should trip Plunger.

7. When replaceable Kanthal Cone rests begin to spread apart noticeably, remove, flip over and re-insert. Or to straighten, remove and heat to redness.

6 — **Junior Cone in place. Note kiln-washed metal parts with cone resting on a flat side well away from porcelain tube.**

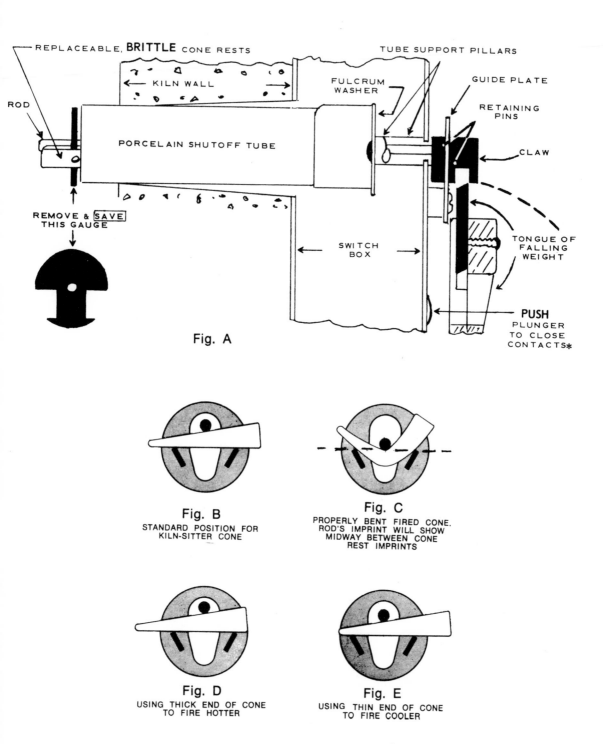

REPLACEABLE, **BRITTLE** CONE RESTS

TUBE SUPPORT PILLARS

KILN WALL

FULCRUM WASHER

GUIDE PLATE

ROD

RETAINING PINS

PORCELAIN SHUTOFF TUBE

CLAW

REMOVE & SAVE THIS GAUGE

SWITCH BOX

TONGUE OF FALLING WEIGHT

PUSH
PLUNGER TO CLOSE CONTACTS*

Fig. A

Fig. B
STANDARD POSITION FOR KILN-SITTER CONE

Fig. C
PROPERLY BENT FIRED CONE. ROD'S IMPRINT WILL SHOW MIDWAY BETWEEN CONE REST IMPRINTS

Fig. D
USING THICK END OF CONE TO FIRE HOTTER

Fig. E
USING THIN END OF CONE TO FIRE COOLER

37. Kiln Sitter, automatic kiln control. Courtesy of Skutt Ceramic Products.

matically switching on the kiln in the early hours of the morning while I was soundly asleep and I then finished off the firing using cones at around midday, which was my most convenient time. I did find that the firing time varied by as much as ½ hour either way, but after a while I could guess approximately how long the firing was likely to take with that particular kiln to within 15 to 20 minutes. This represented little more than one cone variation and with the types of clay and glazes I was using this would not have had catastrophic effects had I relied solely on the time switch. The time switch, incidentally, was set to switch off about 20 minutes after the time at which I had estimated the firing would near completion so that if for some reason I could not be available to attend the kiln as it reached the required temperature, the time switch would automatically switch it off.

Kiln suppliers, such as Skutt and Cress, offer a Limit Timer which comes as part of or can be attached to a Kiln Sitter. The Limit Timer is an electrically driven clock switch mechanism which overrides the Kiln Sitter.

38. *Time switch. Courtesy of Sangamo Weston.*

Other mechanisms available which can be used for automatic kiln starting and cut-off are Amaco's Kiln Starter, the Cress Intermatic Timer and Unique Kiln's Automatic Timer and Controller. All of these turn the kiln on at a pre-set time and can be set to turn the kiln off automatically. Amaco's Kiln-Gard is another mechanical cut-off device, similar to the Kiln Sitter. It is inserted through the spy hole, holding a small cone vertically at the end of a rod. When the cone bends, a switch is activated which turns off the kiln automatically.

These devices are particularly useful in schools, where firings are frequent and the teacher cannot always be present to watch the kiln.

Energy Regulator

The energy regulator, as shown in Figure 39, is an alternative to the three-position switch or infinite control switch. It is purely a retarding medium for controlling the rate of temperature increase, which it does by controlling the heat input to the kiln. It comprises an automatic switching device, the time periods during which the switch contacts are open and closed being infinitely variable. The length of time during which the contacts are closed is controlled by an adjusting knob which is usually calibrated from 0% to 100%. When the knob is set at 100%, the contacts are closed all the time. Therefore, the electricity supply to the elements is never interrupted, and allows the kiln to heat up at its maximum rate.

The energy regulator is mounted either on the kiln or on a separate control panel. A small indicator light is often incorporated in the regulator which goes on when the regulator switch contacts are closed and goes off again when the contacts open. Therefore, when the kiln elements are re-

6
TEMPERATURE CONTROL

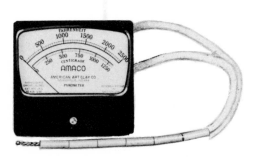

40. *Pyrometer. Courtesy of the American Art Clay Company, Inc.*

Some means of controlling the firing of a kiln is essential to obtain consistently good pottery. Before the intensive study of pyrometric practice, the senses were the only means of determining temperatures; kiln firemen estimated the temperature of a kiln by reference to the degree and color of the glow inside it. The determination of temperature by sight and feel can often be a useful tool for the experienced potter, but in modern times, temperature-measuring and control can be accomplished by the various devices developed for this purpose.

There are basically two methods of controlling a kiln firing: by pyrometers and by pyrometric cones. Pyrometers and pyrometric cones are often used in conjunction as they measure two completely different functions. Pyrometers measure temperature; pyrometric cones measure heat work.

Temperature-measuring instruments are of different types but the ones generally used by studio potters consist of an instrument which transforms the voltages fed into it from a thermocouple into degrees of temperature which are indicated on a scale. The indicating instrument itself is generally one of two types: either a galvanometer (a millivoltmeter) which is similar in design to the ammeter on many automobile dashboards, or a potentiometer. The standard pyrometer generally has a simple galvanometer as the recording instrument whereas the more sophisticated recording instruments generally have potentiometric systems or a combination of the two.

Each of the different types of instruments commonly used by potters in studios and schools has a different function, although some of them offer a more sophisticated means of providing the same control. Obviously the choice of the most suitable type of instrumentation will de-

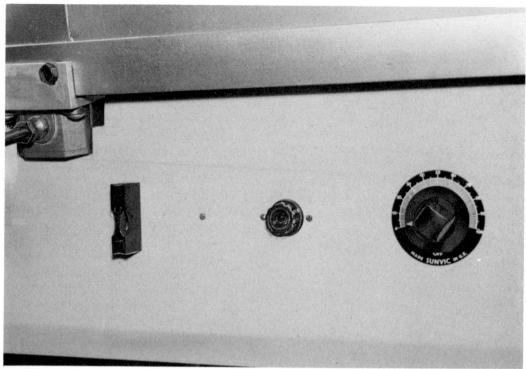

39. *Kiln control panel with door switch and energy regulator.*

ceiving electricity supply the indicator light is burning.

An energy regulator is a very useful piece of equipment for easy control of the rate of temperature increase. If thick-walled pots are being fired, the rate of temperature increase can be reduced. If a pyrometer is fitted to the kiln and the kiln was to be maintained at a particular temperature, the energy regulator setting could be adjusted until a position was found at which the elements were switched on and off at a rate slow enough to prevent any further temperature rise but fast enough to prevent the temperature from dropping. This is alternately called a "hold button."

Door Switch

This is a device which isolates the electrical supply to the kiln elements when the kiln door is open. The switch usually consists of a metal bracket which is fixed to the lower edge of the kiln door and which

depresses a plunger on the front or underside of the kiln; this in turn operates the contactor relay which allows current to flow to the kiln elements. When the door is opened the plunger is released. This switches the contactor relay to off thereby cutting off the electricty supply to the elements.

Door switches are often installed on kilns used in schools and many teachers regard them as an essential item. With most kilns, the elements do not begin to glow for an appreciable time after the kiln has been switched on even if the energy regulator is set at its highest setting. If the kiln has only a rotary switch and this is set at its low position, the elements may never glow but will remain at black heat. Under these conditions there is a risk of electrocution arising from a child's opening the kiln door and placing his hands on the elements. Door switches provide a safety precaution while work is being done on the kiln.

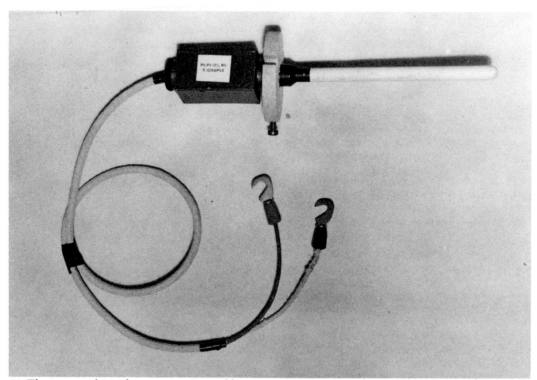

41. *Thermocouple and compensating cables.*

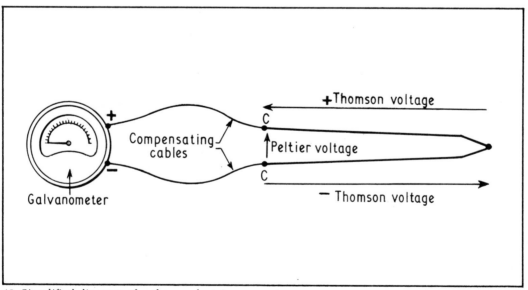

42. *Simplified diagram of a thermoelectric pyrometer.*

pend not only upon the job it has to do but also largely upon personal preference and to a certain degree upon whether the kiln operator can be constantly available or is available only for short periods to attend the kiln. If you have time to change settings, to watch the progress of the firing and to switch the kiln off, then you only really need Orton cones, a three-position switch (or energy regulator), and perhaps also a standard pyrometer.

Pyrometers

The standard pyrometer consists of a galvanometer equipped with a temperature scale, a thermocouple housed inside a porcelain sheath, and two pieces of compensating cable for connecting the two. All brackets and fixing instructions are normally provided, as shown in Figure 40.

When purchasing a new kiln, the factory will normally install the pyrometer at little cost. Otherwise, installation is simple—the metal framework of a kiln is often drilled by the manufacturer at a position suitable for the installation of a thermocouple. All that is necessary is to extend the hole through the brickwork, which is done easily as the brick is very soft, and push the thermocouple into the hole as far as it will go—the metal flange of the thermocouple will then be up against the metal sheeting of the kiln and the thermocouple tip will project into the firing chamber. The galvanometer is connected, by the flanges provided, to the side or roof of the kiln, and the compensating cables are connected between the terminals of the thermocouple and the two terminals on the instrument. Make sure that the red wire is connected to the red terminals and the black to the black. A screw on the front or just underneath the front of the instrument can then be adjusted to set the instrument reading to the room temperature, or, more precisely, the actual temperature inside the kiln, (normally about 18°C.) (64°F.).

When pyrometers are being packed for shipping, a connecting wire is always joined between the pyrometer terminals. This "shunt" wire prevents the indicator needle from swinging about violently if the pyrometer is jolted, and must be removed before the instrument can be used.

A pyrometer must not be positioned where it is subject to radiant heat, drafts, or dampness, and the surrounding temperature should not exceed 35°C. (95°F.). It is also very important to check with a level to ensure that the pyrometer has been mounted perfectly horizontally.

Important Cautions

Do not connect the main electric supply to pyrometer/thermocouple terminals.

Do not run the compensating cables near or parallel to the main electric cable because electric current can be transferred from the main to the compensating cables resulting in inaccurate readings on the pyrometer.

Do not drill holes in the pyrometer case for any purpose whatsoever. If a different mounting is required, the pyrometer should be returned to the factory for modification.

Do not open the pyrometer when dust, dirt, or fumes are in the atmosphere.

Do not use ordinary copper cable for connecting the thermocouple to the pyrometer, because it will not compensate for temperature changes.

Do not shorten or lengthen the cable or thermocouple because the pyrometer has been calibrated for external resistance.

Do not adjust the pyrometer to read zero if the kiln is at room temperature because the temperature inside the kiln is indicated on the pyrometer dial at all times.

Potentiometers

A potentiometer compares minute voltages fed into it from the thermocouple with the precise voltage generated by a battery system inside the instrument. The difference between the two is measured and made to operate a pointer which indicates degrees of temperature. The potentiometer is a more accurate and more robust instrument than the galvanometer, commonly used for the standard pyrometer, which measures the voltage directly from the thermocouple.

Thermocouples ✓

Before discussing the different types of pyrometers that are available to the potter, it is important to cover thermocouples in greater detail; they are the "working end" of the pyrometer, the end that projects inside the kiln and generates the current which is measured by the meter.

When two different metals are drawn into wires, joined together at one end, and heated, a small electric current called voltage is generated. The greater the amount of heat applied to the junction the greater will be the amount of voltage generated in the wires. Conversely, measuring this voltage gives some indication of the amount of heat being applied to the junction of the wires. For example, if the junction of the wires is plunged into boiling water, the voltage recorded on the galvanometer can be marked with the temperature 100°C. (212°F.)—the boiling point of water. Similarly, if the end of the thermocouple is plunged into boiling sulphur, the reading on the galvanometer can be calibrated for 444°C. (809°F.)—the boiling point of sulphur. In this way the galvanometer can be calibrated to read degrees of temperature as well as voltage. If this were done over a range of different temperatures, the resulting instrument would be a "thermoelectric pyrometer" capable of measuring and indicating temperature.

There are several different types of thermocouples and the amount of voltage (measured in millivolts) generated at any particular temperature differs with each type. For this reason, one galvanometer cannot usually be attached to different types of thermocouples. The metals from which the thermocouple wires are made also differ; some of the more commonly used wire combinations are as follows:

Copper and Constantan. Copper for one wire, Constantan (made of 60% copper and 40% nickel) for the other—for temperatures up to 315°C. (600°F.).

Nichrome and Constantan. Nichrome (an alloy of 90% nickel and 10% chromium) for one wire and Constantan for the other—for temperatures up to 870°C. (1600°F.).

Iron and Constantan. Iron for one wire and Constantan for the other—for temperatures up to 870°C. (1600°F.).

Chromel and Alumel. Chromel (a nickel-chromium alloy) for one wire, Alumel (an alloy of nickel, aluminum, manganese, and silicon) for the other—for temperatures up to 1150°C. (2100°F.).

Platinum-Rhodium and Platinum. An alloy of 10% rhodium and 90% platinum for one wire and pure platinum for the other—for temperatures up to 1480°C. (2700°F.).

Platinum-Rhodium and Platinum. An alloy of 13% rhodium and 87% platinum for one wire and pure platinum for the other—for temperatures up to 1480°C. (2700°F.).

Of these, the ones normally used in ceramics are the Chromel-Alumel and the platinum-rhodium and platinum types. Platinum is of course a very expensive metal and for this reason the thermocouples based on platinum are much more expensive than the Chromel-Alumel types. It will be seen that temperatures up to 1150°C. (2102°F.) can be satisfactorily recorded by the use of Chromel-Alumel thermocouples and if you are not going to fire to temperatures higher than this, then for economic considerations this thermocouple would be preferable.

To insulate the thermocouple wires from one another, they are generally passed through small porcelain tubes shown in Figure 41. The insulated wires are then immersed in a refractory sheath, closed at one end, which protects the thermocouple from harmful gases present in the kiln atmosphere. The other end of the sheath terminates in the thermocouple head on which the terminals are located. The wires carrying the voltage back to the galvanometer are connected to these.

The voltage generated by the thermoelectric pyrometer is due to two completely different effects known as the Peltier and Thomson effects. Peltier discovered in 1834 that when two different metals are joined together a difference in voltage exists between them and that this varies with the temperature of the junction. Usually when the junction is heated the voltage generated increases proportionally, but with certain metals the rate of increase of voltage begins to decrease again at certain temperature ranges. In 1854 Thomson discovered that when a length of metallic wire is heated at one end a difference in voltage between the ends is created. Sometimes the heated end is at a higher voltage then the other, but sometimes the reverse is true.

When selecting wires from which to make thermocouples, the manufacturers must ensure that the Peltier and Thomson effects complement one another. They must, therefore, choose two wires whose Thomson effects are in opposite directions and vary uniformly with temperature. They must ensure that the voltage generated by the Peltier effect is such that the wire carrying the negative Thomson voltage must be the positive element as far as the Peltier voltage is concerned. The voltages created by the two different effects will then support one another and will tend to vary uniformly with temperature provided that the cold end of the thermocouple wires is held at a known and constant temperature.

The cold end of the thermocouple is generally referred to as the "cold junction," the end of the thermocouple projecting into the firing chamber being referred to as the "hot junction."

It should always be remembered that the voltage generated by a thermocouple is dependent upon the difference in temperature between the hot and cold junctions and to register temperature accurately it is very important for the cold junction to be kept always at the same known temperature. The reason for this is that the wires referred to as compensating cables which connect the cold junction of the thermocouple to the galvanometer will in themselves generate a small voltage. In this case the galvanometer serves to unite the ends of the compensating cables. The Peltier effect of the compensating cables will vary if the temperature of this junction of the cables is allowed to vary. Similarly, any cold junction variation will affect the voltage created still further. Providing that the cold junction and the galvanometer are kept at a constant temperature, the small Peltier voltage generated by the compensating cables via the galvanometer can be corrected by calibrating the latter.

Since operating errors when using pyrometers are so often due to the cold junction, this subject is worthy of further discussion. Figure 42 shows a typical thermocouple, compensating cable, and galvanometer layout. Assume that this thermocouple is of the Chromel-Alumel type which generates a voltage increasing uniformly with increase in temperature (this is not the case incidentally with platinum-rhodium thermocouples and many other types) and that the hot junction of this thermocouple is at a temperature which results in a reading of 1000°C. (1832°F.) on the galvanometer. Also assume that the galvanometer is at a temperature of 20°C. (68°F.) but that the connections between the thermocouple and the compensating cables labelled "C" on the diagram are at 35°C. (95°F.) as a result of being overheated for some reason. In this example, the cold junction is at "C" and not at the galvanometer.

If heat is applied to the thermocouple or compensating wires at some point along their length, the voltages created by this additional source of heat will tend to cancel themselves out, provided that the respective temperatures of the hot and cold junctions are not affected.

Thermolimit (Pyrolimit)

Shown in Figure 43, this instrument, usually potentiometric, consists of the same type of thermocouple and compensating cable as are used for the standard pyrometer. In addition, the Thermolimit has a bigger dial that has a temperature-indicating pointer (normally black in color) and another pointer (normally red) that can be set manually to any position on the scale. The black pointer indicates the tempera-

ture inside the kiln at all times and when this indicating pointer reaches the setting at which the red pointer has been fixed, the instrument is automatically cut off, which in turn cuts off the electricity supply to the kiln.

Most temperature-indicating instruments are of a delicate nature and the manufacturers stipulate that they should be serviced at regular intervals if accuracy and reliability are to be maintained. Furthermore, it is always a wise precaution to rely for the first few firings on pyrometric cones and to use the instrument solely for a reference—just to ensure that it is functioning correctly.

Controlling Pyrometer

This instrument, which is very similar in design to the Thermolimit, incorporates extra circuits enabling it to act as a thermostat, if necessary, to maintain the kiln at one preset temperature.

This is accomplished with a two-position switch, referred to as a "soak-off" switch. When the switch is set to "soak" the instrument will act as a thermostat, regulating the temperature inside the kiln to correspond to the preset red pointer. If the kiln is at its pre-set temperature and needs to be switched off, all that is necessary is to move the switch to "off" and the kiln will switch off automatically. When the switch is set to "off," the instrument will function like a Thermolimit and automatically switch off the kiln when the black indicating pointer reaches the red one. Moving the switch to "off" before the temperature of the kiln has reached the temperature preset by the red pointer will not override the pointers and turn the kiln off—it will only do this when the black pointer reaches the setting of the red one.

Amaco offers the Temp Tendor, L. & L. Manufacturing Company sells the Alnor

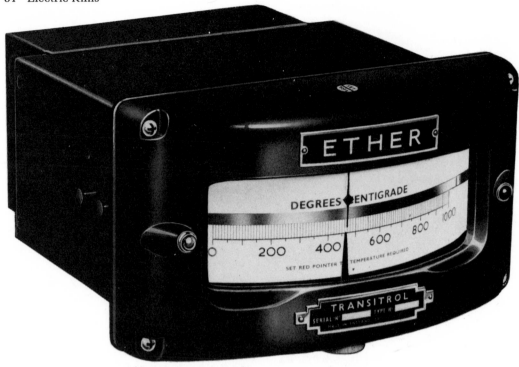

43. *Thermolimit and controlling pyrometer.*

Pyrotac, and Alpine Kilns can be fitted with a West Instrument Corporation Model JL combination high-limit and on-off electronic controller, all of which are electronic instruments which are a combination pyrometer and automatic cut-off designed to shut the kiln off at a predetermined temperature.

Controlling pyrometers are generally slightly more expensive than Thermolimits, depending upon the electrical fittings already on the kiln and the kiln size. A complete instruction book is always supplied with the instrument.

Temperature Regulator

The temperature regulator shown in Figure 44, is different from other pyrometric instruments in that it has a control knob that can be rotated within a scale graduated up to 1400°C. (2552°F.). When the kiln is switched on, no matter how quickly the temperature rises, it will never exceed the temperature indicated on the scale by the control knob. The temperature indicated on the scale by the control knob. The temperature regulator therefore functions exactly like a thermostat on an electric oven which is controlled by a relay to switch the electricity supply on and off.

Two indicating lights are often installed on the temperature regulator: one of these lights up only when the instrument is allowing current to pass to the elements, the other light is on constantly while the instrument is in operation.

I have never been able to understand why this instrument is not much more popular than it is. Perhaps the suppliers are at fault for not advertising it more or perhaps we are all so accustomed to using instruments having moving pointers to indicate temperature continuously that this disadvantage of the temperature regulator is allowed to overshadow completely its compensating advantages. As there is not the delicate mechanism involved in the operation of a movable pointer, the instrument is more rugged than other types of pyrometers. It enables the kiln operator to maintain the kiln at any temperature until it is switched off and it is possible to ap-

44. *Temperature regulator.*

proximate the temperature of the kiln, if necessary, by moving the knob setting and "searching" until a setting is reached at which one light on the instrument begins to switch on and off alternately.

Program Controller

The program controller, shown in Figure 45, which is the most sophisticated and industrially oriented instrument discussed here, is useful when attempting to produce kilnload after kilnload of pieces of the same color, for it will ensure that successive firings are very similar to each other.

The program controller is supplied with aluminum templates or cams which are marked with time and temperature coordinates. It is possible to work out a suitable firing cycle by plotting one of the aluminum cams (drawing a continuous line on the cam very much as one would draw the performance line on a graph) to denote the required rate of temperature increase, maximum temperature, and rate of cooling. The cam is then cut to the contour denoted by the line drawn upon it,

and the cam template fitted to the instrument.

The instrument has a motor that can be switched on and off. When the motor is switched on, the spindle upon which the cam is fitted is caused to rotate very slowly (one revolution per 24 hours or so), turning the cam with it. As the cam turns, it deflects a guide (called the cam follower) which is in constant contact with the edge of the cam. The cam follower in turn causes a deflection of a "regulating" pointer on the temperature scale. Another pointer denotes the actual temperature inside the kiln. Provided the firing cycle indicated by the shape of the cam is within the capabilities of the kiln, the two pointers will move in unison up and down the scale when the kiln is firing. An automatic thermostat control prevents the temperature from exceeding that shown on the regulating pointer.

The shape of the cam controls the rate of heating and cooling in the kiln making it possible to pre-plan any required firing cycle and put it into practice with the pro-

45. Program controller.

gram denoted by the shape of the cam. The cam must be adjusted so that the indicating instrument reads room temperature (or the temperature inside the kiln if this is different from room temperature) before the motor is switched on and the kiln firing started.

Note that the cam will only be driven by the instrument motor while the motor switch is in its "on" position; if the motor is switched off while the kiln is firing, the temperature inside the kiln (which will be indicated on the instrument) will remain constant.

If the cam is rotated until the instrument registers, say, 1100°C. (2014°F.) and the kiln switched on but the motor switch left at "off," the kiln will increase its temperature at the quickest possible rate until it reaches 1100°C. (2014°F.). At this point the kiln temperature will be kept constant until switched off manually or until the instrument motor is switched on.

The program controller has a switching device which can be manually set to turn the kiln off automatically at any desired temperature. An arrow, printed on the face, automatically turns the instrument off when the limit switch lever rotates to a position opposite the arrow.

Program controllers like the one offered by Unique Kilns, Model 740-c, are very sophisticated instruments capable of doing virtually everything required in kiln firing. Consequently, they are the most expensive instruments used by studio potters.

Inaccurate Pyrometer Readings

An inaccurate reading on the pyrometer may be due to incorrect installation, in which case you should check the cautions listed in this chapter.

If the temperature-indicating pointer does not move smoothly up and down the scale with gradual increase and decrease of temperature, if, for example, the pointer sticks at a particular setting and gently tapping the instrument causes the pointer to change to a different setting, then the instrument is definitely faulty and should be returned to the supplier.

Always remember that the temperature indicated by the collapse of pyrometric cones is at best a temperature approximation. These pyroscopes measure heat work and not true temperature as does a pyrometer and consequently a difference of 30°C. (86°F.) or more between the reading on a pyrometer and the temperature suggested by the collapse of a pyrometric cone is quite common.

Pyrometric Cones

Pyrometric cones are heat-work indicators made of ceramic mixtures based on silicates. The chemical nature of silicate mixtures is such that they do not have definite melting points, instead they have a temperature range in which part of the mixture is melted and the remainder is solid. In this temperature range the process of glass formation (vitrification) takes place. When a sufficient degree of vitrification occurs, the pyroscope can no longer support itself and bends or collapses. There are two ways of attaining this result. The first is to heat the pyroscope to a temperature high enough to produce this effect quickly. The second is to heat to a slightly lower temperature but to hold this temperature for a longer time.

Since pyroscopes tend to be of a similar composition to pottery bodies, they offer a very good means of controlling the finishing point of a kiln firing. Pottery is correctly fired when the correct degree of vitrification has taken place. If a kiln firing is done slowly, this will be reached at a lower temperature than when the firing is

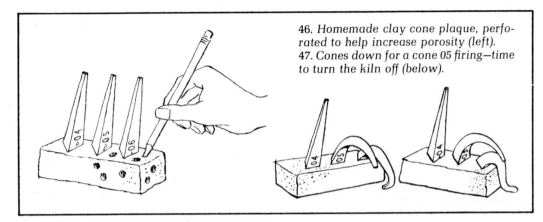

46. *Homemade clay cone plaque, perforated to help increase porosity (left).*
47. *Cones down for a cone 05 firing—time to turn the kiln off (below).*

done very quickly. Thus the reliance on pyrometers alone to determine the finishing point of a kiln firing can be a little misleading. Pyrometric cones offer the most important and useful way of controlling a kiln firing for the studio potter.

The Edward Orton Jr. Ceramic Foundation manufactures the pyrometric cones most commonly used in the United States. Suppliers generally offer Orton cones in two sizes—large or "Standard" cones which are 2½″ tall and have a ½″ base and small or "Junior" cones which are 1 ⅛″ tall with a ¼″ base. The cones themselves are of a three-sided conical shape. They are made of carefully controlled mixtures of ceramic materials. These mixtures are designed to give a graduated scale of fusing temperatures. (You can write to the Edward Orton Jr. Foundation, 1445 Summit Street, Columbus, Ohio 43201 for their booklet which describes exactly how cones are made.) Large and small cones of the same number are of identical composition but the large cones, because of their height and weight bend over sooner (usually about 25°F. lower) than the small ones (see the table in the Appendix for comparative bending temperatures of large and small cones). This difference is usually inconsequential to potters using materials with flexible maturing temperatures, but for consistent results, the Orton Foundation suggests you fire with a consistent cone size.

The cones which melt at lower temperatures contain a higher proportion of fluxes than those melting at higher temperatures, which contain increasingly larger proportions of refractory oxides. This melting or fusing temperature is denoted by a number which is stamped onto the back of the cone. By reference to the table of temperature equivalents for Orton cones in the Appendix, you can obtain an approximate melting point for each of the numbers.

Cones have become a standard measurement for temperature in firing pottery, so much so that potters often refer to the cone which matures at the same time as the fired clay and glazes rather than the degrees Centigrade or Fahrenheit.

It is commonly assumed that Orton cones will always melt at the temperature indicated in the table. This is not so. Orton cones melt and collapse not necessarily when a specific temperature has been attained but when they have been subjected to a certain temperature, or rate of temperature increase, for a certain length of time. Therefore the time factor is very important. For example if you fired a kiln to 1000°C. (1832°F., cone 06) in 3 to 4 hours, the pottery fired in the kiln would not be fired to the same degree as ware fired to the same temperature over a period of 8 to 10 hours. This is rather obvious, but many potters erroneously believe that because the ware has been fired to its recommended temperature the pottery is bound to be fired correctly. If, in the two cases listed above, the fire was being controlled solely by means of a pyrometer, then the kiln would have been switched off in both cases when the temperature reached 1000°C. (1832°F.) and the ware fired in three to four hours would not have been properly fired and, indeed, would probably have been underfired when withdrawn from the kiln. This is where the time factor of Orton cones is so useful. As I have mentioned, Orton cones only collapse when subjected to heat for a certain length of time and if they are fired too rapidly they will not collapse until a temperature is reached which may be considerably above that indicated by the number stamped on the back. Similarly, if the cones are fired too slowly then they will probably collapse at a temperature earlier than that indicated by the cone number. In this way Orton cones give an indication of the amount of heat work applied to the ware and not merely the temperature to which the ware is subjected.

One of the most important considerations in the use of pyrometric cones is the way in which they are mounted. This is generally done by inserting the base of the cones either into special cone holder (in these holders, you insert the cones from beneath) or into a pad of plastic clay which should be about 4″ long, 1″ wide, and ¾″ thick to hold three cones, as shown in Fig. 46. This clay should be quite porous to withstand the shock of firing. You can add grog to the clay and poke pencil holes into the pad to provide further porosity. Regardless of the type of mounting, it is important that all the cones be embedded to the same depth. It is necessary for the cones to be placed at an angle of about 15° to the vertical. This inclination is automatically brought about when the cone is stood upright.

It is usual to use a series of three cones for each firing, as shown in Figure 47: one cone indicating a temperature 20° to 50° (a cone) below the temperature to which the ware is to be fired, one cone indicating the required temperature, and one cone indicating a temperature 20° to 50° (a cone) above the required one (for example cone 04, 05, and 06). In this way the collapse of the lower cone serves as a warning that the temperature is rising to the point at which the second cone will collapse (at which time the kiln should, of course, be switched off). The third cone serves a guard—an indication that the ware has not been overfired. Potters sometimes use an extra warning cone, placed in its own pad, that collapses at a temperature 60° to 80° (2 cones) below the firing temperature.

It is important to place the cones so that the lowest cone, which bends first, bends away from the other two cones. The second cone will then bend on top of the first one. The correct firing of any cone will be indicated when the cone bends over so that its tip is at a level with the base on which the cone is mounted. This is referred to as the "end-point" of the cone. If the temperature continues to increase the cone will collapse still further and eventually melt completely.

Place the cone plaque in the kiln so that it is visible through the spy hole. Be sure to place it back far enough to avoid the draft from the spy hole. If there is any danger of the cones melting onto ware or kiln shelves, you can put the cone plaque on a small piece of firebrick.

You can set more than one plaque in the kiln to ensure uniform firing or to detect uneven temperatures in the kiln. Setting the plaque holding the warning cone in the hotter area of the kiln will indicate that the kiln is about to reach maturing temperature and should be watched closely. It's often helpful to wear sunglasses when checking cones to protect your eyes and also to provide better visibility. Pyrometric cones and pyrometers can be used in conjunction to safeguard against overfiring the kiln.

7

DIFFERENCE IN FIRING TECHNIQUE BETWEEN STUDIO AND INDUSTRIAL POTTERS

There is a considerable difference in firing technique between that practiced by the studio potter and that carried out by his industrial counterpart. Studio potters invariably fire the greenware first in a "biscuit" firing, at a temperature just high enough to make the clay hard yet porous so that a good film is picked up when the pot is dipped into the glaze. This is subsequently followed by a "glaze" firing to a higher temperature than that of the biscuit. Industrial potters, on the other hand, fire their greenware in a "bisque" fire at a higher temperature than the subsequent "glost" fire which is done after the glazes have been applied.

Earthenware and Porous Clays

Clays, like glazes, have a range of temperature to which they must be fired if satisfactory results are to be obtained. For example, earthenware and terracotta have a firing range of 1100° to 1150° C. (2012° to 2102° F., cone 03 to cone 1). Studio potters would generally fire this clay to a biscuit temperature of about 900° to 1050° C. (1652° to 1922° F., cone 010 to cone 05) and then follow this with a glaze firing to 1100° C. (2012° F., cone 03) or higher, which would serve to develop both the body and the glaze at the same time. Industrial potters, however, would fire these clays at a bisque temperature of 1100° C. (2012° F., cone 03) or higher, which would develop the clay, and would then follow this with a glost fire using a glaze that matures at a lower temperature, say 1050° C. (1922° F., cone 05). This produces a clay body which is comparatively inert.

The industrial technique tends to develop more craze-resistance than does the studio pottery technique at these low, earthenware temperatures, the only disadvantage being that after the industrial bisque firing, the bisque ware is compara-

48. *Truck of ware being pushed into tunnel kiln for glost firing at about 1100°C. (2012°F., cone 02).*
Courtesy of Josiah Wedgwood and Sons Ltd.

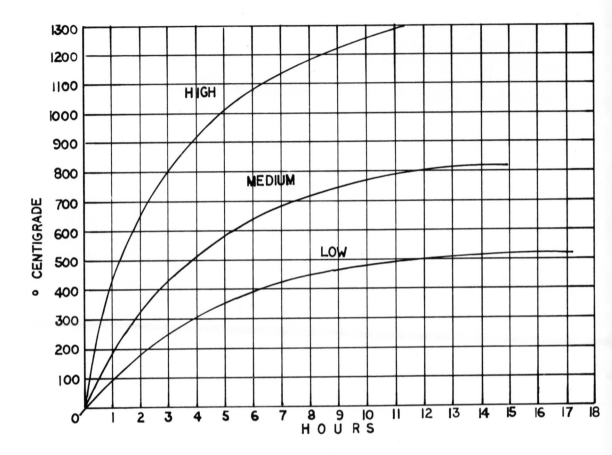

49. *Typical firing curve for each setting on rotary switch; this graph is only intended as a guide and should not be used to determine a specific firing cycle.*

tively vitreous (non-porous) and con-sequently does not pick up a good layer of glaze during the dipping operation. For this reason, industrial concerns always go to great lengths to make sure that the glaze being used in the dipping tubs is of exactly the right consistency to ensure a satisfac-tory pickup of glaze, and for really vit-reous bodies the industrial potters use spraying techniques to apply the glaze coat. The expense of installing spraying equipment is considerable, however, and is often out of the studio potter's range.

Bringing the body to its maturing point on the first firing allows any warpage or distortion to take place during this firing and not during the subsequent glost firing. For example, if a thin, pencil-like object were to be glazed, the industrial potter would do it by firing the clay to its matur-ing temperature during the hard-bisque fire, and during this time the object would be left lying flat on a bat or other suitable support to prevent distortion. During the glost fire, which would be at a lower tem-perature, the same object could be supported merely by its two ends with comparatively little risk of distortion. The studio potter, firing the same piece, would find that it would distort considerably during the glaze fire unless it was supported at points other than at its ends, which would result in marks being left on the glaze surface. With the studio pottery technique, once the temperature of the glaze fire surpasses that of the biscuit, the body itself becomes much more reactive and gives off gases which have to bubble their way through a film of glaze. This may result in pinholes or other glaze blemishes. Because this happens to a much lesser extent with the industrial technique, the appearance of the finished piece tends to be somewhat finer than that produced by the studio potter. On the other hand, the coldness of the non-fusion between glaze and body often discourages the one-of-a-kind or studio potter from using the industrial process.

The studio potter forgoes the advantages of the industrial technique so that he may get high porosity on the biscuit ware which enables him to apply the glaze very easily and also provides a greater warmth and depth to the finished glazed piece, through the glaze thickness and interface (see Chap. 10 for a discussion of interface) of the glaze and body.

Remember that, provided you are using satisfactory glazes and bodies, the temperature to which the body is fired controls the degree of craze-resistance developed by the ware. It is true that crazing difficulties can sometimes be overcome by firing the glaze a little higher than was done with previous glaze firings, but it is generally assumed that the increased craze-resistance arises directly as a result of reactions in the glaze to the extra heat. This is not strictly true; the increased craze-resistance is also due to the in-creased amount of heat applied to the body via the glaze layer.

In addition to the two-fire method (biscuit and glaze), pottery can also be fired by a one-fire process. This involves applying glaze to dry ware and then firing this once to a temperature which is high enough to develop both the body and the glaze at the same time.

Stoneware and Porcelain

The above comments refer to the firing of terracottas, buff clays, and all forms of earthenware. It is also necessary, to fire bone china to the full maturing temperature, 1240° to 1280° C. (2264° to 2336° F., cone 7 to cone 9), during the bisque firing as at this temperature the bone china ware will deform so easily that it has to be placed on special setters or buried in calcined alumina; glazed bone china ware could not of course be treated in this way. With stoneware and porcelain, the pots would be so vitreous after being fired to a full maturing temperature in the bisque that the studio potter would be faced with difficult glaze application problems when using the dipping process. With these bodies therefore, the studio potter fires the ware to a low biscuit temperature, approximately 900° to 1000° C. (1652° to 1832° F., cone 010 to 06), to give the porosity necessary for dipping his pottery successfully. The glaze is then fired to a temperature of approximately 1220° to 1300° C. (2228° to 2372° F., cone 6 to cone 10).

The quality of texture of stoneware and porcelain glazes is often enhanced by the gases which inevitably bubble through from the biscuit ware and also by the reactions which take place between the glaze and the decomposing body. Indeed much stoneware pottery owes its success and appeal to the glaze effects brought about by a high-temperature glaze firing.

8
KILN FURNITURE AND STACKING THE KILN

Stacking a kiln for firing can be an art in itself; with practice you can acquire an eye for using almost all of the available space. Experienced potters can fit a large amount of ware into a small space while still leaving adequate room for air circulation. The ware when stacked actually becomes a part of the kiln construction and dictates the amount and flow of heat retained in the kiln. A tightly packed kiln is more economical to fire and will direct the heat more evenly than a very loosely packed one.

Shelves

In a studio electric kiln, the pottery is placed on shelves that vary according to the size and shape of the firing chamber. Shelves are available for specific kiln sizes from kiln manufacturers and ceramic suppliers. It is a good practice when ordering shelves to indicate your kiln model number. Shelves come in full and half sizes and also can be made to order if necessary. Kiln shelves are manufactured normally in two general firing ranges from two different refractory materials. The lower-fire shelves that withstand temperatures to cone 6 are made from high-alumina mixtures such as cordierite, silimanite, kyanite, and clay. They are very resistant to thermal shock and have low and uniform thermal expansion rates. The best, although unfortunately the most expensive, shelves are made from silicon carbide. They have good hot-load strength and long life but they should be handled with care as they are quite brittle.

You can make your own shelves, although this is a big undertaking and often the resulting shelves have a tendency to warp, producing difficulties in proper stacking. They can be made from a stiff mixture of ½ fire clay and ½ good-sized grog which are packed very densely into a

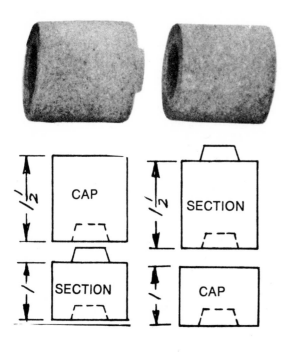

50. *Stack-up post sections and caps, 1¼″ diameter. Courtesy of Skutt Ceramic Products.*

51. *Octagonal shelves and posts.*

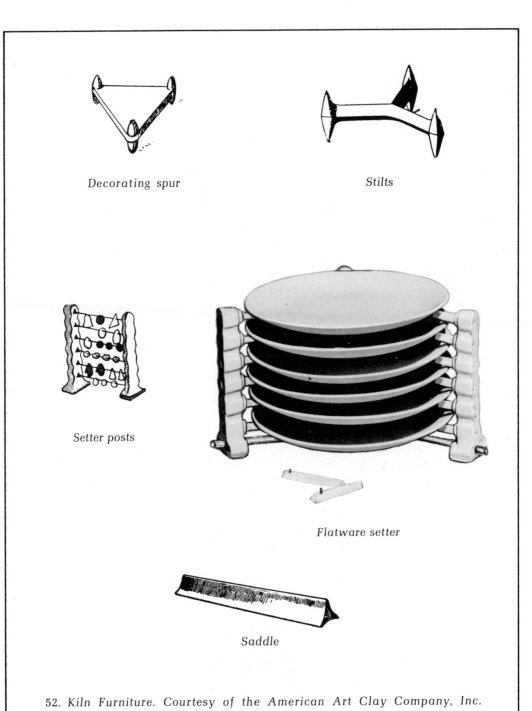

Decorating spur

Stilts

Setter posts

Flatware setter

Saddle

52. Kiln Furniture. Courtesy of the American Art Clay Company, Inc.

mold with a wooden mallet. When dry, the shelves are surrounded with sand or grog and fired to at least cone 11. These shelves will never be as strong as one of similar thickness that are industrially manufactured.

Kiln shelves must be quite dry before being subjected to the normal firing schedule as otherwise they may crack by escaping steam. Sometimes fine cracks may appear in a kiln shelf due to damage during handling or transit. These fine cracks, which may not be apparent but which could be a source of shelf failure, can often be more easily detected by sprinkling a powder such as alumina over the surface of the shelf and then sharply tapping it in the center. This causes the powder to move away from any crack in the shelf, revealing the crack as a line.

If any kiln shelves are cracked, they should either be discarded or broken into two pieces for use as half shelves. If the crack is a minor one it is usually possible to make use of the shelf with very little risk of failure, provided that a support is used to hold the shelf up immediately under the cracked area.

During biscuit firing the pottery shrinks considerably and if warping is to be avoided this shrinking action should not be arrested by any irregularity on the kiln shelf. The best way to assist this shrinkage is to cover the shelf with kiln wash (see Chapter 3 under "First Firing" for how to prepare and apply kiln wash).

Supports

If elements are installed in the floor of the kiln, the pottery should not be placed directly on the floor but on a kiln shelf placed on supports at least ½" above the floor. This prevents possible damage to elements if a pot should break and in addition allows more even heat distribution throughout the kiln. If the pots to be stacked are comparatively small in size, then several shelves may be needed and these are supported one above the other by shelf supports—posts of varying shapes and heights. You can buy posts or make your own.

You can also use soaps which are made from half (cut lengthwise) of a 9" x 5" firebrick. These are very sturdy and can be stacked or cut with a brick saw for varying heights.

The different types of manufactured posts come in heights from ½" to 8" in round, square, triangular, and stacking shapes. It is possible to use a number of small posts, 1" to 1½" in height, to alter the distance between shelves, but a series of posts one above the other is not as stable as one large post of the same height. Sometimes small wads of fireclay can be used to stabilize shelves and posts. You can make your own posts by rolling thick snakes of fireclay and cutting them to uniform heights. Widening each end provides a somewhat sturdier support.

To repair broken kiln furniture, *Ceramic Industry* magazine suggests making a paste of 1 part ball clay, 1 part kaolin, 1 part flint, and 1 part feldspar with sodium silicate (which is a liquid). Mend the piece and allow it to dry. Then fire it to a temperature of the maturation of your clay body or a cone above.

Stacking the Biscuit

Stacking the kiln for a biscuit fire is simpler than stacking one for a glaze fire as all that is really necessary is to place the pots inside the kiln with the object of getting as many pots as possible into the smallest possible space. Be sure you have enough pots to fill the kiln when arranging the stacking—about 1½ kilnloads will provide enough pots for a good arrangement. For easier stacking you can assemble the pots outside the kiln in groups of similar heights. When stacking pots which are both thick and thin, spread them evenly throughout the kiln.

Each shelf should be supported at three points as this prevents rocking which might occur if the shelf was supported at each of its four corners, or at four points on a circular shelf—a three-legged chair or stool will never rock but a four-legged one might. The supports should be arranged in similar positions for each succeeding shelf so that the total weight of the complete set of kiln furniture acts downwards through continuous columns. When stacking two shelves side by side in a large kiln, the heights should be staggered where possible to equalize heat distribution.

I have often found it helpful to have an area of the work bench, or floor, marked out to the exact dimensions of the stacking area including the exact positions of posts and cone plaques. If the layout of posts is different on one shelf to the layout of the posts on the next shelf, then I have also used a full-size diagram drawn on the bench or floor to simulate this alternative arrangement. When this is done the pots can be rearranged within this marked area much more easily than would be the case inside the kiln. The pots can then be viewed from all directions and handled with much more ease. Furthermore, the pots can be arranged in their firing positions while the kiln is actually in use so that when the firing is finished, all that is necessary is just to pick the pots from their places in the marked-out area and place them inside the kiln at their pre-planned position. This can save quite a lot of time and prevent breakage which can occur in moving the pots around inside the kiln.

A most important point is that all ware put into a kiln must be *dry*. If damp pottery is stacked in the kiln, there is a great risk of its cracking or literally exploding during the firing operation, and bits would be scattered over all adjacent pottery pieces, probably damaging them. It is particularly important in a classroom or in group studios where a lot of people are firing ware to be sure that no accidents occur because of damp pots. In this situation, it is often wise to fire the biscuit quite slowly.

A good way of determining whether ware is dry is to place it against your cheek. If it feels cold, then the ware is damp and must be allowed to dry longer. Thick pieces of pottery take longer to dry than thin pieces and they also take longer to fire. If you place thick and thin pieces of pottery in the same kiln, the kiln would have to be fired a little more slowly than would be the case if you were firing thin pieces only.

In the biscuit fire, with all clay except bone china you can stack one pot inside another, for example, a small bowl can be stacked inside a larger one. Do not, however, make the error of packing too many pots inside one another as the largest pot may give way during the firing—you should remember that for a short time during the biscuit fire the pots become weaker than when they were put into the kiln. Experience in stacking will help you determine the amount of weight that a certain pot is capable of holding. Pots can be placed upside down if this is helpful in obtaining tighter packing inside the kiln and if the risk of warping is not increased. Some potters use no shelves at all in the biscuit fire. This can be dangerous though and the stacker should be experienced before attempting to build large towers of pots.

Closed-in shapes such as vases or teapots are comparatively easy to fire because their compact forms have a structural resistance to warping. Fire lidded pots with the lids on to assure equalized shrinkage. Lids may be placed upside down in the biscuit fire if they have high knobs which take up space. Cups and bowls are more liable to warp so identical pairs of these are often "boxed" together, one on top of another (rim to rim). Thin pieces will warp much more easily than thick ones.

When stacking ware for either biscuit or glaze firing, leave a gap of at least 1" between the pot and the nearest element. Failure to do this may produce scorch marks on one side of the pot. It is also advisable to keep shelves ¼" away from the Kiln Sitter and ware ½" away from the sensing rod.

Finally place the cones in position in pads or in the Kiln Sitter and check to ensure that they are placed directly in line with the spy hole. Close the kiln door and you are ready to begin firing.

Stacking the Glaze

Much more care must be taken with stacking the kiln for the glaze fire than for the biscuit fire as the glaze coating will stick the pots together if they are allowed to touch (leave ¼" to ½" between pots). Similarly, should any glaze adhere to the underside or foot of a pot that is place directly on a shelf, the pot will be firmly stuck there after firing. When putting ware directly on the shelf, be sure first that the shelf is covered with an even layer of kiln wash and remove the glaze from the base of the pot by scraping with either a knife or an old toothbrush and cleaning it with a sponge or a damp piece of felt. You can also prevent glaze adhesion on the bottom by dipping the pot into a pan of hot wax (2 or 3 blocks of paraffin mixed with a little kerosene which you can heat in a pan over

a hot plate or in an old electric frying pan; when using a hot plate, be extremely careful when pouring kerosene into the wax—this should be done only when the hot plate is off and unplugged) so that the wax just covers the bottom. Also leave unglazed areas which will be touching during the firing, such as lid rims and flanges.

If you want to glaze the underside of a pot or if you want additional reassurance that no sticking is likely to occur, then several different kinds of furniture can be used on which the pots can be placed to keep them clear of the kiln shelf. Supporting furniture includes items such as stilts, saddles, spurs, triangles, flatware setters, and bead racks as shown in Figure 52. These are available from ceramic suppliers. (see *Suppliers List*). They are quite inexpensive, so it is best to discard them after several firings as the sharp edges of these items tend to become blunt. A new stilt will hardly leave a blemish on the base of a pot even if it is covered with a thin layer of glaze, whereas a stilt which has been in use for several firings may have the points removed and may have to be broken away from the base of the pot after firing, leaving unsightly marks which have to be rubbed down.

Stilts and small saddles are particularly useful in the firing of glazed earthenware, terracotta, and buff and bone china wares to support the pots clear of the kiln shelf. Another advantage of using them is that the air circulation under the pots helps to reduce the temperature variation between the top and bottom of the pot. This will help to prevent the occurrence of cracking or dunting (pottery faults are discussed in Chapter 11).

The three marks on the underside of a saucer between the rim and the foot ring are the three points at which the saucer was supported on special "cranks" during

53. Glazed pots supported inside the kiln.

the glost fire in an industrial kiln. These cranks are refractory racks into which identical plates or saucers can be very tightly placed, and they are extensively used throughout the ceramic industry. They can be used to advantage with glazed earthenware, terracotta, or bone china wares but not with stoneware or porcelain. Likewise the use of stilts, spurs, or saddles can raise problems in firing stoneware or porcelain. If they are fired to the full maturing temperature, the pots may begin to sag or squat over the stilts and for this reason stoneware and porcelain pots (which are normally left unglazed at the base) are stood directly on the kiln shelf—particularly with large pieces.

When stacking glazed ware into the kiln, hold the pieces firmly, although not by the rim; trying to hold pieces delicately with thumb and finger is much more likely to result in the glaze film becoming damaged, unless the pots are very small. If any glaze is knocked away during the stacking, then apply more touched on with either a finger or a soft brush and rubbed smooth when dry.

Put the posts on the shelf that you are stacking first to allow for the space that they take up. Then stack similar sized pots together. In stacking a top-loading kiln, be sure that the shelf will clear all pot rims and lids before lowering it onto the posts.

Whe stacking stoneware pots for the glaze fire keep in mind to allow for the further shrinkage that is going to occur. Some kiln furniture is of a much wider diameter at the base then it is at the tip and pots can be stacked so that they overhang the base. When these pots shrink they sometimes sink down onto the furniture with the re-sult that they are stuck firmly after the firing has been completed.

It is best to avoid as much as possible stacking pots of different colors in the same firing. If this cannot be avoided, then try to keep white and highly pigmented glazes, for instance black, as far away from each other as possible because volatilization of the metallic oxides such as chrome or copper in the glaze from one pot can influence the color of its neighbor to a noticeable degree.

Make certain that any kiln wash painted on the shelves is dry before beginning to stack pots into the kiln; it is surprising how damp kiln wash gets onto the fingers and then onto the glazed pots. It is not usually necessary to give a complete coating of kiln wash to the shelves after every firing but spots of glaze sticking to the shelves must be chipped or ground away and the area painted over with a new layer of wash. Periodically it is a good idea to rub away the layer of kiln wash with a flat grinding stone (not the Carborundum type) and then to carefully brush off the shelves, subsequently giving them a new coat of wash.

In any case the kiln furniture should be checked after each firing and any loose particles of kiln wash lightly brushed away. Also check for cracks in the kiln shelves. This regular check is important and should always be done to prevent accidents.

Set the cones making sure that when they collapse they will not fall against a pot that has been placed too close to them, close the door or lid of the kiln, and you are ready to begin firing.

9
FIRING THE KILN

Most kiln manufacturers recommend an average rate of temperature increase of not more than 100°C. (212°F.) per hour, except for the first 2 or 3 hours firing time when the rate of temperature increase must be slower than this. Most potters fire the biscuit for 5 to 7 hours at cone 09 to cone 04. Comparatively thin pieces of pottery—of a maximum thickness of ¼" to ½"—can be fired quite safely with this schedule, but very thick pieces—thicker than ¾"—will need a lower firing rate, particularly in the early stages.

It is common practice to select a set firing cycle based upon the experience of the first few firings and then to keep to this for all future firings for a similar type of ware (see Chapter 3, "First Firing" for instructions on "breaking in" your new kiln). A typical firing schedule could be: 2 hours on low with the spy-hole plug out followed by 3 hours on medium (after 1 or 2 hours insert the spy-hole plug), followed by switching to high. (Skutt recommends leaving the top spy-hole plug out during the entire biscuit firing.)

Schools particularly may have a problem in not having sufficient time to complete a firing. If this is so, it is possible with most kilns to leave the kiln at its low setting overnight as the kiln temperature will not rise above 400° to 500°C. (752° to 932°F.) at this setting. Then the following morning the kiln can be switched directly to its medium or high setting thereby completing the firing later in the afternoon.

As kiln manufacturers generally provide a graph with each kiln showing how quickly the kiln temperature will rise at various settings of the energy regulator, infinite control, or rotary switch, it is possible to calculate roughly how long a firing to a certain temperature under a set firing procedure will take.

Watching the kiln during the first few

54. Econo-Kiln firing (the cord is improperly connected because it must span the kiln in order to plug in). This kiln has been moved around and operated to cone 5 and cone 6 for five years without repair.

biscuits firings is important. You will soon learn how to tell temperature by the color of the firing chamber and you can often gauge when a biscuit firing is done by the diasppearance of shadows on pot shoulders or under overhanging lids.

Clay Firing Temperatures

It should be remembered that the firing temperatures of earthenware and terracotta clays vary. Most earthenware clays have a firing range of 1100° to 1150°C. (2014° to 2109°F., cone 03 to cone 1), but the terracotta types can vary more widely. Stoneware and porcelain temperatures range from 1250° to 1460°C. (2282° to 2660°F., cone 5 to cone 16). In the biscuit, stoneware and porcelain should be fired to about 900° to 1100°C. (1652° to 2012°F., cone 010 to cone 03). Firing them much higher than this will make them too vitreous to glaze easily. If Orton cones are being used in the firing, the ones selected should obviously be those corresponding to the required firing temperature.

During the period of time that the pottery is being fired, several very complicated chemical reactions take place and the firing schedule should be such that these reactions can take place unhindered. For all practical purposes however, these reactions can be grouped into two phases: the first phase being the formation of steam and the second phase being the burning away of all the organic (carbonaceous) material present in the clay. Most of the steam which is formed in the clay is generated over the first 100° to 300°C. (212° to 572°F.) or so and firing should consequently be done comparatively slowly over this range. Most of the burning away of organic materials takes place immediately afterwards and continues up to about 900°C. (1641°F.).

The most important of these two phases is the first one—the liberation of steam, as the rate of temperature increase of kilns is usually not so rapid that all the carbonaceous matter cannot be burned away. I know of many potters who merely take care over the first hour or so after the kiln is switched on and then allow the kiln to continue its temperature rise at a medium or high rate with apparently no bad effects. A lot does depend upon the kiln, the amount of ware inside the kiln, and particularly the thickness of the ware being fired.

About 90% of the pots fired by school and studio potters are not thicker than ½". If the pottery is thicker than this, then the rate of temperature increase of the kiln must be slower in order to allow the heat generated inside the kiln to soak completely into the ware.

Biscuit Firing

After all the ware has been safely loaded in the kiln, the cones set, and the kiln door closed (it is recommended in some top loading round kilns to prop the lid open with a brick wedge during the initial stages of the biscuit firing), you are ready to commence firing.

In the beginning, the spy hole should be left open. If an energy regulator or other timing device is installed on the kiln, this should be set at a fairly low setting; if the kiln is equipped merely with a three-position (low, medium, high) switch, then the switch should be set at low.

The object of this procedure is to ensure that during the early stages of firing the water vapor chemically held inside the clay, which is converted into steam, is allowed to escape unimpeded. The rate of temperature increase should be fairly slow and certainly not greater than about 100°C. (212°F.) per hour for the thinner pieces of pottery. The thicker pieces will demand a much slower temperature increase—perhaps as low as 50° to 70°C. (122°F. to 158°F.) per hour.

The kiln will now gradually increase in temperature and large amounts of steam (which may not be seen) will be escaping from the spy holes. After about 2 to 4 hours the kiln can be switched to medium on the three-position rotary switch or, if an energy regulator or infinite control switch if fitted instead of this, the regulator can be turned up to a reading of about 60% on the scale. At this point the temperature should be 150° to 350°C. (302° to 662°F.).

At the same time the spy-hole plug can be placed firmly in position. If there is a large amount of organic matter in the clay (as is generally the case with stoneware or fireclays) or if the pots are very tightly packed inside the kiln, it may be better to delay putting the spy-hole plug in position for another hour or so. In any event kilns are not airtight and gases will escape even when the spy-hole plug is in firmly.

The actual brickwork lining of the interior of the kiln will begin to glow a red color at a temperature of about 600°C. (1112°F., cone 022), and at about 650° to 700°C. (1202° to 1292°F., about cone 019 to cone 018) will be noticeably glowing. When it has been on the medium setting for 1 to 3 hours, the kiln can be switched to high to finish the firing for terracotta and earthenware types of clays. For stoneware clays, it is normally best to allow the kiln to remain on medium for another hour or so, since many of these clays contain a comparatively high amount of carbon—particularly those containing fireclay.

After switching to high (or 100% of the energy regulator or infinite control switch), the kiln will begin to increase in temperature at its maximum speed. If experience shows that this rate of temperature increase is too rapid, then it may be best in the future to use the 90% setting (or less) of the regulator or control.

In most electric toploading kilns, it is hotter at the top than at the bottom. You may want to leave the top switch on medium and turn the bottom switch to high to equalize the temperature.

The kiln interior by now will be glowing brightly and after another 2 or 3 hours the temperature will probably be in the region of 800° to 1000°C. (1472° to 1832°F.). If the kiln is equipped with a pyrometer, it will help to determine the point at which you should start looking into the kiln to check the cones. This normally happens when the reading on the pyrometer gives an indication of some 30° or so before the first cone is due to collapse. Without a pyrometer, you must rely upon glancing into the kiln through the spy-hole about every ½-hour or so until the first cone begins to collapse. Often when the ware reaches the proper biscuit temperature, it will begin to glow red. When this happens look into the kiln every 10 minutes and switch the kiln off the moment the cone to which the ware is being fired has collapsed.

Cooling

The rate at which kilns cool varies from model to model and also depends upon the temperature and amount of ware and shelves inside the kiln. It is best to leave the kiln as it is until the interior temperature drops to about 150° to 100°C. (302° to 212°F.) at which time the spy-hole plugs can be removed and the door can be opened in stages (or propped up with a brick wedge in a top-loading kiln). In general, the kiln should be cooled for the same amount of time that it took to fire.

Inspection

When the pots are taken from the kiln, examine them closely. If any of them appear to be a greyish color, there is probably still some organic matter inside them, in which case you will know that the temperature increase of future biscuit firings must be retarded by leaving the kiln on its medium setting for a longer period of time. If the pots are extensively cracked, one possible cause is that steam pressure built up inside the pot has had to rupture the pot to burst its way out. If this is the case then the kiln must be allowed to remain on low for longer in future firings or you should check more carefully to make sure the greenware is not damp. Clay cracking, however, can be caused by a very "short" (not very plastic) clay body, by working with the clay when it is too dry, by not drying the pots evenly, or by drying them too quickly. In these cases, the cracks will be present in the greenware before it is stacked in the kiln, although they may be too fine to be detected. The biscuit firing will usually open them up.

Glaze Firing

Each glaze has a maturing temperature to which it should be fired no matter at what temperature the biscuit firing was done. When firing stoneware and porcelain, for example, the glaze firing will be done at 1250° to 1300°C. (2282° to 2372°F., cone 7 to cone 10), the greenware having been fired to a biscuit temperature of 900° to 1100°C. (1652° to 2012°F., cone 010 to cone 03).

After stacking the glaze as described in Chapter 8, switch the kiln to low for 1 hour to drive away surplus moisture retained by the biscuit ware as a result of glaze application. This may not be necessary if the dipped ware is allowed to dry thoroughly before stacking the kiln. Many potters also leave the spy-hole plug out during the initial firing period to allow steam to escape

more easily but it is usually not necessary, particularly if the dipped ware has been dried out.

Switch the kiln to medium or about 50% to 70% on the energy regulator or infinite control switch and leave on this setting for 1 hour or so before switching to high. Here again, many people dispense with the medium position altogether during the glaze firing and switch the kiln to its highest setting at the earliest possible time. This is all right provided that no cracking or dunting of the ware is experienced. If the kiln has a vent plug this should be firmly in position until the kiln is switched off.

As the kiln temperature approaches the required glaze firing temperature, gas bubbles will still be escaping through the glaze layer and forming craters in the glaze. If the firing has proceeded very rapidly up to this stage, there may not be sufficient time for these craters to heal over before the kiln is switched off. The best thing to do is to slow down the rate of temperature increase over the last 50° to 100° or so if the kiln has been fired at a faster rate than about 100° per hour, and then to observe the results when the kiln has cooled. If the glaze surface is pinholed, has an "eggshell" or "orange peel" effect, or contains a large number of bubbles, reduce the rate of temperature increase during the latter stages of the next firing, or "soak" the kiln for half an hour or so before switching off (see chapter 5 on soaking with a Kiln Sitter). This can be done by turning down the setting of the energy regulator or switching the three-position switch to medium at frequent intervals. Do not remove the spy-hole plug to slow down the rate of temperature increase as this will result in a wide temperature variation inside the kiln and could cause cracking or crazing of the glaze surface.

Cooling

When the glaze firing is completed—as indicated by the collapse of the cones or the correct firing temperature indicated on the pyrometer—the kiln should be switched off. The speed with which kilns then cool varies widely from one type of kiln to the next. After soaking, if necessary, the kiln should be left tightly closed to cool for about the same length of time as it was fired.

If the kiln takes too long to cool to 750°C. (1382°F.) the surface of a *glossy* glaze is likely to be comparatively dull and there may be evidence of devitrification; on the other hand a comparatively slow cooling rate is necessary to obtain best results from *matt* glazes. Consequently one should vary the rate of cooling to conform to the type of ware being fired. For glossy glazes, the cooling cycle may be speeded up by partial or complete removal of the spy-hole plug, but the plug must be replaced when the temperature of the kiln has dropped to 750°C. (1382°F.). Below this, the kiln should be allowed to cool slowly (with the spy-hole plug in position) until the temperature drops to about 130°C. (266°F.) when, if desired, the cooling rate can be speeded up again by removing the spy-hole plug or progressively opening the kiln door. (I mention that cooling can be speeded up once the temperature has dropped to 130°C. (266°F.), because many teachers particularly have to conform to a tight time-schedule and it is essential to remove the fired pottery from the kiln at the earliest possible time.) The door must *not* be flung open as the cold air suddenly entering the kiln may crack the pots or the kiln shelves: open the door in stages—no more than merely releasing the tight seal around the door at first followed by opening the door slightly about fifteen minutes later.

(For further discussion on glossy and matt glazes, see chap. 11.) For a regular glaze firing, allow the kiln to cool slowly to about 100° to 200°C. (212° to 392°F.), then remove the spy-hole plugs, and slowly open the door. Opening up the kiln after a glaze firing to observe the results is one of the thrills of the potter's craft and all too frequently impatience is allowed to get the upper hand.

I should perhaps end this chapter by saying that you will generally be able to obtain very satisfactory results with your kiln in the glaze firing merely by switching it on to a medium to high setting of the rotary switch or energy regulator, switching it off again when the required temperature has been reached, and opening up the kiln when it has cooled approximately to room temperature. There must be very many potters who fire their kilns with complete satisfaction by following this basic, very simple procedure. Indeed, when kilns are fired with the aid of an instrument such as a Thermolimit, temperature regulator, or controlling pyrometer they are normally fired and cooled at a more or less constant rate. You will however generally be able to obtain even better results if you appreciate what is happening inside your kiln at any particular time and can act as the catalyst in adjusting the kiln to make the firing cycle more appropriate to the immediate requirements.

10
BASIC EFFECTS OF HEAT ON CLAY AND GLAZES

With the exception of some terracottas and a few stoneware clays, most of the clays used by potters are not merely clays dug up from the ground and purified, but are mixtures of different types of clay and other materials. For example, prepared earthenware clays are made from a mixture of two or three different types of ball clay, two or three different types of china clay, flint, and Cornwall (Cornish) stone, all of which are mixed together in liquid form in carefully controlled amounts. The mixture is then sieved and passed over powerful magnets before being passed to the filter presses, where surplus water is removed to convert the clay from its liquid state to a plastic condition, like the consistency of plasteline. This plastic clay is then passed through a pug mill where the clay is thoroughly sliced and mixed to give it a very homogenous consistency. Prepared clay is generally referred to as a "body" rather than as a clay, and particularly so once the clay has been fired.

When making your own clay body, mix the clays together either by hand or in a clay (cement or dough) mixer and spread it out to dry on plaster bats. Homogenous consistency is attained through wedging the clay—either slicing it many times and slamming it together or kneading it.

Each of the constituents of prepared pottery clays plays a different role. Ball clays are generally introduced to make the body plastic and to give it good workability. China clays add whiteness to the body and are always appreciably more refractory than ball clays. Flint, as we shall see later, supplies silica and is introduced mainly to develop craze-resistance, and feldspar or Cornwall stone serves as the flux which melts and holds the other particles together. When the clay has been fired it should not be considered as one homogeneous mass but more as a mixture

54A. *Lidded pot by Harry Stringer, 1968. Granular manganese slip under lead-borate tin glaze. Photo courtesy of the artist.*

of different materials suspended in a fluid which upon cooling has solidified, thereby holding all the particles firmly in position. Other materials are very frequently used in bodies, for example, nepheline syenite is often used as a substitute for feldspar, and quartz, or even sand, is sometimes used as a substitute for flint.

Ware should always be dry before being fired. When clay is fired it undergoes several complex changes and, even though it is dry when being stacked in the kiln, a considerable amount of water vapor will be driven off during the firing operation. This volume of water driven off may be about fifty times the volume of the kiln and is not water which can be dried away before firing. This is water which is chemically held by the clays present in the body. All clays, of course, shrink as they are being dried and they shrink still further during the firing operation. This degree of shrinkage varies from clay to clay but is generally higher in those bodies which have higher firing temperatures. The more clay present in the body, the greater will be the degree of shrinkage.

Vitrification and Porosity

Potters speak of some clays as being more refractory than others. By this they mean that the firing temperature of maturing range is higher for certain clays than for others—for example, stoneware bodies which have to be fired at temperatures of about 1250° to 1300°C. (2282° to 2372°F., cone 7 to cone 10) are more refractory than earthenware bodies which fire at 1100° to 1150°C. (2012° to 2102°F., cone 04 to cone 1). Potters also use the terms, "vitrification" and "porosity" to describe the degree of water retentivity of the body after firing. A vitrified body is one that is dense having a very low porosity or is completely nonporous. The porosity of a body decreases as it is fired to higher temperatures.

A body is correctly fired when it has been heated to its maximum degree of vitrification without deforming or has been fired to a temperature where the body can develop a sufficient coefficient of contraction to enable glazes to be used without crazing (see Chapter 11 on pottery faults for a discussion of crazing). The temperature or, more correctly, the range of temperatures at which this stage is reached varies from one type of body to another and is referred to as the firing range, maturing range, or vitrification point of the clay. Some clays, for example stoneware, will be almost completely vitrified when this point has been reached, others such as earthenware and terracotta, will still possess an appreciable degree of porosity.

Importance of Silica

Silica is possibly the most important material used in ceramics—indeed, it is sometimes regarded as the basis of the pottery industry and it is fortunate for the potter that the majority of the earth's crust contains supplies of silica in one form or another. Flint pebbles found in the chalky strata of parts of southern England are traditionally used by the British potter to introduce silica into the body recipe after the pebbles have been calcined (burned), crushed, and ground to a powder. In other parts of Europe and in America, quartz or sand is used for the same purpose. Silica also occurs abundantly in igneous rock and consequently also in feldspar, the decomposition product of igneous rock, and in sandstone.

As far as the potter is concerned the most important characteristic of silica is its behavior when heated. Just as silica can be located in so many different materials, so does the silica crystal itself occur in several different forms of modifications. When silica is heated some of it changes from one form to another only to revert to the original form when it is subsequently cooled. Other modifications of silica effect permanent change to a new form which remains when the silica is cooled.

Modifications of Silica

The most important crystal modifications of silica are as follows:

α(alpha) quartz   β (beta) quartz

α(alpha) tridymite   β (beta) tridymite

α(alpha) cristobalite   β(beta) cristobalite

Of these the alpha and beta quartz and the alpha and beta cristobalite modifications are of particular concern. Whenever these silica forms change from one modification to another under the influence of heat, an expansion takes place; similarly when the silica is subsequently cooled and beta quartz, for example, reverts to its original form of alpha quartz, a contraction of the silica mass takes place as shown in Figure 55.

Let us now look at this behavior in more detail. When silica is heated it gradually expands until a temperature of approximately 225°C. (437°F.) is reached. Here it suddenly expands considerably as the alpha cristobalite content changes to beta cristobalite, which has the same chemical composition but larger volume. As heating is continued another sudden expansion occurs at a temperature of approximately 550° to 575°C. (1022° to 1067°F.) when alpha quartz changes to beta quartz.

However, as heating continues, other forms of silica begin to change into beta cristobalite, this conversion progressing with increasing rapidity as the temperature is raised. If silica is heated above 1200°C. (2192°F.) for example, most of it is converted into beta cristobalite. Thus the higher the temperature to which a pottery clay or body is fired, the more cristobalite is developed. This is a very important phenomenon.

As silica is cooled it gradually contracts until a temperature of approximately 575° to 550°C. (1067° to 1022°F.) is reached, at which point the beta quartz content reverts to its original alpha quartz form accompanied by a sudden contraction. 225°C. (437°F.) is the point at which beta cristobalite changes back to alpha cristobalite. This beta to alpha cristobalite change causes another sudden volume contraction.

These sudden expansions at certain temperatures when the silica is heated and the sudden contractions at the same temperatures when it is cooled occur every time the silica, or a body containing silica, is fired. They therefore occur during glaze firings as well as biscuit ones. If heating or cooling of the pottery is proceeding too quickly, the stresses set up by the above silica "inversions" can, and often do, result in cracks known as "dunting" that go straight through the piece (this is discussed further in the next chapter).

The formation of an appreciable amount of cristobalite renders pottery clays and bodies craze-proof. This is because the beta to alpha cristobalite change as the glaze-fired ware is being cooled suddenly shrinks the biscuit ware, causing the glaze covering it to be placed in a state of compression.

Stages in Biscuit Firing

Water smoking covers the period from the beginning of the firing up to a temperature of about 150°C. (302°F.). During this period any remaining mechanically held water present in the clay is boiled away. Re-

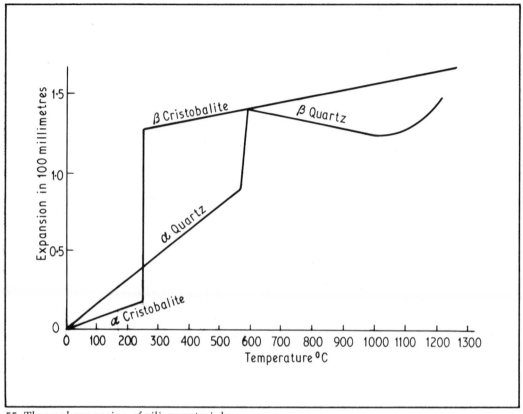

55. *Thermal expansion of silica materials.*

moval occurs in two ways: first, the body continues to contract until each particle touches its neighbor and, secondly, water is removed from between the particles.

Dehydration occurs from 150°C. (302°F.) to 600°C. (1112°F.). The chemically combined water present in the clay mostly comes away from the body between about 200°C. (392°F.) and 460° to 600°C. (860 to 1112°F.) but traces are still present up to 900°C. (1652°F.). During this period, the amount of steam given off from the ware will be about fifty times the interior volume of the kiln and this must be allowed to escape easily. If the kiln is heated too

quickly from the commencement of firing up to the end of the dehydration period, steam formed inside the body may not be able to get to the surface quickly enough and may build up to such a pressure that the pottery is blown apart. Firing should therefore be at a fairly slow rate over this temperature range.

Oxidation occurs at 400° to 900°C. (752° to 1652°F. cone 09), when most of the carbon present in the greenware burns away. If the oxidation of the carbon content is not complete, the result may be the formation of what is referred to as a black core inside the body. This can sometimes be seen on building bricks. Insufficient oxidation can also produce small black holes on the surface of pottery or turn the glaze on bone china green. By 800°C. (1472°F. cone 015) the clay is as porous as a sponge as it has now lost most of its chemically held water and most of the carbon without any readjustment of the other ingredients. At this stage the body is, in fact, lighter in weight than it was when first loaded in the kiln and is extremely porous. If the tip of the tongue is touched against the pottery the tongue will stick because of the suction caused by the dryness of the biscuit. This phenomenon is used by experienced industrial potters to give a rough guide as to whether the biscuit ware has been fired to a high enough temperature. If the bicuit is too porous it has not been fired hard enough, if too vitreous it has been overfired.

Vitrification occurs from about 900° C. (1652°F. cone 09) up to the firing temperature of the clay. The fluxes present in the body now tend to soften and begin to react with the clays; as the temperature is increased they begin to melt more and more until eventually, if the temperature were taken beyond the vitrification point of the body, gases would be given off which would lead to bloating or blistering. When this happens the fluxes in the body would be literally boiling.

Matching Glazes

Glazes are suspensions in water of materials which will subsequently melt together to form a glasslike coating.

Glazes have to be "matches" to the body to which they are applied if good craze-resistance is to be obtained—that is, the rate of expansion and contraction of the glaze must be similar to that of the body, otherwise one will crack away from the other if the fired pot is suddenly heated or cooled. The rate of expansion of a galze depends upon the quantity and rate of expansion of each material used in its composition. Various materials have very different rates of expansion and by careful selection it is possible, within limits, to design a glaze to have a specific rate of expansion and contraction. If the rate of expansion of the body is known, a glaze can be calculated to suit it and this glaze would then be "matched" to the body. In actuality, the glaze is designed to have a slightly lower coefficient of expansion than the body upon which it is to be used. Therefore, during the cooling, the glaze will contract a little less than the body thereby "squeezing" it—the contraction of the body puts the glaze under a small amount of compression. This gives the glaze a built-in resistance against crazing, (compression and tension in glazes are discussed in the next chapter).

Eutectics

Some very strange things can happen when materials are heated, and glaze constituents are no exception. Silica, for example, which is a constituent of nearly all glazes, has a melting point of 1713° C. (3115° F., cone 32) and is therefore a very refractory material. However, when it is mixed with other materials and melted in the kiln, they combine to form new compounds which together have a much lower melting point—very often lower than the melting points of any of the materials in the original mixture. This formation is called "eutectics"—mixtures which have a melting temperature lower than that of any of their constituents.

When a glaze is heated, the materials from which it is made begin to combine together long before the glaze becomes completely molten. The glaze itself gradually melts and becomes increasingly more molten as heating is continued until eventually it becomes so fluid that it runs almost like water. When the glaze is cooled it becomes progressively more viscous until, at a temperature of approximately 800° to 600° C. (1472° to 1112° F., cone 015 to cone 022), depending on the type of glaze, it becomes rigid and ceases to flow.

It would not be strictly true to refer to the glaze as now being a solid. Solids have definite melting points: lead, for example, suddenly melts at a temperature of 327°C (620°F.), copper melts at 1084°C.(1983°F. about cone 04). Glazes, like glasses, are known as supercooled liquids which are solid at normal temperatures—they do not have a definite melting point but gradually soften over a wide range of temperature.

Interface

As the glaze becomes more and more molten it increasingly attacks the body to which it is which it is applied. This reaction between the body and the glaze is very important. It results in a layer called the "interface," which is part glaze and part body and which helps to fix the glaze firmly to the body. Instead of having a definite layer of glaze on a definite body, like a sheet of water on a block of aluminum, a layer of glaze merges with a layer of part glaze part body which merges with the body. A good interface helps to anchor the glaze thereby preventing it from cracking away from the body.

If the biscuit ware has not been properly fired so that excess gases must be given off during the glaze firing, these gases can dislodge the glaze film and rupture it. When this happens the glaze may roll back to leave a bare patch, this fault is known as crawling. Grease, dust, or dirt on the biscuit ware can also cause crawling, as can the overlapping of two dissimilar glazes (see the next chapter for further discussion of glaze and body faults).

Bubbles and Craters

During the heating of a glazed piece, gases escape not only from the body but also from the glaze itself as it decomposes under the influence of heat. When the glaze begins to melt, the escape of these gases becomes increasingly difficult until the gases eventually have to bubble their way through the molten glaze. The speed with which they do this varies from glaze to glaze and depends upon the thickness and fluidity of the glaze layer, but when they eventually do reach the surface they burst and this results in the formation of small craters. The purpose of subsequent heating (soaking) of the glaze is to enable it to become just fluid enough for it to flow and fill in these craters. If the glaze firing is done very rapidly the gas bubbles can be trapped inside the glaze as there is not enough time for them to escape through the molten glaze before the kiln is switched off and the glaze becomes solid again. Furthermore, because the glaze would not become fluid enough to allow the craters to be filled in, the glaze would have a pinholed appearance. To achieve a nice smooth glaze surface, free of bubbles and blemishes, it is therefore often necessary to fire the kiln comparatively slowly just before it has reached the maturing temperature of the glaze being used, or alternatively to hold the kiln at its firing temperature for ½ hour or so (see instructions on soaking with a Kiln Sitter in Chapter 5).

Effects of Cooling

In general the kiln should cool about as long as it took to fire the ware to maturity. With matt and opaque glazes, a very rapid cooling is never necessary and in fact with opaque glazes it may hinder the development of the correct amount of opacity.

For glossy glazes, while the glaze is molten, some of the constituents are being vaporized and if this were allowed to continue unnecessarily, the glossy glazes would become very dull and lack shine. As the glaze cools towards the point at which it becomes a solid mass this rate of vaporization decreases considerably. To obtain a good glossy glaze the kiln should be cooled, after an initial drop of about 100° C. (212° F.), fairly quickly down to about 750° C. (1382° F., a dull-red color) at which temperature most glazes will be rigid. Any stresses or strains created in the glaze by this rapid rate of cooling will be easily absorbed, for the glaze is molten and any stresses will just flow away. However, as the glaze becomes increasingly more rigid it becomes a very different story; the glaze is now able to crack—and will do so if stresses and strains are caused by cooling too quickly. It is therefore best to fix an arbitrary point of 750° C. (1382° F.) and to cool as quickly as possible down to this point followed by a much slower rate of cooling. Once the temperature drops below 750 C. (1382° F.), care must be taken to ensure that the rate of cooling is slow enough to prevent the ware from cracking. There are two particularly dangerous temperature ranges—at about 575° C. (1067° F.) and at about 225° C. (437° F.). At these points, for technical reasons discussed in the previous chapter, the silica present in the body undergoes a sudden contraction as it is being cooled, with the result that the body and the glaze layer fixed to it suddenly contract. If all of the body and the glaze covering it reached these temperature points at the same time, and thus shrank at the same time, no problems would occur but this ideal state is never reached in practice. While one part of the pot may be at one of these critical temperature points, another part of the same pot may well be at a temperature 10, 20, 30, or even more degrees different. During the cooling operation the inside of the pot is, for example, usually hotter than the outside; similarly, during the cooling operation, the foot of a pot resting on the shelf is usually hotter than the outside; similarly, during the cooling operation, the foot of a pot resting on the shelf is usually hotter than the top of the same pot standing in free air, due to the great amount of heat retained by the shelf. These temperature differences inevitably produce strains which are so magnified by the sudden shrinkage of the pot when part of it reaches the critical temperature points mentioned above, that cracking often takes place. These cracks, due to heat stresses, are known as dunts and usually penetrate all the way through the pot, making it fit only for the scrap heap.

To prevent this cracking, you must allow the pot to absorb these stresses over as long a period of time as possible and this can only be done by cooling slowly when the temperature of the kiln approaches 575°C. (1067°F.) and again when the kiln temperature approaches 225°C. (437°F.).

11
SOME POTTERY FAULTS AND HOW TO OVERCOME THEM

Most pottery faults are caused by incorrect making or firing procedures, incorrect materials, or ignorance on the part of the potter. However, many of these defects can be influenced considerably by adjusting the firing conditions or the firing cycle to which the ware is subjected.

This chapter lists some of the common faults which will befall even the best of potters from time to time. They have been included in this book because when these problems occur, it is important for the potter to determine how to overcome them and to decide what role the kiln can play in their cause and correction. Many pottery faults are often wrongly attributed to incorrect heat treatment in the kiln.

Crazing

Crazing takes the form of very fine cracks spread throughout the glaze, especially in the areas that are more thickly glazed than others. These cracks permit moisture to enter the body if it is porous, and this is, of course, unhygienic. For pottery which is used decoratively rather than functionally crazing can, however, be regarded as a decoration.

The fundamental cause of both crazing and peeling is a difference in the degree of contraction of the body and the glaze covering it. If the coefficients of expansion (the degree of expansion and contraction) of the body and of the glaze were exactly the same, crazing and shivering or peeling would never occur. However, when pottery is being used it is often heated and cooled—especially when it is used as a receptacle for hot food and then subsequently washed in hot water. When this happens the first part of the pottery to be affected by the heat will be the surface, the heat gradually soaking through to the interior of the body. The glaze will therefore expand or contract a little sooner than the body, and these stresses could cause crazing. Glasses and glazes, however, can withstand far more compression than tension without cracking. This is to say that they can withstand being squeezed, without giving way, much more easily than they could withstand the same force trying to pull the glaze apart. It follows then that suddenly chilling a hot pottery surface is much more likely to cause the glaze to crack than suddenly heating it. This characteristic of glasses and glazes to withstand compressive forces more easily than tensil ones is used by industrial ceramists. To prevent crazing from occuring they deliberately attempt to put the glaze film into a state of compression. As the ware is heated, the glaze compresses and therefore the cooling operation is aimed at reducing the compressive forces present in the glaze rather than putting the glaze into tension.

Chapter 10 explains that the formation of cristobalite in the body is due to the body being fired to comparatively high temperatures and that this formation takes place slowly and results from the conversion of silica in the body. It also explains that cristobalite contracts very sharply at about 225°C. (437°F.) when being cooled and expands again at the same point when being heated. Pottery bodies containing cristobalite therefore contract rather sharply when cooled to about 225°C. (437°F.). After a piece has been fired in the glaze kiln, the body, with the glaze covering it, contracts as soon as the kiln has been switched off and cooling begins. The glaze at this stage, however, is molten and will therefore absorb any stresses or strains set up by the gradual contraction of the body. The glaze will gradually become more and more viscous as the temperature drops and will remain in a semifluid condition down to about 750°C. (1382°F.). As

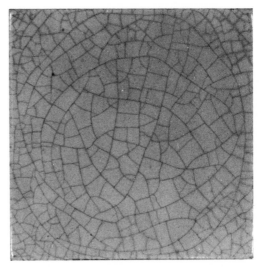

56. *Crazing.*

cooling continues below this temperature the glaze becomes solid and can no longer absorb any stresses and strains as it could when in a semimolten condition. When a temperature of 225°C. (437°F.) or thereabouts is reached, the body contracts very rapidly (because of the rapid contraction of cristobalite) and this has the effect of putting the glaze into compression. This compression remains in the glaze when the ware is taken from the kiln.

Crazing therefore occurs when there is not sufficient compressive stress in the glaze to withstand frequent heating and cooling. If cristobalite has not been allowed to develop properly in the body, there may be little or no compression in the glaze and crazing will take place very easily. If, therefore, the biscuit is fired to a low temperature, lower than that recommended, and then the glaze is fired to a low temperature, the insufficient cristobalite formation probably will not prevent the glaze from subsequently crazing.

Figures 57 and 58 provide a visual summary of the occurrence of compression and tension. A shows a slab of biscuit

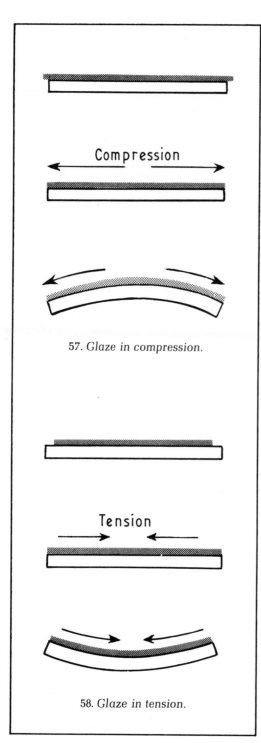

57. *Glaze in compression.*

58. *Glaze in tension.*

ware with a high rate of expansion and contraction on which has been placed a glaze having a lower rate. The glaze wants to spread itself out over a greater surface than that offered by the biscuit slab. By firing the two together we arrive at B where both glaze and body occupy the same area and the glaze is in a state of compression. If the body was very thin or elastic this compression would relieve itself by the glaze forcing the body to bend as in C. D illustrates a glaze having a higher expansion and contraction than that of the body which, when fired together, results in E where the glaze is being stretched by the body in an attempt to cover it. This is the condition of tension in which crazing can occur. The glaze tension tries to relieve itself by bending the body as in F, which is the opposite of C.

The most common cause of crazing is through not firing the pottery to a high enough temperature or, if the pottery is fired to this temperature, not allowing enough time for the heat to really soak into the ware. Crazing can also be caused by applying the glaze far too thickly or adding to the glaze, materials which have a very high coefficient of expansion. Some of the biggest offenders in this latter respect are soda (Na_2O), potash (K_2O), and most other alkali compounds. Alkaline glazes tend to contain comparatively high amounts of these oxides and this is why they seldom develop as much craze resistance as other glazes.

Obviously it is possible to affect crazing resistance by changing the composition or type of body. Generally speaking, the finer the particle size of tle material, the more reactive it becomes. If the silica present in pottery bodies is not ground finely enough, less cristobalite will tend to be formed.

Silica can be added to a porous body to increase the expansion of forming more cristobalite and yet can be added to the glaze to decrease expansion. In a glaze, silica is converted to silicate which has a low expansion. Adding silica to either or both the glaze and the body can therefore help to overcome crazing.

Pure silica will not form cristobalite until a temperature of 1450°C. (2642°F.) has been reached, but in tle presence of feldspar, cornwall stone, whiting, dolomite, talc, and also iron oxide, cristobalite may form at temperatures as low as 900° to 950°C. (1652° to 1742°F., cone 010 to cone 08). Talc tends to have a marked effect in this respect.

Porous bodies will continually absorb moisture from the atmosphere causing them to swell until the expansion of the body releases all the compression in the glaze. The glaze then goes into tension which, as the body continues to swell results in crazing. This is often seen on industrial tiles used in bathrooms or kitchens, after they have been in use for a long time.

Shivering

Shivering or peeling is the reverse of crazing and is caused by the glaze having far too much compression. Shivering appears as very fine cracks in the glaze the edges of which ride over one another or overlap. It tends to take place particularly on the edges of pottery such as the rim of cups. The sharp edges of glaze can be felt with the hand and often break away. Shivering is usually due to using a clay having too high a coefficient of expansion and/or a glaze not having a high enough coefficient.

This is, incidentally, a comparatively uncommon fault. Ways to overcome it include reducing the biscuit and glaze firing temperature or adding a material such as an alkaline frit that has a high coefficient of expansion to the glaze.

Crawling

This is the name given to the tendency of the glaze to roll away from certain areas of the pottery after firing, leaving behind a bare patch of biscuit ware. It is generally caused by the presence of oil, grease, or deposits of dust or similar materials on the biscuit ware before dipping. These either allow the glaze to run away from the affected area during dipping or result in a very poor bond between the glaze and the body, allowing the glaze to roll away during firing. It is also commonly caused by knocking or otherwise damaging the unfired glaze surface. This again may release the bond between the biscuit and the glaze which results in the dislodged portion of glaze either falling away from the pot when in the kiln or melting with the rest of the glaze film and then being pulled away by surface tension.

Another common cause of crawling is the addition of materials to the glaze which will cause a considerable shrinkage of the glaze layer as it dries out after application. Siccatives or "binders" such as starch, Karo syrup, gelatin, sodium silicate, gum arabic, and gum tragacanth, will

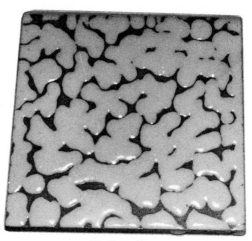

59. *Crawling.*

all cause high shrinkage rates as also will excessive additions of clays—for example, china clay and bentonite. Most of the binders are of a vegetable nature and will ferment if the liquid glaze is allowed to stand for several days or weeks, particularly in hot weather; if this is likely, add a little formaldehyde to the glaze.

Other possible causes of crawling are:

Soluble salts in the body causing a deposit on the surface of the ware. In this case barium carbonate should be added to the body.

Soluble salts present in the water supply used when "sponging" the ware or when "throwing" pots on the wheel. This can be cured by adding a little vinegar to the water.

Glaze applied too thickly.

Glaze applied when ware is not at the correct degree of dryness—especially with once-fired ware.

Thick and thin sections of ware.

Overlapping of incompatible glazes.

Cut Glaze

This is another form of crawling and generally results from the glazed surface being scratched or otherwise marked after dipping. When the ware is fired, cut glazes show as a bare streak of biscuit through the glaze in the same place as the damage caused to the unfired glaze film. A thin smear of oil or grease can give the same effect and because of this there is often confusion between crawling and cut glaze.

Scumming

This is due to the presence of soluble salts in the body that are generally introduced from the water supply. As the body dries after the pottery has been made, the water escaping from the body brings the soluble salts with it and since these cannot be vaporized into the atmosphere they are left behind on the surface of the pottery as a fine scum or powder which can sometimes be felt with the finger. For some reason this scum tends to be deposited around the edges of pottery such as the rim of a cup.

The effect is that either the glaze runs away from the scummed portion after dipping, or, more commonly, the glaze flakes away from this area after firing.

Scumming is a surprisingly common fault and can be overcome by converting the soluble salts present in the body into an insoluble form so that the moisture content of the body does not carry the salts with it when the water is being evaporated during drying. The method used most often to convert soluble salts to insoluble ones is to add about 1% to 2½% barium carbonate to the body.

Soluble salts are more likely to be troublesome when water is taken from a static tank. When this happens the proportion of soluble salts in the tank water tends to increase because of loss of water by evaporation.

Incidentally, it is not unknown for the normal main water supply in certain areas to contain a comparatively high proportion of soluble salts. These may precipitate scumming on large pieces or cause difficulty in preparing casting slips to the recommended recipe.

Dunting

This is the name given to a crack which generally passes completely through the pot—through both glaze and body—and is caused by thermal shock or stress. The fracture line of a dunt is nearly always gently curved having no sharp corners.

It is usually possible to tell whether a dunt has occurred when pottery is being heated in the kiln or whether it occurred in the cooling operation by inspecting the edges of the crack. If a dunt occurred when the pottery was being heated, the edges of the crack will be rounded as the glaze subsequently melted during the firing operation. If the dunt occurred during the cooling operation, the edges will be sharp and the dunt may be very difficult to see.

Dunts hardly ever occur during the biscuit firing, being largely confined to the glaze firing and particularly to the cooling cycle. They can be caused by having too much flint present in the body, the dunt then occurring usually at either the quartz or cristobalite inversions. The usual cause, however, is either trying to cool the kiln too quickly or trying to take pots out of the kiln before they are cool enough. In the desire to inspect the finished ware, discretion is too often cast to the winds and the kiln opened too soon. The results can be disastrous. (See Chapter 9 for instructions on properly cooling the kiln.)

There are other factors that can cause dunting during the glaze fire. Pots that are fairly thick at the base and have a much thinner cross-section near the top may often dunt when the base of the pot is placed flat upon the kiln shelf. During the firing, the bottom of the pot takes considerably longer to heat up than the top; this gives rise to a stress between the top and the bottom of the pot which may in turn lead to a dunt. If you are firing pots of this nature, try supporting them on stilts or saddles so that there is a gap between the base of the pot and the kiln shelf.

Some bodies are specially prepared to fire satisfactorily at earthenware temperatures of 1100° to 1150°C (2012° to 2102°F., cone 06 to cone 05), but can also be fired at

60. *Dunting.*

stoneware temperatures. The manufacturer sometimes adds cristobalite to these bodies to give satisfactory craze resistance at the lower temperature, but cristobalite naturally formed in the body at the higher temperatures can result in an excess of cristobalite, which can cause dunting. With bodies of this type used for stoneware, it is best to fire the glaze as rapidly as possible.

Other possible causes of dunting are:

Ware made with curves of too sharp radius—particularly on rim or foot of bowls.

Thick and thin sections of ware.

Overfiring.

Cracking

Often cracks present in a piece of pottery immediately after making may not be noticeable to the naked eye. The biscuit firing however, will make them open up. If cracks are found, particularly along the edges or rims of pottery pieces, when these pieces are withdrawn from the kiln, the cause can usually be attributed to cracks present in the clay before firing. This in turn may be due to rapid or uneven drying, trimming clay with a blunt knife, or using a clay that is too short—not plastic enough—and so on.

If, however, the kiln is fired too quickly over the "water smoking" period, the moisture escaping from the clay may not be able to come out quickly enough and steam generated inside the greenware may reach such a pressure that it has to burst its way through. When this happens the pottery either cracks or may literally explode.

Incidentally, a small hole should be poked in an enclosed piece while it is still leather hard. If this is not done, the air trapped inside the pot will expand when heated in the kiln and can blow the pot apart.

Pinholed Glaze

Pinholing is usually a body defect and not due to glaze. A very common cause is not firing the greenware to a high enough biscuit temperature, followed by a glaze firing at a higher temperature than the biscuit one. During the glaze firing, gas bubbles generated within the biscuit burst their way through the glaze surface, causing deep pinholes. Try firing the biscuit ware to a slightly higher temperature but do not exceed the maturing temperature of the clay.

With cast pottery, pinholes can be caused by introducing air bubbles into the casting slip—usually by mixing too vigorously. The industrial practice is to keep the prepared casting slip under slow agitation in a large tank or "ark," so that the pinholes trapped in the slip slowly escape to the surface. Air bubbles can also be forced into incorrectly wedged or pugged clay. Damp the greenware sponging incorrectly will usually smooth out any craters present on the surface of the pot. However, avoid the use of excess water or very dirty water, for this can also lead to pinholing problems.

Other possible causes of pinholing are:

Casting pottery in dirty or very old molds. (Similarly the first cast or two in new molds may cause trouble.)

The addition of too many dry scraps from previous casting operations to the slip.

Underglaze color applied to heavily.

Dry ingredients that are not thoroughly mixed.

Soluble salts in the body.

Ware not dry before dipping—especially biscuit ware.

Excessive agitation of the glaze, that forces air bubbles into it.

It is best to "soak" the glaze firing for a period of ½ hour or so (see Chapter 5) at the maximum firing temperature, as this allows the glaze more time to flow and fill in any pinholes or craters formed in it. If pinholing still persists and appears to be due to the glaze, then use a longer soaking time and cool the glaze more slowly.

Devitrification

Occasionally when pottery is taken from the glaze kiln it is found that the transparent glaze has turned a little milky—particularly where the glaze is most thickly applied. This milkiness occasionally takes on a pinkish or purplish discoloration when the transparent glazes are used over red bodies. This fault is referred to as devitrification.

It is generally caused by crystallization

taking place in the glaze, forming calcium and zinc silicates or calcium borate. This crystallization takes place when the kiln is being cooled and while the glaze is still comparatively molten. Once the temperature of the kiln drops to below about 750°C. (1382°F.), the glaze is normally solid and no further devitrification can take place.

Calcium borate is formed by a reaction between calcium present in the body and boron present in the glaze. It therefore follows that those glazes low in boron will tend to form less calcium borate. Leadless glazes generally contain far more boron than low-solubility types (low-lead glazes that pass the British regulations for safe lead content) and devitrification is consequently much less likely to occur with a low-solubility glaze.

If the biscuit is fired to a temperature at least as high as that of the subsequent glaze fire, as is done in industry, the biscuit ware will tend to become comparatively non-reactive during the glaze fire and calcium cannot be leached out so easily, thus decreasing the likelihood of calcium borate formation.

To overcome devitrification, try firing the biscuit to higher temperatures. If the trouble persists, which is unlikely, try adding alumina to the glaze or reducing the amounts of certain oxides such as zinc, calcium, barium, or magnesium. A higher firing can clear up clouding but can also reduce opacity in the glaze.

Glossy and Matt Glazes

Matt glazes logically go hand in hand with opaque glazes. Additions of clay or whiting to glazes can cause them to become more matt. These additions have the tendency to raise the maturing temperature of the glaze thereby producing a matt surface by underfiring. Conversely, overfiring is a common cause of matt glazes firing to a glossy finish.

The matt surface of some glazes is effected by the development of fine crystals in the glaze. Slow cooling is important for producing a soft, matt "crypto-crystalline" glaze, which has hardly discernible crystals as opposed to those glazes with large crystals. (See Chapter 9 on slow cooling of the glaze kiln.)

Blow-out

This is the name given to a crater formed in the clay body by a piece of material being literally blown away from the surface. It is caused by the presence of foreign particles in the body which give off gases fairly suddenly, thereby generating a great deal of pressure inside the body. To relieve this pressure, a small part of the surface bursts away. This fault is usually confined to biscuit ware but if the ware is glazed, the piece blown out will, of course, take a portion of the glaze with it.

Common potter's plaster is a likely cause of blow-out and if you usually mix scrap clay from molds with your working clay, you should make sure that you are not introducing plaster into the body. Minute specks of plaster generally will not cause any trouble, but small nodules will.

This fault is also far more likely to occur with natural clays dug from the ground and used for pottery making, as these obviously contain a far higher portion of impurities than the prepared bodies sold by manufacturers.

Sulphuring

This appears as a dull scum or discoloration on the surface of the glaze. In very slight cases it may be possible to rub this scum away with the fingers but usually it is permanent.

As the name implies, this fault is due to

61. *Bloating.*

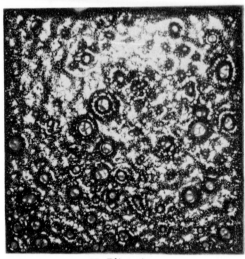

62. *Blistering.*

the interaction of sulphur gases present in the kiln atmosphere, with the glaze. It is most common in glazes containing calcium or barium. These sulphur gases can arise in several different ways and can be introduced into the kiln from the products of combustion of oil, gas, and solid fuels. Sulphur is one of the normal gases given off by most pottery clays during the firing operation. Some clays and glazes contain considerably more sulphur compounds than others and to prevent sulphuring taking place these gases should be allowed to escape easily from the kiln. The usual way to overcome sulphuring is therefore to let the kiln cool a little more quickly by allowing a little more ventilation which at the same time lets the sulphur gases escape and reduces the length of time the pottery is open to attack in the kiln.

With the studio pottery technique of firing, the body becomes reactive again during the glaze fire once the temperature of the biscuit fire has been passed. The sulphur gases coming away from the clay at that point can often cause sulphuring. Firing the biscuit to a higher temperature may consequently prevent this problem.

Bloating

This fault is generally confined to the body and is nearly always due to overfiring. When the body is overfired, the flues begin to boil and the body becomes semimolten. Gases formed by the boiling of the fluxes then begin to form bubbles inside the body resulting in "lumps" all over the surface of the body. In extreme cases the body swells considerably. I have seen small tiles which have bloated to literally twice the original size.

Blistering

This is a fault similar to bloating but the bubbles are smaller and are formed in the glaze. Blistering is also generally due to the glaze being badly overfired so that boiling and bubbling takes place. These bubbles in the glaze usually burst leaving a crater which may show the bare clay body underneath.

To remedy both bloating and blistering, either reduce the glaze firing temperature or, if this is not possible, use glazes that have a higher firing range.

Dull Underglaze Colors

Underglaze colors are normally painted on unglazed biscuit ware, which is then glazed when the color has dried out, (see Chapter 12 for more discussion on underglaze colors). The glaze should preferably be of the low-solubility type for these contain a certain proportion of lead which is compounded in the glaze in such a way that the risk of lead poisoning is negligible. This lead content of the low-solubility glaze produces a very glossy glaze and enhances the color of any pigment used in or under the glaze. By comparison, leadless glazes often produce colors that are dull and lifeless.

Most underglaze colors remain stable at temperatures up to about 1120° to 1150°C. (2048° to 2109°F., cone 02 to cone 1). At temperatures above this, many of them begin to change color, become duller, and burn away, although now there is a range of colors available which have been specially prepared to withstand stoneware temperatures up to 1300°C. (2381°F., cone 10).

Underglaze colors are usually prepared for painting by mixing them with a special medium until the paint is of a suitable consistency. This medium contains a gum which can cause the glaze to "crawl" away from the color to leave an area bare of glaze. To prevent this, industrial potters fire the painted, unglazed biscuit ware to a temperature of about 650°C. (1202°F. between cone 020 and cone 019). This "hardening-on" fire as it is called, serves to burn away the medium and at the same time fixes the painted design firmly to the pottery. The ware can then be dipped without risk of the glaze crawling away or smudging the painted design.

Underglaze colors can be painted on to the surface of the greenware prior to biscuit firing or applied to the surface of unfired glazed ware. With the latter procedure if a glossy color is desired it is best to mix some transparent glaze with the color, otherwise the colors will fire dull.

Dull Overglaze Colors

Over-glaze colors are normally mixed with an oil medium to allow them to be applied easily. When the oil is burned away during the firing operation the fumes given off must be allowed to escape easily or the quality of the colors will be affected considerably. When firing over-glaze enamels the spy-hole plug should be left open until the kiln interior has risen to (662° to 752°F.) about 350° to 400°C. or until the characteristic smell of burning oil medium can no longer be detected coming from the kiln. Not allowing these gases to escape is the usual cause of dull over-glaze colors.

Many colors, however, will become a little dull as a result of overfiring. Over-glaze enamels should be fired at a temperature of about 730° to 750°C. (1346° to 1382°F. about cone 017); at temperatures higher than this the colors (particularly reds) will begin to change their tone and to lose their gloss. If the temperature continued to rise beyond this point the colors will be burned away.

12
EXPERIMENTAL GLAZING AND MULTIPLE FIRING

One of the advantages of electric kiln firings and the major reason for the widespread use of electric kilns in industry is the predictability and continuity of result in a controlled atmosphere. For the studio potter, it is easy to rely on the unpredictable results of natural-fuel firings to provide a degree of spontaneity and surprise to finished ware; the neutralizing atmosphere of the electric kiln can seem bland and dull in comparison. Nonetheless, more and more in recent times, potters are beginning to find that startling and varied results can be obtained by combining some traditional glazing techniques with modern industrial technology or by application of controlled glazes. This chapter will present a survey of some of these possibilities in an attempt to inspire potters to reexamine electric kilns for their potential.

Reduction

In *The Complete Book of Pottery Making* (Pitman Publishing, London), John B. Kenny relates the story of a potter who lived in China many centuries ago. The potter specialized in making vases covered with a green copper oxide glaze. His work was in constant demand and so he employed several assistants to maintain his output. One day he loaded his kiln with ware, just as he had done so many times before, but because of insufficient draft in the chimney he couldn't get the fires to draw properly. Moreover, once the fires were burning, there was still a poor draft in the kiln and almost as much smoke escaped out of the firemouths as went up the chimney. Naturally the firing took considerably longer than usual and during all this time the air was filled with an unpleasant smelling smoke.

The potter knew that much of his pot-

63. Moon Dog Dream *by Patti Warashina, 1971. Low-fire clay and glazes, luster, handbuilt. Photo by Bob Hanson, courtesy of the Museum of Contemporary Crafts.*

tery would be ruined, and sure enough, after the firing, pot after pot was taken out blackened and dull and fit only for the scrap heap. However, right in the middle of the kiln was one pot the likes of which had never been seen before: it was a remarkably beautiful red color.

Being a very patriotic sort, the potter decided that the Emperor should have it and so it was duly packed and dispatched. The Emperor, in turn, was so delighted with it that he had the vase carefully broken and cut into small pieces which were then mounted on rings as though they were precious stones. Then he sent an order to the potter for more vases.

Now the potter's troubles began: try as he might he just could not reproduce that vase. The Emperor, however, did not like to be kept waiting and demanded quick results. Still the potter tried but to no avail; nothing that he could do would produce more of those red vases. Eventually the Emperor could wait no longer and sent a message demanding the vases be delivered, or else!

The poor potter was terrified. Every experiment he had tried had failed; nevertheless, he decided he would try firing his kiln just once more. Half way through the firing the Emperor's messenger called again threatening dire consequences if the potter did not produce the goods after this firing. This was simply too much for the poor potter who, deciding to end it all, opened the door of the kiln and jumped in. His assistants rushed to save him but it was too late and all they could do was close the dampers and wait for the kiln to cool. The kiln, in the meantime had filled with an acrid smoke which spread over everything once the dampers were closed. Lo and behold, when the kiln was opened it was full of beautiful red pots.

On subsequent firings the potters ex-periments with throwing dead animals on the fire and closing the dampers slightly and they continued to obtain beautiful red pots. Eventually they tried wet straw, wood, and other burnable materials and still they obtained red pots. According to the legend, this was how the secret of reduction was discovered.

Effect of Reduction

A reducing atmosphere results when the air inside the kiln becomes overloaded with carbon. This happens when the fuel does not receive enough oxygen to complete combustion. Under this condition, the clay bodies and the glazes "fight" among themselves, thereby forcing some of them to give up part of their oxygen content. For example, green copper oxide loses some of its oxygen and becomes red copper oxide. Similarly red iron oxide becomes black iron oxide. The red color produced by the reduction of copper oxide results in the beautiful *sang-de-boeuf* or oxblood color whereas black iron oxide, formed by the reduction of red iron oxide, can produce a green or grayish green color known as celadon.

Effect on Elements

Reduction firing traditionally has been the provenance of gas, oil, or wood burning kilns; so much as been said in the past about the great danger to electric kilns elements that it is commonly assumed that reduction either cannot be done, or cannot be done economically in an electric kiln. This is not necessarily so provided that certain basic pointers are observed. I have mentioned in Chapter 3 that the Kanthal elements used in most electric kilns, and for all those kilns fired over a temperature of 1150°C. (2102°F., cone 1) are covered with a protective oxide layer when in use. This oxide layer is grayish in color and

64. Deep Cove, *landscape storage jar by Wayne Higby, 1973. Earthenware, Raku technique.* *Photo courtesy of the artist.*

serves to seal off the element metal from harmful gases in the kiln atmosphere which would otherwise seriously attack the metal and shorten element life considerably. During a reduction firing this protective grey coating thins out and eventually it disappears. However, usually two or three firings are necessary for this coating to be removed to such an extent that the element metal is exposed. The protective coating is restored to the elements after an oxidation firing. It is therefore possible to create a reduction atmosphere in an electric kiln without excessively rapid element failure provided that the protective coating on the elements is not allowed to seriously deteriorate. In practice, after a reduction firing you should observe the element coating to see if the film is becoming thin. If there is any evidence of this, an oxidizing fire must be carried out to restore the coating to its usual thickness. It may take two or three oxidizing firings to restore the coating or only one firing may be necessary. If the reduction atmosphere is not very powerful it may indeed be possible to carry out two or three reduction firings before an oxidation firing is necessary. Reduction firings, then, can be carried out with electric kilns with reasonable economy provided that these elementary precautions are observed. Element life will certainly be reduced even if these precautions are observed but nowhere near as quickly as would be the case if reduction firings were carried out haphazardly.

I am often asked to give my opinion on how much element life will be reduced by reduction firings. How can I possibly answer a question like that? So much depends upon the length of the firing, the degree of atmosphere reduction, and so on that it is impossible to give a positive answer. It is even impossible to give an estimated firing life for elements under normal oxidizing conditions—I have known elements to fail after a few months' use yet I have a friend in Tunbridge Wells who has been firing two or three times per week for eight years without ever needing an element replacement.

Even the element wire manufacturers cannot give any guidance on this point, but the general feeling is that under conditions of reduction one can expect about half the element life obtained under oxidizing conditions.

Formation of Reducing Atmosphere

This can be done by putting enough highly organic material—any material which has a high carbon content and which demands a lot of oxygen to burn and produce heat and carbon dioxide—in the kiln to use up most of the oxygen in the atmosphere leaving little or none at all for the clay bodies and glazes. Several materials that potters could use are charcoal, twigs, and sugar cubes. Moth balls can be used to produce a reduction atmosphere very efficiently but the gases given off are dangerous as they are highly toxic. Moreover, they tend to make the kiln very dirty inside resulting in a slight glazing effect on the brickwork and elements. Local reduction can also be obtained on the pot by adding 1% to 4% very finely ground silicone carbide to a suitable alkaline glaze; 1% copper added to the glaze will result in a fairly good copper red.

The glaze constituents are in their most reactive state and thus most susceptible to the effects of a reduction atmosphere when the glaze is at a high temperature and in a molten condition. Sufficient reduction can usually be obtained by introducing the carbonaceous material immediately after switching off the kiln, continuing additions until the ware has cooled to about 750°C. (1350°F.).

This may all sound very simple but in actual practice it is not very easy to introduce carbon into the kiln at these high temperatures. Dropping a lump of charcoal in the kiln could easily damage the pots. Many potters overcome this problem by placing a receptacle in the kiln to catch the pieces of charcoal. Charcoal can be introduced either through the spy hole or through the vent hole at the top or back of the kiln. To maintain a reducing atmosphere inside the kiln it is necessary to replace the vent plug or the spy-hole plug as soon as the charcoal has been safely lowered in. After about ½ hour add more charcoal to the kiln.

The British Ceramic Manufacturing Company, Podmore and Sons, has developed a special reduction bung which they can fit as an optional extra to kilns during manufacture. This takes the form of a comparatively large brick containing a spy hole which can be removed from the door of the kiln while the kiln is being fired. This "bung" has a receptacle built into it which can be loaded with charcoal and then inserted into the kiln—just like replacing the spy-hole plug. Podmore's recommend the use of two of these so that while the charcoal in one is being used up inside the kiln the other one can be loaded, so that rapid replacement can be made. (An American equivalent of this is not available at this time according to Amaco.)

Usually reduction is used for high-fire stoneware to obtain the special colors mentioned above. At low temperatures, and particularly when low-solubility or other lead-containing glazes are being used, a reducing atmosphere should be avoided, for the lead content of the glaze will be reduced, forming an unpleasant grayish black discoloration in the glaze.

A reduction color *cannot* be obtained by adding materials already in reduced form to the glaze and then firing in an oxidizing atmosphere. For example, red copper oxide cannot be added to a glaze to be fired in oxidation with the expectation of achieving a copper red color. In the neutral atmosphere, the red copper will be oxidized resulting in the usual copper green color.

Raku

Raku, a low-fire technique that produces a variegated and pleasing glaze texture by surface reduction after firing, can be done simply and cleanly in an electric kiln.

The actual glaze texture is achieved when the clay body and glazes have reached maturity in the kiln. At this "red hot" stage, the piece is removed from the kiln with tongs (*take care when inserting the tongs next to elements not to touch the elements!*) held by asbestos gloves. The piece is then treated by any number of different methods, such as blowing on the glaze, sinking the piece in tea or in a non-combustible container of sawdust, straw, or seaweed. A lid must be kept handy with which to completely cover the container to stop the burning and cut off the oxygen to produce a reducing atmosphere. (For further information and instructions on performing the raku firing, consult the *Bib-

65. *Honey pot with dipper by Katie Kazan, 1973. Cone 6 porcelain and colored oxides. Photo by Alida Conin.*

66. *Covered jars by Byron Temple, 1973. Kazan cone 6 porcelain with rolled and paddled clay design and transparent glaze. Photo by Jeff Hannigan.*

liography; there is also a good, concise description of raku for school use in the April 1971 issue of *Ceramics Monthly* magazine, pages 17 and 18.)

Wayne Higby, a potter who work primarily in raku surfaces and whose pots are shown in Figure 64, says: "An electric kiln would be good in heating up as you could get a completely oxidizing (clear, no extra fuel) atmosphere. I would like this in that I try very hard to get good, clean, fresh color. Color is very important to me and I find that the cleaner I can keep the kiln in heating up the piece the fresher the color is. An electric kiln would serve as an advantage in this case. Also an electric kiln will heat evenly and this is a great help in firing complicated pieces not only in the glaze (raku) firing but also in the biscuit firing."

A small electric kiln, with approximately a 12" x 12" x 12" firing chamber, either front or top loading, is convenient for achieving raku temperatures in a short time (1 to 2 hours). Amaco offers a "Portable Raku Ceramic Unit" which includes all the necessary equipment for firing raku ware: a small electric kiln, a cart with a handle, reduction and water buckets, clay and glazes, decorating colors, tongs, kiln gloves, and an asbestos mitten.

If a small kiln is not available, it is possible to build a false floor in a larger kiln, which does not divert the flow of heat, but which centralizes it to a smaller area for quicker heat increase. A very rapid temperature increase is an advantage for maturing raku glazes. The kiln floors and shelves should be heavily coated with kiln wash for raku projects.

Clay Body Variation

Clay bodies used in an oxidizing atmosphere can attain a textured, variegated or colored surface by the addition of colored oxides, rough materials such as sand or grog, or by combining hand-formed shapes with thrown shapes. Figures 65, 66 are pots made from a cone 6 porcelain clay body that contains macaloid, an ingredient which makes otherwise nonworkable bodies workable. The pots were covered with a transparent or tinted glaze and fired in an electric kiln.

Luster

Lusters deposit a thin coating of metal or metallic oxide onto the surface of a glaze. Metal luster colors, which take on a sheen like gold, silver, platinum, or metallic colors, can be achieved in an oxidizing atmosphere with the use of a reducing agent. Lusters can be purchased ready-to-use in liquid form from a ceramic supplier. They are applied with a brush or a spraying apparatus onto the surface of a glaze. The pot is then fired to red heat—(about 650° to 750°C. (1200° to 1380°F., use the cone suggested by the supplier). The piece should be allowed to dry or be preheated slightly to burn out the oily medium which could discolor the luster.

Underglaze and Overglaze Colors

Underglaze colors, available in liquid or dry powdered form, provide a selection of brilliant opaque hues with which to decorate pottery and ceramics. They can be brushed, silk screened, or sprayed on greenware or biscuited ware to be fired alone or covered with a translucent or a white glaze. They can also be mixed with transparent or white glazes to make colored glazes.

Underglaze colors can be used to make a distinct line or linear design on a piece where a colored glaze could melt and blur into others. They also afford brilliant colors in a uniform blend. The colors can also be brushed on as a water-

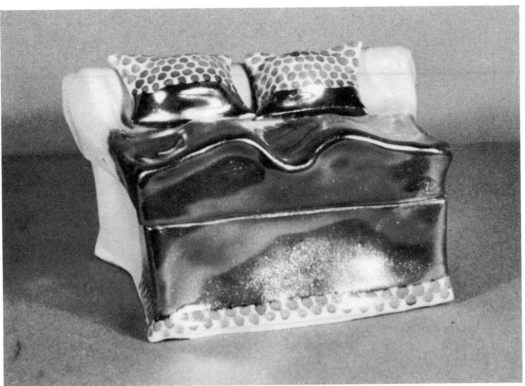

67. *Double Bed by Kit-Yin Snyder, 1969. Porcelain with platinum and red lusters. Photo courtesy of the artist.*

color wash and used with wax resist or in sgrafitto decoration. Other applicators available for underglaze decoration include crayons, pencils.

When applying underglaze colors, consistency can be improved by adding glycerine, a few drops to each tablespoon of liquid color. A drop of dextrine or gum arabic helps to keep the color from smudging after it has been applied to the pot. Apply the colors in a thin coat; if applied too thickly, they have a tendency to crawl. If crawling of the glaze over the color becomes a problem, it can be remedied to some extent by the addition of a small amount of flux, such as a low-melting frit. This is best determined by tests.

Underglaze pigments are somewhat more expensive than colored oxides, but their tints are stronger. Colors are the same before and after painting, which is often not true of colored oxides, therefore the final result can be more clearly ascertained.

Underglaze colors are fired to the maturing temperature of the clay and glazes to which they are applied.

Overglaze colors, often used on whiteware (porcelain or china clay) but which also may be used on stoneware or earthware, can be applied to a glaze before or after firing. The lusters previously mentioned in this chapter fall into this latter category as do overglaze enamels and china paint which are available ready-to-use in powder or semimoist form from ceramic suppliers. These are applied and fired in a separate low-temperature firing—usually 720° to 800°C. (1328° to 1472°F., cone 018 to cone 015)—after the glaze has matured.

A rapid firing in 3 hours is usually a sufficient time to fire these colors and an electric kiln is ideal for this.

Jane Pieser, whose china-painted clock is shown in Figure 69, fires her overglazed pieces to cone 017. She says: "Overglaze

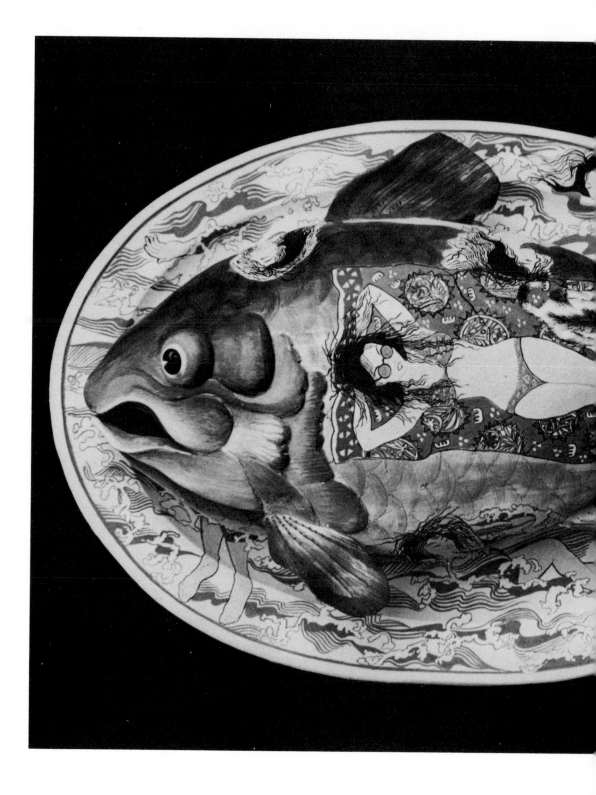

69. China-painted clock by Jane Peiser, 1972. Handbuilt porcelain, fired to cone 10 reduction, decorated with overglaze and flower decals and refired to cone 017 oxidation. Photo by Evon Streetman.

68. Dish on a Fish, (left) covered fish plate by Patti Warashina, 1973. Low-fire clay and glaze and underglaze. Photo courtesy of the artist.

70. *Untitled (mailed plate) by Ken D. Little, 1972. Multiple-fired earthenware and mixed media. Photo courtesy of the artist.*

71. *Car Kiln by Patti Warashina, 1970. Low-fire clay and glaze, underglaze, and luster. Photo courtesy of the artist.*

has the advantage of being applied *after* the pot has been fired to maturity. Thus you can have a good sturdy high-fired pot with bright colors as well. It can also be done by someone who can paint but not pot as on commercial tiles and plates. I wipe the area to be painted with alcohol, mix the powdered china paint with painting medium on a tile with a spatula, allow overnight drying before firing, and fire in an electric kiln preferably with an automatic shut off. I leave the lid up until atmosphere clears. The firing takes 12 hours and cooling takes the same amount of time. I like thin-walled hexagonal electric kilns rather than thick square ones because they cool faster and more evenly.

"I have done some china painting on salt pots. I glaze the areas that I want to paint and unless the salt is very heavy the glazed areas do not 'orange peel' like the rest of the piece. The overglaze on these pots is limited to the faces, so it's not a really large part of the process."

Multiple Firings

The possibilities of multiple firings with earthenware, stoneware, porcelain, or any clay body and glaze are of course limitless. Multiple firings can produce brilliance and depth of surface. When building up processes on ware, it is often advisable to start with a white or light-colored clay body so that the subsequent colors and images can be clearly seen.

Ken Little, whose "Untitled (Mailed Plates)" are shown in Figure 70, fires his pieces as many as 25 times. He claims that he has "had no trouble firing pieces many times as long as there was no sudden thermal shock. The plates were heated and cooled at a fairly even rate especially during the early stages of the firing. Electric kilns provide a very even controllable heat at this critical beginning of the firing process. They are limited by their size but should be considered a tool of a very flexible nature with plenty of room for experimentation."

Commercial decals, transfer paper, rubber stamps, and silk screen printing can also be used for decorating pottery surfaces. Photographic images can be made with a silk screening process which involves the use of a dot-screened halftone print. This is exposed onto a photo stencil film which has a special emulsion for adhesion to the screen. It is very important to expose this film on the correct side to make a positive transfer. You can perform this process yourself using hydrogen peroxide to develop the film and transferring it to the screen while still wet, or you can have a commercial silk screen house make the stencil for you. The stencil is printed either directly on a flat or slightly curved pottery surface or on a transfer sheet with an underglaze color mixed to the consistency of paint from a tube with an oily medium made of equal parts varnish, turpentine, and boiled linseed oil. In this case, there should be a hardening on firing as mentioned above. Or it can be printed as an overglaze enamel and fired to the overglaze temperature.

Photographic transfers can also be made by using a liquid photo emulsion which is painted on the ware under darkroom conditions, exposing the pot as a piece of photosensitized paper and developing it in the usual photo chemicals. Contact a photographic store for specific products.

TEMPERATURE EQUIVALENTS FOR ORTON STANDARD PYROMETRIC CONES

AS DETERMINED AT THE NATIONAL BUREAU OF STANDARDS

CONE NUMBER	LARGE CONES				CONE NUMBER	SMALL CONES	
	60°C	108°F	150°C	270°F		300°C	540°F
022	585°C.	1085°F.	600°C.	1112°F.	022	630°C.*	1165°F.*
021	602	1116	614	1137	021	643	1189
020	625	1157	635	1175	020	666	1231
019	668	1234	683	1261	019	723	1333
018	696	1285	717	1323	018	752	1386
017	727	1341	747	1377	017	784	1443
016	764	1407	792	1458	016	825	1517
015	790	1454	804	1479	015	843	1549
014	834	1533	838	1540	014	870*	1596
013	869	1596	852	1566	013	880*	1615
012	866	1591	884	1623	012	900*	1650
011	886	1627	894	1641	011	915*	1680
†010	887	1629	894	1641	†010	919	1686
09	915	1679	923	1693	09	955	1751
08	945	1733	955	1751	08	983	1801
07	973	1783	984	1803	07	1008	1846
06	991	1816	999	1830	06	1023	1873
05	1031	1888	1046	1915	05	1062	1944
04	1050	1922	1060	1940	04	1098	2008
03	1086	1987	1101	2014	03	1131	2068
02	1101	2014	1120	2048	02	1148	2098
01	1117	2043	1137	2079	01	1178	2152
1	1136	2077	1154	2109	1	1179	2154
2	1142	2088	1162	2124	2	1179	2154
3	1152	2106	1168	2134	3	1196	2185
4	1168	2134	1186	2167	4	1209	2208
5	1177	2151	1196	2185	5	1221	2230
6	1201	2194	1222	2232	6	1255	2291
7	1215	2219	1240	2264	7	1264	2307
8	1236	2257	1263	2305	8	1300	2372
9	1260	2300	1280	2336	9	1317	2403
10	1285	2345	1305	2381	10	1330	2426
11	1294	2361	1315	2399	11	1336	2437
12	1306	2383	1326	2419	12	1355	2471

* Temperatures approximate. See Note 3. N.D. — not determined.

† Iron-free (white) are made in numbers 010 to 3. The iron-free cones have the same deformation temperatures as the red equivalents when fired at a rate of 60 Centigrade degrees per hour in air.

Notes:

1. The temperature equivalents in this table apply only to Orton Standard Pyrometric Cones, *when heated at the rates indicated, in an air atmosphere.*

2. Temperature Equivalents are given in degrees Centigrade (°C.) and the corresponding degrees Fahrenheit (°F.). The rates of heating shown at the head of each column of temperature equivalents were maintained during the last several hundred degrees of temperature rise.

3. The temperature equivalents were determined at the National Bureau of Standards by H. P. Beerman (See Journal of the American Ceramic Society, Vol. 39, 1956), with the exception of those marked (*).

4. The temperature equivalents are not necessarily those at which cones will deform under firing conditions different from those under which the calibrating determinations were made. For more detailed technical data, please write the Orton Foundation.

5. For reproducible results, care should be taken to insure that the cones are set in a plaque with the bending face at the correct angle of 8° from the vertical, with the cone tips at the correct height above the top of the plaque. (Large Cone 2"; small and P.C.E. cones 15/16")

TABLE 1.   *Courtesy of The Edward Orton Jr. Ceramic Foundation.*

COLOR/TEMPERATURE RELATIONSHIPS

Temp. °C.	Approximate Orton Large cone no.	Color	Effect on clay	Type of ware and glazes
225	–	no visible color– "black heat"	Alpha to beta cristobalite inversion	
575	–		Alpha to beta quartz inversion	
600	022			
750	017	Dull red		Firing temperature for on-glaze enamels (china paints)
830	014			
850				
875	012	Cherry red		Luster glazes
920	09		Most of organic matter burnt away by this time	
960	08	Cherry red/ orange		Low firing lead glazes sometimes opacified with tin oxide (majolica)
1000	06		Terracottas mature	Porous bisque earthenware
1060	04			
1100	03	Orange changing to yellow/orange	Earthenware matures	Industrial earthenware biscuit and bone china glost
1150	1			
1200	5	Distinct yellow orange	Terracottas melt; increasing beta cristobalite formation	Semi-porcelain
1250	7			Salt glazes
1280	9	Slight white tinge		Bone china biscuit, stoneware and some porcelain
1300	10			
1350	13	Intense yellow-white		Porcelain
1460	16			

TABLE 2.

BIBLIOGRAPHY

Building Electric Kilns

Alfred University. *Kiln Drawings and Material Lists*. Alfred, New York, 1965.

Engineering Station, University of New Hampshire. *Making an Electric Kiln*. Publication #1, 4th ed. Durham, New Hampshire, 1951.

———, Laurance E. Webber. *Making Studio Electric Kilns*. Reproduced in its entirety in Chapter 4, 1954.

Norton, F. H. *Ceramics for the Artist Potter* (pp. 288–289). Reading, Massachusetts: Addison-Wesley, 1956. Here Norton changes his plan for the wire-wound electric kiln described in *Elements of Ceramics*, see next entry, to make a more rugged, easier to construct model. This change calls for eight commercial 1000-watt heating units wound with Kanthal wire to replace the Kanthal A-1 ribbon allowing the kiln to be fired to cone 10.

Norton, F.H. *Elements of Ceramics*. 2nd ed. (pp. 215–220). Reading, Massachusetts: Addison-Wesley, 1957. Norton gives designs and succinct instructions (which are made apparent through very clear line drawings) for building a test kiln with an 8″ x 8″ x 9″ firing chamber which can be fired to cone 4 and a "wire-wound electric box kiln" with eight times the cubic capacity of the test kiln. This kiln is designed with two doors for ease in loading and can be fired to cone 10, but to lengthen the life of the kiln, it's recommended that it be fired at a maximum of cone 4. He also gives instructions for constructing a small and a large electric globar kiln.

Turoff, Muriel. *How to Make Pottery* (pp. 74–77). New York: Crown, 1949. Turoff presents an "inexpensive electric kiln" with plans originated by Frank W. Smith. These plans are somewhat vague, not explaining the temperature at which this kiln can be fired nor its actual size, although this could easily be computed from the information given.

General Information about Electric Kilns

Nelson, Glenn C. *Ceramics: A Potter's Handbook* (pp. 282–284). New York: Holt, Rhinehart and Winston, 1971.

Rhodes, Daniel. *Kilns: Design, Construction and Operation* (pp. 141–150). Philadelphia: Chilton, 1968. Rhodes' chapter on electric kilns gives diagrams and detailed information about electric current.

Instruction Manuals

Amaco (American Art Clay Company, Inc.) *Instruction Book No. 2*. Indianapolis, Indiana, 1973.

HED Industries, Inc. *General Instruction Manual, Unique Kilns*. Pennington, New Jersey, 1973.

Skutt Ceramic Products. *How to Operate and Care for Your Skutt Kiln*. Portland, Oregon, 1973.

Technical Information

The Edward Orton Jr. Ceramic Foundation. "Orton Pyrometric Cones and Their Importance to the Hobby Potter" and other literature. 1445 Summit Street, Columbus, Ohio 43201 (telephone 614-299-4104).

The Kanthal Corporation, Bethel, Connecticut 06801

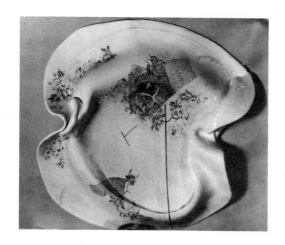

Floral Whiteware Platter by Kathy Dambach, 1973. Underglaze powder rubbed on biscuit and sprayed with transparent glaze, fired to cone 04. Photo transfers applied and refired to cone 04. Gold markings applied and fired to cone 018. Photo courtesy of the artist.

SUPPLIERS LIST

Kilns and Accessories

A.D. Alpine, Inc.
353 Coral Circle
El Segundo, California 90245
(213) 772-2557

AMACO (American Art Clay Company, Inc.)
447 West 16th Street
Indianapolis, Indiana 46222
(317) 244-6871

Cress Electric Kilns
available from Seeley's Ceramic Service, Inc.
9 River Street
Oneonta, New York 13820
(607) 432-3812

Evenheat Kiln, Inc.
6949 Legion Road
Caseville, Michigan 48725
(517) 856-4040

L & L Manufacturing Company
142 Conchester Road
Chester P.O. Box 348
Twin Oaks, Delaware County
Pennsylvania 19016
(215) 485-6334

Skutt Ceramic Products
2618 East Steele Street
Portland, Oregon 97202
(503) 235-8010

Unique Kilns
HED Industries, Inc.
P.O. Box 176
Pennington, New Jersey 08534
(609) 446-3006

Westby Kilns, Ceramic Supplier
and Manufacturing Company
408 NE 72nd Street
Seattle, Washington 98115
(206) 523-8300

Ceramic Suppliers

AMACO (American Art Clay Company)
4717 West 16th Street
Indianapolis, Indiana 46222
(217) 244-6871

Jack D. Wolfe Company, Inc.
724 Meeker Avenue
Brooklyn, New York 11222
(212) 387-3604

Kemper Manufacturing, Inc.
Ceramic Tools
P.O. Box 545
Chino, California 91710
(714) 628-6822

Newton Potter's Supply, Inc.
96 Rumford Avenue
West Newton, Massachusetts 02165
(617) 893-1200

Podmore and Sons Ltd.
Shelton
Stoke-on-Trent, England

Sculpture House
38 East 30th Street
New York, New York 10016
(212) 679-7474

Standard Ceramic Supply Company
P.O. Box 4435
Pittsburgh, Pennsylvania 15205
(412) 923-1655

GLOSSARY AND INDEX *All numbers in italic refer to illustrations*

Alkaline: frit, 119; glazes, 118, 130
Automatic shut-off. *See* Kiln Sitter *and* Pyrometer, controlling.

Baffle. *See* Muffle.
Bag wall (wall built inside the kiln that deflects the flame from the ware), 20
Barium, 123, 125; carbonate, 120
Bentonite, 20
Biscuit firing (first low-temperature firing which makes the clay very porous for glazing; used primarily by craft potters), 17, 90, 92, 93, 102, 103–105, 106, 122, 124, 132; shrinkage of ware during, 97, 111; stacking, 97–99.
Bisque firing (first firing at clay-maturation temperature; used primarily in industry), 90, 92, 93
Black heat (warmth without noticeable color), 77
Blistering (glaze fault which forms small bubbles), 124
Bloating (pottery fault where the clay body swells, resulting in lumps on the surface of the glaze), 124, 125
Blow-out (glaze fault where small particles of the surface break away), 123
Bone china, firing, 93, 99
Bricks, refractory. *See* Refractory bricks.
Brickwork, 38, 40, 41, 103; cracking of, 49; cutting, 40; fireproof mortar, 40

Calcium borate, 123
Carborundum (trade mark of the Carborundum Co., Niagara Falls, which pioneered the industrial synthesis of silicon carbide), 101. *See also* Silicon carbide.
Casting slips, 120, 122
Celadon, 128
China clay, 108, 120
China paint (overglaze color), 133, 137
Clay body: preparation, 108; variation, 132
Cold junction, 82
Color, glaze, 132; of kiln interior while firing, 49, 77, 102, 105
Compensating cable(s), (wires which connect the cold junction of the thermocouple to the galvanometer), 81–83
Compression, 11, 117–119
Cone. *See* Pyrometric cone.
Continuous kiln. *See* Kiln(s), continuous.
Contraction of clay and glaze, 117, 118
Cooling: biscuit, 105; glaze, 107, 114, 115, 117, 123, 124
Cornwall (Cornish) Stone, 108
Counterflow (tunnel-kiln recycling system). *See* Kiln(s), tunnel.
Cracking (pottery fault), 99, 106, 114, 121, 122; during cooling, 107, 115; in the interior brickwork, 49

Cranks, 99, 101
Craters. *See* Pinholing.
Crawling (glaze fault where surface rolls away from clay body), 114, 119, 120, 125
Craze-resistance, developing: in clay body, 108, 111, 121; in firing, 90, 93; in glaze, 113, 117, 118
Crazing (pottery fault which produces fine cracks throughout the glaze), 93, 110, 115–119; causes of, 118. *See also* Craze-resistance, developing.
Cristobalite, 111, 117, 121
Crypto-crystalline (glaze having a matt surface and hardly discernible crystals), 123
Crystallization, 122, 123
Cut glaze (fault similar to crawling, where glaze is scratched or marked during dipping), 120

Decals, commercial 137
Dehydration, 112
Devitrification (glaze fault where transparent glaze turns milky), 122, 123
Dextrine (a gummy substance used in underglaze colors to keep them from smudging), 433. *See also* Gum arabic.
Door switch (device which automatically isolates the electrical supply to the kiln when the door is opened), 77
Draft, in a kiln, 14
Dryness of pots: determining, 98; for applying glaze, 120; for firing, 110
Dunting (glaze fault which produces a crack throughout the piece), 99, 106, 111, 120, 121

Earthenware, firing, 90, 92, 93, 99, 101, 105; temperature for, 102, 110, 121
Edward Orton Jr. Ceramic Foundation, 88
Electric kilns. *See* Kiln(s), electric.
Element(s), electrical (two wires wound or coiled to produce voltage and generate heat in a kiln), 37, 40; brittleness of, 46, 47; connectors, 41; deterioration, 47; effect of reduction on, 128–130; failure tests, 47; grooves, 46, 47; humming, 47; Kanthal, 37, 42, 47, 128; Nichrome, 37, 42; placement of ware near, 97; regulating, 42; repairing, 46, 47; replacing, 32, 36, 37; sags, 46, Silicon carbide, 42
End-point of pyrometric cones, 89
Energy regulator (mechanism for controlling the rate of temperature increase in a kiln), 46, 76, 77, 102, 103, 106, 107
Eutectic (mixture having a melting point lower than that of its constituents), 113
Evolution of kilns, 12–29
Expansion of clay and glaze, 117–119

Feldspar, 108, 110

Firemouth(s), 14, 17, 20, 29

Firing, 102–107; chamber, 14, 17; color, 49, 77, 102; cost, 35; earliest records of clay, 12; first (bake-out), 47, 49; incorrect, 116; multiple, 137; over, 124; techniques, 90–93; temperature, 17, 23, 30, 32, 35, 37, 102. *See also* Biscuit; Bisque; Glaze; Glost; *and* Earthenware; Porcelain; Stoneware; Terracotta.

Flatware setter, 99

Flint, 108, 110. *See also* Silica.

Flue, 17, 21

Formaldehyde, added to preserve glaze, 120

Fuel, for firing kilns, 12, 14, 20, 21, 23, 29; loading, 17

Gas(es): bubbles, 122, 124; developed in glaze, 114, 125; exhaust, 14

Galvanometer (device for calculating reference points between voltage and degrees of temperature), 80; calibrating, 81

Glaze (thin glassy layer melted and matured on a dry or biscuited clay body); cooling, 107, 114, 115; experimental, 126–137; firing, 90, 92, 93, 106; matching, 113, 114; stacking, 99, 101; studio and industrial techniques, 92, 93

Glossy glaze(s), 123, 125; cooling, 107, 115

Glost firing (melting and maturation of a glassy layer on a clay body which has been fired to a hard, high bisque temperature), 90, 92, 93

Greenware (unfired pottery), 90, 106, 122; leather-hard, 122

Grog (fired clay which has been ground into fine particles), 132; making shelves with, 97

Grounding the kiln (connecting the kiln to a wire that extends to the ground), 35

Gum arabic (used in underglaze color to keep it from smudging), 125, 133. *See also* Dextrine.

Hard-bisque. *See* Bisque firing.

Hearth(s), 12, 17; open, 12

Heat: loss, 38; work, measured by pyrometric cones, 88

High-temperature firing. *See* Porcelain *and* Stoneware.

Higby, Wayne, *129*, 132; quoted, 132

Hot junction, 82

Hydrogen peroxide (used to develop photofilm for silk screening), 137

Industrial firing techniques, 23, 25, 90, 92, 93

Inspection, of fired pots, 105; of new kiln, 37

Interface (layer between glaze and body), 114

Intermittent, periodic kiln. *See* Kilns, periodic.

Inversion, silica. *See* Silica, modifications.

Iron oxide, black and red, 128

Kazan, Katie, *131*

Kiln(s): bottle, 19, 20, *22*; continuous, 14, 23, 25; downdraft, 14, 21; Egyptian, *13*; evolution of, 12–29; Far-Eastern climbing, 14, *15*; first, 14; floor, 12, *16*, 34; Hanley, *18*, 19; horizontal, 14, *15*; modern studio, 29; periodic, 14; primitive, *15*, 25, 29; Roman, 14, *16*, 17, 29; roller conveyor, 25; through-draft, 14; top hat, 25, *28*; tunnel, 23, 25, *26*, 27; updraft, 14, 17, 19, 29; vertical intermittent, 14, 17, 24

Kiln(s), electric: choosing, 30–37; cost, 30, 33, 35; diagrams, *38*, *44*, 45; electricity consumption, 30, 34, 35; electrical requirements, 34, 35; framework, 38, *39*, 73; hexagonal, 137; making studio (booklet), 50–71; sectional, 34; shipping, 37; site and access, 32–34; size and capacity, 30, 32; switch, 47; top-loading, 33, 101, 105; weight, 33

Kiln furniture, 94–101; cranks, 99, 101; flatware setter, 99; posts, 97–98, 101; repair, 97; saddles, 99, 121; spurs, 99; stilts, 99, 121; triangles, 99. *See also* Silicon Carbide.

Kiln site, 32–34

Kiln Sitter (device for automatically shutting off the kiln which utilizes a small pyrometric cone), 49, 72, 73, 76, 99; diagram *74*, 75

Kiln wash (a slurry of water mixed with ½ part kaolin or china clay and ½ part silica or flint), 49, 97, 101

Leather-hard, *See* Greenware.

Little, Ken, *136*, 137; quoted, 137

Low-solubility (low-temperature glaze that meets British standards for lead content), 121, 123, 125

Luster (thin coating of metal applied to a glaze), 132

Macaloid (product which acts as a binder for clay bodies), 132

Matt glaze(s), 107, 114, 115, 123

Muffle (baffle) (refractory internal shell which protects ware from contact with combustion gases), 14, 23, 46

Overglaze colors, 125, 132, 133, 137

Oxidation, (kiln atmosphere made up primarily of oxygen), 112, 113, 128, 129, 131

Peeling. *See* Shivering.

Peltier effect (the discovery that two different metals joined together create difference of voltage between them and this varies with the temperature of the junction), 82

Phase (single, two power leads and one ground; three, three power leads and one ground, providing heavy-duty service), 34, 35

Piccolpasso (Italian who wrote the first book on pottery methods in the 16th century), 17

Pieser, Jane, 133, *135*, 137; quoted, 137

Pinholing (pottery fault causing small holes in the glaze surface), 114, 122

Plaster, as cause of blow-out, 123

Porcelain, 133; firing, 93, 101; temperature, 102, 106

Porosity (measure of proportion of pores in ceramic material—ability of a ceramic piece to absorb moisture), 90, 110, 119

Posts. *See* Supports.

Potentiometer (instrument which measures minute voltages and operates a pointer to indicate them on a temperature scale), 81

Program controller (sophisticated device for automatically designing a firing cycle), 85, 86

Pyrolimit. *See* Thermolimit.

Pyrometer(s) (instrument for measuring temperature inside the kiln), 49, 78, 105; controlling, 83, 107; inaccurate readings, 87; installing, 80, 81; standard, 80, 81

Pyrometric cone(s), (pyroscopes: graduated ceramic devices for measuring heat work inside the kiln), 49, 78, 83, 87–89, 99; diagram, *79*; mounting in a plaque, 89; setting, 101

Pyroscope. *See* Pyrometric cone.

Quartz. *See* Silica.

Raku (Japanese technique of low-fire pottery), 131, 132; glaze maturation, 132

Reduction (reducing the oxygen in the kiln while firing), 126–131; in an electric kiln, 128–131. *See also* Elements, effect of reduction on.

Refractory (resistant to high temperatures), 110; boxes (saggars), 17; bricks, 37, 40, 41

Rotary switch (kiln-operating device with four settings: off, low, medium, high), 72, 102, 107

Saddles, 99, 121

Saggar (refractory clay box in which to place ware in a kiln), 17

Salts, soluble, 120, 122

Sand, 97, 132. *See also* Silica.

Sang de boeuf (ox blood, the red color produced by the reduction of copper oxide), 128

Scumming (film produced on the glaze by the presence of soluble salts in the clay body), 120

Sectional kiln (kiln which can be taken apart and to which extra rings can be added to expand the firing chamber). *See* Kiln(s), electric: sectional.

Shelf(ves), kiln, 94, 97, 121; cracking, 97; making, 94, 97; refractory, 25, 94; silicon carbide, 94; warping, 94, 97

Shivering (also called peeling); glaze fault producing fine surface cracks that tend to overlap), 106, 116, 119, 137

Short clay (not sufficiently plastic), 106, 122

Shrinkage, 101, 110, 111, 120; during cooling, 115

Silica, 110, 111, 119; modifications, 111. *See also* Flint.

Silicon carbide (articial compound of silicon and carbide made from baked sand and coke, used to make kiln shelves and furniture; it can also be mixed in a glaze to effect local reduction; it can also be mixed in a glaze to effect local reduction), 130; shelves, 94

Silk screening, 137; photographic, 137

Smoke, causes of in firing, 49

Snyder, Kit-Yin, *133*

Soaking (half hour or so period after the kiln has reached maturation when it is kept at its maximum temperature to effect a desired degree of vitrification or chemical reaction), 73, 106, 114

Spurs, 99

Spy hole(s), 21, 38, 76, 130; plugs, 102, 103, 106, 107, 125, 130

Stacking (arranging ware in a kiln), 94, 97–101; biscuit, 97–99; glaze, 99, 101, 106; how to hold pots while, 101

Staggering kiln shelves, 98

Stilts, 99, 121

Stoneware, firing, 93, 101, 105, 108; temperature, 102, 106, 110, 121

Stringer, Harry, *109*

Sulphuring (glaze fault producing a dull scum or discoloration), 123

Supports (posts), 97; making, 97; how many to use, 98; placing, 101

Switch, rotary, 72, 102, 107; door, 77; infinite control, 103, 106; time, 73, 76

Switching schedule (standard: one hour on low, one hour on medium, one hour on high or until kiln reaches maturity), 49, 72, 73

Temperature: control 78–89; distribution, 29; external, 34; maximum at which to fire electric kiln, 30; range, 110; rate of increase, 102, 106; variation, 17, 46, 99, 103, 106. *See also* Firing temperature *and* Cooling.

Temperature regulator (thermostatic type device for controlling the temperature by switching the kiln on and off), 84, 85, 107

Temple, Byron, *131*

Tension, 117–119

Terracotta, firing, 90, 99, 101, 103, 108

Test lamp (voltmeter), for determining element failure, 47, *48*

Thermocouple(s) (the part of the pyrometer that projects into the kiln and measures voltages on the basis of the electric current generated when the junction between two dissimilar conductors is heated), 46, 80, 81; wires used for, 81, 82

Thermolimit (also called Pyrolimit, a pyrometric instrument with two pointers, red and black, which is capable of turning off the kiln when the required temperature has been reached), 83, 107

Thickness of ware, 98, 102, 120, 121

Thompson effect (the discovery that heating a length of metallic wire at one end creates a difference of voltage between the ends), 82

Time switch (device with 24-hour graduated scale which can be set to turn off the kiln by the action of two pointers), 73, 76

Transfers, 137

Triangles, 99

Underglaze colors, 122, 125, 132, 133

Vent plug, 106

Visibility of cones during firing, 89

Vitrification, 102, 110, 113

Voltage, 81, 82; supply needed for electric kiln, 35

Voltmeter. *See* Test lamp.

Warashina, Patti, *127*, *134*, *135*, *136*

Warping, kiln shelf, 94, 97

Water-smoking period (temperature range of 100° to 250°C. [212° to 482°F.] when the mechanically held water in the clay is being dispersed), 102, 111, 112, 121

Webber, Laurance, E. (*Making Studio Electric Kilns*), 50, 51

Wedging (process of kneading clay to a homogenous consistency), 14; incorrect, 122

Whiteware. *See* Porcelain *and* China clay.

Wiring requirements of electric kilns, 34, 35, 41, 42; chart, *43*

Zinc, 123